This set of exploratory texts draws together significant expertise and sets the scene for future thinking. In the midst of global imperatives to learn, to be more entrepreneurial, it is a most welcome contribution to the debate.

Andy Penaluna, *Professor and Director, International Institute for Creative Entrepreneurial Development, University of Wales, UK*

In this insightful and timely publication, Rae and Wang explore entrepreneurial learning from its inception as a field of academic inquiry right through to its development in contemporary entrepreneurship literatures. The authors bring together a collection of complementary perspectives on entrepreneurial learning, and in so doing, map out a challenging future research agenda. This text should be of value to researchers and educators alike, as well as to those studying entrepreneurial learning as part of a taught programme.

Colette Henry, *Professor, Dundalk Institute of Technology, Ireland*

I highly recommend this text, which provides a fresh perspective on the area of entrepreneurial learning, exploring new research, practice and pedagogical practices. The contributing authors include some of the thought leaders in the entrepreneurship discipline and this work offers new insights that will be of great interest to the academic community, policy makers and enterprise support agencies.

Paul Jones, *Associate Professor, Plymouth University, UK*

Entrepreneurial Learning

This book explores the development of the rapidly evolving field of entrepreneurial learning by bringing together contributions from an international team of researchers, who offer new understanding of its emerging
development and its potential scope for the future. Using the three domains
of theory, education, and learning-in-practice, this book offers differing
and complementary perspectives on entrepreneurial learning:

- Conceptual work which reviews and summarises prior work in the
  field and advances theoretical understanding of entrepreneurial learning research, enabling a review of the development of research in this
  area over time.
- Applied work around entrepreneurship education which develops
  understanding of teaching and learning practices in educational and
  institutional contexts.
- Exploration of learning in the 'real' business contexts, including new
  venture creation, family business and small business development, and
  'intrapreneurial' learning in larger organisations.

Using global perspectives, originating from the different cultural contexts
of the USA, UK, Nordic and Chinese perspectives, the chapters converge to
address issues, questions and opportunities for the future development of
entrepreneurial learning. This book will be of interest to educators and
researchers in the areas of entrepreneurship, enterprise education and
entrepreneurial development, as well as policy makers and business advice
and support agencies.

David Rae is Dean of the Shannon School of Business, Cape Breton University, Canada and former Editor-in-Chief of the *International Journal of
Entrepreneurial Behaviour and Research*.

Catherine L. Wang is Professor of Strategy and Entrepreneurship at Royal
Holloway University of London, UK.

Routledge studies in entrepreneurship

Edited by Jay Mitra
Essex University, UK
and
Zoltan Acs
George Mason University, USA

This series extends the meaning and scope of entrepreneurship by capturing new research and enquiry on economic, social, cultural and personal value creation. Entrepreneurship as value creation represents the endeavours of innovative people and organisations in creative environments that open up opportunities for developing new products, new services, new firms and new forms of policy making in different environments seeking sustainable economic growth and social development. In setting this objective the series includes books which cover a diverse range of conceptual, empirical and scholarly topics that both inform the field and push the boundaries of entrepreneurship.

Entrepreneurial Learning

New perspectives in research, education and practice

Edited by David Rae and
Catherine L. Wang

Routledge
Taylor & Francis Group

LONDON AND NEW YORK

First published 2015
by Routledge
2 Park Square, Milton Park, Abingdon, Oxon OX14 4RN

and by Routledge
605 Third Avenue, New York, NY 10017

First issued in paperback 2020

Routledge is an imprint of the Taylor & Francis Group, an informa business

British Library Cataloguing in Publication Data
A catalogue record for this book is available from the British Library

Library of Congress Cataloging in Publication Data
Entrepreneurial learning: new perspectives in research, education and
practice / edited by David Rae and Catherine L. Wang.
    pages cm. – (Routledge studies in entrepreneurship)
    Includes bibliographical references.
    1. Entrepreneurship. 2. Organizational learning. I. Rae, David,
    II. Wang, Catherine L.
    HB615.E597453 2015
    658.3'124–dc23   2014030450

ISBN 13: 978-0-367-73854-9 (pbk)
ISBN 13: 978-0-415-72324-4 (hbk)

Typeset in Sabon
by Wearset Ltd, Boldon, Tyne and Wear

Contents

Figures

Tables

Contributors

Cinla Akinci is Lecturer in Management at the University of St Andrews, UK. Her research is focused on the role of intuition in managerial decision making and organisational learning. Her research on intuition has received several awards and has been published in international management journals.

Per Blenker is an Associate Professor at the iCARE group at Aarhus University. His primary research and teaching interests are in entrepreneurship and enterprise education.

Dermot Breslin is a Lecturer in Entrepreneurship at the University of Sheffield University, and Visiting Professor at Tor Vergata University, Rome. His research focuses on the emergence and co-evolution of practices within organisations. He is currently Associate Editor for the *International Journal of Management Reviews*.

Harveen Chugh is a specialist in entrepreneurship for PA Consulting Group. She was previously a Lecturer in Entrepreneurship and Strategy at Royal Holloway University of London and she gained her Ph.D. in Entrepreneurship from Imperial College Business School.

William A. Drago is Professor of Management at the University of Wisconsin – Whitewater.

Mark D'Souza-Mathew is the Knowledge Transfer Partnership Associate. He has a Ph.D. in Chemical Engineering and is certified in Professional Innovation Management. His research interests include functional surfaces, innovation capture systems and strategic goal implementation.

Jeff Gold is Professor of Organisation Learning at Leeds Business School. His research interests include management and leadership development, HRD and SME development and professional learning.

Dilani Jayawarna is a Senior Lecturer at the University of Liverpool Management School. She is Co-Chair of the British Academy of Management (BAM) Entrepreneurship Special Interest Group and a Consulting

Editor for the *International Small Business Journal*. Her recent publications are in the areas of entrepreneurial human capital, entrepreneur life course and bootstrapping/resourcing start-up businesses.

Oswald Jones is Professor of Entrepreneurship at the University of Liverpool Management School and Head of the Organisation and Management group. He is a member of the British Academy of Management (BAM) Council and Co-Editor, with Caroline Gatrell, of the *International Journal of Management Reviews*. Recent publications have focused on organisational learning in small firms, entrepreneurial learning, networks and networking, bootstrapping/resourcing start-up businesses, and enterprise education.

Rita G. Klapper is an entrepreneurial teaching and learning specialist using innovative and creative pedagogy, drawing upon art, music, theatre, yoga and mindfulness. She graduated with a Ph.D. in Entrepreneurship from Leeds University Business School and is currently a Lecturer in Enterprise at the Manchester Enterprise Centre, the University of Manchester, UK.

Xiaoqing Li is Lecturer in Strategy and Entrepreneurship at Brunel Business School, Brunel University, UK. Her research interests include strategic alliances in the higher education sector, internationalisation of services, international cooperative strategy, and internationalisation of firms in emerging markets.

Allan Macpherson is Associate Professor of Management at the University of Wisconsin – La Crosse. He has published a range of articles investigating the evolution of business knowledge, nascent entrepreneurship and learning from crises in small firms. His other work investigates strategic organisational learning in communities of practice and learning and change during, and following, extreme events.

Ian McKeown is a Senior Lecturer in Entrepreneurship based at the University of Wolverhampton. His research publications include entrepreneurial learning in SME management teams, team learning and mentoring, and coaching in small firms. He has been involved in supporting small firms through numerous Business Link consultancy projects, KTP and KEEN partnerships.

Howard Pickard is Director and Managing Director at Leeds Bradford Boiler Company.

Robert Pickard is Director and Manager at Leeds Bradford Boiler Company.

David Rae is Dean of the Shannon School of Business, Cape Breton University, Canada and former Editor-in-Chief of the *International Journal of Entrepreneurial Behaviour and Research*.

Mohammed Rafiq is Professor of Marketing at the Business School, University of Roehampton. His research areas include e-service quality, relationship quality, e-loyalty, internal marketing, town centre retail image, market orientation, innovation and new product development.

Deema Refai is Lecturer in Entrepreneurship in the Department of Strategy and Marketing at the University of Huddersfield. Deema specialises in enterprise education and the utilisation of experiential and interactive learning approaches as means for developing graduates' enterprise skills, with a special interest in healthcare disciplines.

Sarah Robinson is Associate Professor and educational anthropologist at the Centre for Teaching Development and Digital Media in the Faculty of Arts at Aarhus University in Denmark. She has researched entrepreneurship teaching and learning in higher education using ethnographic methods for the past two years.

Claus Thrane is an economist and researcher and teacher of entrepreneurship. His Ph.D. in entrepreneurship was on new venture creation and he holds significant expertise in entrepreneurial pedagogy and didactics as well as experience in cross-disciplinary course development in entrepreneurship.

Jeff Vanevenhoven, Ph.D., is an Associate Professor and coordinator of the entrepreneurship major at the University of Wisconsin – Whitewater. He received his Ph.D. from the University of Wisconsin – Milwaukee. His work has appeared in the *Strategic Management Journal* and the *Journal of Small Business Management*.

Catherine L. Wang is Professor of Strategy and Entrepreneurship at the School of Management, Royal Holloway University of London. Her research areas include entrepreneurial learning, entrepreneurial orientation, organisational ambidexterity, dynamic capabilities and innovation.

Lorraine Watkins-Mathys BA (Hons.), PGCE, MA, Ph.D. is Head of the School of Applied Management and Law at Buckinghamshire New University. Owing to her professional and international experience Lorraine has undertaken much of her research in transition and emerging economies focusing on international entrepreneurship and management issues.

Yu Zheng is Lecturer in Asian Business and International Human Resource Management at the School of Management, Royal Holloway University of London. Her research interests include international human resource management, comparative employment relations, Japanese multinational corporations, foreign direct investment in China and emerging human resource management models.

Acknowledgements

The editors wish to thank all of the contributors to this book for their insights, dedication and patience in finalising their work. We thank the publishing team at Routledge for their timely guidance and assistance. We thank our families for the time we have given this project. Finally, we acknowledge the founding contribution of Dr Jason Cope to the study of entrepreneurial learning since we began.

1 Introduction

David Rae and Catherine L. Wang

One of the editors of this book vividly recalls, as a neophyte in a business school back in around 1997, declaring the intention to research entrepreneurial learning, and the response received was: 'Why would you want to do that? No one will be interested and you won't get it published!' Undeterred, conducting such research became an entrepreneurial journey in itself. Fortuitously, others were simultaneously engaging in the field. Deakins (1996) had set a marker by noting the lack of understanding of how entrepreneurs learn, and by organising a series of conferences which brought together early contributors to the field; their work was published in annual special issues of the *International Journal of Entrepreneurial Behaviour and Research* (1998, 1999, 2000). There had been a few earlier contributors, with Reuber and Fischer (1993), Young and Sexton (1997) and Mitton (1997) starting to address the topic from a North American perspective.

It is possible to go further back, and to locate an interest in the entrepreneur's ability to learn in the economic theories of Schumpeter (1934) and Kirzner (1973), albeit as a necessary step in presaging entrepreneurial action rather than as their primary focus. However, the period from the late 1990s onwards brought growing interest in what we may term the human and social dynamics of entrepreneurship. This was distinct from the previous dominance of economics-based work which generally focused on the study of small businesses rather than on people.

During this period a change of government occurred in the UK, heralding a 'New Labour' administration which had spent much time and been heavily influenced by entrepreneurship policy and development in the United States. The policy focus moved away from its main concentration on supporting existing small firms, to address the potential of 'The Entrepreneurial Society' (Gavron *et al.*, 1998), which led to a significant increased interest in entrepreneurship education in schools and higher education, in support of new venture creation, business incubation and entrepreneurship in hitherto little-recognised sectors, such as the creative and cultural industries, and, in due course, social entrepreneurship. This led to major government investments in education, especially in higher education which was seen to have a major role to play in social change, the democratisation of entrepreneurship, as well as unlocking intellectual capital for business creation. The development of these policy initiatives in the UK was accompanied by similar movements at the European level, and indeed by other supranational organisations, and by many national governments. Writers such as Allan Gibb, in particular, have influenced this movement significantly.

All of these developments required an understanding of the roles of human agency, learning and capital in entrepreneurship. A fundamental shift was the realisation that entrepreneurship was not simply the unrelated actions of individuals in search of personal economic rewards, or the classic US 'Free Enterprise' model, but that entrepreneurship could be understood more usefully in sociological terms as a social and cultural collective movement, composed of disparate but like-minded individuals. In parallel with this realisation, researchers started to use a wider range of methodological perspectives and approaches than those which had previously been applied in studying entrepreneurship. These were informed by disciplines and traditions including sociology, psychology, education, cultural studies such as anthropology, and indeed others.

Many people have found the scope to develop career opportunities in enterprise education, in business support projects and organisations for entrepreneurship, and in researching these policies and processes. This led to significant and continuing growth in conferences, professional network organisations, and in publishing activity centred on entrepreneurship. Research into entrepreneurial learning has grown and continues to evolve rapidly, at a scale which no one was likely to anticipate in the early years of interest in the topic, before the year 2000, for example.

The purpose of this book

Given this continuing growth of interest in the topic as a field of academic enquiry as well as of educational development and empirical application in society, there is some value in taking stock of what work has been done, and to invite new perspectives and explorations in the field. This book therefore aims to explore the development of the field since its inception in the 1990s and to bring together contributions which offer new understandings of its potential development and scope for the future. Entrepreneurial learning is an arena in which multiple perspectives are created and offered. This has been the case from the outset: there has never been a single theoretical model or framework, though there have been attempts to create one. The field is diverse, and one reason for this is that no single accepted theory of human learning exists; as entrepreneurship is simply a domain or context within which human learning takes place, differing conceptualisations of entrepreneurial learning are inevitable.

This issue of context is important. The early years of study in this topic tended to be dominated by a polarity between North American and British writing, generally located in their domestic educational and cultural contexts. Mainland European writers quickly engaged in the topic and made important contributions. As the notion of entrepreneurship as a movement for social and cultural as well as economic transformation has become prevalent worldwide, interest in the learning process of entrepreneurship has accompanied this notion. This book has incorporated an international perspective, but we as editors would have wished to go further, and to include contributions from a wider range of international and cultural perspectives, which may be an ambition for the future.

One question which has to be addressed in a book such as this is: when we talk of entrepreneurial learning, what do we mean? How do we define the term and the territory?

Both editors, as well as the contributors and writers cited in this book, have provided definitions in order to operationalise their own research in the field, as well as to enable educators, students and practitioners to understand what we are talking about. As a starting point, we suggest that entrepreneurial learning is a process in which individuals, groups (such as venture teams or even communities) and organisations develop and practise the knowledge, skills and capabilities they require to take entrepreneurial actions, and to achieve outcomes which may transform themselves, their ventures, and their social, cultural and economic context. Learning is necessary and inevitable within entrepreneurship.

The question of definitions is addressed more fully in Chapter 2, 'Entrepreneurial learning: past research and future challenges', in which Catherine Wang and Harveen Chugh provide a comprehensive review of the literature on entrepreneurial learning as a foundation for the book. Their systematic analysis evaluates the contributions of the diverse literature. Based on this, they propose three pairs of key learning types that merit attention in future research, namely individual and collective learning; exploratory and exploitative learning; and intuitive and sensing learning. This typology is used to articulate three key challenges for future research in entrepreneurship and organisational learning. While a few other comprehensive reviews of the entrepreneurial literature exist (e.g. Erdelyi, 2010), this chapter provides a valuable starting point for the book, in which it becomes explicit that connections between different types of learning, domains of knowledge, and traditions of research and methodologies have to be made in order to understand the work in the field.

Structure and overview

The structure of the book reflects three themes. These themes were selected having reviewed the development of research in the field of entrepreneurial learning over the past fifteen years, including work of both a conceptual nature, work which reviews and summarises prior research in the field to advance theoretical understanding of entrepreneurial learning research, and work of an applied, empirical and situated nature.

- Human-centred naturalistic, lifelong and career learning (three chapters).
- Entrepreneurial learning in education: concepts and paradigms (three chapters).
- Entrepreneurial learning in organisations, including international perspectives (five chapters).

These three themes each reflect differing contexts in which learning occurs. The first centres on the entrepreneurial person, situated in their biography and whole-life experience. The second is situated in an educational context of organised, institutional and expected learning. The third is again organisational, but, rather than being detached from business, centres on learning within organisations as entrepreneurial environments. These three themes include perspectives on conceptualising and theory building, formalised learning in institutional settings and informal learning-in-practice, which are manifested in comparable ways in different cultural and national contexts.

The first theme, human-centred learning, includes three quite different and important contributions which offer new perspectives on entrepreneurship as a lifelong learning process in which context plays a significant role. In the opening chapter, Chapter 3, Dilani Jayawarna, Oswald Jones and Allan Macpherson explore the hitherto-unexplored role of childhood and adolescent human capital learning to become an entrepreneur. Using a long-term dataset on child development, they argue that the processes through which human capital influences entrepreneurial prospects begin during children's early school years, and they propose that cognitive ability and creative potential are powerful influences on subsequent entrepreneurial career prospects in adulthood. Hence, promoting creative abilities in early childhood is a predictor of subsequent entrepreneurship. In addition, the roles of parental employment, in particular self-employment, and economic status are decisive in subsequent entrepreneurship. The authors conceive entrepreneurial learning as a constantly unfolding process, intersecting with social factors to influence an individual's life course, and requiring further research on structural and social influences which determine entrepreneurial learning opportunities and trajectories.

In Chapter 4, Cinla Akinci proposes the role of entrepreneurial intuition in decision making, based on Crossan et al.'s (1999) organisational learning process model, which connects individual, group and organisational learning through a framework of intuiting, interpreting, integrating and institutionalising learning. This highlights the role of intuitive learning through affect and cue recognition in the identification and discovery of opportunities, based on the prior experience and learning of entrepreneurs. It aims to bridge the fields of entrepreneurial and organisational learning research, and the discovery of opportunities.

In Chapter 5, David Rae suggests that recognising 'the moment' may be used in understanding entrepreneurial processes of learning and creativity. The significance of 'the aha moment' in entrepreneurial behaviour is widely used at a popular level but has not been well explored in relation to human learning. In this chapter he reflects on momentary perspectives from literature, philosophy, social psychology and neuroscience, proposing that human behaviour operates 'in the moment', and the significant role played by unconscious, intuitive and emotional processes in entrepreneurial behaviour. The results of two limited-scale studies of entrepreneurs and entrepreneurship educators are used to develop a conceptualisation of human behaviour in the moment, which may be applied to understand how entrepreneurial activities such as learning, creative thinking and decision making are enacted.

The second theme, 'Entrepreneurial learning in education: concepts and paradigms', also offers three contributions. There has been extensive writing on enterprise and entrepreneurship education, much of which has been of an empirical and applied nature, sharing understanding of teaching and learning practices in educational contexts of primary, secondary, tertiary, vocational and higher education. However, too much of this has failed to cross the divide between classroom learning and entrepreneurial practice, or to conceptualise in ways which have utility and value beyond the limitations of the case. In selecting contributions for this theme, we have aimed to move beyond these bounded contributions to address wider issues. In Chapter 6, Jeff Vanevenhoven and William Drago report the results of a global survey into the structure and scope of entrepreneurship education programmes in higher education with the aim of informing definitions of best practices and effectiveness metrics. Based on responses from over 300 universities internationally, the results provide new understanding of the range and diversity of educational provision, analysing differences between types of courses, faculty positions, infrastructure, location in the university and external support.

Chapters 7 and 8 introduce new and generalisable conceptualisations of entrepreneurial learning in education. In 'Progression and coherence in enterprise education: an overall framework supporting diversity', Per Blenker, Sarah Robinson and Claus Thrane propose a framework which allows educators to communicate more clearly the diversity of roles and relationships between different entrepreneurship courses and modules, based on their experiences in a large international research project. Using observations from anthropologists, they offer a research-based model of enterprise learning activities built on an explicit learning philosophy, organised with an emphasis on progression and differentiated pedagogy. Their methodological contribution demonstrates how different research methods may be used in combination to develop entrepreneurship course contents and pedagogy.

There is an interesting comparison possible with the next chapter from Rita Klapper and Deema Refai, which is founded on the premise that entrepreneurial learning needs to be considered from a holistic perspective in which each dimension contributes to the others to create a sense-giving 'Gestalt'. Wenger's social theory of learning (2009) is also deployed, together with guiding principles for educational design, which influence the impact and quality of entrepreneurship education and students' motivation for studying and learning. By bringing these together with Gestalt theory and Wenger's social theory of learning, they advocate a comprehensive way of designing entrepreneurship teaching programmes, to bring the learner closer to the realities of entrepreneurial practice.

The third theme explores learning in the 'real' contexts of business organisations, including new venture creation, owner-manager and small business development, and 'intrapreneurial' learning in larger corporations. It also introduces an international perspective on entrepreneurial learning, from the different cultural contexts of the UK and Chinese perspectives. The five chapters in this theme offer quite different views of entrepreneurial learning in organisations, albeit with points of connection and comparison.

First, in Chapter 9, Ian McKeown introduces a study of entrepreneurial learning and unlearning in the context of small firm management teams. He explores the difficulties which members of the management team in a small firm collectively face in trying to share their experiences, while co-constructing knowledge and understanding of their environment which subsequently creates or reveals opportunities for the small firm. Field research produced a longitudinal qualitative case study of an management team involved in an entrepreneurial manufacturing firm. This informed the development of a workable model of entrepreneurial learning from a team perspective, contributing to existing theoretical conceptualisations of the process of entrepreneurial learning. What also emerged from this model was a complex, often messy picture of entrepreneurial learning involving a dynamic interplay between three core issues of team participation, shared practices and the influence of situated power and valuing of what is learned.

The theme of complex, messy learning is also apparent in Chapter 10, which articulates the 'struggle' for product development and innovation in a family-owned business. Jointly authored by the associate of a Knowledge Transfer partnership, Mark D'Souza-Mathew, two family firm members, Robert and Howard Pickard, and the researcher Jeff Gold, this is a comparable and co-created account of learning through the technical and social processes of innovation and new product development in a small firm. The case is distinctive within the book, illustrating in fine detail how learning can be highly specific, situated and related to the value-creating technology of the firm. The chapter offers lessons for the product development and innovation process in family-owned businesses.

Chapter 11 moves from the specific to a more philosophical and epistemological view of this territory, in which distinct connections and comparisons can be made with both of the preceding chapters. The author, Dermot Breslin, relates how social science works to study socio-cultural change, in which this approach has reconceptualised the small business's struggle for survival as an evolutionary process in which the entrepreneur must 'learn to evolve'. The chapter develops an evolutionary perspective on entrepreneurship by exploring the use of evolutionary language and reinterpreting entrepreneurial learning as the co-evolution of components of knowledge through the mechanisms of variation-selection-retention. It argues that, if knowledge co-evolves and entrepreneurs become aware of this evolution, they can learn to adapt, and to influence the wider evolutionary process within the firm and beyond.

The book closes with two chapters which move the exploration of entrepreneurial learning to the rapidly changing context of Chinese private businesses. While the two chapters share this context however, the perspectives they provide are quite different, and again merit comparison to generate fresh and revealing insights between empirical exploration and philosophical reflection.

First, in Chapter 12, Catherine Wang, Mohammed Rafiq, Xiaoqing Li and Yu Zheng provide an overview of two case studies of Chinese high-technology private enterprises. They use this evidence to advance the understanding of the emerging concept of 'entrepreneurial preparedness' as a cumulative, social and purposeful learning process, highlighting the roles of experiential learning, social learning and entrepreneurial goals as mechanisms to enable entrepreneurial preparedness in new venture creation and management. Their findings reveal that the social and purposeful nature of entrepreneurial preparedness is integral to and interwoven within the cumulative learning process, deepening the understanding of how and under what conditions entrepreneurial preparedness occurs in new venture creation and management. Their findings illustrate the positive and negative double-edged role of prior experience, especially when context changes, and reflect on the extent to which entrepreneurs' personal backgrounds influence firm development in the context of change, while balancing learning and performance goals in relation to the needs of firm development.

Finally, in Chapter 13 Lorraine Watkins-Mathys examines entrepreneurial learning in the Chinese social, cultural and business context. Examining the Eastern mindset and Confucian approaches to learning and entrepreneurship, these are compared with Western approaches to entrepreneurial learning, attributes and behaviours. She proposes that the Confucian cultural heritage lends itself to meaning-oriented learning and interpretation, in which behaviour and learning is driven by a value-based belief system that places a strong moral obligation on the entrepreneur who is expected to have a strong moral character; a strong sense of loyalty to family and country. The institutional framework is considered in relation to Chinese society, as is the role of structural holes and disconnections which are created as a consequence of how resources are organised for respective industries, providing opportunities for Chinese entrepreneurs and ways to obtain those resources. 'Guanxi' or relational familial and market networks play an important role in helping entrepreneurs maximise such business opportunities.

Conversations, issues and questions for the future

The contributions which have been requested and offered for this book provide a range of perspectives on entrepreneurial learning. Each provides distinctive insights and possibilities for future investigation. Rather than providing a closing chapter, we feel it is appropriate in this final section of the Introduction to signal some proposed lines of enquiry for the future. After nearly twenty years, entrepreneurial learning can no longer be considered a new or even emerging field of study, but rather one that has become established and has in turn been subdivided into a number of related topics.

We set out three themes in this book with the intention that these are theoretically, empirically and practically engaged, such as through the processes of creating and sharing knowledge and practice; the roles of social networks, entrepreneurial cultures, communities and society; and the applications of digital technologies which enable connection, communication and social learning. Together with changing economic, contextual and intellectual movements, these themes enable the book's contributors to suggest emerging new perspectives in entrepreneurial learning.

However, the continuing evolution and changing nature of entrepreneurship, and of the contexts within which entrepreneurial practitioners, learners, educators, advisers and researchers operate, mean that the subject remains relevant, fluid and without a single unifying or definitive theory or explanation. We therefore suggest that the following issues and questions are ones of growing value and importance for researchers to consider.

The book aims to offer an internationally informed perspective, but at this point it is only partially successful in achieving this aim. Much more needs to be known about how entrepreneurs learn in the conditions of developing countries. In particular, we know little about entrepreneurial learning in the context of adverse economic, social and political environments, and those where there are unstable and volatile conditions. At the time of writing, we started to see entrepreneurial development in countries such as Burma and Somalia, small signs of street market micro-preneurship even in the most hostile conditions of North Korea, and adversity being experienced in Pakistan, Palestine, Afghanistan and other zones. This question is of increasing urgency: how does entrepreneurial learning occur in such conditions of adversity and instability?

There is some work appearing on entrepreneurial learning and gender, but more work needs to be done in this field. There is scope to explore female and gendered perspectives in entrepreneurial learning. Related to this, the learning experiences and process of ethnic minority women and men is an under-researched field, as is the learning experiences of entrepreneurs with disabilities.

In relation to entrepreneurship education and learning in the context of organisations, there is more to do in understanding the translation and relationships between education and workplace learning, including the use of social networks, technologies, and how the impact and effectiveness of entrepreneurial learning may be assessed. As new business models and media emerge, how does entrepreneurial learning occur in, for example, distributed or shared economy businesses? There is increasing work on enterprise education in developing countries which needs systematic review and analysis to inform research, policy and practice.

In relation to types of organisations and forms of entrepreneurship, the period since 2008 has seen continuing advances in social entrepreneurship and social innovation, together with the related but distinct field of sustainable entrepreneurship. The ethical and value base of entrepreneurship is changing, yet the learning dimension of this is not well understood. More knowledge is needed, not least to inform education and support, on how entrepreneurial learning occurs in communities and organisations where the philosophy is explicitly ethical, socially accountable and participative.

Although there is progress in understanding the relationships, at theoretical and practical levels, between entrepreneurial and organisational learning, more conceptual and contextual research is needed to understand more effectively the nature of entrepreneurial learning in large corporations, and in public and third-sector organisations which are aiming to transform themselves into entrepreneurial organisations. There are many such instances in the educational, health, government agency and local government arenas, and a need for enhanced understanding of the relationships between management development and entrepreneurial learning.

These are simply reflections on future possibilities and imperatives which arise from the editors' reflections upon reading the contributions to this book. Finally, we wish to thank the authors for their contributions, and to say that it has been a privilege to work with them on developing their distinctive perspectives. We also wish to thank the editorial and publishing team at Routledge for their advice and support over the past three years in which this book has progressed from idea to reality. We commend the book to you, and hope that you draw knowledge, insights and inspirations from it.

References

Crossan, M.M., Lane, H.W. and White, R.E. (1999). An Organizational Learning Framework: From Intuition to Institution. *The Academy of Management Review*, 24(3), 522–537.

Deakins, D. (1996). *Entrepreneurship and Small Firms*. Maidenhead: McGraw-Hill.

Erdelyi, P. (2010). The Matter of Entrepreneurial Learning: A Literature Review. In International Conference on Organizational Learning, Knowledge and Capabilities (OLKC), 3–6 June, Northeastern University, Boston, MA.

Gavron, R., Cowling, M. and Westall, A. (1998). *The Entrepreneurial Society*. Institute for Public Policy Research.

International Journal of Entrepreneurial Behaviour and Research (1998). Volume 4, Issue 2 (Special issue): Learning and the Entrepreneur.

—— (1999). Volume 5, Issues 3–4 (Special issue): Papers from the Second Enterprise and Learning Conference, Parts 1 and 2.

—— (2000). Volume 6, Issue 3 (Special issue): Papers from the Second Enterprise and Learning Conference.

Kirzner, I. (1973). *Competition and Entrepreneurship*. Chicago, IL: University of Chicago Press.

Mitton, D. (1997). Entrepreneurship: One More Time – Non-cognitive Characteristics that Make the Cognitive Click. In *Frontiers of Entrepreneurship Research*, Wellesley, MA: Babson College, pp. 189–203.

Reuber, R.A. and Fischer, E.M. (1993). The Learning Experiences of Entrepreneurs. In N.C. Churchill *et al.* (eds), *Frontiers of Entrepreneurship Research*. Wellesley, MA: Babson College, pp. 234–245.

Schumpeter, J. (1934). *The Theory of Economic Development*. Cambridge, MA: Harvard University Press.

Wenger, E. (2009). A Social Theory of Learning. In D.C. Philips and J.F. Soltis, *Perspectives on Learning*. New York: Teachers' College Press, pp. 209–218.

Young, J.E. and Sexton, D.L. (1997). Entrepreneurial Learning: A Conceptual Framework. *Journal of Enterprising Culture*, 5(3), 223–248.

2 Entrepreneurial learning

Past research and future challenges

Catherine L. Wang and Harveen Chugh

Introduction

Entrepreneurial learning (EL) has emerged as a promising area of research at the interface between learning and the entrepreneurial context (Harrison and Leitch 2005). Central to EL research are issues pertinent not only to *what* entrepreneurs should or do learn during the process of exploring and exploiting an entrepreneurial opportunity in the creation of new ventures or management of existing firms, but, more importantly, the specific processes of learning that take place (Cope 2005). Simply put, *how* learning takes place and *when* learning takes place is fundamental to our understanding of the entrepreneurial process. As Minniti and Bygrave (2001, p. 7) assert, 'entrepreneurship is a process of learning, and a theory of entrepreneurship requires a theory of learning'.

EL research has flourished over the past decade, and demonstrates several characteristics. First, while EL is broadly positioned at the interface of entrepreneurship and organisational learning, existing studies have drawn from a wide range of theoretical insights, including experiential learning (e.g. Minniti and Bygrave 2001; Cope 2003; Clarysse and Moray 2004), organisational learning (e.g. Lant and Mezias 1990; Covin *et al.* 2006; Wang 2008), social cognitive theory (i.e. Erikson 2003), population ecology (i.e. Dencker *et al.* 2009) and configuration theory (i.e. Hughes *et al.* 2007), employing different methods to study different entrepreneurial contexts. While this may signal the vivacity of the field, it is important to take inventory of the work to date through a systematic literature review, and identify key research themes and developmental patterns to provide an overview of EL literature for further research to build on.

Second, accompanying the characteristic of diversity of EL research is its highly individualistic and fragmented nature, resulting in incongruence in many aspects of EL, such as its definitions. For example, although EL is often referred to as learning in the entrepreneurial process (Ravasi and Turati 2005; Politis 2005; Holcomb *et al.* 2009), its definitions span from 'venture learning' (Berglund *et al.* 2007, p. 178), 'learning to recognise and act on opportunities, and interacting socially to initiate, organise and manage ventures' (Rae 2005, p. 324), to 'the variety of experiential and cognitive processes used to acquire, retain and use entrepreneurial knowledge' (Young and Sexton 2003, p. 156). While we recognise that the diversity, individuality and inconsistency reflects individual researchers' epistemological, ontological and methodological background, it is important to take stock of the EL literature and identify the key research gaps and challenges for future research.

Third, the rise of EL research has revitalised entrepreneurship research by focusing on the learning and developmental process of entrepreneurship (Deakins 1996), and who an entrepreneur may become through learning (Cope 2005; Rae 2000). As Cope (2005, p. 379) commented, 'it is through learning that entrepreneurs develop and grow'. This responds to the failure of past entrepreneurial research on traits, which was unsuccessfully preoccupied with 'who an entrepreneur is' and precluded an entrepreneur's ability to learn, develop and change (Gartner 1988). However, more research is needed to understand the role of learning in entrepreneurship (Blackburn and Kovalainen 2009), how EL can help one understand the key challenges in the entrepreneurship literature, and to cross-fertilise the entrepreneurship and organisational learning literatures.

This study aims to help fill the above three research gaps by focusing on three key objectives. First, we conduct a systematic analysis of the EL literature in business and management studies to take stock of the theoretical and empirical development, and to identify EL research themes and developmental patterns. In particular, our systematic literature review is based on pre-defined themes often used in traditional and systematic literature reviews to elicit developmental patterns in terms of publication distribution, theoretical perspectives, EL definitions, types of learning, entrepreneurial contexts, and methods and units of analysis. We aim to provide an overview of the EL research and a foundation for future researchers to build on. As Low and MacMillan (1988) argue, a periodical review of a particular field is necessary for deriving maximum benefit from future research. Second, we discuss three pairs of learning types that deserve more attention in future research, namely individual and collective learning, exploratory and exploitative learning, and intuitive and sensing learning. These learning types correspond to the key EL research gaps identified in our systematic literature review as well as the key challenges at the centre of debate in the entrepreneurship literature, providing fruitful avenues for future research. We follow the paths of Gibb Dyer (1994) and Cope (2005) and aim to identify key challenges that help direct future EL research towards more fruitful research avenues. Third, through exploring the three pairs of learning types and the key challenges that correspond to the learning types, we draw further insights from entrepreneurship and organisational learning to advance EL research. We also feed back to the entrepreneurship literature by discussing how these learning types help us understand the key challenges in entrepreneurship. Therefore, this chapter helps to further cross-fertilise the entrepreneurship and organisational learning literatures as well as advancing EL research. In sum, our main aim is to take stock of EL research to provide a foundation for future EL research to proliferate and prosper, while recognising its current diversity and individuality.

Literature analysis: themes and trends

We started with a broad definition of EL as 'learning in the entrepreneurial process' (Ravasi and Turati 2005; Politis 2005; Holcomb *et al.* 2009) to guide our literature search and analysis. We defined the entrepreneurial process as 'the process by which individuals – either on their own or inside organizations – pursue opportunities without regard to the resources they currently control' (Stevenson and Jarillo 1990, p. 23). Opportunity exploration (as well as discovery, recognition or development) and opportunity exploitation are widely recognised as the two generic, heterogeneous processes of entrepreneurship (Stevenson and Jarillo 1990; Shane and Venkataraman 2000). Specifically, opportunity exploration entails the search for information leading to the creation of new knowledge (Alvarez and Busenitz 2001), while opportunity exploitation requires a firm to commit resources in order to build efficient business systems for full-scale operations for producing, and gaining returns from, the new product arising from the opportunity (Choi and Shepherd 2004).

Literature search

Accordingly, our literature search focuses primarily on the following entrepreneurial contexts in which an entrepreneurial opportunity is explored and exploited. (1) Opportunity exploration and exploitation in start-up entrepreneurship or new venture creation (SE). As new venture creation is central to entrepreneurship (Ireland *et al.* 2005), research has studied how an entrepreneurial opportunity is explored and exploited in the process of new venture creation. (2) Opportunity exploration and exploitation in established firms (EE), including small and medium-sized businesses and large corporations. Since entrepreneurship is not necessarily constrained in the new venture creation stage, but may span the entire life cycle of the firm (Reuber and Fischer 1999), research has studied how an entrepreneurial opportunity is explored and exploited in established firms. Finally, (3) opportunity exploration and exploitation in general entrepreneurship (GE); that is, without specifying if this takes place in start-up or established firms.

We searched academic journal articles listed in the Association of Business Schools (ABS) Academic Journal Quality Version 4 by Subject Area (Kelly *et al.* 2010) published during the period up until and including August 2012, primarily in the following categories of the business and management discipline: 'Entrepreneurship and Small Business Management' as the primary source of our literature search; and 'General Management', 'Strategic Management', 'Organization Studies', 'Innovation', and 'Management Development and Education' as our secondary literature sources, since these categories include journals that occasionally publish entrepreneurship research. We conducted searches using the electronic databases Business Source Complete, Science Direct, JSTOR and Wiley Online Library, covering the period up until and including August 2012. We searched the Title and Abstract fields using the primary Boolean search terms of 'entrepreneur* AND learn*', and the secondary search term of 'opportunity AND learn*' to identify all articles within our conceptual boundaries. This process resulted in a total of seventy-five academic journal articles (fifty-two empirical and twenty-three conceptual articles) that were included in our final analysis resulting in the emergence of a number of publication patterns and themes.

Publication distribution

This section reports three key findings from the analysis of the thematic codes 1–4 ((1) Name(s) of the authors; (2) Year of publication; (3) Country of authors' institution(s) at time of publication; and (4) Journal title). First, there has been a sharp increase of scholarly interest in EL since 2000 (see Figure 2.1). The 2005 Special Issue of *Entrepreneurship Theory and Practice* (ET&P) is a key contributor to the growth, as seven of the articles in our analysis were from this issue. Second, the key publication outlets include the US-based ET&P (eighteen articles) and *Journal of Business Venturing* (JBV) (seven articles); and the UK-based *International Journal of Entrepreneurship Behaviour and Research* (IJEB&R) (seven articles) and *Journal of Small Business and Enterprise Development* (JSB&ED) (seven articles). The conceptual development by Minniti and Bygrave (2001) and the Special Issue on EL edited by Harrison and Leitch (2005) have been particularly influential in shaping EL research. Among sixty-one articles published after 2001, twenty-three reference Minniti and Bygrave (2001), while among forty-three articles published after 2005, fourteen reference Harrison and Leitch (2005). Third, it is evident that research collaboration (as indicated by co-authorship) has largely been within the same country or region and very little collaboration exists between North American and European researchers with few exceptions (e.g. Schildt *et al.* 2005; Gruber *et al.* 2008; Dencker *et al.* 2009). Although there is a small percentage of European-based authors published in ET&P (five out of eighteen articles) and JBV (four out of seven articles), the authors publishing in JSB&ED and IJEB&R are all European-based (with the exception of Erikson (2003), who was affiliated with both Norway and the USA). The overall analysis of publication distribution shows that EL research has gained momentum in the past decade, with the North American and

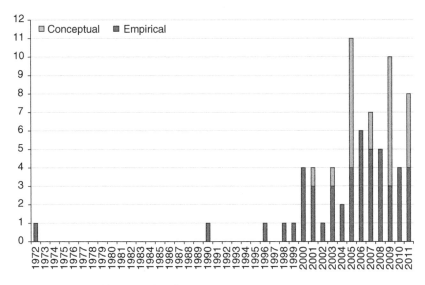

Figure 2.1 EL publication distribution (1972–2011).

Note
While our literature search included articles published up until and including August 2012, we have only included articles up until 2011 in this figure, so that we do not give an inaccurate representation of the articles published in 2012. NB: There have been three empirical articles and one conceptual article published from January to August 2012.

European research in two camps in terms of publication outlets. We discuss this point further in the summary of this section.

Theoretical perspectives

EL research has drawn upon a wide range of theoretical perspectives. Specifically, two theoretical perspectives play a dominating role. First, several articles build on experiential learning (i.e. Lamont 1972; Minniti and Bygrave 2001; Cope 2003; Clarysse and Moray 2004; Corbett 2005, 2007; Dimov 2007; Politis and Gabrielsson 2009; Lévesque *et al.* 2009). These studies have largely drawn on the work of Kolb (1976, 1984, 1985, 1999) and his colleagues (e.g. Kolb and Kolb 2005; Kolb *et al.* 1984, 1995; Kolb and Kolb 2001). Second, several articles have drawn on theories of organisational learning, including exploratory and exploitative learning (March 1991), single- and double-loop learning (Argyris and Schön 1978), organisational learning (consisting of four constructs: knowledge acquisition, information distribution, information interpretation and organisational memory) (Huber 1991), absorptive capacity and external learning (Cohen and Levinthal 1990; Zahra and George 2002; Jones 2006), the fifth discipline of the learning organisation (Senge 1990), higher level or lower level learning (Fiol and Lyles 1985), and organisational learning in terms of information processing and decision making (Cyert and March 1963; Levitt and March 1988; March and Simon 1958; March and Olsen 1975, 1976). Organisational learning theory has been applied to EL studies in a wide variety of ways; for example, whether entrepreneurial firms use higher order learning (Chaston *et al.* 2001), how the theory of organisational learning helps conceptualise entrepreneurship (Lant and Mezias 1990), and how intentionality drives opportunity development from the organisational learning perspective (Dimov 2007). Several authors (e.g. Covin *et al.* 2006; Wang 2008; Zhao *et al.* 2011) study learning in corporate contexts and find that entrepreneurship research benefits from the application of organisational learning theory (Dutta and Crossan 2005). However, very little insight exists to advance the conceptualisation of EL, especially how organisational learning processes differ in entrepreneurial firms from non-entrepreneurial firms. We discuss how EL can draw further insights from organisational learning theory in the next section.

Definitions of entrepreneurial learning

While forty-seven of the seventy-five articles used the term 'entrepreneurial learning', the remaining twenty-eight articles refer generally to learning in the entrepreneurial process and do not provide a definition of EL. Of the forty-seven articles that do use the term 'entrepreneurial learning', eleven define EL explicitly, ten define EL implicitly, and the remaining twenty-six articles do not define EL either explicitly or implicitly. These definitions are incongruent and include 'venture learning' (Berglund *et al.* 2007), learning that 'informs the entrepreneur's quest for new opportunities' (Franco and Haase 2009, p. 634), 'how entrepreneurs accumulate and update knowledge' (Minniti and Bygrave 2001, p. 8), 'learning to work in entrepreneurial ways' (Rae 2000, p. 151), and 'learning experienced by entrepreneurs during the creation and development of a small enterprise, rather than a particular style or form of learning that could be described as "entrepreneurial"' (Cope 2005, p. 374). The definitions reflect a wide range of focuses such as learning by the venture team (Berglund *et al.* 2007), the learning processes involved in the development of a new venture (Ravasi and Turati 2005), learning experienced by entrepreneurs (Cope 2003; Cope and Watts 2000), what, how and why entrepreneurs learn (Parker 2006), recognising and acting on opportunities (Rae 2006), and a process related to knowledge acquisition, assimilation and organisation (Holcomb *et al.* 2009; Minniti and Bygrave 2001; Politis 2005). These definitions demonstrate the different frames of reference that researchers have applied to understanding EL. However, a closer examination of these definitions reveals that they are primarily related to what and how individual entrepreneurs learn, with very few papers studying team- or organisational-level learning, or beyond. In other words, little is known about how collective learning takes place in entrepreneurial teams or firms. Overall, there is a general lack of consensus on what EL is and EL at the organisational level is under-researched. We discuss individual and collective learning in the next section.

Types of learning

In this section, we analyse the learning mechanisms used in EL research. Experiential learning, in addition to being applied as a theoretical lens for EL, is widely referred to as a mechanism for learning in thirty-two out of seventy-five articles. Among the thirty-two articles, fourteen draw from the work of Kolb (1984) (e.g. Cope 2005; Politis 2005; Corbett 2005, 2007; Dimov 2007). Experiential learning in the remaining articles does not refer to Kolb and his colleagues' work, but to 'learning-by-doing' (Cope 2003; Balasubramanian 2011), learning from past business experience (Lamont 1972), learning from positive and negative experiences (Minniti and Bygrave 2001), learning from past experience (Rerup 2005; Sardana and Scott-Kemmis 2010), and learning from participation and from the experience of others (i.e. vicarious learning) (Lévesque *et al.* 2009). In addition, several individual or organisational learning theories have been used to understand the entrepreneurial process: (1) March's (1991) exploratory and exploitative learning (cited by twenty-two articles); (2) Argyris and Schön's (1978) single-loop/adaptive and double-loop/generative learning (twenty-one articles); (3) Huber's (1991) organisational learning (twenty-two articles); (4) Cohen and Levinthal's (1990) absorptive capacity and external learning (sixteen articles), and Zahra and George's (2002) reconceptualisation of absorptive capacity (eight articles); (5) situated learning and communities of practice by Lave and Wenger (1991) and Wenger (1998) (eight and five articles respectively), and Brown and Duguid's (1991) work in the same area (eight articles); (6) Senge's (1990) the fifth discipline of the learning organisation (sixteen articles); (7) Fiol and Lyles' (1985) higher level or lower level learning (eleven articles); and (8) organisational learning in terms of information processing and decision making include the work by Cyert and March (1963) (ten articles), Levitt and March (1988) (nine articles), March and Simon (1958) (three articles), March and Olsen (1975) (two articles), and March and Olsen (1976) (two articles). There is a need to understand the respective roles and contributions of different types of learning in the advancement of EL research, which we discuss in the next section.

Entrepreneurial context

In this section, we report our analysis of EL research with particular reference to the 'entrepreneurial context' as defined in the Methods section. First, twenty-one articles fall under the SE context (start-up entrepreneurship).

Within this context, the research focus spans independent new start-ups (e.g. Nicholls-Nixon *et al.* 2000; Honig 2001; Huovinen and Tihula 2008; Karataş-Özkan 2011), university spin-offs (Clarysse and Moray 2004) and start-ups in incubators (Hughes *et al.* 2007). These articles focus primarily on individual learning in start-up entrepreneurship. Given the prominence of teams in the start-up process (Timmons and Spinelli 2006), there is a scarcity of research on learning in the process of forming a founding team (with very few exceptions, such as Karataş-Özkan 2011).

Second, twenty-three articles fall under the EE context (entrepreneurship in established firms) (Table 2.1). Among these articles there is a relatively balanced focus on small, medium or large firms; for example, Cope (2003) studied the effect of discontinuous events on learning outcomes in the context of small business management and growth; Schildt *et al.* (2005) examine the antecedents of exploratory versus exploitative learning from external corporate ventures in large firms; and Lee and Williams (2007) focus on dispersed entrepreneurship in large multinational corporations. In particular, studies in the EE context have already started to explore how the learning process and the entrepreneurial process interact to have an impact on firm performance (e.g. Covin *et al.* 2006; Hughes *et al.* 2007; Wang 2008; Rhee *et al.* 2010; Zhao *et al.* 2011). For example, it has been found that firms cannot sustain dual-dominant orientations of exploitative learning and entrepreneurial orientation (Hughes *et al.* 2007), a learning orientation must be in place in order to realise the effect of entrepreneurial orientation on firm performance (Wang 2008), and learning from strategic mistakes may be of more particular value to conservative firms than to entrepreneurial firms (Covin *et al.* 2006).

Third, thirty out of seventy-five articles fall under the GE context (general entrepreneurship) without reference to start-up or established firms. These include the following. (1) Four articles that focus primarily on the general process of opportunity exploration (discovery, recognition and development) (i.e. Lumpkin and Lichtenstein 2005; Politis 2005; Sanz-Velasco 2006; Corbett 2005, 2007; Dimov 2007). (2) Four articles that deal with both exploration and exploitation despite more emphasis on exploration (i.e. Rerup 2005; Dutta and Crossan 2005; García-Cabrera and García-Soto 2009). For instance, Dutta and Crossan (2005) provide an insightful 4I framework for understanding different learning processes involved in opportunity discovery and exploitation, but their emphasis lies primarily in the exploration process at the level of individual entrepreneurs. The only article that explicitly deals with the different needs of opportunity discovery and exploitation is by Rerup (2005), which compares the influence of entrepreneurs' prior experience on opportunity discovery and exploitation. (3) Seventeen articles that specifically emphasise how individual entrepreneurs learn to explore and exploit opportunities, although with no reference to any specific entrepreneurship context (e.g. Rae and Carswell 2001; Minniti and Bygrave 2001; Young and Sexton

2003; Parker 2006; Thorpe *et al.* 2006; Lévesque *et al.* 2009). Finally, (4) four articles that do not specify any entrepreneurial context and one editorial for a journal special issue (Harrison and Leitch 2005). We discuss the need for understanding learning in opportunity exploration and exploitation in the next section.

Methods and the unit of analysis

In this section we report on the methods and unit of analysis employed by the studies. The studies employ a wide range of methods ranging from case studies and surveys to mixed methods studies. When examining the methods and unit of analysis in connection with the entrepreneurial context (see Table 2.1), we found that across the three entrepreneurial contexts forty-three out of seventy-five articles focus on 'individuals' or 'entrepreneurs' as the unit of the analysis and twenty-seven focus on firm-level analysis. Among the twenty-seven firm-level studies there is a clear emphasis on quantitative analysis (thirteen articles) as opposed to qualitative analysis (six articles), while methods used to study individual entrepreneurs are diverse. Articles studying entrepreneurial projects, teams, dyads and communities are few and far between. These include Lee and Williams' (2007) study on learning at the level of entrepreneurial communities in large multinational corporations, and Almeida *et al.*'s (2003) study on the role of firm size in learning about start-ups from external sources based on the dyad between start-ups and other start-ups and incumbents.

A summary of the key challenges for future research

In addition to the key themes and developmental patterns of EL research that we have summarised above, we draw attention to three key challenges in EL research that have emerged from our analysis of the literature. First, as discussed in the themes 'Theoretical Perspectives', 'Types of Learning' and 'Entrepreneurial Context', while a large body of work explains what and how individual entrepreneurs learn, more research is needed to advance EL research at the team and organisational levels and beyond. EL research builds on a wide range of individual and organisational learning theory and practice. Consequently, it has inherited the long-standing problem in the organisational learning literature: how individual learning can be integrated into collective learning. This is a challenge, although it is widely recognised that organisational learning is not equal to the sum of learning of individuals (Cohen and Levinthal 1990). This challenge is highly relevant and to some extent is exacerbated in entrepreneurship because entrepreneurs are often motivated by individualistic drive and energy. While acknowledging the role of enterprising individuals in opportunity discovery and exploitation (Venkataraman 1997), the entrepreneurship literature recognises that it is often an entrepreneurial team, rather

Table 2.1 Entrepreneurial context, methods, and the unit of analysis

	Opportunity exploration and exploitation in start-up entrepreneurship (SE)				Opportunity exploration and exploitation in established firms (EE)				Opportunity exploration and exploitation in general entrepreneurship (GE)				Subtotal
	Quality	Quantity	Mixed	Conceptual	Quality	Quantity	Mixed	Conceptual	Quality	Quantity	Mixed	Conceptual	
Individual	3[c]	6[b]	2	1	3	1[b]	2	2	8	3		14[d]	45
Project					1								1
Team	2[c]												2
Organisation	1	5	1		4	8[a]	1	2	1	1		3[d]	27
Dyad		1											1
Community								1					1
Unspecified												1	1
Subtotal 1	6	12	3	1	8	9	3	5	9	4	0	18	78[b, c, d]
Subtotal 2	22				25				31				

Notes

a These include one paper using simulation methods (Lant and Mezias, 1990).

b Honig (2001) studies both nascent entrepreneurs and intrapreneurs within established firms; this paper is recorded in both the SE and the EE domains (and is therefore counted twice).

c Karataş-Özkan (2011) studies both the micro-level analysis of entrepreneurs; and meso-relational level analysis of entrepreneurial teams (and is therefore counted twice);

d Westhead and Wright (2011) discuss both the entrepreneur and the firm (and is therefore counted twice).

than an individual, that drives the entrepreneurial process, even in the early stages of new venture creation (Kamm *et al.* 1990). Integrating individual entrepreneurial behaviours and actions within collective efforts at the team or organisational levels is indeed a thorny issue (Zahra 1993). This poses a key challenge: how individual opportunity-seeking behaviour may be integrated with organisational advantage-seeking behaviour (Hitt *et al.* 2001). In the next section, we discuss the relationship of individual and collective learning, drawing on further insights from entrepreneurship and organisational learning, as well as how these learning types help us understand the key challenge.

Second, our analysis of 'Definitions of Entrepreneurial Learning', 'Types of Learning' and 'Entrepreneurial Context' highlights that, while EL scholars have called for a greater understanding of entrepreneurs' learning processes in the opportunity discovery and exploitation processes (Corbett 2005, 2007; Davidsson *et al.* 2001), there remains a paucity of studies on learning in this area, especially the opportunity-exploitation process. This EL research gap corresponds to another challenge in the entrepreneurship literature: while it is widely recognised that the processes of exploring and exploiting an opportunity are heterogeneous (Stevenson and Jarillo 1990; Shane and Venkataraman 2000), more research is needed to understand how to develop the skills and resources required to explore and exploit opportunities. Entrepreneurs who create new ventures are not necessarily those who lead the new ventures through growth and prosperity. Opportunity exploration and exploitation require different sets of skills and resources (Choi and Shepherd 2004) and involve different types of learning (Wang and Rafiq 2009). Therefore, in the next section, we discuss the relationship of exploratory and exploitative learning, as well as their contribution to the opportunity exploration and exploitation processes.

Third, as discussed in 'Theoretical Perspectives', 'Types of Learning' and 'Methods and the Unit of Analysis', the diversity, individuality and inconsistency of EL research reflects researchers' different ontological and epistemological positions, which in turn underpin another key challenge: how entrepreneurial opportunities come about – which is at the centre of debate in entrepreneurship research (Busenitz *et al.* 2003; Buenstorf 2007; Short *et al.* 2010). The extent to which a researcher believes that the physical world exists independently of our understanding or awareness of it (ontology) and that our knowledge of the physical world depends on our prior conceptions and experiences (epistemology) influence a researcher's fundamental research philosophies and methodological approaches. Understanding the ontological, epistemological and methodological differences pertinent to researchers' perceptions of where entrepreneurial opportunities are from and how entrepreneurs learn in exploring and exploiting opportunities is another key challenge. The North American and European methodological divide on EL research to some extent reflects such ontological and epistemological differences. Specifically, European researchers often emphasise the subjective nature of knowledge and adopt a qualitative approach to understanding the experiential nature of EL (e.g. Clarysse and Moray 2004; Cope 2003, 2005; Cope and Watts 2000; Deakins and Freel 1998; García-Cabrera and García-Soto 2009; Huovinen and Tihula 2008) and the socially constructed nature of EL (e.g. Lee and Jones 2008; Lee and Williams 2007; Rae 2000, 2005, 2006; Rae and Carswell 2001; Taylor and Thorpe 2004; Thorpe et al. 2006). Conversely, North American researchers often stress the objective nature of knowledge and adopt a quantitative approach to examine to what extent an existing learning theory plays a role in different entrepreneurial contexts (e.g. Almeida et al. 2003; Covin et al. 2006; Nicholls-Nixon et al. 2000). Motivated by the different approaches to understanding entrepreneurial opportunities and how entrepreneurs learn in opportunity exploration and exploitation, we discuss a third pair of learning types: intuitive learning (learning through discovering possibilities) and sensing learning (learning through understanding and analysing facts) in the next section.

The key learning types in entrepreneurial learning

We discuss three pairs of learning types, namely individual and collective learning, exploratory and exploitative learning, and intuitive and sensing learning (see Figure 2.2). We choose to discuss these key learning types for three reasons – because they: (1) derive from the key research gaps based on our systematic literature analysis and correspond to the key challenges in the entrepreneurship literature; (2) help to draw insights from the entrepreneurship and organisational learning literatures and hence to further cross-fertilise the two literature bodies to advance EL research; and (3) feed back into the entrepreneurship literature by providing insights on how these learning styles help us understand the key entrepreneurial problems. These learning types are not an exhaustive list of key learning types, but those that help to address the current EL research gaps and the key research challenges thereby deserving more attention in future study. We next discuss each pair of learning types in detail before summarising them in Table 2.2.

Individual and collective learning

In relation to the first challenge, namely how to integrate individual opportunity-seeking behaviour with organisational advantage-seeking behaviour (Hitt et al. 2001), we discuss the respective roles of individual and collective learning as well as their relationship (see Table 2.2). Individual learning is the process in which individuals acquire data, information, skill or knowledge, whereas collective learning may be defined as a 'social process of cumulative knowledge, based on a set of shared rules and procedures

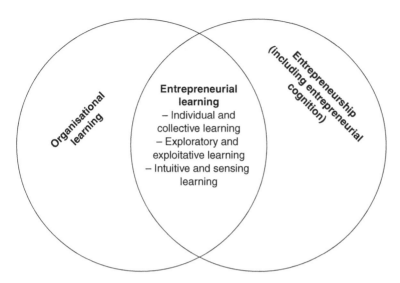

Figure 2.2 EL: boundaries and key learning types.

which allow individuals to coordinate their actions in search for problem solutions' (Capello 1999, p. 354). Collective learning may take place at the team level, the organisational level (Nelson and Winter 1977), the regional level such as within regional innovation milieus (Capello 1999), or any other unique social milieux (Easterby-Smith and Araujo 1999). What differentiates collective learning from learning (or individual learning) is its social nature of learning; collective learning is cumulative, interactive and public, and acts as a vehicle for temporal and spatial knowledge transmission (Capello 1999). The social nature also indicates that collective learning is reliant on an effective combination of know-what and know-how as well as know-who (i.e. formal and informal contacts and networks that provide access to know-what and know-how) (Gibb 1993, 1997; Jones *et al.* 2010). March (1991, p. 73) also stresses the social context in which a mutual learning process takes place between an organisation and the individuals in it: 'organizations store knowledge in their procedures, norms, rules and forms. They accumulate such knowledge over time, learning from their members. At the same time, individuals in an organization are socialized to organizational beliefs.' Recent research concludes that entrepreneurs experience a high level of learning when there is a combination of high learning challenge (i.e. the distance between the entrepreneur's prior knowledge and the role in the venture team) and a high level of learning support (i.e. team composition with strong prior knowledge providing a rich learning milieu) (Sardana and Scott-Kemmis 2010). This provides further evidence on the importance of social context in which entrepreneurs learn.

Table 2.2 A summary of the key learning types

Key learning type	Definitions of learning type	Key challenge	Example links with entrepreneurship and learning literatures	Example future research questions
Individual learning	The process in which individuals acquire data, information, skill or knowledge	How to integrate individual opportunity-seeking behaviour with organisational advantage-seeking behaviour (Hitt *et al.* 2001)	• Team learning, organisational learning (Nelson and Winter 1977), learning within regional milieux (Capello 1999) or unique social milieux (Easterby-Smith and Araujo 1999) • Social nature of learning: cumulative, interactive and public (Capello 1999); emphasis on the social context in which mutual learning takes place (March 1991) and social interactions are enabled (Easterby-Smith and Araujo 1999; Jones and Macpherson 2006) • Effective combination of know-what, know-how and know-who (Gibb 1993, 1997; Jones *et al.* 2010) • The processes of integrating and institutionalising (Dutta and Crossan 2005) • The importance of a shared vision (Wang 2008); shared understanding of the collective activity (Easterby-Smith *et al.* 2000) • Developing collective cognitions consisting differentiation and integration (West 2007) • Effective organisational systems for knowledge sharing (Jones and Macpherson 2006), and the political will and skill to influence and institutionalise system changes (Macpherson and Jones 2008)	• How does the entrepreneurial team composition affect individual and organisational learning? • What organisational conditions simultaneously promote individual and collective learning in entrepreneurial firms? • How is a collective cognition formed through a learning process in an entrepreneurial team or firm? • How does learning occur within an entrepreneurial cluster, community or network? • How does learning help shape an entrepreneurial cluster, community or network?

continued

Collective learning	'A social process of cumulative knowledge, based on a set of shared rules and procedures which allow individuals to coordinate their actions in search for problem solutions' (Capello 1999, p. 354)		
Exploratory learning	Focus on discovery through enactment and interpretation to generate enough variations that some will prove ex post to yield desirable results (variance-seeking learning that increases performance variance) (McGrath 2001)	How to develop skills and resources required for opportunity exploration and exploitation - two heterogeneous processes of entrepreneurship (Stevenson and Jarillo 1990; Shane and Venkataraman 2000)	• Difference between exploration and exploitation (March 1991) • Cognitive properties required for opportunity exploration and exploitation (Shane and Venkataraman 2000); cognitive heuristics and biases of entrepreneurs (Baron 1998); creativity-based cognitive approaches (Ward 2004) • Single-loop (adaptive) and double-loop (generative) learning (Argyris and Schön 1978); lower and higher level learning (Fiol and Lyles 1985) • Unlearning (Hedberg 1981; Zahra *et al.* 2011) • Acquisitive learning through acquiring and assimilating external knowledge and experimental learning through internal transformation (Kreiser 2011)
Exploitative learning	Emphasis on directed search that is amenable to ex-ante planning and control to limit variety achieved by honing in on and deepening initial insights as experience increases (mean-seeking learning that improves mean performance and decreases variance) (McGrath 2001)		

• How does the learning of entrepreneurs or entrepreneurial firms differ in the process of exploration and exploitation?

• What and how do entrepreneurs or entrepreneurial firms unlearn?

• What organisational contexts are more conducive to exploratory or exploitative learning?

• What cognitive processes do entrepreneurs go through in different learning contexts?

• How do the cognitive processes of entrepreneurs differ in exploratory and exploitative learning?

Table 2.2 Continued

Key learning type	Definitions of learning type	Key challenge	Example links with entrepreneurship and learning literatures	Example future research questions
Intuitive learning	Learning by knowing relationships of facts through discovering possibilities (abstract, conceptual thinking) (Felder and Silverman 1988)	How entrepreneurial opportunities come about – discovered or created (Eckhardt and Shane 2003; Buenstorf 2007; Short et al. 2010)	• Psychological types (Jung 1971; Myers and McCaulley 1985) • Individuals' cognitive (intuitive or analytical) processing styles (Corbett 2002) • The discovery approach to entrepreneurial opportunities following the positivist school of thought (Kirzner 1979) • The creation approach to entrepreneurial opportunities following the interpretive or social constructionist school of thought (Gartner 1988; Rae 2000; Cope 2005) • Opportunities as objective realities but their discovery may require a creative act by entrepreneurs (Shane 2003). • Effectuation approach to entrepreneurship (Sarasvathy et al. 2003) • Experiential learning (Kolb 1984, 1985) • Situated learning theory (Lave and Wenger 1991; Wenger 1998); the social theory of learning (Rae and Carswell 2001; Taylor and Thorpe 2004; Rae 2005, 2006; Thorpe et al. 2006; Cope 2005); social learning theory (Bandura 1977) • Vicarious learning (Lévesque et al. 2009)	• What factors play a key role in each stage of the experiential learning cycle, especially the transformation of an entrepreneur's concrete experience to abstract conceptualisation? • What and how do entrepreneurs or entrepreneurial firms learn from experience (successes and failures) of other entrepreneurs/entrepreneurial firms? • To what extent is the entrepreneurial decision-making process based on intuitive or analytical skills of the entrepreneur? • How do creative and analytical skills affect learning in the entrepreneurship process? • How do entrepreneurs or entrepreneurial firms search and acquire external information, and make sense of the information in the learning process?
Sensing learning	Learning by knowing facts or details based on external contacts through sights, sounds and physical sensations (concrete, analytical thinking) (Felder and Silverman 1988)			

Integrating individual learning with collective learning is an especially challenging task for entrepreneurial firms given the individualistic nature of entrepreneurs. The EL literature has started to address how collective learning takes place in organisations. For example, Dutta and Crossan (2005, p. 434) highlight two important processes of EL: integrating as 'the process of developing shared understanding amongst individuals and the taking of coordinated action through mutual adjustment'; and institutionalising as 'the process of ensuring that routinized actions occur'. These processes enable individual entrepreneurs to act as learning agents to evaluate what is possible within the organisation, develop a coherent and collective action plan, and pool organisational resources to pursue identified opportunities (Crossan *et al.* 1999). Empirical evidence supports the fact that entrepreneurial activities are more likely to bear fruit when individuals are committed to common organisational goals (Wang 2008). From a social constructionist perspective, organisations are sites of collective activity in which individuals are required to develop a shared understanding of that activity (Easterby-Smith *et al.* 2000), and it is through interaction within unique social milieux that learning occurs (Easterby-Smith and Araujo 1999). To facilitate effective social interactions among individuals, organisations need to have effective systems in place for knowledge sharing (Jones and Macpherson 2006), as well as the political will and skill to influence and institutionalise system changes that help transform a divided organisation into a practice-based community engaged in collective learning (Macpherson and Jones 2008). Karataş-Özkan (2011) found that new venture team members develop 'a feel for the game', understanding their own strengths and weaknesses and adjusting their roles in the new venture. Such practice is associated with increased entrepreneurial learning at individual and team level (Karataş-Özkan 2011).

The recent development of corporate entrepreneurship places a considerable emphasis on how organisations can instil a culture and implement systems to align individual opportunity-seeking behaviour with organisational advantage-seeking behaviour (Hitt *et al.* 2001). The ability of organisations to align individuals' interests, motivate them to search for opportunities, encourage them to cooperate in the creation of new resource combinations and to exploit them successfully is a critical discriminator between prosperous entrepreneurial firms and non-entrepreneurial firms (Chung and Gibbons 1997). Moreover, entrepreneurial cognition within the entrepreneurship literature highlights the need for collective cognitions, broadly defined as 'the content of the combination of individual perspectives and the structural characteristics of that combination' (West 2007, p. 84). The structure of the combination is critical for integrating individual perspectives. In particular, the structure must provide a unique goal that is clearly differentiated from other goals and promote a consistent understanding of the goal among individual members; these dual characteristics of the structure of collective cognitions are referred to as differentiation and integration (West 2007). Collective cognitions are developed through the ongoing comprehension of unfolding events by teams of interacting individuals (Weick and Roberts 1993). Further, Lee and Jones (2008), extending Nahapiet and Ghoshal's (1998) notion of cognitive social capital (i.e. social norms, values, attitudes and beliefs), bridges the gap between individual cognition and the distributed nature of organising; they argue that entrepreneurs' perceptions of shared language, codes and narratives are critical for developing shared understanding and common values leading to efficient and effective social relations.

Despite the insights from entrepreneurship and organisational learning on the integration of individual and collective learning, several questions deserve more attention; for example, 'How does the entrepreneurial team composition affect individual and organisational learning?', 'What organisational conditions simultaneously promote individual and collective learning in entrepreneurial firms?', and 'How is a collective cognition formed through a learning process in an entrepreneurial team or firm?' More research is also needed to understand how learning takes place in entrepreneurial clusters, communities and networks, and how learning helps to shape an entrepreneurial cluster, community or network.

Exploratory and exploitative learning

The second challenge is how to develop skills and resources required for opportunity exploration and exploitation as two heterogeneous processes of entrepreneurship (Stevenson and Jarillo 1990; Shane and Venkataraman 2000). In relation to this we discuss the respective roles of, and the relationship between, exploratory and exploitative learning (see Table 2.2). According to McGrath (2001), exploratory learning emphasises discovery through enactment and interpretation to generate enough variations that some will prove ex post to yield desirable results, while exploitative learning focuses on directed search that is amenable to ex ante planning and control to limit variety achieved by honing in on and deepening initial insights as experience increases. Exploratory learning (variance-seeking learning) increases performance variance, while exploitative learning (mean-seeking learning) improves mean performance and decreases variance (McGrath 2001). Exploratory learning (also experimental learning) often results from the internal transformation through developing new knowledge (Kreiser 2011; Zhao *et al.* 2011) and could involve firms breaking away from a successful action pattern (i.e. deviance-error learning) (Bingham and Davis 2012). Exploitative learning (also acquisitive learning) often results from the acquisition and assimilation of knowledge that exists outside the firm (Kreiser 2011; Zhao *et al.* 2011), and is associated with trial-and-error learning (Bingham and Davis 2012). Exploratory and exploitative learning corresponds to the learning processes involved in exploration and exploitation, as March (1991, p. 71) describes: exploration involves 'search, variation, risk taking, experimentation, play, flexibility, [and] discovery', while exploitation entails 'refinement, choice, production, efficiency, selection, implementation, [and] execution'. Although exploratory and exploitative learning are both required to generate new ideas, select ideas, and eventually implement a chosen idea in an entrepreneurial process, the existence of positive performance effects derives from the balanced application of exploration and exploitation (March 1991; Sirén *et al.* 2012).

The entrepreneurship and especially entrepreneurial cognition literature lends some insights, with a particular emphasis on opportunity exploration (discovery, recognition and evaluation). Opportunity discovery relies on the possession of prior knowledge required to recognise the opportunity and the cognitive properties required to value it (Shane and Venkataraman 2000). Compared with non-entrepreneurs, entrepreneurs are more likely to think and reason based on cognitive heuristics and biases (e.g. self-serving bias and counterfactual thinking) due to the highly uncertain conditions that entrepreneurs tend to encounter (Baron 1998). Moreover, entrepreneurs are more likely to use creativity-based cognitive approaches (i.e. conceptual combination, analogical reasoning, abstraction and problem formulation) to generate novel ideas (Ward 2004). The high level of creativity is particularly fitting with the exploratory learning process. However, such cognitive style may cause frustration and burnout as the venture goes through the exploitation phase (Brigham and De Castro 2003), and hence becomes counterproductive in the exploitative learning process.

The demand of exploratory and exploitative learning on organisations is echoed in other organisational learning theories, such as Argyris and Schön's (1978) single-loop (adaptive) and double-loop (generative) learning, and Fiol and Lyles' (1985) higher and lower level learning. Adaptive and lower level learning involves modifying actions according to the difference between expected and obtained outcomes (hence exploitative in nature), whereas generative and higher level learning involves questioning the values, assumptions and policies that led to the actions in the first place, and searching and discovering new solutions (hence exploratory in nature). The latter entails a higher level of unlearning (Hedberg 1981; Zahra *et al.* 2011); that is, deliberately learning not to do something. In particular, learning from failure is a function of distinctive learning processes that enable higher level learning outcomes (Cope 2011). Although the two types of learning may occur in any organisation, entrepreneurial firms are prone to a higher level of exploratory and generative learning (and hence unlearning) compared with non-entrepreneurial firms, since they often operate in a highly uncertain environment.

Overall, exploratory and exploitative learning are key learning types for understanding what and how entrepreneurs learn in the opportunity exploration and exploitation processes. However, despite the insights from the organisational learning and entrepreneurship literatures, many research questions require further investigation; for example, 'How does the learning of entrepreneurs or entrepreneurial firms differ in the processes of exploration and exploitation?', 'What and how do entrepreneurs or entrepreneurial firms unlearn?', 'What organisational contexts are more conducive to exploratory or exploitative learning?', 'What cognitive processes do entrepreneurs go through in different learning contexts?', and 'How do the cognitive processes of entrepreneurs differ in exploratory and exploitative learning?'

Intuitive and sensing learning

To discuss the third challenge, namely how entrepreneurial opportunities come about – discovery or creation (Eckhardt and Shane 2003; Buenstorf 2007; Short *et al.* 2010) – we discuss two relevant learning types: intuitive and sensing learning (see Table 2.2). The concepts of intuitive and sensing learning styles were initially developed by Jung (1971) in his psychological types, later operationalised by Myers and McCaulley (1985), and are currently used widely in education research. Sensing learning involves learning by knowing facts or details based on external contacts through sights, sounds and physical sensations, while intuitive learning involves learning by knowing relationships of facts through discovering possibilities (Felder and Silverman 1988). Sensing learners are considered to be concrete and practical thinkers, implying that they are more prone to discover and identify an opportunity that exists in the environment through understanding and analysing the relationships of market conditions. Conversely, intuitive learners are considered to be abstract thinkers, suggesting that they are more likely to create a new opportunity based on a high level of conceptual thinking and discovering possibilities. Intuitive learning is akin to what Bingham and Davis (2012, p. 613) describe as improvisational learning – 'a real-time learning process in which firms learn to solve unexpected problems or capturing surprising opportunities in the moment' (Miner *et al.* 2001). Research has found that the more an individual's cognitive processing style tends towards 'intuitive' and away from 'analytical', the more opportunities an individual is likely to identify (Corbett 2002). These learning types are instrumental to the understanding of how entrepreneurial opportunities (Venkataraman 1997; Eckhardt and Shane 2003) come about – a key theme of the entrepreneurship research.

In a recent review, Short *et al.* (2010) conclude that little agreement exists about the definition, the nature and the role of opportunities (Buenstorf 2007; Eckhardt and Shane 2003; Short *et al.* 2010). One of the several conflicting views is whether entrepreneurial opportunities are discovered or created (Buenstorf 2007). The discovery approach is positioned in the positivist school of thought predominant among North American researchers, suggesting that opportunities exist in the environment independent of the entrepreneur. What differentiates entrepreneurs from non-entrepreneurs is 'entrepreneurial alertness' – the ability to see the gap where products or services do not exist (Kirzner 1979). In contrast, the creation approach, typically represented by the European research, is centred in the interpretivist or social constructionist school of thought, postulating that opportunities emerge as a result of the entrepreneur's perception, interpretation and understanding of the environment (Gartner *et al.* 2003). This stream of literature focuses on the developmental nature of entrepreneurial behaviour; that is, an entrepreneur's ability to learn, grow and change (Gartner 1988; Rae 2000; Cope 2005), such as in unfolding entrepreneurial events. To address the limitations of the two opposing approaches, Shane (2003) argues that opportunities may exist as objective realities even though their discovery may require a creative act by the entrepreneur (Shane 2003). Furthermore, effectual entrepreneurs can use their expertise to recognise, discover or create opportunities dependent on market conditions (Sarasvathy *et al.* 2003). This suggests that opportunity exploration may involve both intuitive and sensing learning.

A number of learning theories complement the understanding of intuitive and sensing learning. First, Cook *et al.* (2009) note that the sensing and intuitive learning types are similar to the concrete-abstract learning dimension of Kolb's (1984, 1985) experiential learning theory, which has been widely used in the EL research. The experiential learning cycle also helps fill the gap of how concrete experience is transformed to abstract conceptualisation (i.e. through reflective observation), which through active experimentation modifies the next occurrence of concrete experience (Kolb 1984, 1985). However, how this full experiential learning cycle occurs among entrepreneurs or in entrepreneurial firms requires further research, since the majority of the experiential learning research has not fully addressed this issue as pointed out in our literature analysis. Second, several other learning theories from the social constructivist perspective, such as the situated learning theory (Lave and Wenger 1991; Wenger 1998; Brown and Duguid 1991) and the social theory of learning (e.g. Rae and Carswell 2001; Taylor and Thorpe 2004; Rae 2005, 2006; Thorpe *et al.* 2006; Lee and Williams 2007) help explain the intricacies of sensing learning. These theories essentially argue that knowledge or learning is evident in situated activity or 'knowing' (Macpherson and Jones 2008). Learning is a process of social interaction (Fang *et al.* 2010) or co-participation, dependent on social, historical and cultural factors (Taylor and Thorpe 2004), and hence is 'an integral and inseparable aspect of social practice' (Lave and Wenger 1991, p. 31). More specifically, social learning theory also suggests that learning occurs through close contact with other people, and the observation and imitation of role model behaviours (Bandura 1977). That is, learning can take place vicariously (Lévesque *et al.* 2009). Entrepreneurs' self-efficacy, managerial experience, business skills and education levels are all influenced by the socialisation process (Jones and Tullous 2002), and hence affected by the social groups to which the entrepreneur is related (Cope 2005). Social processes in which entrepreneurs seek to repair relational damage caused by venture failure are associated with their regression and gradual re-emergence, leading to social affirmation that may support rehabilitation (Cope 2011).

In sum, the roles of intuitive and sensing learning have not been fully addressed in the EL literature. This is an important research area, given that these learning types help enhance our understanding of the debate on how opportunities are discovered or created, and how the rational and the effectuation approaches to entrepreneurial behaviours can be explained. Future research may address questions such as 'What factors play a key role in each stage of the experiential learning cycle, especially the transformation of an entrepreneur's concrete experience to abstract conceptualisation?', 'What and how do entrepreneurs or entrepreneurial firms learn from the experience (successes and failures) of other entrepreneurs or entrepreneurial firms?', 'To what extent is the entrepreneurial decision-making process based on intuitive or analytical skills of the entrepreneur?', 'How do creative and analytical skills affect learning in the entrepreneurship process?', and 'How do entrepreneurs or entrepreneurial firms search for and acquire external information, and make sense of the information in the learning process?'

In sum, the three pairs of learning types (see Table 2.2) are fundamental to the understanding of entrepreneurial behaviours, namely individual opportunity seeking and organisational advantage seeking, opportunity exploration and exploitation, and the discovery or creation approaches to entrepreneurial opportunities. The respective roles of these learning types are dependent on the individual, team, organisational, social and environmental contexts in which EL takes place, as discussed above. Literature suggests that firms may combine different types of learning over time in the form of learning sequences, which are in turn influenced by initial learning conditions (Bingham and Davis 2012).

Discussion: the state of entrepreneurial learning

Despite the scholarly call for building EL theory (Krueger 2003), the EL literature is fragmented and ad hoc in nature (Harrison and Leitch 2005). Macpherson (2009) echoes the concern of the highly individualistic approaches to EL. Our analysis of the EL literature clearly reveals the diverse philosophical, theoretical and methodological approaches used to study the learning process in the entrepreneurial context. We summarise the key aspects covered in the literature to consolidate and delineate the domain of EL set out in our objectives.

The domain of EL research

First, EL relies not only on know-what and know-how, but also know-who. Know-what and know-how focus on information, knowledge and experience, for example, accumulating or updating knowledge (Minniti and Bygrave 2001), the development of new knowledge (Politis 2005), accumulating and organising knowledge and information (Ravasi and Turati 2005), and acquiring new knowledge (Holcomb *et al.* 2009). Know-who provides formal and informal contacts and networks, and hence access to know-what and know-how (Gibb 1993, 1997; Jones *et al.* 2010). Accordingly, EL occurs when entrepreneurs make sense of the world around them and change it in some arresting manner (Starbuck 1983; Thorpe *et al.* 2006); when entrepreneurs interact socially to initiate, organise and manage ventures (Rae 2005); when entrepreneurs transform experience into action in a business setting (Lee and Jones 2008); and when entrepreneurs construct new meaning in the process of recognising and acting on opportunities (Rae and Carswell 2001).

Second, the mechanisms (or the types of learning) by which learning takes place (i.e. *how* learning occurs) are primarily drawn from the individual and organisational learning literature. Individual learning styles include experiential learning specifically defined by Kolb (1984), as well as experiential learning as a broad learning process encapsulating learning-by-doing (Cope 2003), trial-and-error learning (Lant and Mezias 1990), learning from past experience (Lamont 1972; Minniti and Bygrave 2001; Rerup 2005), and learning from participation and the experience of others (i.e. vicarious learning) (Lévesque *et al.* 2009). Several influential organisational learning mechanisms include single-loop/adaptive and double-loop/ generative learning (Argyris and Schön 1978), higher level or lower level learning (Fiol and Lyles 1985), and exploratory and exploitative learning (March 1991). Each type involves the development or modification of new or existing insights and behaviours.

Third, the processes of EL are intertwined in the processes of exploring and exploiting an entrepreneurial opportunity. For example, EL is defined as 'what informs the entrepreneur's quest for new opportunities' (Franco and Haase 2009). Depending on the individual, team, organisational, social or environmental contexts, EL processes may be present in different forms. For example, EL may entail learning by an independent entrepreneur, an entrepreneurial team and firm; or learning by an individual, team or firm to behave or work in an entrepreneurial way (Rae 2000). Moreover, EL may involve a dynamic process characterised by ongoing knowledge acquisition, organisation, development and creation (also see Minniti and Bygrave 2001); this could be a continuous learning process made of multiple learning epochs (Voudouris *et al.* 2011), a sporadic process where learning occurs from moments in which an individual is situated (Rae 2013), or due to critical events (see Cope and Watts 2000). Moreover, EL is referred to as a lived experience involving a cumulative series of interdependent events (Morris *et al.* 2012). Pittaway and Thorpe (2012) point out that Jason Cope contributed significantly to the theorising of the lived experience of entrepreneurs through understanding discontinuous events, and such events could well be venture failure (Cope 2011).

Fourth, the outcome of EL generally involves the development of new insights and behaviours or the modification of existing insights and behaviours, which may be embedded in multi-faceted entrepreneurial activities. For example, EL is often associated with the implementation of an opportunity leading to the creation and development of a new venture (Berglund *et al.* 2007; Cope 2005; Hughes *et al.* 2007; Nicholls-Nixon *et al.* 2000), a spin-off from an existing organisation (Clarysse and Moray 2004; Lamont 1972), a renewal of an existing organisation (Covin *et al.* 2006; Corbett *et al.* 2007), or even exiting an entrepreneurial venture which has learning effects enhancing the entrepreneur's accumulated knowledge base (Breslin 2008). The array of contents, mechanisms, processes and outcomes depict the domain of EL research within a growing body of literature.

The role of EL in the organisational learning and entrepreneurship literatures

Based on our literature analysis, we have identified and discussed three pairs of key learning types that correspond to three key challenges which emerged from our literature analysis: (1) individual and collective learning that helps to integrate individual opportunity-seeking behaviour with organisational advantage-seeking behaviour; (2) exploratory and exploitative learning that helps to resolve the paradox of opportunity exploration and exploitation as two heterogeneous entrepreneurial processes; and (3) intuitive and sensing learning that helps us understand how entrepreneurial opportunities come about. We have also identified some fruitful avenues for future research to help move EL research forward. As discussed, these learning types can draw insights from, and also feed back to, the organisational learning and entrepreneurship literatures. In particular, although EL has become a promising research area attracting an increasing number of scholarly publications, there is a high level of interest in applying experiential and organisational learning theories in the entrepreneurship process rather than building new EL theory as revealed in our analysis. As a result, the boundary of exchange between EL and organisational learning remains largely unspecified. In other words, little is known about how the learning processes or mechanisms of entrepreneurs or entrepreneurial firms differ from non-entrepreneurs and non-entrepreneurial firms. Through our key EL learning types, we highlight that entrepreneurial firms are more likely to face the challenge of integrating individual learning with collective learning given the individualistic nature of entrepreneurs. Given that collective learning is social and interactive by nature (Capello 1999), entrepreneurial firms are considered as sites of collective activity in which individuals interact socially (Jones and Macpherson 2006) to develop a shared understanding of that activity (Easterby-Smith *et al.* 2000). We also stress that compared with their non-entrepreneurial counterparts, entrepreneurial firms are more likely to use creativity-based, variance-seeking learning (i.e. exploratory learning) (McGrath 2001) as well as unlearning (Hedberg 1981), since they often operate in a dynamic environment. Therefore, entrepreneurs are likely to possess a high level of cognitive heuristics and biases, such as counterfactual thinking (Baron 1998), especially in the opportunity exploration process. Finally, intuitive learners are more likely to create a new opportunity based on a high level of conceptual thinking, while sensing learners are more prone to discover an opportunity by scanning the environment and analysing the relationships of market conditions. These learning types help to explain how entrepreneurial opportunities come about; following Shane (2003) and Sarasvathy *et al.*'s (2003) arguments on the combination or an effectuation process of opportunities as objective realities and as the creative discovery of entrepreneurs, intuitive and sensing learning complement each other in the opportunity exploration and exploitation process.

On the other hand, EL has risen to the fundamental paradigmatic shift of entrepreneurship from a static, trait-based approach to a dynamic, learning-based approach. The three pairs of learning types help us to understand some of the challenges, namely the problem of integrating individuals' opportunity-seeking behaviour with the firm's advantage-seeking behaviour (Hitt *et al.* 2001), the paradoxical demands between opportunity exploration and exploitation, and the discovery or creation approaches to entrepreneurial opportunities. The learning types we discussed help to cross-fertilise the literatures of entrepreneurship and organisational learning. The advancement of EL may contribute to a further paradigmatic shift of entrepreneurship towards becoming a more 'interdisciplinary' arena, which is supported by Steyaert (2005) and Schindehutte and Morris (2009).

EL research thus far has focused on applying existing theories in the entrepreneurial context. Future research may place more emphasis on theory building in certain under-researched areas; for example, how the three different pairs of learning types come into play in different entrepreneurial contexts. This requires more qualitative, phenomenon-driven research, which is especially effective in addressing 'how' and 'why' in unexplored or under-explored research areas with little viable theory and empirical evidence (Eisenhardt and Graebner 2007). Greater research collaboration between North America and Europe is needed to facilitate knowledge exchange and cross-fertilisation of EL research. This comes with the caveat that there will be challenges to overcome between the two research camps as they both come from different philosophical stances. Possible ways to cross-fertilise North American and European research on EL include using mixed methods to mitigate the limitations of using quantitative or qualitative methods alone, or research collaboration where researchers interact and socialise to build on the strengths of their philosophical and methodological differences. However, it is argued that researchers' different philosophical beliefs and preferred research approaches may be incommensurable. Therefore, it is challenging for a researcher working within one philosophical and methodological approach to work within another. Alternatively, cross-fertilisation could also be achieved by encouraging theory developed in one research camp (i.e. European) based on qualitative, phenomenon-driven research to be tested by researchers in another (i.e. North American) using quantitative research.

Conclusion

EL has become an important research area at the interface of entrepreneurship and organisational learning. This chapter has identified a critical mass of EL research. However, the EL literature is highly individualistic and fragmented, calling for both theoretical and empirical development. Based on a systematic analysis of the literature, we identified key EL research themes and developmental patterns. Moreover, we identified three key EL research gaps and discussed three pairs of learning styles that deserve more attention in future research, namely individual and collective learning, exploratory and exploitative learning, and intuitive and sensing learning. The three pairs of learning styles correspond to three key challenges in the entrepreneurship literature, namely the need for integrating individual opportunity-seeking behaviour with organisational advantage-seeking behaviour; the need for developing skills and resources required for opportunity exploration and exploitation; and the need for understanding how entrepreneurial opportunities come about. Therefore, the three pairs of learning styles help to advance EL research and also feed back to the entrepreneurship literature.

Acknowledgement

A full version of this chapter has been published in the *International Journal of Management Reviews*, 2014, Vol. 16, No. 1, pp. 24–61. It is reproduced with kind permission of John Wiley & Sons.

References

Almeida, P., Dokko, G. and Rosenkopf, L. (2003). Startup size and the mechanisms of external learning: Increasing opportunity and decreasing ability? *Research Policy*, 32(2), pp. 310–315.

Alvarez, S.A and Busenitz, L.W. (2001). The entrepreneurship of resource-based theory. *Journal of Management*, 27, pp. 755–775.

Argyris, C. and Schön, D.A. (1978). *Organizational Learning: A theory of action perspective*. Reading, MA: Addison-Wesley.

Balasubramanian, N. (2011). New plant venture performance differences among incumbent, diversifying, and entrepreneurial firms: The impact of industry learning intensity. *Management Science*, 57(3), pp. 549–565.

Bandura, A. (1977). *Social Learning Theory*. Englewood Cliffs, NJ: Prentice Hall.

Baron, R.A. (1998). Cognitive mechanisms in entrepreneurship: Why and when entrepreneurs think differently than other people. *Journal of Business Venturing*, 13(4), pp. 275–294.

Berglund, H., Hellström, L. and Sjölander, S. (2007). Entrepreneurial learning and the role of venture capitalists. *Venture Capital*, 9(3), pp. 165–181.

Bingham, C.B. and Davis, J.P. (2012). Learning sequences: Their existence, effect, and evolution. *Academy of Management Journal*, 55(3), pp. 611–641.

Blackburn, R. and Kovalainen, A. (2009). Research small firms and entrepreneurship: Past, present and future. *International Journal of Management Reviews*, 11(2), pp. 127–148.

Breslin, D. (2008). A review of the evolutionary approach to the study of entrepreneurship. *International Journal of Management Reviews*, 10(4), pp. 399–423.

Brigham, K.H. and De Castro, J.O. (2003). Entrepreneurial fit: The role of cognitive misfit. In J.A. Katz and D.A. Shepherd (eds), *Cognitive Approaches to Entrepreneurship Research*. Oxford: Elsevier, pp. 37–71.

Brown, J.S. and Duguid, P. (1991). Organizational learning and communities-of-practice: Towards a unified view of working learning and innovation. *Organization Science*, 2(1), pp. 40–47.

Buenstorf, G. (2007). Creation and pursuit of entrepreneurial opportunities: An evolutionary economics perspective. *Small Business Economics*, 28, pp. 323–337.

Busenitz, L.W., West, G.P., Shepherd, D., Nelson, T., Chandler, G.N. and Zacharakis, A. (2003). Entrepreneurship research in emergence. *Journal of Management*, 29, pp. 285–308.

Capello, R. (1999). Spatial transfer of knowledge in high technology milieux: Learning versus collective learning processes. *Regional Studies*, 33, pp. 353–365.

Chaston, I., Badger, B. and Sadler-Smith, E. (2001). Organizational learning: An empirical assessment of process in small U.K. manufacturing firms. *Journal of Small Business Management*, 39(2), pp. 139–151.

Choi, Y.R. and Shepherd, D.A. (2004). Entrepreneurs' decisions to exploit opportunities. *Journal of Management*, 30, pp. 377–395.

Chung, L.H. and Gibbons, P.T. (1997). Corporate entrepreneurship: The roles of ideology and social capital. *Group and Organization Studies*, 22, pp. 10–30.

Clarysse, B. and Moray, N. (2004). A process study of entrepreneurial team formation: The case of a research-based spin-off. *Journal of Business Venturing*, 19(1), pp. 55–79.

Cohen, W.M. and Levinthal, D.A. (1990). Absorptive capacity: A new perspective on learning and innovation, *Administrative Science Quarterly*, 35(1), pp. 128–152.

Cook, D.A., Thompson, W.G., Thomas, K.G. and Thomas, M.R. (2009). Lack of interaction between sensing-intuitive learning styles and problem-first versus information-first instruction: A randomized crossover trial. *Advances in Health Science Education*, 14, pp. 79–90.

Cope, J. (2003). Entrepreneurial learning and critical reflection: Discontinuous events as triggers for 'higher-level' learning. *Management Learning*, 34(4), pp. 429–450.

—— (2005). Toward a dynamic learning perspective of entrepreneurship. *Entrepreneurship Theory and Practice*, 29(4), pp. 373–397.

—— (2011). Entrepreneurial learning from failure: An interpretative phenomenological analysis. *Journal of Business Venturing*, 26(6), pp. 604–623.

Cope, J. and Watts, G. (2000). Learning by doing: An exploration of experience, critical incidents and reflection in entrepreneurial learning. *International Journal of Entrepreneurial Behaviour and Research*, 6(3), pp. 104–124.

Corbett, A.C. (2002). Recognizing high-tech opportunities: A learning and cognitive approach. In W.D. Bygrave *et al.*, *Frontiers of Entrepreneurship Research*. Wellesley, MA: Babson College, pp. 49–61.

—— (2005). Experiential learning within the process of opportunity identification and exploitation. *Entrepreneurship Theory and Practice*, 29(4), pp. 473–491.

—— (2007). Learning asymmetries and the discovery of entrepreneurial opportunities. *Journal of Business Venturing*, 22(1), pp. 97–118.

Corbett, A.C., Neck, H.M. and DeTienne, D.R. (2007). How corporate entrepreneurs learn from fledgling innovation initiatives: Cognition and the development of a termination script. *Entrepreneurship Theory and Practice*, 31(6), pp. 829–852.

Covin, J.G., Green, K.M. and Slevin, D.P. (2006). Strategic process effects on the entrepreneurial orientation – sales growth rate relationship. *Entrepreneurship Theory and Practice*, 30(1), pp. 57–81.

Crossan, M.M., Lane, H.W. and White, R.E. (1999). An organizational learning framework: From intuition to institution. *Academy of Management Review*, 24(3), pp. 522–537.

Cyert, R.M. and March, J.G. (1963). *A Behavioral Theory of the Firm*. Englewood Cliffs, NJ: Prentice Hall.

Davidsson, P., Low, M.B. And Wright, M. (2001). Editor's introduction: Low and MacMillan ten years on: Achievements and future directions for entrepreneurship research. *Entrepreneurship Theory and Practice*, 25(4), pp. 5–17.

Deakins, D. (1996). *Entrepreneurship and Small Firms*. Maidenhead: McGraw-Hill.

Deakins, D. and Freel, M. (1998). Entrepreneurial learning and the growth process in SMEs. *The Learning Organization*, 5(3), pp. 144–155.

Dencker, J.C., Gruber, M. and Shah, S. (2009). Pre-entry knowledge, learning, and the survival of new firms. *Organization Science*, 20(3), pp. 516–537.

Dimov, D. (2007). From opportunity insight to opportunity intention: The importance of person–situation learning match. *Entrepreneurship Theory and Practice*, 31(4), pp. 561–583.

Dutta, D.K. and Crossan, M.M. (2005). The nature of entrepreneurial opportunities: Understanding the process using the 4I organizational learning framework. *Entrepreneurship Theory and Practice*, 29(4), pp. 425–449.

Easterby-Smith, M. and Araujo, L. (1999) Organizational learning: Current debates and opportunities, in M. Easterby-Smith, J. Burgoyne and L. Araujo (eds), *Organizational Learning and the Learning Organization: Developments in theory and practice*. London: Sage, pp. 1–22.

Easterby-Smith, M., Crossan, M. and Nicolini, D. (2000) Organizational learning: Debates past, present and future. *Journal of Management Studies*, 37(6), pp. 783–796.

Eckhardt, J.T. and Shane, S.A. (2003). Opportunities and entrepreneurship. *Journal of Management*, 29(3), pp. 333–349.

Eisenhardt, K.M. and Graebner, M.E. (2007). Theory building from cases: Opportunities and challenges. *Academy of Management Journal*, 50(1), pp. 25–32.

Erikson, T. (2003). Towards a taxonomy of entrepreneurial learning experiences among potential entrepreneurs. *Journal of Small Business and Enterprise Development*, 10(1), pp. 106–112.

Fang, S-C., Tsai, F-S. and Lin, J.L. (2010). Leveraging tenant-incubator social capital for organizational learning and performance in incubation programme. *International Small Business Journal*, 28(1), pp. 90–113.

Felder, R.M. and Silverman, L.K. (1988) Learning and teaching styles in engineering education. *Engineering Education*, 78(7), pp. 674–681.

Fiol, M. and Lyles, M. (1985). Organizational learning. *Academy of Management Review*, 10(4), pp. 803–813.

Franco, M. and Haase, H. (2009). Entrepreneurship: An organizational learning approach. *Journal of Small Business and Enterprise Development*, 16(4), pp. 628–641.

García-Cabrera, A.M. and García-Soto, M.G. (2009). A dynamic model of technology-based opportunity recognition. *Journal of Entrepreneurship*, 18(2), pp. 167–190.

Gartner, W.B. (1988). 'Who is an entrepreneur?' Is the wrong question. *American Journal of Small Business*, 13(1), pp. 11–32.

Gartner, W.B., Carter, N.M. and Hills, G.E. (2003). The language of opportunity. In C. Steyaert and D. Hjorth (eds), *New Movements in Entrepreneurship*. Cheltenham: Edward Elgar, pp. 103–124.

Gibb, A.A. (1993). The enterprise culture and education. Understanding enterprise culture and its links with small business, entrepreneurship and wider educational goals. *International Small Business Journal*, 11(3), pp. 11–34.

—— (1997). Small firms' training and competitiveness. Building upon the small business as a learning organisation. *International Small Business Journal*, 15(3), pp. 13–29.

Gibb Dyer, W. Jr. (1994). Toward a theory of entrepreneurial careers. *Entrepreneurship Theory and Practice*, 19(2), pp. 7–21.

Gruber, M., Macmillan, I.C. and Thompson, J.D. (2008). Look before you leap: Market opportunity identification in emerging technology firms. *Management Science*, 54(9), pp. 1652–1665.

Harrison, R.T. and Leitch, C.M. (2005). Entrepreneurial learning: Researching the interface between learning and the entrepreneurial context. *Entrepreneurship Theory and Practice*, 29(4), pp. 351–371.

—— (2008). *Entrepreneurial Learning: Conceptual frameworks and applications*. London: Routledge.

Hedberg, B. (1981). How organizations learn and unlearn. In P.C. Nystrom and W.H. Starbuck (eds), *Handbook of Organizational Design*, No. 1. London: Oxford University Press, pp. 3–27.

Hitt, M.A., Ireland, R.D., Camp, S.M. and Sexton, D.L. (2001). Guest Editors' introduction to the Special Issue strategic entrepreneurship: Entrepreneurial strategies for wealth creation. *Strategic Management Journal*, 22, pp. 479–491.

Holcomb, T.R., Ireland, R.D., Holmes Jr., R.M. and Hitt, M.A. (2009). Architecture of entrepreneurial learning: Exploring the link among heuristics, knowledge, and action. *Entrepreneurship Theory and Practice*, 33(1), pp. 167–192.

Honig, B. (2001). Learning strategies and resources for entrepreneurs and intrapreneurs. *Entrepreneurship Theory and Practice*, 26(1), pp. 21–35.

Huber, G.P. (1991). Organizational learning: The contributing processes and the literatures. *Organization Science*, 2(1), pp. 88–115.

Hughes, M., Hughes, P. and Morgan, R.E. (2007). Exploitative learning and entrepreneurial orientation alignment in emerging young firms: Implications for market and response performance. *British Journal of Management*, **18**(4), pp. 359–375.

Huovinen, J. and Tihula, S. (2008). Entrepreneurial learning in the context of portfolio entrepreneurship. *International Journal of Entrepreneurial Behaviour and Research*, **14**(3), pp. 152–171.

Ireland, R.D., Reutzel, C.R. and Webb, J.W. (2005). From the editors: Entrepreneurship research in AMJ: What has been published, and what might the future hold? *Academy of Management Journal*, **48**(4), pp. 556–564.

Jones, K., and Tullous, R. (2002). Behaviors of pre-venture entrepreneurs and perceptions of their financial needs. *Journal of Small Business Management*, **40**, pp. 233–249.

Jones, O. (2006). Developing absorptive capacity in mature organizations: The change agent's role. *Management Learning*, **37**(3), pp. 355–376.

Jones, O. and Macpherson, A. (2006). Inter-organizational learning and strategic renewal in SMEs: Extending the 4I framework. *Long Range Planning*, **39**(2), pp. 155–175.

Jones, O., Macpherson, A. and Thorpe, R. (2010). Learning in owner-managed small firms: Mediating artefacts and strategic space. *Entrepreneurship and Regional Development*, **22**(7–8), pp. 649–673.

Jung, C.G. (1971) *Collected Works of C.G. Jung*, Vol. 6: *Psychological Types*, edited and translated by G. Adler and R.F.C. Hull. Princeton, NJ: Princeton University Press.

Kamm, J.B., Shuman, J.C., Seeger, J.A. and Nurick, A.J. (1990). Entrepreneurial teams in new venture creation: A research agenda. *Entrepreneurship Theory and Practice*, **14**(4), pp. 7–17.

Karataş-Özkan, M. (2011). Understanding relational qualities of entrepreneurial learning: Towards a multi-layered approach. *Entrepreneurship and Regional Development*, **23**(9–10), pp. 877–906.

Kelly, A., Morris, H., Rowlinson, M. and Harvey, C. (eds) (2010). *Association of Business Schools Academic Journal Quality Guide*, Version 4. London: The Association of Business Schools.

Kirzner, I.M. (1979). *Perception, Opportunity, and Profit: Studies in the theory of entrepreneurship*. Chicago, IL: University of Chicago Press.

Kolb, A. and Kolb, D.A. (2001). *Experiential Learning Theory Bibliography 1971–2001*. Boston, MA: McBer and Company.

—— (2005). *The Kolb Learning Style Inventory – Version 3.1*. Boston, MA: HayGroup.

Kolb, D.A. (1976). *The Learning Style Inventory: Technical manual*. Boston, MA: McBer and Company.

—— (1984). *Experiential Learning: Experience as the source of learning and development*. Englewood Cliffs, NJ: Prentice Hall.

—— (1985). *Learning-style Inventory: Self-scoring inventory and interpretation booklet*, Boston, MA: McBer and Company.

—— (1999). *Learning Style Inventory – Version 3: Technical Specifications*. Boston, MA: TRG Hay/McBer, Training Resources Group.

Kolb, D.A., Boyatzis, R.E. and Mainemelis, C. (2001). Experiential learning theory: Previous research and new directions. In R.J. Sternberg and L.F. Zheng (eds),

Perspectives on Thinking, Learning, and Cognitive Styles. Mahwah, NJ: Lawrence Erlbaum, pp. 227–247.

Kolb D.A., Osland J. and Rubin, I. (1995). *Organizational Behavior: An experiential approach to human behavior in organizations* (6th edition). Englewood Cliffs, NJ: Prentice Hall.

Kolb, D.A., Rubin, I.M. and MacIntyre, J.M. (1984). *Organization Psychology: An experiential approach to organizational behavior* (4th edition). Englewood Cliffs, NJ: Prentice Hall.

Kreiser, P.M. (2011). Entrepreneurial orientation and organizational learning: The impact of network range and network closure. *Entrepreneurship Theory and Practice*, 35(5), pp. 1025–1050.

Krueger, N.F. Jr. (2003). The cognitive psychology of entrepreneurship. In Z.J. Acs and D.B. Audretsch (eds), *Handbook of Entrepreneurship Research: An interdisciplinary survey and introduction*. Dordrecht, The Netherlands: Kluwer Academic Publishers, pp. 105–140.

Lamont, L.M. (1972). What entrepreneurs learn from experience. *Journal of Small Business Management*, 10(3), pp. 36–41.

Lant, T.K. and Mezias, S.J. (1990). Managing discontinuous change: A simulation study of organizational learning and entrepreneurship. *Strategic Management Journal*, 11(Special Issue), pp. 147–179.

Lave, J. and Wenger, E. (1991). *Situated Learning: Legitimate peripheral participation*. New York: Cambridge University Press.

Lee, R. and Jones, O. (2008). Networks, communication and learning during business start-up: The creation of social cognitive capital. *International Small Business Journal*, 26(5), pp. 559–594.

Lee, S.H. and Williams, C. (2007). Dispersed entrepreneurship within multinational corporations: A community perspective. *Journal of World Business*, 42(4), pp. 505–519.

Lévesque, M., Minniti, M. and Shepherd, D. (2009). Entrepreneurs' decisions on timing of entry: Learning from participation and from the experiences of others. *Entrepreneurship Theory and Practice*, 33(2), pp. 547–570.

Levitt, B. and March, J.G. (1988). Organizational learning. *Annual Review of Sociology*, 14, pp. 319–340.

Low, M.B. and MacMillan, I.C. (1988). Entrepreneurship: Past research and future challenges. *Journal of Management*, 14(2), pp. 139–161.

Lumpkin, G.T. and Lichtenstein, B.B. (2005). The role of entrepreneurial learning in the opportunity-recognition process. *Entrepreneurship Theory and Practice*, 29(4), pp. 451–472.

Macpherson, A. (2009). Book review: *Entrepreneurial Learning: Conceptual frameworks and applications*. *International Journal of Entrepreneurial Behaviour and Research*, 15(6), pp. 622–628.

Macpherson, A. and Jones, O. (2008). Object-mediated learning and strategic renewal in a mature organization. *Management Learning*, 39(2), pp. 177–201.

March, J.G. (1991). Exploration and exploitation in organizational learning. *Organization Science*, 2(1), pp. 71–87.

March, J.G. and Olsen, J.P. (1975). The uncertainty of the past: Organizational learning under ambiguity. *European Journal of Political Research*, 3, pp. 147–171.

—— (1976). *Ambiguity and Choice in Organizations*. Bergen: Scandinavian University Press.

March, J.G. and Simon, H.A. (1958). *Organizations*. New York: Wiley.

McGrath, R.G. (2001). Exploratory learning, innovative capacity, and managerial oversight. *Academy of Management Journal*, 44(1), pp. 118–131.

Miner, A.S., Bassoff, P. and Moorman, C. (2001). Organizational improvisation and learning: A field study. *Administrative Science Quarterly*, 46, pp. 304–337.

Minniti, M. and Bygrave, W. (2001). A dynamic model of entrepreneurial learning. *Entrepreneurship Theory and Practice*, 25(3), pp. 5–16.

Morris, M.H., Kuratko, D.F., Schindehutte, M. and Spivack, A.J. (2012). Framing the entrepreneurial experience. *Entrepreneurship Theory and Practice*, 36(1), pp. 11–40.

Myers, I.B. and McCaulley, M.H. (1985). *Manual: A guide to the development and use of the Myers-Briggs Type Indicator*. California: Consulting Psychologists Press.

Nahapiet, J. and Ghoshal, S. (1998). Social capital, intellectual capital, and the organizational advantage. *Academy of Management Review*, 23(2), pp. 242–266.

Nelson, R. and Winter, S. (1977). In search of a useful theory of innovation. *Research Policy*, 6, pp. 36–76.

Nicholls-Nixon, C.L., Cooper, A.C. and Woo, C.Y. (2000). Strategic experimentation: Understanding change and performance in new ventures. *Journal of Business Venturing*, 15(5–6), pp. 493–521.

Parker, S.C. (2006). Learning about the unknown: How fast do entrepreneurs adjust their beliefs? *Journal of Business Venturing*, 21(1), pp. 1–26.

Pittaway, L. and Thorpe, R. (2012). A framework for entrepreneurial learning: A tribute to Jason Cope. *Entrepreneurship and Regional Development*, 24(9–10), pp. 837–859.

Politis, D. (2005). The process of entrepreneurial learning: A conceptual framework. *Entrepreneurship Theory and Practice*, 29(4), pp. 399–424.

Politis, D. and Gabrielsson, J. (2009). Entrepreneurs' attitudes towards failure: An experiential learning approach. *International Journal of Entrepreneurial Behaviour and Research*, 15(4), pp. 364–383.

Rae, D. (2000). Understanding entrepreneurial learning: A question of how? *International Journal of Entrepreneurial Behaviour and Research*, 6(3), pp. 145–159.

—— (2005). Entrepreneurial learning: A narrative-based conceptual model. *Journal of Small Business and Enterprise Development*, 12(3), pp. 323–335.

—— (2006). Entrepreneurial learning: A conceptual framework for technology-based enterprise. *Technology Analysis and Strategic Management*, 18(1), pp. 39–56.

—— (2013). The contribution of momentary perspectives to entrepreneurial learning and creativity. *Industry and Higher Education*, 27(6), pp. 407–420.

Rae, D. and Carswell, M. (2001). Towards a conceptual understanding of entrepreneurial learning. *Journal of Small Business and Enterprise Development*, 8(2), pp. 150–158.

Ravasi, D. and Turati, C. (2005). Exploring entrepreneurial learning: A comparative study of technology development projects. *Journal of Business Venturing*, 20(1), pp. 137–164.

Rerup, C. (2005). Learning from past experience: Footnotes on mindfulness and habitual entrepreneurship. *Scandinavian Journal of Management*, 21, pp. 451–472.

Reuber, A.R. and Fischer, E. (1999). Understanding the consequences of founders' experience. *Journal of Small Business Management*, 37(2), pp. 30–45.

Rhee, J., Park, T. and Lee, D.H. (2010). Drivers of innovativeness and performance for innovative SMEs in South Korea: Mediation of learning orientation. *Technovation*, 30, pp. 65–75.

Sanz-Velasco, S. (2006). Opportunity development as a learning process for entrepreneurs. *International Journal of Entrepreneurial Behaviour and Research*, 12(5), pp. 251–271.

Sarasvathy, S.D., Dew, N., Velamuri, S.R. and Venkatamaran, S. (2003). Three views of entrepreneurial opportunity. In Z.J. Acs and D.B. Audretsch (eds), *Handbook of Entrepreneurship Research*. Boston, MA: Kluwer, pp. 141–160.

Sardana, D. and Scott-Kemmis, D. (2010). Who learns what? A study based on entrepreneurs from biotechnology new ventures. *Journal of Small Business Management*, 48(3), pp. 441–468.

Schildt, H.A., Maula, M.V.J. and Keil, T. (2005). Explorative and exploitative learning from external corporate ventures. *Entrepreneurship Theory and Practice*, 29(4), pp. 493–515.

Schindehutte, M. and Morris, M.H. (2009). Advancing strategic entrepreneurship research: The role of complexity science in shifting the paradigm. *Entrepreneurship Theory and Practice*, 33(1), pp. 241–276.

Senge, P.M. (1990). *The Fifth Discipline: The art and practice of the learning organisation*. New York: Currency Doubleday.

Shane, S. (2003). *A General Theory of Entrepreneurship*. Cheltenham: Edward Elgar.

Shane, S. and Venkataraman, S. (2000). The promise of entrepreneurship as a field of research. *Academy of Management Review*, 25(1), pp. 217–226.

Short, J.C., Ketchen, D.J., Jr., Shook, C.L. and Ireland, R.D. (2010). The concept of 'opportunity' in entrepreneurship research: Past accomplishments and future challenges. *Journal of Management*, 36(1), pp. 40–65.

Sirén, C.A., Kohtamäki, M. and Kuckertz, A. (2012). Exploration and exploitation strategies, profit performance, and the mediating role of strategic learning: Escaping the exploitation trap. *Strategic Entrepreneurship Journal*, 6, pp. 18–41.

Starbuck, W.H. (1983). Organizations as action generators. *American Sociological Review*, 48(1), pp. 91–102.

Stevenson, H.H. and Jarillo, J.C. (1990). A paradigm of entrepreneurship: Entrepreneurial management. *Strategic Management Journal*, 11(Summer Special Issue), pp. 17–27.

Steyaert, C. (2005). Entrepreneurship: In between what? On the 'frontier': As a discourse of entrepreneurship research. *International Journal of Entrepreneurship and Small Business*, 2(1), pp. 2–16.

Taylor, D.W. and Thorpe, R. (2004). Entrepreneurial learning: A process of co-participation. *Journal of Small Business and Enterprise Development*, 11(2), pp. 203–211.

Thorpe, R., Gold, J., Holt, R. and Clarke, J. (2006). Immaturity: The constraining of entrepreneurship. *International Small Business Journal*, 24(3), pp. 232–252.

Timmons, J.A. and Spinelli, S. (2006). *New Venture Creation: Entrepreneurship for the 21st century* (7th edition). Boston, MA: McGraw-Hill Higher Education.

Venkataraman, S. (1997). The distinctive domain of entrepreneurship research: An editor's perspective. In J. Katz and R. Brockhaus (eds), *Advances in Entrepreneurship, Firm Emergence, and Growth*, 3, pp. 119–138. Greenwich, CT: JAI Press.

Voudouris, I., Dimitratos, P. and Salavou, H. (2011). Entrepreneurial learning in the international new high-technology venture. *International Small Business Journal*, 29(3), pp. 238–258.

Wang, C.L. (2008). Entrepreneurial orientation, learning orientation, and firm performance. *Entrepreneurship Theory and Practice*, 32(4), pp. 635–656.

Wang, C.L. and Rafiq, M. (2009). Organizational diversity and shared vision: Resolving the paradox of exploratory and exploitative learning. *European Journal of Innovation Management*, 12(1), pp. 86–101.

Ward, T.B. (2004). Cognition, creativity, and entrepreneurship. *Journal of Business Venturing*, 19(2), pp. 173–18.

Weick, K.E. and Roberts, K.H. (1993). Collective mind in organizations: Heedful interrelating on flight decks. *Administrative Science Quarterly*, 38(3), pp. 357–381.

Wenger, E. (1998). *Communities of Practice: Learning, meaning, and identity.* New York: Cambridge University Press.

West, G.P. III (2007). Collective cognition: When entrepreneurial teams, not individuals, make decisions. *Entrepreneurship Theory and Practice*, 31(1), pp. 77–102.

Westhead, P. and Wright, M. (2011). David Storey's optimism and chance perspective: A case of the emperor's new clothes? *International Small Business Journal*, 29(6), pp. 714–729.

Young, J.E. and Sexton, D.L. (2003). What makes entrepreneurs learn and how do they do it? *Journal of Entrepreneurship*, 12(2), pp. 155–182.

Zahra, S.A. (1993). A conceptual model of entrepreneurship as firm behavior: A critique and extension. *Entrepreneurship Theory and Practice*, 17, pp. 5–21.

Zahra, S.A. and George, G. (2002). Absorptive capacity: A review, reconceptualization, and extension. *Academy of Management Review*, 27(2), pp. 185–203.

Zahra, S.A., Abdelgawad, S.G. and Tsang, E.W.K. (2011). Emerging multinationals venturing into developed economies: Implications for learning, unlearning, and entrepreneurial capability. *Journal of Management Inquiry*, 20(3), pp. 323–330.

Zhao, Y., Li, Y., Lee, S.H. and Chen, L.B. (2011). Entrepreneurial orientation, organizational learning, and performance: evidence from China. *Entrepreneurship Theory and Practice*, 35(2), pp. 293–317.

3 Becoming an entrepreneur

The unexplored role of childhood and adolescent human capital

Dilani Jayawarna, Oswald Jones and Allan Macpherson

Introduction

Research on the creation of new businesses has focused largely on human capital acquired through higher education and employment (Ucbasaran *et al.*, 2008). However, Heinz (2002) argues that the individual's future outcomes arise from personal, family and work histories rather than from achievements fixed in time. Evidence across the social sciences suggests that early childhood is a crucial period for effective educational investment; building skills early in life produces lasting effects (Esping-Anderson, 2008). Research also suggests that cognitive stimulation in childhood is strongly influenced by social origins (Bradley and Corwyn, 2002). Despite this general agreement about the importance of childhood education and socialisation, there is a limited understanding of how early-stage human capital is linked to entrepreneurship. Recently, Obschonka *et al.* (2012) claimed that the process related to entrepreneurial career development starts early in life and encouraged entrepreneurship researchers to incorporate childhood competences in entrepreneurship studies.

This chapter offers an important contribution to knowledge about the development of human capital across various stages of an individual's life course and the influence on entrepreneurial potential in adulthood. We use data from the National Child Development Study (NCDS) to highlight childhood, adolescent and early adulthood educational and human capital pathways (including family) to entrepreneurship. Overall, we argue that the processes through which human capital influences entrepreneurial prospects begin during the early school years and are not confined to credentials and work experience in adulthood, as suggested elsewhere (Chandler and Hanks, 1998; Davidsson and Honig, 2003). Studies that focus exclusively on secondary school attainment or university education miss an important part of the story. In particular, this chapter demonstrates that children's cognitive ability and creative potential are powerful influences on their entrepreneurial career prospects. This is an observation that is best understood with reference to family resources and associated support of childhood educational attainments. Currently there has been little focus on the processes through which children with creative abilities are selected (or select themselves) for entrepreneurial success. In studying this process, it is important to understand how socially patterned interactions between children and their parents shape various types of human capital that are important for careers in entrepreneurship. An account of human capital accumulation over the life course that is attentive to both socially structured variations in experience, and to the role of individuals in creating their own pathways, offers substantial promise in understanding entrepreneurial careers. The successful realisation of this account requires that researchers broaden their focus to acknowledge the importance of childhood resources and the role of parental influence on children's entrepreneurial career trajectories.

We suggest that a better understanding of human capital developed in childhood and early adulthood is important for a number of theoretical and practical reasons. Currently, there is a very limited understanding of the way in which early educational experiences contribute to a future career in entrepreneurship (Obschonka *et al.*, 2012). Furthermore, the role which families play in this process is largely ignored (see Aldrich and Yang, 2012). From a more practical perspective, politicians and policy makers place tremendous emphasis on creating an appropriate environment for entrepreneurship (Bennett, 2008; Huggins and Williams, 2009). However, as pointed out by many critics, policies to promote entrepreneurship have actually had a limited impact on the number of people who engage in business start-ups (Bridge, 2010; Shane, 2009; Storey, 2011). Equally, in the UK at least, there is little evidence to indicate that those who do set up new ventures have the skills or motivation to develop businesses with real potential for growth (Anyadike-Danes *et al.*, 2011). Literature suggests that cognitive and non-cognitive (initiative and communication skills) abilities developed during childhood provide a strong influence on future career success (Farkas, 2003; Carneiro and Heckman, 2003) and more specifically enhancing adults' life chances as entrepreneurs (Athayde, 2009). Hence, the policy challenge is to ensure that all children have the appropriate support to increase entrepreneurial activity at a national level. Policy interventions to develop childhood activities and behaviours can influence the behaviours, actions, identities and self-definitions of adults (Down, 2012), and are therefore essential in promoting entrepreneurship in adulthood.

The structure of the chapter is as follows. We begin with a brief review of UK policies designed to promote entrepreneurship. This is followed by a summary of key contributions to the human capital literature. Largely following career development literature we then argue the case for the importance of studying human capital acquisition during the life course of the entrepreneur and the parental influence on human capital development in childhood and adolescence. Following our research methods, we present the data analysis and discuss the implications of this research for theory, practice and policy.

Policies to promote entrepreneurship

Most governments are concerned to encourage entrepreneurship both directly and indirectly (Audretsch *et al.*, 2007). The UK has initiated a number of schemes through which to support those engaged in business start-ups. For example, Jayawarna *et al.* (2011) discuss how the 'New Entrepreneur Scholarship' helped those from disadvantaged areas establish new businesses. Earlier, publication of the Bolton Report (1971) stimulated interest in small firms and entrepreneurship from both academics and policy makers in the UK. Huggins and Williams (2009) in their evaluation of Labour government policies to promote entrepreneurship reach a number of conclusions. First, enterprise policy moved away from the support of small business into a wider interpretation of entrepreneurship. Second, the desire to promote enterprise led to an 'explosion' of uncoordinated initiatives, which was detrimental to their impact. Third, the Labour government concentrated on longer term socially driven initiatives (cultural change) rather than shorter term economic drivers (Huggins and Williams, 2009). The authors sum up by pointing out that entrepreneurship policies can have a detrimental impact upon overall economic performance by encouraging some individuals to engage in unproductive entrepreneurship (see Shane, 2009). Bennett (2008) also examines policy support for SMEs in the UK and reaches different conclusions. First, he finds that there is little evidence to support the view that there is major market failure in terms of support for SMEs. He does, however, acknowledge that there may be some gaps in support 'for very small businesses and for start-ups' (Bennett, 2008, p. 294). Second, he finds little evidence that the government's *Business Link* (now disbanded) initiative achieved very much in terms of market penetration or effectiveness. Third, similar to Huggins and Williams, Bennett acknowledges that the constant restructuring of government support for smaller businesses has a negative impact upon both take-up and effectiveness. Despite this rather negative evaluation of policy initiatives in the UK, there is no doubt that some programmes have been extremely effective and cost-efficient. The New Entrepreneur Scholarship (NES) – which was an initiative to help those from disadvantaged backgrounds set up their own businesses (Taylor *et al.*, 2004) – is a good example. Jayawarna *et al.* (2011) calculated that the regional benefits in terms of gross value added (GVA) of the NES programme far exceeded the investment of public funding.

Bridge (2010) examines both the nature of policy initiatives and their impact on economic performance. He suggests that there are very few useful evaluations of policies designed to create new businesses and stimulate employment. He develops an alternative approach to enterprise policy which rejects ideas associated with 'standard economic theory'. What this means is that individuals are assumed to make rational economic choices about engaging in business start-ups based on risk assessments of the expected returns from entrepreneurship (Shane, 2003). In contrast, Bridge claims that social factors are much more important than economic factors in terms of influencing whether or not individuals engage in entrepreneurship. He also suggests that we can divide the population into three distinct groups: (1) an active group of entrepreneurs; (2) a group who will never consider entrepreneurship; (3) those who could be encouraged to become entrepreneurial. The key assumption is that an individual's decision to become an entrepreneur is influenced primarily by his or her close ties (family, friends and other influential people such as teachers). Conventional factors designed to promote entrepreneurship including various enterprise support agencies, training, finance and reductions in 'red tape' are unlikely to change attitudes towards entrepreneurship. We broadly agree with Bridge's assertion that social influences are important in terms of encouraging individuals to consider entrepreneurship. Our view is that in addition to family and friends, primary, secondary and higher education have an increasingly important role to play in promoting entrepreneurship to younger people. We also believe that it is extremely important for policy makers to instigate initiatives that encourage young entrepreneurs to build viable businesses rather than becoming self-employed (or undertaking 'necessity entrepreneurship'). This means that nascent entrepreneurs need the skills and competences to establish the appropriate foundations for start-up businesses to become 'gazelles' (Anyadike-Danes *et al.*, 2011; Jones *et al.*, 2014).

In the international context, various World Bank documents have recognised education as a key enabling factor for entrepreneurship. Most of these documents accept that knowledge is a resource, and education is a means to generate or make use of this resource. Here they argue in favour of promoting an entrepreneurial culture through the field of education and encourage the production, distribution and management of education programmes to suit people of different ages, coming from different social backgrounds and with varying life expectations. For example, Wolfensohn (2002) in his report to the World Bank made the entrepreneurship and childhood link more explicit when he noted that to create the conditions for entrepreneurship, investment in education including early childhood education is essential. The OECD also places particular emphasis on the number participating in business-related education at the tertiary level and the proportions of young people trained in business start-up (OECD, 2008).

Although current policy explicitly identifies the need for an innovative, focused and targeted 'education for entrepreneurship' programme, no country was successful in capturing the key ingredients to make this a reality. Vetrivel (2010) stated that a clearer understanding of the interrelation between entrepreneurship and the institutional, cultural and social environment and context is the driver for an effective and comprehensive entrepreneurship education policy. Development of entrepreneurial capabilities among younger people has become increasingly important for most counties. For example, in the past ten years, UK universities have placed much more emphasis on enterprise education designed to develop and enhance the skills of students. A number of dedicated programmes have also been introduced in the UK to promote entrepreneurship among young people. For example, Young Enterprise offers enterprise education through primary, secondary and university level programmes to people aged from four to twenty-five years, based on the principle of 'learning by doing' and thereby trying to develop positive aptitudes in business start-up from a young age. The Prince's Youth Business Trust is another high-profile and well-resourced youth enterprise programme in the UK. This programme targets young people aged from eighteen to twenty-five who are disadvantaged to help them achieve economic independence by means of soft support and hard finance. An experimental study to evaluate the Young Enterprise Company Programme delivered at secondary school level in the UK revealed an encouraging impact; it fostered positive attitudes towards self-employment and participants displayed higher levels of enterprise potential than non-participants. However, Greene (2009) in his youth enterprise programme evaluation revealed that, while simpler forms of evaluation tend to provide positive outcomes, more sophisticated evaluations are not so positive (Greene, 2009).

Our question is as follows. To what extent can research influence policies related to improving the process of human capital acquisition for entrepreneurship? There are two major insights from contemporary research and policy evidence that offer guidance. One comes from extensive research which suggests a powerful relationship between early childhood education and later labour market success (Pryor and Schaffer, 2000). For example, Heckman's (2006) learning-begets-learning dictum states that the effectiveness of later learning is a function of a child's early cognitive development. The second insight comes from research which highlights parental time dedication and cognitive stimulus that results in unequal outcomes both in terms of educational attainment and later-life career paths. Thus the acquisition of 'cultural capital' in the parental home, including parental socio-economic status and quality of parental stimulation, is an important element of human capital that helps children convert education into positive employment results (see Esping-Andersen, 2008).

Human capital

According to Nahapiet (2011), human capital is a term used by 'neoclassical economists' to describe the stocks of knowledge and skills that enable individuals to create economic value. The foundations for our understanding of human capital were established by economists such as Adam Smith, J.S. Mill and Alfred Marshal, in particular, the recognition that people as well as machines, building and land were 'productive resources'. Adam Smith's (1776) identification of the division of labour as a key element in enhancing the 'dexterity of workers' was central to the development of efficient systems of production (see 1993 edition). Human capital came to prominence in the 1960s with the work of Schultz (1961) and Becker (1964), although explicit use of the term is attributed to Pigou (1928). Schultz (1961) argued that post-war economic recovery was the result of healthy and well-educated populations. Individuals accrue human capital when they invest in their education, health and experience. Daniel Bell's (1973) work on the nature of 'post-industrial society' stressed the importance of knowledge workers to organisations and to the economy. Parnes' (1984) definition is useful, since he refers to human capital as the productive capabilities of individuals acquired at some cost and that can command a price in the labour market. Elaborating on this definition, Cetindamar et al. (2012) highlight at least three elements that make human capital the most critical resource that economic actors possess in the labour market (Hitt et al., 2001). First, capital in the form of skills and knowledge enhances labour productivity by providing people with the ability and know-how to perform services and create value. When new economic opportunities exist, individuals with better human capital should have a higher likelihood of identifying and exploiting those opportunities. Second, human capital is a long-term investment that carries both out-of-pocket and opportunity costs. With the correct level and quality of human capital, individuals can make positive gains from that investment. Third, because human capital is transferable and valuable to other actors in the market, it commands a price and is a valuable asset for any individual.

Explanations of the relationship between human capital and labour market outcomes differ according to various academic disciplines. Economists promote formal education as a credential for employability and therefore treat it as a fixed asset that enables individuals to maximise utility from their occupations (Blundell et al., 2005; Almond and Currie, 2009). From a management perspective, Becker (1964) distinguished between general human capital (basic literacy and numeracy) and specific human capital, which is applicable to one company or a particular sector. Following on from Becker's seminal contribution, education remains the focus of most human capital research (Keeley-Brown, 2007). Becker (2011) argues that the human capital approach, which he helped pioneer, led to an entirely new way of examining labour markets. Human capital theory is based on the principle that the more workers invest in education and training, the higher their earnings. Von Krogh and Wallin (2011, p. 267) suggest that there is a curvilinear relationship between time spent in schooling and lifetime earnings because of opportunity costs. As Nahapiet (2011) points out, educational credentials have limitations in acting as proxies for an individual's skills and competences. Sociologists, on the other hand, tend to focus on socialisation influences during children's educational careers. Consequently, there has been growing interest in examining learning in a wider context including on-the-job training as well as the role of family and community groups (Eraut and Hirsh, 2007). This more social view of human capital led to links with work on social capital (Swedberg and Granovetter, 2001). For example, the emergence of the communities-of-practice literature stresses the interaction of knowledge and relational attributes (Lave and Wenger, 1991). In contrast, psychologists highlight the behavioural influences on learning experiences and related career prospects (Masten and Coatsworth, 1998; Gutman *et al.*, 2003). Although the ideas from these disciplines are conceptually related, they have different influences on understanding and explaining the underlying human capital production function (Caspi *et al.*, 1998).

Esping-Andersen (2008) investigates links between childhood human capital and future career opportunities. It is suggested that a very large proportion of young people in developed countries lack both formal qualifications and the cognitive/non-cognitive abilities that are essential for knowledge-based economies. This is particularly important given the recent OECD (2013) report, which indicated that sixteen- to twenty-four-year-olds in the UK lag behind those in most other European countries in terms of literacy and numeracy. While formal education is certainly important in developing the appropriate skills and knowledge, there are other equally salient factors. Although cognitive skills have a genetic component, they are also developed through appropriate nurturing and environmental stimulation (Bjorklund *et al.*, 2006). Parental investment in children helps create appropriate cultural capital, which contributes to school success (de Graaf, 1998). According to Esping-Andersen (2008, p. 28) cultural capital is more important than socio-economic status in accounting for cognitive differences between fifteen year olds. Esping-Andersen (2008) goes on to argue that investment in the pre-school phase yields the highest possible rates of return on future skills development. Such investment should include improvement of non-cognitive skills, including communication and initiative, as well as conventional cognitive skills comprising memory, problem solving, motor skills and analytical abilities. We suggest that there are strong links between human capital acquired in early childhood and the likelihood of entrepreneurial success in later life.

Human capital and entrepreneurship

The qualities that entrepreneurs bring to new ventures largely depend on the resources built up through education and experience (Gibb, 1996). Teece (2011) agrees that there are strong links between entrepreneurship and human capital. He draws on Schumpeter's concept of 'creative destruction' to identify the key role of well-educated individuals in restructuring the economy:

> Whether one is focusing on creating value or capturing it, in recent decades the numerati and literati (expert talent) and entrepreneurs have become more important for the creation and management of technology in the global economy.
>
> (Teece, 2011, p. 531)

At the same time, Teece acknowledges that the ability to create or sense new opportunities is not something that is 'universally distributed'. Researchers have focused on measuring the effects of human capital endowments by examining the influence of educational attainment and organisational experience on financial performance, growth and innovation (Wiklund and Shepherd, 2003; de Clercq and Arenius, 2006; Shrader and Siegel, 2007). Formal education is an important component of human capital (Schuller, 2001) for individuals intending to become entrepreneurs. In addition to developing critical thinking, effective communication and sound decision-making skills in the entrepreneur (Gupta and York, 2008a), education also provides credentials and legitimacy to run a successful venture (Kim *et al.*, 2006; Zott and Huy, 2007).

A significant share of any individual's human capital is built up through on-the-job training, experience and increased responsibilities. Kolb's (1984) experiential learning theory (ELT) has certainly been extremely influential in the study of entrepreneurship (Cope and Watts, 2000; Cope, 2005). In addition to assisting in accumulating new knowledge and skills, formal education helps potential entrepreneurs acquire other resources, including financial, social and physical capital, which increase an individual's abilities to discover and exploit business opportunities (Van Praag *et al.*, 2013). Entrepreneurial activity also depends on specific capabilities (such as technical skills) acquired during employment and developed through interaction with others (Rae and Carswell, 2001); other writers have stressed the importance of learning from failure (Cope, 2011). Effective entrepreneurs make changes to their strategy as a result of both experience and experimentation (Nicholls-Nixon *et al.*, 2000). Prior knowledge of markets and a clear understanding of how to address customer needs appear to aid this process of discovery (Shane, 2000). Human capital provides the resources necessary to implement the strategies needed to improve the performance of new firms (Hitt *et al.*, 2001).

The entrepreneurial ability to connect knowledge and opportunities requires a very specific set of skills and insight (Venkataraman, 1997). In addition, existing stocks of human capital are the basis of sense-making resources through which people conceive and execute their actions (Weick, 1995). This means that an individual's existing abilities and knowledge have the potential to enable (or constrain) an individual's capacity to conceptualise alternative priorities (Williams and Lombrozo, 2013). While human capital comprises an entrepreneur's knowledge and experience, his or her learning trajectories also depend upon motivation and resourcefulness

(Shepherd and Douglas, 2002; Hmieleski and Corbett, 2006). Learning from experience through both reflection and reflexivity (Cunliffe, 2002) has the potential to enhance an entrepreneur's human capital and thus provide opportunities for the individual to translate experience into innovation. Managerial and technical competences are important, but the ability and willingness to engage in critical reflection is an essential component through which creativity can be achieved to promote organisational learning (Cope, 2005). Individuals can thus enhance their own human capital endowments through experience, education and critical reflexivity.

Analysis of entrepreneurial stories demonstrates the interdependence of the entrepreneur and employees within an institutional context (O'Connor, 2002). Thus, in order to enact change within their firm, entrepreneurs must use their human capital to engage with others and foster what Sadler-Smith *et al.* (2001) describe as a 'learning orientation'. Using human capital requires entrepreneurs to collaborate with others in order to embed learning in shared activities (Macpherson and Jones, 2008; Zhang *et al.*, 2006). It is these collaborative routines that potentially support firm-level innovation and performance. In addition, these types of social skills (human capital) are important for converting 'weak ties' into the strong ties that provide access to valuable resources (Granovetter, 1973; Hite, 2005; Larson and Starr, 1993). Previous business experience also helps to create intangible assets (such as reputation), which can give entrepreneurs credibility with other actors (De Carolis and Saparito, 2006; Shaw *et al.*, 2008). In addition, if entrepreneurs are to enlist the support of others to join their firms, to help make and sell their products or services, and to help them realise imagined futures (Gold *et al.*, 2002), this requires the social and human capital to get other stakeholders engaged in their business. Entrepreneurs, then, must also possess social skills to enable them to interest other stakeholders in the potential of a new venture (Baron and Tang, 2008; Zott and Huy, 2007). Taken together, this means that human capital is the accumulated effect of prior experience and education, as well as the social skills and motivation to engage with others. This in turn influences the nature of collaborative learning that shapes collective activity within the firm (Jones *et al.*, 2010).

In summary, the entrepreneurship literature acknowledges links between human capital and effective entrepreneurship. According to the conceptual model developed by Jones *et al.* (2010), entrepreneurial knowledge and experience is central to enhancing absorptive capacity, social capital and, ultimately, firm performance. However, in this chapter, our argument is that it is also important to consider early educational experiences and family background if we are to develop a clear understanding of the role of human capital in promoting entrepreneurship. Jayawarna *et al.* (2011) posit a cumulative model of the production of human capital that allows for the possibility of differing human capital investment stages along the life course of the entrepreneur. In this model, the interactive nature of building human capital and family endowments/investments is highlighted. It further suggests that human capital accumulation in earlier stages in life bolsters the development of human capital in later stages. Recently, there has been an emerging literature which suggests that entrepreneurship has a strong genetic component (Nicholau *et al.*, 2008; Shane *et al.*, 2010). They provide evidence to confirm White *et al.*'s (2007) claim that at least part of the reason why some people, and not others, become entrepreneurs is innate. Shane *et al.* (2010) acknowledge that genetic factors can have both positive and negative influence on the person–job fit. However, their empirical evidence confirms that 'entrepreneurs whose genetic endowment predisposes them to develop personality characteristics favourable to entre-preneurship perform better at running their own businesses' (Shane *et al.*, 2010: 474). At the same time, their statistical evidence for a genetic com-ponent in entrepreneurship is at best very modest (Jones *et al.*, 2014). Research shows that some of the variance across the 'big five' personality attributes is accounted for by the skills, competences and experiences acquired during the life course and, therefore, can change in response to life experiences and other educational or training interventions (Almlund *et al.*, 2011).

Research methods

In this chapter we use prospective data from the National Child Develop-ment Study (NCDS), a longitudinal study of the entire cohort of children (approximately 17,000) born in Britain in the first week of March 1958. During the course of the study these individuals have been followed up seven times, when they were aged seven, eleven, sixteen, twenty-three, thirty-three, forty-three and fifty. The first three follow-ups obtained information from children/cohort member, parents, schools and local medical authorities, while the remaining follow-ups surveyed only the sub-jects. We used the entire NCDS sample followed up to 1991. This selection process left us with a final sample of 10,970 out of which 1596 reported self-employment as their economic activity. Of the 1,596 self-employed population at age thirty-three, 998 individuals who reported business ownership are included in the study. However, after cross-validation of some of the data to check the respondents' 'true' employment status, a number of those who claimed employed or business ownership were found to be unemployed and therefore removed from the dataset. In addition, those cases with over 50 per cent of missing data related to study variables were also removed from the dataset to allow meaningful data interpreta-tion at bivariate level. A final sample of 835 business owners at age thirty-three are therefore compared against the reference group of 7,790 wage-employed population at age thirty-three.[1] Fifty-three per cent of the employee population and 66.8 per cent of the business ownership popula-tion are male. Chi-square and ANOVA tests are used along with relevant descriptive statistics (percentage and mean scores) to study the difference in the level of human capital competency measured at different stages of respondents' life course between business owners and wage-employment population.

Accumulation of human capital over the life course of the entrepreneur

There is persuasive evidence to suggest that human capital investment in early childhood can lead to large and persistent gains (Abington and Blankenau, 2013), and human capital accumulation beyond childhood is more costly. Nevertheless, academic and policy advice on human capital related to entrepreneurship is largely skewed towards the provision and impact of education during young adulthood. With human capital investments largely concentrating in later years (with higher education institutions now taking a major role) and development opportunities arising early in life (e.g. childhood), there is a clear mismatch between the provision and acquisition of human capital. Abington and Blankenau (2013) proposed a two-stage hierarchical education system in which endowment of *early human capital* at stage one is a function of government spending, exogenous family effects and family spending in early childhood. Accumulated knowledge at childhood nurtured through family and government funding later on in life (stage two) generates *general human capital* important to be successful in the labour market. Cunha and Heckman (2007) in their review of human capital investment over an individual life course stress the importance of modelling human capital accumulation as a hierarchical process where early childhood education sets the stage for productive education in late childhood. Skills attained early on in life leave a learner better prepared to take advantage of later opportunities to develop skills that are more refined. IQ, an essential human capital for entrepreneurs to discover and exploit business opportunities, is essentially set by age ten (Cunha and Heckman, 2007) and investment in IQ development later in life is less productive. From a business ownership perspective, Obschonka *et al.* (2012) argue that the process related to entrepreneurial career development starts early on in life and they emphasise the relevance of considering childhood competences in entrepreneurship studies. More specifically, Schmitt-Rodermund (2007) linked adults' entrepreneurship to age-appropriate entrepreneurial competence acquired through early developmental stages, including adolescence. Consequently, individuals are channelled into entrepreneurial careers as a result of the stimulation of such early competences.

The consensus is that expenditures on early childhood education programmes constitute worthy social investments in the human capital for entrepreneurs to start and run successful businesses. Within this premise, we also assert that qualifications and experience acquired in secondary and tertiary education can influence entrepreneurship prospects through the acquisition of employment-related skills (Greene and Saridakis, 2008). Formal educational qualifications are helpful in entering valuable social networks, as they act as a seal of assurance for finance providers, including banks and venture capitalists (Zott and Huy, 2007). Jayawarna *et al.* (2011) found that degree-level education provided access to a wider network of resources in support of early stages businesses, which also facilitated longer term development. The relationship between formal education and entrepreneurship has however found mixed support in empirical research (Davidsson and Honig, 2003). While conventional wisdom suggests that higher levels of formal education, largely measured by qualification and duration of schooling, are beneficial for new entrepreneurs (Delmar and Davidsson, 2000), it does not guarantee success in business; entrepreneurial activity is also confounded by a number of factors outside credentials (Davidsson and Honig, 2003). However, in terms of career choice, formal qualifications may create more attractive opportunities for waged employment rather than a career in entrepreneurship. While Kim *et al.* (2006, p. 16) noted that 'too much education discourages attempted entrepreneurship', Davidsson and Honig (2003, p. 321) hypothesised that 'individuals with higher amounts of human capital ... may feel the risks are lower for them [in entrepreneurship], in that they are more easily re-absorbed by the market should their venture fail'. It is not surprising, therefore, that links between human capital, as a fixed level of educational attainment, and entrepreneurship are confusing (Unger *et al.*, 2011).

Just as business experience provides human capital for entrepreneurs when they set up their own companies (Rae and Carswell, 2001), it is possible that part-time work, job training or even starting a fledgling business will provide the type of human capital appropriate for developing an entrepreneurial career later in life (Hickie, 2011). Vocational courses in early adulthood can help to exploit the potential to turn IQ early on in life to specific entrepreneurial skills in later life. The influence of a number of childhood, adolescent and early adulthood human capital predictors in selecting people into business ownership versus conventional employment at age thirty-three were studied using NCDS data (Table 3.1).

Of the childhood human capital measures, numeracy skills, cognitive ability, creative ability and literacy skills at age seven make a significant contribution to differentiate business ownership from paid employment at age thirty-three. While the former three measures enable an entrepreneurial career path, children who display a high level of literacy skills have a higher likelihood of entering paid employment. Work experience from spare-time work during adolescence seems to capture a large part of the human capital responsible for starting an entrepreneurial career. The effect of numeracy skills persists over time. The significant effect that having entrepreneurial parents has on business foundation illustrates how norms

Table 3.1 Human capital for business ownership vs. paid employment: childhood, adolescent and early adulthood human capital

	Business owners	*Employed*	*ANOVA F/ Chi-square (sig)*
Childhood			
Age 7 – problem arithmetic test score	5.54 (2.42)	5.25 (2.45)	11.459***
Age 7 – cognitive ability	7.48 (1.84)	7.09 (1.96)	22.124***
Age 7 – creative design test score (creative ability)	24.80 (6.87)	23.88 (6.94)	9.037***
Age 7 – reading test score	23.65 (6.59)	24.08 (6.63)	(n.s)
Adolescence			
Age 11 – mathematics test score	17.73 (10.15)	17.62 (9.86)	(n.s)
Age 11 – total score on general ability	44.62 (15.25)	44.98 (15.42)	(n.s)
Age 16 – hours spare time jobs takes/week	3.37 (1.56)	2.98 (1.34)	18.079***
Did spare-time work at 16	56.3%	49.7%	11.767***
Parents in business (age 16)	9.1%	4.5%	40.34***
Age 16 – total O level A–C, CSE1	2.17 (2.99)	2.26 (3.04)	(n.s)
Early adulthood			
Age 23 – number of FT/PT jobs	3.02 (1.95)	2.64 (1.75)	35.44***
Total months economically active (age 16–23)	67.08 (26.68)	64.93 (26.06)	5.088*
Had prior SE experience (measured at 23)	16.4%	1.2%	787.023***
First job in SE/Family business	4.2%	0.5%	148.567***
Had an apprenticeship	35.3%	19.8%	110.29***
Educational qualifications			10.689**
• degree/postgraduate qualifications	9.9%	11.1%	
• upper secondary	49.5%	43.7%	
• below secondary or no qualifications	40.5%	45.2%	

Notes
* $p < 0.05$.
** $p < 0.01$.
*** $p < 0.001$.
Mean values are given; values in parenthesis are standard deviations.

are transferred between generations. This suggests that start-up entrepreneurship is established as a feasible life project early on through role-modelling (Kim *et al.*, 2006; Western and Wright, 1994). The data also suggest that a *higher level* of achievement in GCSE+CSE (A–C grades) negatively affects choosing an entrepreneurial career, although the effects are not significant at a conventional level. There was also support for the hypothesis that achieving a solid school education (upper secondary qualifications) rather than higher level credentials was important for following a career in entrepreneurship. The importance of a solid school education is further supported by the finding that children who studied to below secondary, or who lacked any formal qualifications, have a lower tendency to choose an entrepreneurial career path when compared to those selected into paid employment. In relation to experience-based determinants, both the number of jobs and the duration of economically active episodes early on in adulthood are significant predictors for becoming an entrepreneur as an adult. In addition, previous business experience, self-employment or business as a first career were significant predictors of starting a career in entrepreneurship during adulthood. Experience and knowledge gained through an apprenticeship programme also seemed to be a strong determinant of entrepreneurship; the effect is over and above all other human capital measures at early adulthood, apart from a previous career in business/self-employment.

Our research provides evidence that basic education (primary and secondary schooling), but not higher education has a positive association with engagement in entrepreneurship. This, together with Kim *et al.*'s (2006, p. 16) assertion that 'too much education discourages attempted entrepreneurship', provides some justification for the need to understand the human capital accumulation along the life course, specifically at the early stage of schooling. Our results confirm that academic abilities, especially in the form of mathematical skills and creative skills, are important in the complex operations involved in entrepreneurial activities (Baum *et al.*, 2007; Hartog *et al.*, 2010).

One obvious possible explanation is that basic academic achievement and cognitive test scores from childhood persist over time. In turn, this raises the question of what stages in people's life course affect various aspects of development, including cognitive skills, personality traits like conscientiousness, and work experience and responsibilities. Although the literature on the effects of childhood education has drawn upon several different models of human development, literature on cognitive developments for entrepreneurship at this stage of the life course is virtually absent. Our data provide support for the long argued proposition that the highly educated face a high opportunity cost at start-up. We also find that parental business experience, economic activity, business experience and taking part in apprenticeship programmes during adolescence and early adulthood are positively related to start-up. This leads us to suggest that an intervening form of human capital – *enterprise skills* – may enable some to apply their education to career success *and* make them more likely to apply their human capital to start-up.

Parental influence and entrepreneurial careers

We found that idiosyncratic knowledge obtained through education (at primary, secondary and higher levels) as well as prior work experiences stimulate the identification and exploitation of entrepreneurial opportunities. We also argue in this chapter that parental investments of time and money towards promoting education, work experience and work values in childhood and adolescence serve as a significant source of idiosyncratic knowledge for potential entrepreneurs. Researchers have found that family capital is positively associated with entrepreneurship (Cetindamar *et al.*, 2012; Aldrich and Cliff, 2003), and that parental involvement can channel children with different academic abilities into more positive developmental pathways (Kokko and Pulkkinen, 2000).

Even though there is widespread agreement about the importance of parents to their children's propensity to become entrepreneurs, there is very little discussion on how this effect operates. Our arguments are therefore largely based on discussions in career development studies which suggest that life experiences and skills encouraged by parenting practices are associated with cognitive development in childhood, which continue into adulthood (Bradley and Corwyn, 2002; Pérez-Rodrigo and Aranceta, 2001). A stimulating family environment that pays attention to future employability encourages higher aspirations in children (Bradley and Corwyn, 2002) and shapes the preferences of their career choices. In particular, effective child-rearing (measured in terms of parental involvement, stimulation and appreciation of education) is a major driver for channelling children into economically viable career pathways (Esping-Andersen, 2008). Parental socio-economic status (SES) is also linked to early competences as children from more privileged socio-economic backgrounds show higher levels of academic attainment, generalised self-efficacy and social skills. Differences in family SES mean that children have varying levels of access to material and social resources, which in turn influences their cognitive development. According to De Garmo *et al.* (1999), higher SES status is associated with better parenting, which in turn affects school achievement via skill-building activities and school behaviour. Parents in successful careers encourage learning and credentials, and transmit positive attitudes about employment to their children (Becker and Tomes, 1986; Mortimer *et al.*, 1986). As Esping-Anderson (2008) noted, resource-rich parents can offer secure futures for even the least gifted children. Despite high ability, low SES children are on average concentrated towards the bottom of skill distribution tables due to fewer opportunities provided by their disadvantaged status (Currie and Thomas, 1997). In entrepreneurship, there is also a credible case to be made that familial 'cultural capital' may be of equal, if not greater, importance to childhood human capital (Esping-Andersen, 2008). Familial cultural capital, or what Esping-Anderson (2008) called the family 'learning milieu', can operate through various channels. In addition to parents' education level, quality of stimulation and parents' appreciation of their child's education, growing up in a family business is a particularly important predictor for children who become entrepreneurs, or who join the family business as an adult (Athayde, 2009; Niittykangas and Tervo, 2005). Indeed, a recent study by Fairlie and Robb (2007) found that those with parents who owned small firms were significantly more likely to enter business themselves. Parents in business pass on valuable experiences, confidence and other elements of managerial human capital to their offspring, thus increasing the likelihood that they will pursue entrepreneurial careers (Zellweger *et al.*, 2011; Laspita *et al.*, 2012; Aldrich and Yang, 2012). This inter-generational link is important because the strongest parental influence is argued to be human capital rather than finance (Dunn and Holtz-Eakin, 2000).

We use data from NCDS to argue that parental influence in a child's human capital could operate through 'exposure', 'involvement', 'appreciation' and 'capital' mechanisms, in that those exposed to parents running businesses in childhood, receiving parental support in education and born to educated parents are more likely to tip into an entrepreneurial career when compared to those who seek conventional employment (Table 3.2). Our research is largely guided by the work of authors who suggest that career pathways linking early socialisation and the role of multiple interacting parental influences are predictors of entrepreneurial behaviour in later life (Aldrich and Kim, 2007; Aldrich and Yang, 2012; Schoon and Duckworth, 2012). Related to the influences from the above mechanisms is the role which parental socio-economic status plays in facilitating the acquisition of necessary human capital by the entrepreneurs during childhood/adolescence.

The results clearly suggest that children with parents in self-employment at childhood are more likely to follow an entrepreneurial career as opposed to selecting a career in conventional employment in adulthood. Growing up in a family with role models who exemplify possible career choices is important in child development (Flouri *et al.*, 2002), and this is particularly the case for children whose parents are running successful businesses (Mungai and Velamuri, 2011). In relation to parental involvement in child education, we found that it was the time commitment (especially mothers) rather than the level of engagement that determined the propensity to become a business owner (as opposed to paid employment). In relation to the parental involvement and appreciation hypotheses which we tested, the results, albeit not strong, do point in the anticipated direction: parental cultural capital is a powerful influence for entrepreneurial career attainment. Previous research has also documented the extent to which parents, especially the mother, act as gatekeepers for their children's education (Flouri and Buchanan, 2002), and findings suggest that maternal employment when children are in education is a significant risk factor for poor intellectual development and educational attainment. In relation to parental capital, interestingly NCDS data confirm a primary, socio-economic pathway to entrepreneurship, one that emerges from the inter-generational

Table 3.2 Parental influence on childhood human capital for business ownership vs. paid employment

	Business owners	*Employed*	*ANOVA F/ Chi-square (sig)*
Parental exposure			
Parents in business at age 11	9.8%	4.6%	41.84***
Parental involvement			
Mother not in work until child age 11	49.6%	44.3%	7.55**
Parents reading to child (age 7)	1.7597	1.7557	(n.s)
Parents offer substantial help for child education (age 7)	53.3%	53.1%	(n.s)
Parents' appreciation of education			
Parents make no initiative to discuss education with child (age 11)	36.5%	39.6%	8.27*
Parents interest in child education (composite measure)	1.9701	1.9678	(n.s)
Parental human capital			
Both parents stayed at school after minimum age	20.5%	15.1%	18.37***
Parental socio-economic status			
Parental financial capabilities (composite measure)[1]	2.71	2.52	3.771***

Notes
* $p < 0.05$.
** $p < 0.01$.
*** $p < 0.001$.
1 a composite measure of parent education, income (house ownership + benefits + financial hardships) and social class.

transmission of human and financial resources from parents. In addition, the relationships we found (results not provided) between acquisition of childhood human capital (acquisition of mathematical, creative and cognitive skills) and both parental human capital and socio-economic status further confirm the inter-generational transmission of parental capital to children when selecting an entrepreneurial career in adulthood.

Policy discussion

Since extensive public funds are invested in the education system, closer examination is warranted to identify how education may contribute more directly and effectively to boost the human capital necessary to promote entrepreneurship. Esping-Andersen (2008), for example, suggests that spending per student rises 'monotonically' from pre-school to tertiary education and argues that the best rates of return on skill development would be achieved by more investment in pre-school education. Several aspects of the findings from our study are relevant for human capital investment policy. First, we highlight the importance of the early targeting of children if entrepreneurship as a career choice is to be promoted in adulthood. Children's early skills have a lasting effect on human capital in adulthood (Jayawarna et al., 2012). Policies that are almost exclusively directed at credentials through formal education have no real value in promoting an entrepreneurial culture. This research points to the fact that human capital investments across the early life course of children are critical in this endeavour and that schools need to be properly equipped to promote and encourage entrepreneurial behaviours. As Juhn et al. (1993) suggest, higher returns from early education lie mainly in unobserved abilities and cognitive stimulation, and therefore promotion of creative abilities in early childhood are important predictors for entrepreneurial careers in adulthood. Second, childhood human capital endowments interact with work experiences during adolescence to shape the development of an entrepreneurial career. Third, in terms of developing childhood human capital for a future career as an entrepreneur, parental and family circumstances and involvement have a very strong influence. Childhood human capital development is widely centred in the family. Thus, the role of parents, their employment and economic status are decisive factors in tipping children into entrepreneurship when they mature.

Importantly, this study identifies the importance of promoting academic skills such as literacy and numeracy and the importance of nurturing cognitive and non-cognitive abilities. As Shane et al. (2010) note, cognitive skills are partially transmitted genetically and partially nurtured through education programmes and parental stimulus. Cetindemar et al. (2012) propose that the relationship between human capital and entrepreneurship may be affected by the level of a country's economic development. Because differences at the country level cannot be attributed to genetics, it is evident that policy and institutions matter greatly in providing the necessary human capital base for entrepreneurship (Esping-Andersen, 2008). Here the role of schools, parents and human capital investors needs to be recognised. Given the potential payoff from early education and the importance of early skills in forecasting later school and labour market success, supporting low-income children's participation in high-quality early childhood education may well constitute a wise investment.

Our finding that the effects of parental and early childhood education investments on outcomes in relation to seeking entrepreneurial careers in adulthood will be largest for children experiencing low socio-economic status (supplementary analysis) is particularly relevant here. Those children whose skill development may be compromised by economic disadvantage, or low-quality home environments, are predicted to benefit more from early childhood education programmes than more advantaged children. Early childhood education programmes should therefore be designed to provide the kinds of enrichment that low-income children most need to do well in school and succeed in the labour market. At the same time, the evidence suggests that the inter-generational transmission of entrepreneurial resources means that children, irrespective of their upbringing and economic status, should be provided with the necessary skills at a younger age to enhance their entrepreneurial intentions, thereby increasing the probability of starting businesses in adulthood.

Finally, since a sound general education and exposure to entrepreneurial activity and apprenticeship programmes seem to be predictors of future successful entrepreneurship, it is also worth considering how we support broader entrepreneurial learning through policy. The findings above suggest that policy should support potential entrepreneurs from an early age, because learning to become an entrepreneur and embedding the skills and attitudes necessary to succeed is a lifelong process. This does not mean entrepreneurial learning opportunities later in life are not valuable and should not be supported through policy. Rather, it suggests a conceptual re-imagining about how, and when, entrepreneurial learning occurs. Entrepreneurial learning is not a process confined to those working in and on a business, but we can conceive of it as a constantly unfolding process which intersects with many social factors that influence an individual's life course (Centidamar *et al.*, 2012). Thus, a fuller understanding is required about different types of life courses that support successful entrepreneurial learning in order to devise more effective policy interventions (Jayawarna *et al.*, 2011). In other words, we need further research on the structural influences within societies that determine entrepreneurial learning opportunities and trajectories.

Conclusions

Research on childhood education suggests that rates of return from educational investment rise exponentially the younger the child, suggesting that early-school investments yield disproportionally high net returns (Carneiro and Heckman, 2003). The foundations of entrepreneurship education policy should therefore lie in the realisation that human capital for entrepreneurship is formed early on in life starting from childhood. Overall, our results provide strong support for the need to re-evaluate education/human capital policy taking into account cognitive developments from early life stages and incorporating mechanisms to aid families in the quest for improved skills, knowledge and experience to facilitate and promote entrepreneurship. Our findings highlight the role of early competences as well as contextual influences in selecting and shaping career development as an entrepreneur. There are three key policy issues to address: (1) the importance of government investment and support for childhood education; (2) enhance family capacity to invest in childhood education; and, (3) encourage parental influence and involvement in the educational outcome. In addition, the research evidence highlights the importance of vocational training and early work experience during adolescence.

In this chapter we argue that inequalities in schooling and career attainment remain powerfully influenced by social origins – especially in the early life stages. Here at least four main mechanisms influence entrepreneurial opportunities: family socio-economic status, parental human capital, parental dedication, and what we might call 'learning milieu' within which children grow up (exposure to entrepreneurial culture within the family). We identified a strong enterprise life course pathway from direct inter-generational transmission of parental financial and human capital. This initial advantage enables the continued accrual of high levels of human capital (not necessarily credentials) and this positive pathway helps children tip over into business founding as a sustained route of socio-economic privilege. Previously for the UK, Gregg *et al.*'s (1999) data show that financial difficulties during childhood reduce by about half children's likelihood of advanced vocational training and poor children are three times less likely to attain higher academic degrees. While we generally agree that Gregg *et al.*'s (1999) data provide explanations for childhood resources and entrepreneurial career relationship, our findings further extend the understanding of the development of necessary and relevant entrepreneurial human capital at childhood and the parental role in childhood education and subsequent entrepreneurial career prospects.

Therefore, we suggest that this study helps explain why earlier policies to promote entrepreneurship have, apparently, had very little influence on start-up rates (Shane, 2010; Storey, 2011). As Bridge (2010) asserts, social factors are very important influences on the attitudes of younger people towards entrepreneurship. What our data indicate is that a more focused approach to entrepreneurship education and support would lead to the creation of a larger number of successful business start-ups. Students with good numeracy skills and a solid record of achievement in secondary education have a sound basis for becoming entrepreneurs. When such skills are combined with support from parents who are committed to the development of their children's cultural capital (Esping-Andersen, 2008) and early work experience, however mundane (Hickie, 2011), then there is a far greater likelihood that these individuals will become successful entrepreneurs.

Note

1 Although smaller in size, business ownership probability of 0.107 is similar in size to self-employment proportions in other studies using NCDS data (see e.g. Burke *et al.*, 2002).

References

Abington, C. and Blankenau, W. (2013) Government education expenditures in early and late childhood. *Journal of Economic Dynamics and Control* 37: 854–874.

Aldrich, H.E. and Cliff, J.E. (2003) The pervasive effects of family on entrepreneurship: Towards a family embeddedness perspective. *Journal of Business Venturing* 18: 573–596.

Aldrich, H.E. and Kim, P.H. (2007) A life course perspective on occupational inheritance: Self-employed parents and their children. *The Sociology of Entrepreneurship* 25: 33–82.

Aldrich, H.E. and Yang, T. (2012) Lost in translation: Cultural codes are not blueprints. *Strategic Entrepreneurship Journal* 6(1): 1–17.

Almlund, M., Duckworth, A.L., Heckman, J.J. and Kautz, T. (2011) Personality Psychology and Economics. IZA Discussion Paper 5500.

Almond, D. and Currie, J. (2009) Human Capital Development Before Age Five. *Working Paper Series*, Columbia University.

Athayde, R. (2009) Measuring enterprise potential in young people. *Entrepreneurship Theory and Practice* 33(2): 481–500.

Anyadike-Danes, M., Bonner, K. and Hart, M. (2011) *Job Creation and Destruction in the UK: 1998–2012*. Department for Business Innovation and Skills, UK.

Athayde, R. (2009) Measuring enterprise potential in young people. *Entrepreneurship: Theory and Practice* 33(2): 481–500.

Audretsch, D.B., Grilo, I. and Thurik, A.R. (eds) (2007) *The Handbook of Research on Entrepreneurship Policy*. Cheltenham, and Northampton, MA: Edward Elgar.

Baron, R. and Tang, J. (2008) Entrepreneurs' social skills and new venture performance: Mediating mechanisms and cultural generality. *Journal of Management* 35(2): 282–306.

Baum, J.R., Frese, M. and Baron, R.A. (2007) *The Psychology of Entrepreneurship*. Englewood Cliffs, NJ: Erlbaum.

Becker, G.S. (1964) *Human Capital: A theoretical and empirical analysis, with special reference to education*. New York: Columbia University Press.

—— (2011) Foreword. In A. Burton-Jones and J.-C. Spender (eds), *The Oxford Handbook of Human Capital*. Oxford: Open University Press.

Becker, G.S. and Tomes, N. (1986) Human capital and the rise and fall of families. *Journal of Labor Economics* 4: S1–S39.

Bell, D. (1973) *The Coming of Post-industrial Society*. New York: Basic Books.

Bennett, R. (2008) SME policy support in Britain since the 1990s: What have we learnt? *Environment and Planning C: Government and Policy* 26(2): 375–397.

Bjorklund, A., Lindahl, M. and Plug, E. (2006) The origins of intergenerational associations: Lessons from Swedish adoption data. *The Quarterly Journal of Economics* 121(3): 999–1028.

Blundell, R., Dearden, L. and Sianesi, B. (2005) Evaluating the effect of education on earnings: Models, methods and results from the National Child Development Survey. *Journal of the Royal Statistical Society. Series A (Statistics in Society)* 168(3): 473–512.

Bolton, J.E. (1971) *Report of the Committee of Enquiry on Small Firms*. London: HMSO.

Bradley, R.H. and Corwyn, R.F. (2002) Socioeconomic status and child development. *Annual Review of Psychology* 53: 371–399.

Bridge, S. (2010) *Rethinking Enterprise Policy: Can failure trigger new understanding?/Simon Bridge, Online access with purchase: Palgrave Connect (Business & Management Collection)*. Basingstoke: Palgrave Macmillan.

Burke, A.E., Fitzroy, F.R. and Nolan, M.A. (2002) Self-employment wealth and job creation: The roles of gender, non-pecuniary motivation and entrepreneurial ability. *Small Business Economics* 19(3): 255–270.

Carneiro, P. and Heckman, J. (2003) 'Human capital policy'. In J. Heckman and A. Krueger (eds), *Inequality in America*. Cambridge, MA: MIT Press.

Caspi, A., Bradley, R., Wright, E., Moffitt, T.E. and Silva, P.A. (1998) Early failure in the labor market: Childhood and adolescent predictors of unemployment in the transition to adulthood. *American Sociological Review* 63(3): 424–451.

Cetindamar, D., Gupta, V.K., Karadeniz, E.E. and Egrican, N. (2012) What the numbers tell: The impact of human, family and financial capital on women and men's entry into entrepreneurship in Turkey. *Entrepreneurship and Regional Development* 24(1–2): 29–51.

Chandler, G. and Hanks, S. (1998) An examination of the substitutability of founders' human and financial capital in emerging business ventures. *Journal of Business Venturing* 13: 353–369.

Cope, J. (2005) Towards a dynamic learning perspective of entrepreneurship. *Entrepreneurship: Theory and Practice* 29(4): 373–397.

—— (2011) Entrepreneurial learning from failure: An interpretative phenomenological analysis. *Journal of Business Venturing* 26: 604–623.

Cope, J. and Watts, G. (2000) Learning by doing – An exploration of experience, critical incidents and reflection in entrepreneurial learning. *International Journal of Entrepreneurial Behaviour and Research* 6(3): 104–125.

Cunha, F. and Heckman, J.J. (2007) The technology of skill formation. *American Economic Review* 97(2): 31–47.

Cunliffe, A. (2002) Reflexive dialogical practice in management learning. *Management Learning* 33(1): 35–61.

Currie, J. and Thomas, D. (1997) Early Test Scores, Socioeconomic Status and Future. Working paper.

Davidsson, P. and Honig, B. (2003) The role of social and human capital among nascent entrepreneurs. *Journal of Business Venturing* 18: 301–331.

De Carolis, D.M. and Saparito, P. (2006) Social capital, cognition, and entrepreneurial opportunities: A theoretical framework. *Entrepreneurship: Theory and Practice* 30(1): 41–56.

De Clercq, D. and Arenius, P. (2006) The role of knowledge in business start-up activity. *International Small Business Journal* 24(4): 339–358.

De Garmo, D.S., Forgatch, M.S. and Martinez, C.R. (1999) Parenting of divorced mothers as a link between social status and boy's academic outcomes: Unpacking the effects of socioeconomic status. *Child Development* 70: 1231–1245.

de Graaf, P. (1998) Parents' financial and cultural resources, grades, and transitions to secondary school. *European Sociological Review* 4(3): 209–221.

Delmar, F. and Davidsson, P. (2000) Where do they come from? Prevalence and characteristics of nascent entrepreneurs. *Entrepreneurship and Regional Development* 12(1): 1–23.

Down, S. (2012) Evaluating the impacts of government policy through the long view of life history. *Entrepreneurship and Regional Development* 24(7–8): 619–639.

Dunn, T. and Holtz-Eakin, D. (2000) Financial capital, human capital, and the transition to self employment: Evidence from intergenerational links. *Journal of Labor Economics* 18: 282–305.

Eraut, M. and Hirsh, W. (2007) *The Significance of Workplace Learning for Individuals, Groups and Organizations.* Oxford and Cardiff: ESRC Centre on Skills, Knowledge and Organizational Performance.

Esping-Andersen, G. (2008) Childhood investments and skill formation. *International Tax and Public Finance* 15: 19–44.

Fairlie, R.W. and Robb, A. (2007) Families, human capital, and small business: Evidence from the characteristics of business owners survey. *Industrial and Labor Relations Review* 60(2): 225–244.

Farkas, G. (2003) Cognitive skills and noncognitive traits and behaviours in stratification process. *Annual Review of Sociology* 29: 541–562.

Flouri, E. and Buchanan, A. (2002) Childhood predictors of labor force participation in adult life. *Journal of Family and Economic Issues* 23(2): 101–120.

Flouri, E., Buchanan, A. and Bream, V. (2002) Adolescents' perceptions of their fathers' involvement: Significance to school attitudes. *Psychology in the Schools* 39: 575–582.

Gibb, A. (1996) Entrepreneurship and small business: Can we afford to neglect them in the twenty-first century business school. *British Journal of Management* 7: 309–321.

Gold, J., Holman, D. and Thorpe, R. (2002) The role of argument analysis and story telling in facilitating critical thinking. *Management Learning* 33(3): 371–388.

Gold, J., Holt, R. and Thorpe, R. (2008) A good place for a CHAT: Activity theory and MBA education. In M. Reynolds and R. Vincent, *The Handbook of Experiential Learning and Management Education.* Oxford: Oxford University Press.

Granovetter, M. (1973) The strength of weak ties. *American Journal of Sociology* 78(6): 1360–1380.

Greene, F.J. (2009) Assessing the impact of policy interventions: The influence of evaluation methodology. *Environment and Planning C: Government and Policy* 27: 216–229.

Greene, F.J. and Saridakis, G. (2008) The role of higher education skills and support in graduate self-employment. *Studies in Higher Education* 33(6): 653–672.

Gregg, P., Harkness, S. and Machin, S. (1999) *Child Development and Family Income.* York: Joseph Roundtree.

Gupta, V.K. and York, A.S. (2008) The effects of geography and age on women's attitudes towards entrepreneurship: Evidence from the state of Nebraska. *International Journal of Entrepreneurship and Innovation* 9(4): 251–262.

Gutman, L.M., Sameroff, A.J. and Cole, R. (2003) Academic growth trajectories from 1st grade to 12th grade: Effects of multiple social risk factors and preschool child factors. *Developmental Psychology* 39: 777–790.

Hartog, J., van Praag, M. and van der Sluis, J. (2010) If you are so smart, why aren't you an entrepreneur? Returns to cognitive and social ability: Entrepreneurs versus employees. *Journal of Economics and Management Strategy* 19: 947–989.

Heckman, J.J. (2006) Skill formation and the economics of investing in disadvantaged children. *European Sociological Review* 4: 209–221.

Heinz, W. (2002) Transition discontinuities and the biographical shaping of early work careers. *Journal of Vocational Behaviour* 60: 220–240.

Hickie, J. (2011) The development of human capital in young entrepreneurs. *Industry and Higher Education* 25(6): 469–481.

Hite, J.M. (2005) Evolutionary processes and paths of relationally embedded network ties in emerging entrepreneurial firms. *Entrepreneurship: Theory and Practice* 29(1): 113–144.

Hitt, M.A., Ireland, R.D., Camp, M. and Sexton, D.L. (2001) Strategic entrepreneurship: Entrepreneurial strategies for wealth creation. *Strategic Management Journal* 22: 479–491.

Hmieleski, K. and Corbett, A. (2006) Proclivity for improvisation as a predictor of entrepreneurial intentions. *Journal of Small Business Management* 44: 45–63.

Huggins, R. and Williams, N. (2009) Enterprise and public policy: A review of labour government intervention in the United Kingdom. *Environment and Planning C: Government and Policy* 27(1): 19–41.

Jayawarna, D., Jones, O. and Macpherson, A. (2011) New business creation and regional development: Enhancing resource acquisition in areas of social deprivation. *Entrepreneurship and Regional Development* 23(9/10): 735–761.

Jones, O., Macpherson, A. and Jayawarna, D. (2014) New Venture Creation: Creating Dynamic Entrepreneurial Learning Capabilities. Routledge-ISBE Masters in Entrepreneurship Series.

Jones, O., Macpherson, A. and Thorpe, R. (2010) Promoting learning in owner-managed small firms: Mediating artefacts and strategic space. *Entrepreneurship and Regional Development* 22(7/8): 649–673.

Juhn, C., Murphy, K. and Pierce, B. (1993) Wage inequality and the rise in returns to skill. *Journal of Political Economy* 101: 401–442.

Keeley-Brown, L. (2007) *Training to Teaching in the Learning and Skills Sector.* Harlow: Pearson Education.

Kim, P.H., Aldrich, H.E. and Keister, L.A. (2006) Access (not) denied: The impact of financial, human, and cultural capital on entrepreneurial entry in the United States. *Small Business Economics* 27(1): 5–22.

Kokko, K. and Pulkkinen, L. (2000) Aggression in childhood and long-term unemployment in adulthood: A cycle of maladaptation and some protective factors. *Developmental Psychology* 36: 463–472.

Kolb, D.A. (1984) *Experiential Learning: Experience as the source of learning and development.* Englewood Cliffs, NJ: Prentice-Hall.

Larson, A. and Starr, J.A. (1993) A network model of organization formation. *Entrepreneurship: Theory and Practice* 17(2): 5–15.

Laspita, S., Breugst, N., Heblich, S. and Patzelt, H. (2012) Intergenerational transmission of entrepreneurial intentions. *Journal of Business Venturing* 27(4): 414–435.

Lave, J. and Wenger, E. (1991) *Situated Learning: Legitimate peripheral participation.* New York: Cambridge University Press.

Macpherson, A. and Jones, O. (2008) Object-mediated learning and strategic renewal in a mature organization. *Management Learning* 39(2): 177–201.

Masten, A.S. and Coatsworth, J.D. (1998) The development of competence in favorable and unfavorable environments: Lessons from research on successful children. *American Psychologist* 53(2): 205–220.

Mortimer, J.T., Lorence, J. and Kumka, D.S. (1986) *Work, Family and Personality Transition to Adulthood*. Norwood, NJ: Ablex.

Mungai, E. and Velamuri, S.R. (2011) Parental entrepreneurial role model influence on male offspring: Is it always positive and when does it occur? *Entrepreneurship: Theory and Practice* 35(2): 337–357.

Nahapiet, J. (2011) A social capital perspective: Exploring the links between human capital and social capital. In A. Burton-Jones and J-C. Spender (eds), *The Oxford Handbook of Human Capital*. Oxford: Open University Press.

Nicholls-Nixon, C.L., Cooper, A.C. and Woo, C.Y. (2000) Strategic experimentation – Understanding change and performance in new ventures. *Journal of Business Venturing* 15(5): 493–521.

Nicolaou, N., Shane, S., Cherkas, L., Hunkin, J. and Spector, T.D. (2008) Is the tendency to engage in entrepreneurship genetic? *Management Science* 1: 167–179.

Niittykangas, H. and Tervo, H. (2005) Spatial variations in intergenerational transmission of self-employment. *Regional Studies* 39: 319–332.

O'Connor, E. (2002) Storied business: Typology, intertextuality, and traffic in entrepreneurial narrative. *Journal of Business Communication* 39(1): 36–54.

Obschonka, M., Silbereisen, R.K. and Schmitt-Rodermund, E. (2012) Explaining entrepreneurial behaviour: Dispositional personality traits, growth of entrepreneurial resources and business idea generation. *The Career Development Quarterly* 60: 178–190.

OECD (2013) *OECD Skills Outlook 2013: First results from the survey of adult skills*. OECD Publishing, http://dx.doi.org/10.1787/9789264204256-en.

Parnes, H.S. (1984) *People Power*. Beverly Hills, CA: Sage.

Pérez-Rodrigo, C. and Aranceta, J. (2001) School-based nutrition education: Lessons learned and new perspectives. *Public Health Nutrition* 4: 131–139.

Pigou, A. (1928) *A Study in Public Finance*. London: Macmillan.

Pryor, F. and Schaffer, D. (2000) *Who's Not Working and Why?* Cambridge: Cambridge University Press.

Rae, D. and Carswell, M. (2001) Towards a conceptual understanding of entrepreneurial learning. *Journal of Small Business and Enterprise Development* 8(2): 150–158.

Sadler-Smith, E., Spicer, D.P. and Chaston, I. (2001) Learning orientations and growth in smaller firms. *Long Range Planning* 34(2): 139–158.

Schmitt-Rodermund, E. (2007) The long way to entrepreneurship: Personality, parenting, early interests, and competences as precursors for entrepreneurial activity among the 'termites'. In R.K. Silbereisen and R.M. Lerner (eds), *Approaches to Positive Youth Development*. London: Sage.

Schoon, I. and Duckworth, K. (2012) Who becomes an entrepreneur? Early life experiences as predictors of entrepreneurship. *Development Psychology* 48(6): 1719–1726.

Schuller, T. (2001) The complementary roles of human and social capital. *Canadian Journal of Science* 312(5782): 1900–1902.

Schultz, T.W. (1961) Investment in human capital. *American Economic Review* 1(2): 1–17.

Shane, S. (2000) Prior knowledge and the discovery of entrepreneurial opportunities. *Organization Science* 11(4): 448–469.

—— (2003) *A General Theory of Entrepreneurship: The individual–opportunity nexus*. Cheltenham: Edward Elgar.

—— (2009) Why encouraging more people to become entrepreneurs is bad public policy. *Small Business Economics* 33(2): 141–149.

Shane, S., Nicolaou, N., Cherkas, L. and Spector, T.D. (2010) Genetics, the Big Five, and the tendency to be self-employed. *Journal of Applied Psychology* 95(6): 1154–1162.

Shaw, E., Lam, W. and Carter, S. (2008) The role of entrepreneurial capital in building service reputation. *Service Industries Journal* 28(7/8): 899–917.

Shepherd, D. and Douglas, E. (2002) Self-employment as a career choice: Attitudes, entrepreneurial intentions, and utility maximization. *Entrepreneurship Theory and Practice* 26(3): 81–90.

Shrader, R. and Siegel, D.S. (2007) Assessing the relationship between human capital and firm performance: Evidence from technology-based new ventures. *Entrepreneurship: Theory and Practice* 31(6): 893–908.

Storey, D.J. (2011) Optimism and chance: The elephants in the entrepreneurship room. *International Small Business Journal* 29(4): 303–321.

Swedberg, R. and Granovetter, M. (2001) Introduction to the Second Edition. In M. Granovetter and R. Swedberg (eds), *The Sociology of Economic Life*. Cambridge, MA: Westview Press.

Taylor, D.W., Jones, O. and Boles, K. (2004) Building social capital through action learning: An insight into the entrepreneur. *Education and Training* 46(4/5): 226–235.

Teece, D.J. (2011) Human capital, capabilities, and the firm: Literati, numerati, and entrepreneurs in the twenty-first century enterprise. In A. Burton-Jones and J-C.Spender (eds), *The Oxford Handbook of Human Capital*. Oxford: Oxford University Press.

Ucbasaran, D., Westhead, P. and Wright, M. (2008) Opportunity identification and pursuit: Does an entrepreneur's human capital matter? *Small Business Economics* 30(2): 153–173.

Unger, J., Rauch, A., Frese, M. and Rosenbusch, N. (2011) Human capital and entrepreneurial success: A meta-analytical review. *Journal of Business Venturing* 26(3): 341–366.

Van Praag, M., van Witteloostuijn, A. and van der Sluis, J. (2013) The higher returns to formal education for entrepreneurs versus employees. *Small Business Economics* 40: 375–396.

Venkataraman, S. (1997) The distinctive domain of entrepreneurship research: An editor's perspective. In J.A. Katz (ed.), *Advances in Entrepreneurship: Firm emergence and growth* (Vol. 3). Greenwich, CT: JAI Press.

Vetrivel, S.C. (2010) Entrepreneurship and education: A missing key in development theory and practice. *Advances In Management* 3(8): 18–22.

Von Krogh, G. and Wallin, M. (2011) The firm, human capital and knowledge creation. In A. Burton-Jones and J-C. Spender (eds), *The Oxford Handbook of Human Capital*. Oxford: Oxford University Press.

Weick, K. (1995) *Sensemaking in Organizations*. Thousand Oaks, CA: Sage.

Western, M. and Wright, E.O. (1994) The permeability of class boundaries to intergenerational mobility among men in the United States, Canada, Norway and Sweden. *American Sociological Review* 59: 606–629.

White, R., Thornhill, S. and Hampson, E. (2007) A biosocial model of entrepreneurship: The combined effects of nurture and nature. *Journal of Organizational Behavior* 28: 451–466.

Wiklund, J. and Shepherd, D. (2003) Knowledge-based resources, entrepreneurial orientation, and the performance of small and medium-sized businesses. *Strategic Management Journal* 24(13): 1307–1314.

Williams, J.J. and Lombrozo, T. (2013) Explanation and prior knowledge interact to guide learning. *Cognitive Psychology* 66(1): 55–84.

Wolfensohn, J.D. (2002) *A Time to Act: Address to the Board of Governors*. Washington, DC: World Bank, September.

Zellweger, T., Sieger, P. and Halter, F. (2011) Should I stay or should I go? Career choice intentions of students with family business backgrounds. *Journal of Business Venturing* 26(5): 521–536.

Zhang, M., Macpherson, A. and Jones, O. (2006) Conceptualizing the learning process in SMEs: Improving innovation through external orientation. *International Small Business Journal* 24(3): 299–323.

Zott, C. and Huy, Q.N. (2007) How entrepreneurs use symbolic management to acquire resources. *Administrative Science Quarterly* 52: 70–105.

4 Entrepreneurial learning through intuitive decision making

Cinla Akinci

Introduction

In recent years there has been a growth of interest in the role played by intuition in entrepreneurial cognition and behaviour (Allinson *et al.*, 2000; Baron and Ward, 2004; Dutta and Crossan, 2005; Krueger, 2007; Mitchell *et al.*, 2005). However, the field of entrepreneurship has been overly concerned with the individual entrepreneur to the detriment of ignoring the possibilities of entrepreneurial activities occurring at the group and organisational levels (Shane and Venkataraman, 2000). To address this shortcoming, the question of 'how do entrepreneurs learn?' may be better understood by adopting a multi-level organisational learning perspective. In this respect, this chapter aims to conceptualise entrepreneurial learning, with a focus on intuitive decision making, through the 4I (i.e. intuiting, interpreting, integrating, institutionalising) organisational learning framework developed by Crossan *et al.* (1999). As key to the discussion within this chapter, the 4I model acknowledges that there is an element of preconscious intuition that assumes importance in the discovery of a specific opportunity at a particular instance in time. Essentially, the 4I framework is a process model of individual, group and organisational learning; it thus incorporates within itself an interaction of knowledge flow between levels, offering useful insight into how ideas transcend from the enterprising individuals to a wider organisational system.

In this chapter, I first address entrepreneurial cognition based on various conceptualisations of intuition in judgement and decision making. A central message to be conveyed is the dynamic interplay of intuition and analysis, as well as cognition and affect in the intuitive decisions of entrepreneurs. As such, the dual-process theories (i.e. System 1 and System 2) provide the foundation upon which the discussion of entrepreneurial decision making is formed. Furthermore, particular attention is given to the role of affect in the experiential (i.e. intuitive) system in the identification and discovery of opportunities through recognition of the cues, drawing from the extensive experience and learning base of entrepreneurs. Finally, the chapter proposes that it is imperative to view the process of entrepreneurial opportunities from a social as opposed to solely individual perspective, offering a conceptual framework of intuitive entrepreneurial decision making which draws upon the 4I framework to provide understanding of entrepreneurs' cognition and behaviour as a multi-level learning process. The chapter concludes with a set of recommendations for the effective use of intuitions in entrepreneurial decision making, and proposes future directions for research to bring together the fields of entrepreneurship, decision making and organisational learning.

Entrepreneurial cognition

Management scholars have offered a variety of definitions of intuition over the past few decades (see Akinci and Sadler-Smith, 2012 for a historical review of intuition in management research) (a selection of definitions are provided in Table 4.1). Simon (1987, p. 63) defined intuitions as 'analyses frozen into habit and the capacity for rapid response through recognition' emphasising the experience-based nature of intuition. This was neatly encapsulated and consolidated by Kahneman and Klein (2009) as 'intuitive expertise' or 'expertise-based intuition' (Salas *et al.*, 2010). Dane and Pratt (2007, p. 40) defined intuitions as 'affectively charged judgements that arise through rapid, non-conscious, and holistic associations', thereby drawing attention to the view of 'intuition-as-affect', and also echoing Polanyi's assertion that cognition can be 'unconscious' to the extent that 'we can know more than we can tell' (Polanyi, 1966, p. 4).

Sadler-Smith and Shefy (2004) suggested that intuition relies on both expertise (through explicit and implicit learning processes, manifested as subconscious decision heuristics) and feelings (manifested as affect associated with particular stimulus), a view consistent with the dual-process theories. The authors called these two notions 'intuition-as-expertise' and 'intuition-as-feeling' respectively. The former is consistent with Simon's (1987, p. 63) assertion of intuition as 'analyses frozen into habit' whereas the latter is consistent with Epstein's (1998) notion of experiential processing (i.e. intuitive) which involves affect. Simon (1987) acknowledged this distinction by asserting that the intuition of the emotion-driven manager is very different from the intuition of the expert: the latter's behaviour is the product of learning and experience, and is largely adaptive; whereas the former's behaviour is a response to urges which may not necessarily lead to the right judgement and choice.

A distinctive aspect of entrepreneurial cognition is that entrepreneurs are said to have a 'knack for sensing an opportunity where others see chaos, contradiction and confusion' (Timmons, 1989, p. 1). Entrepreneurs also thrive on change, are adventurous, pursue opportunities, generate ideas, are proactive and innovative, and are 'of necessity intuitive because of the characteristics [i.e. incomplete information, time pressure, ambiguity and uncertainty] of the environment in which they are operating' (Allinson *et al.*,

Table 4.1 Definitions of intuition (in alphabetical order of authors)

Definition of intuition	Source
A powerful human faculty, perhaps the most universal natural ability we possess.	Bastick (1982, p. 2)
A perception of coherence at first not consciously represented but which comes to guide our thoughts towards a 'hunch' or hypothesis.	Bowers *et al.* (1990, p. 74)
Affectively charged judgements that arise through rapid, non-conscious and holistic associations.	Dane and Pratt (2007, p. 40)
Intuition is manifested in the fluent, holistic and situation-sensitive way of dealing with the world.	Dreyfus and Dreyfus (1986, p. 56)
The essence of intuition or intuitive responses is that they are reached with little apparent effort, and typically without conscious awareness. They involve little or no conscious deliberation. Intuition is the result of learning.	Hogarth (2010, p. 339)
A psychological function that unconsciously yet meaningfully transmits perceptions, explores the unknown, and senses possibilities which may not be readily apparent.	Jung (1933, pp. 567–568)
Intuition as 'holistic hunch' (judgement made through a subconscious synthesis of information drawn from diverse experiences) and intuition as 'automated expertise' (recognition of a familiar situation and the straightforward but partially subconscious application of previous learning related to that situation).	Miller and Ireland (2005, p. 21)
Intuitions are implicitly or tacitly informed by considerations that are not consciously noticed or appreciated.	Polanyi (1964, p. 24)
Intuition may be the direct result of implicit, unconscious learning: through the gradual process of implicit learning, tacit implicit representations emerge that capture environmental regularities and are used in direct coping with the world.	Reber (1989, p. 232)
Intuition is knowledge gained without rational thought. It comes from some stratum of awareness just below the conscious level and is slippery and elusive. Intuition comes with a feeling of 'almost, but not quite knowing'.	Rowan (1986, p. 96)
A capacity for attaining direct knowledge or understanding without the apparent intrusion of rational thought or logical inference.	Sadler-Smith and Shefy (2004, p. 77)
A feeling of knowing with certitude on the basis of inadequate information and without conscious awareness of rational thinking.	Shirley and Langan-Fox (1996, p. 564)
'Analysis frozen into habit' and the capacity for rapid response through recognition.	Simon (1987, p. 63)
Intuition has the characteristics of being implicit, inaccessible and holistic. Intuition and skill are not expressible in linguistic forms and constitute a different kind of capacity, reflecting 'sub-symbolic' processing.	Smolensky (1988, p. 82)
Knowing without being able to explain how we know, in four discrete levels of awareness: physical, emotional, mental and spiritual.	Vaughan (1979, pp. 27–28)
Intuition involves awareness of things perceived below the threshold of conscious perception.	Westcott (1968)

Source: adapted from Hodgkinson *et al.* (2008).

2000, pp. 32–33). In situations where there are no clear criteria against which to evaluate the merits of an idea, intuition may be the only way to 'sense direction' (Adaman and Devine, 2002, p. 341) and fill in the gaps in objective knowledge (Goop *et al.*, 2006) with subjective, albeit informed, judgements and creative insights (Baron and Ward, 2004). A successful entrepreneur must be able to not only perceive opportunities which have potential commercial value (Baron, 2004) but also be able to discriminate between opportunities that have a value worth pursuing and those that do not. In this regard there is a 'need for a better understanding of exactly how entrepreneurs identify and exploit opportunities' (Thorpe *et al.*, 2006, p. 233).

Entrepreneurial cognition is distinctive to the extent that it is concerned with cognitive processes relating to: (1) discovery: entrepreneurs require sufficient a priori knowledge to combine extant ideas in novel and creative ways in order to discover new opportunities; (2) evaluation: entrepreneurs require the cognitive ability to be able to appraise the viability and potential for value creation of a discovered opportunity; (3) exploitation: entrepreneurs must have the motivational, cognitive and social abilities, skills and resources to engage in the exploitation of viable discoveries (Mitchell *et al.*, 2005).

'Entrepreneurial alertness', described as the mental representations and interpretations, give entrepreneurs a unique insight into the value of a given resource (Kirzner, 1979). It is a dimension of individual difference, possessed by certain types of individuals enabling them to perceive cues (e.g. marked needs or underemployed resources) which others do not see. Alertness may be the product of 'genetic makeup, background and experience, and/or in the amount and type of information they possess about a particular opportunity' (Ardichvili *et al.*, 2003, p. 110), and is part of an intangible cognitive infrastructure necessary for organisations to be able to successfully perceive and act upon new opportunities (Krueger, 2000). Alertness is a useful concept in addressing the question raised by Thorpe *et al.* (2006) – 'How do entrepreneurs identify and exploit opportunities?' – since it shares several of the features of entrepreneurial intuition, but is not equivalent to entrepreneurial intuition.

In their recognition of viable new venture opportunities, successful entrepreneurs are commonly portrayed as relying heavily upon nonlinear thinking modes such as intuition, feelings and emotion, creativity, imagination, and optimism (Bird and Baron, 2005; Blume and Covin, 2005). Similarly, Dutta and Crossan (2005) argued that implicit in Schumpeter's (1934) view of the entrepreneur is the notion that he or she is high in terms of the cognitive abilities of creativity and intuition, as well as the social and emotional skills to overcome scepticism and hostility. In this respect, it is recognised that entrepreneurship is inherently a cognitive, affective and social process. Existing research shows that successful entrepreneurs possess a predominant nonlinear thinking and decision-making style compared with other successful professionals. For example, an empirical study by Allinson *et al.* (2000) concluded that entrepreneurs reflected a more intuitive cognitive style than the general population of managers; were no different in cognitive style than senior managers and executives; and were more intuitive than middle and junior managers. Furthermore, studies by Blume and Covin (2005) and Corbett (2002) indicated that entrepreneurs possess a greater intuitive thinking style, whereas managers prefer a more systematic, rational and analytical approach to processing information and making decisions.

However, successful entrepreneurs cannot be considered to rely exclusively on their intuition or analysis, or indeed cognition or affect (Baron and Ward, 2004); rather, two interacting and mutually reinforcing processes (i.e. intuition and analysis) functioning interdependently must serve to structure intention and action (see Akinci, 2014a). Empirical findings by Groves *et al.* (2008, 2011) suggest that entrepreneurs utilise much greater balance and versatility in linear and nonlinear thinking than their professional actor and accountant counterparts, whose predominant thinking style profiles followed expected patterns (i.e. actors prefer a nonlinear thinking style and accountants prefer a linear style). Overall these results suggest that entrepreneurs possess linear and nonlinear thinking style balance in both their alertness to diverse sources of information and the cognitive processing of such information to facilitate decision making and problem solving.

The dual-process perspective

The dual-process perspective provides a potentially useful account of individual differences in decision makers' use of intuitive or analytical judgements and the creative facet of entrepreneurial intuition. Although dual-process theories come in a number of forms, what they have in common is the idea offered by Stanovich and West (2000) that there are two different modes of cognitive systems in thinking and reasoning (Evans, 2003). In order to emphasise the prototypical view adopted, the two systems have simply been generically labelled System 1 and System 2. System 1 is characterised as contextually dependent, automatic, largely unconscious, associative, intuitive and implicit in nature. Thus, it is relatively undemanding in terms of its use of scarce cognitive resources. This system has the ability to model other minds in order to read intention and to make rapid interactional moves based on those modelled intentions. In contrast, System 2 processing is contextually independent, analytic, rule-based and explicit in nature. Hence, it is relatively slow and makes greater demands on cognitive resources than its System 1 counterpart.

According to the Cognitive-Experiential Self Theory (CEST: Epstein, 1994), behaviour and conscious thought are guided by the joint operations of these two systems, with their relative influence being determined by various parameters including the nature of the situations, individual differences in style of thinking and the degree of emotional involvement. In CEST terms, the 'analytical system' uses algorithms and normative rules, such as probability calculus, formal logic and risk assessment. It is relatively slow, effortful, and requires conscious control. In contrast, the 'experiential system' is intuitive, fast, mostly automatic, and not accessible to conscious awareness.

There is a ubiquitous influence of automatic thinking outside of awareness on conscious thinking and behaviour (Epstein, 1994). In most situations, the automatic processing of the experiential system (i.e. System 1, intuitive) is dominant over the rational system (i.e. System 2, analytical) because it is less effortful and more efficient, and accordingly it is the default option. Moreover, because it is generally associated with affect, it is apt to be experienced as more compelling than is dispassionate logical thinking. The rational and experiential systems normally engage in seamless integrated interaction, but they sometimes conflict, experienced as a struggle between feelings and thoughts (Denes-Raj and Epstein, 1994). However, certain situations are readily identified as requiring analytical processing (e.g. solving mathematical problems), whereas others are more likely to be responded to in an automatic, experientially determined manner (e.g. interpersonal behaviours). Holding such situational features constant, the greater the emotional involvement, the greater the shift in the balance of influence from the rational to the experiential system (Denes-Raj and Epstein, 1994).

The output of the intuiting process (i.e. intuition) is an involuntary and immediate affective response in conscious awareness that can be 'the feeling of liking an entity or a feeling of risk' which provides a powerful means of communication within the organism (Betsch, 2008, p. 4). The valence associated with this recognition manifests as a 'gut' reaction which serves as a criterion for selecting (positive valence) or rejecting (negative valence) a particular option. In the case of a negative somatic state, the sense arrived at is of a threat or too great a risk and signals avoidance (e.g. preventing an entrepreneur from making a potentially risky investment); whereas a positive somatic state gives rise to a sense of opportunity and promise, and thereby signals attraction (e.g. proceeding with the business investment) (Le Doux, 1996). Therefore, affective gut feeling plays a significant role in influencing the actions of the decision maker, sometimes leading to success and sometimes leading to failure.

Role of affect in experiential system

Affect plays a central role in dual-process theories (see Chaiken and Trope, 1999) of thinking, knowing and information processing (Slovic *et al.*, 2002, 2007). In order to explicate the affective aspects of entrepreneurial intuition it is necessary to draw upon concepts and theories from neurology and cognitive neuroscience. The term 'affect' is used to refer to the specific quality of 'goodness' or 'badness' experienced as a feeling state (with or without consciousness), and demarcating a positive or negative quality of a stimulus (Slovic et al., 2002, p. 397). Reliance on such feelings may be characterised as the 'affect heuristic'. Decision makers use an affect heuristic to make judgements drawing from representations of objects and events in their minds which are 'tagged' (Slovic et al., 2002, p. 400) to varying degrees with affect. In the process of making a judgement or decision, people consult or refer to an 'affect pool' containing all the positive and negative tags consciously or unconsciously associated with the representations. Affective reactions to stimuli are often the very first reactions, occurring automatically and subsequently guiding information processing and judgement, indicating that all perceptions contain some affect (Zajonc, 1980).

Affect may serve as a cue for many important judgements and decisions (Kahneman et al., 1982). Affective responses tend to occur rapidly and automatically. Using an overall, readily available affective impression can be far easier and more efficient than weighing the pros and cons, or retrieving from memory many relevant examples, especially when the required judgement or decision is complex or mental resources are limited (Slovic et al., 2002). Therefore, an entrepreneur's non-conscious appraisal of a potential business opportunity may result in either positive affective feelings, giving rise to positive assessment and evaluation of an acceptable level of risk or potential for high payback; or negative affective feelings, giving rise to negative assessment and evaluation of an unacceptable level of risk (Slovic et al., 2002) guiding judgement and decision making.

Although affect has long played a key role in many behavioural theories, it has rarely been recognised as an important component of human judgement and decision making (Finucane et al., 2000). The main focus of descriptive decision research has been cognitive rather than affective. Despite this cognitive emphasis, the importance of affect is being recognised increasingly by decision researchers (Isen, 1993; Janis and Mann, 1977; Johnson and Tversky, 1983; Loewenstein et al., 2001; Slovic et al., 2002, 2007; Zajonc, 1980).

> It was the experiential system, after all, that enabled human beings to survive during their long period of evolution. Long before there was probability theory, risk assessment, and decision analysis, there were intuition, instinct, and gut feeling to tell us whether an animal was safe to approach or the water was safe to drink.
>
> (Slovic et al., 2004, p. 313)

Slovic and colleagues (2004) contended that human beings possessed intuitive skills long before they were equipped with rational logic. As life became more complex and humans gained more control over their environment, analytic tools were invented to 'boost' the rationality of our experiential thinking. Subsequently, analytical thinking was placed on a pedestal and portrayed as the fundamental nature of rationality. However, current wisdom suggests that the rational and experiential systems operate in parallel and each seems to depend on the other for guidance (i.e. the dual-process view). Studies have demonstrated that analytic reasoning cannot be effective unless it is guided by emotion and affect (Slovic *et al.*, 2004).

Blume and Covin (2011) scrutinise entrepreneurs' attribution to intuition (as opposed to actual use of intuition) in the venture founding process, suggesting it is critical for entrepreneurs to be able to differentiate between affective responses or gut feelings associated with true intuition and equivalent affective responses associated with other phenomena or stimuli. While distinguishing between these possibilities is not always easily accomplished, an important basis when inferring the use of intuition as a decision driver is the acknowledgement that intuition is rooted in what we learn from our experiences (Dreyfus and Dreyfus, 1986; Simon, 1987). The experiential (i.e. intuitive) system is intimately associated with the experiences of affect, including 'vibes' which refer to subtle feelings people are often unaware of, representing events in the form of concrete exemplars and schemas inductively derived from emotionally significant, intense or repetitive past experiences (Epstein, 1994). Damasio's (1994) work is particularly relevant to the present discussion of the role of affect in intuitive decision making. Somatic-Marker Hypothesis (SMH) offers a physiological explanation to the operation of the experiential system. The key point of this hypothesis is that decision making is a process guided by emotions, and that in reality many decisions are influenced by the power of 'gut feel'. Before any kind of rational analysis is applied to a judgemental problem, if a bad outcome connected with a particular response comes to mind, an unpleasant gut feeling is experienced. Since this feeling is about the body, it is called a 'somatic-marker' (Damasio, 1994, p. 173) from 'soma', the Greek word for body, and 'marker' because the gut feeling marks an image which serves to focus our attention on the potential outcome. Somatic markers are a special instance of feelings generated from secondary emotions. The affective charge (or the emotional tag) that may be inferred from the SMH is one possible means of accounting for the 'gut feeling' that accompanies the non-conscious recognition and judgement of complex patterns; that is, informed intuition grounded in prior learning and experience (Sadler-Smith, 2008). Therefore, these emotions and feelings play a crucial role by helping entrepreneurs filter various possibilities quickly, even though the conscious mind may not be aware of it.

Recognition of entrepreneurial opportunities

Entrepreneurial opportunities are defined as 'a set of environmental conditions that lead to the introduction of one or more new products or services in the marketplace by an entrepreneur or by an entrepreneurial team through either an existing venture or a newly created one' (Dutta and Crossan, 2005, p. 426). Previous research on entrepreneurial opportunities assumed one of the two contrasting ontological positions: the Kirznerian view versus the Schumpeterian view. The Kirznerian view is that opportunities exist independently in the environment, waiting to be discovered, i.e. the 'discovery approach' (e.g. Busenitz, 1996; Gaglio, 1997; Gaglio and Katz, 2001; Kaisch and Gilaad, 1991; Shane and Venkataraman, 2000). Researchers within this position are concerned with factors such as the entrepreneur's personality traits, social networks and prior knowledge as being the primary antecedents of an entrepreneur's alertness to business opportunities. This perspective holds that opportunity recognition cannot occur in the absence of the entrepreneur's day-to-day knowledge. Accordingly, alertness and day-to-day knowledge go hand-in-hand in order for opportunities to be discovered by the entrepreneur. Alertness, as expressed in terms of the operation of the intuitive system, pattern recognition and related somatic processes, has the potential to add to our understanding of entrepreneurial intuition (Sadler-Smith et al., 2008). Kirzner (1979, 1997) focused not only on entrepreneurial alertness and the idiosyncratic knowledge base of the individual, but also on how this knowledge combines with entrepreneurial imagination and interpretation in order to lead to opportunities. On the contrary, the Schumpeterian view suggests that entrepreneurial opportunities emerge on the basis of the entrepreneur's perception, interpretation and understanding of environmental forces, i.e. the 'enactment approach' (e.g. Gartner, 1985; Gartner et al., 1992; Hill and Levenhagen, 1995; Levenhagen et al., 1993; Weick, 1979). This view highlights that entrepreneurial opportunities are created rather than discovered. In addition, in the overall process of the emergence of entrepreneurial opportunities, entrepreneurs' personal attributes rather than their personal knowledge resources play the most critical role.

In the discovery of opportunities, knowledge-based factors including 'maturity' (Thorpe et al., 2006) or expertise (Ericsson and Charness, 1994) contribute significantly to individuals' propensity to entrepreneurship through an impact on self-efficacy and confidence to take action (de Clercq and Arenius, 2006). Successful entrepreneurs are capable of discerning patterns consisting of cues that are seemingly irrelevant and incoherent to others. In Baron and Ward's (2004, p. 559) terms, they are able to 'connect the dots'. Baron and Ensley (2006, p. 1332) state that 'applying pattern recognition to the identification of business opportunities, it seems possible that specific persons recognise opportunities for new ventures because they perceive connections between apparently independent events and then detect meaningful patterns in these connections'. In this regard, from the Kirznerian standpoint, it is logical to assume that a given business opportunity must have existed in an entrepreneur's environment as a potentially discernible pattern of cues, waiting to be discovered.

Working within the Naturalistic Decision Making (NDM) context, Klein (2003) described intuitive judgement as an 'alarm bell inside the head' set off by intuitions built up through many years of learning and repeated experiences that accumulate to form complex patterns composed of sets of multiple and interacting cues. This accords with Simon's view of intuition as 'analyses frozen into habit and the capacity for rapid response through recognition' (1987, p. 63). Because patterns may be subtle, people often cannot describe what they noticed, or how they judged a situation as typical or atypical, leading to Klein's (1998, p. 33) view of intuition as 'recognising things without knowing how we do the recognising'.

Klein's (1997) work gave rise to the development of the Recognition Primed Decision (RPD) model which emphasised the crucial role of situation awareness in field settings. This has the potential to add to our understanding of entrepreneurial intuition through pattern recognition. Accordingly, people size up the situation and immediately know how to proceed, which goals to pursue, what to expect and how to respond. Within Klein's RPD model, affect is also of vital importance. This is the case, for instance, when an experienced decision maker's contextual awareness results in a particular combination of cues not 'feeling' right, but without him or her being able to say why. Klein (1998) claims that intuition grows out of experience and the RPD model is a model of intuition. Some aspects of intuition come from the ability to use experience to recognise situations and know how to handle them. However, intuition is not infallible: our experience will sometimes mislead us, and we will make mistakes that add to our experience base. This may contribute to the development of the entrepreneur's informed intuition through exposure, learning, trial and error and feedback, all according well with the notion of 'maturity' (Thorpe *et al.*, 2006).

In Simon's words, 'intuition is nothing more and nothing less than recognition' (1992, p. 155); it enables the expert's rapid recognition of and response to situations that are marked by familiar cues, and thereby gives access to large bodies of knowledge assembled through training and experience (Simon, 1983, 1997). Information organised in a production system of this kind can produce expert behaviour (Simon, 1992). This assertion is backed up by expertise researchers (e.g. Ericsson and Charness, 1994) who have found that experts may hold as many as 50,000 patterns in long-term memory and that these provide the basis for informed intuitions built up over ten or more years of dedicated practice. As such, the RPD model describes the decision strategy used most frequently by people with experience. This application involves some explicit reasoning (sometimes mental simulations to check feasibility of solutions), but the key to intelligent action is the automatic retrieval process (Evans, 2007). This strategy allows experts to quickly make difficult decisions by saving them the time they would otherwise have used to decompose the situation into basic elements, and to perform analyses and calculations based on those elements (Beach *et al.*, 1997; Howell, 1997).

Similarly, expertise in general cannot be captured in rule-based expert systems. Since expertise is based on the making of immediate, unreflective situational responses, 'intuitive judgement is the hallmark of expertise' (Dreyfus and Dreyfus, 2005, p. 779). These scholars suggest that deliberation is certainly used by experts if time permits, but it is done for the purpose of improving intuition, not replacing it. Therefore, pattern recognition through intuition is a vitally important process in identifying entrepreneurial opportunities (Baron, 2004) potentially being a source of competitive advantage which is valuable, rare and difficult to imitate (Barney, 1991).

Entrepreneurial opportunities as a learning process

To successfully exploit a discovered business opportunity, an entrepreneur needs to have at his or her disposal a blend not only of cognitive abilities but social skills as well (Bird, 1988). The ability to express intuitions metaphorically or imagistically is part of the social and emotional skills set needed to build shared interpretations and evaluations, and to overcome scepticism and hostility. Indeed, the building of shared meaning may be one way in which firms can foster the collective cognitions (West, 2007) and shared intuitions (Dutta and Crossan, 2005) that allow them to move quickly in markets as opportunities arise.

Dutta and Crossan (2005) conceptualise entrepreneurial opportunities as a learning process (i.e. 'socially constructed' and grounded in the cognitive and behavioural capability of individuals): the underlying notion is that in engaging with opportunities, entrepreneurs essentially follow a path of self- and organisational learning. As such, the scholars have adopted an organisational learning perspective by employing the 4I framework (intuiting, interpreting, integrating, institutionalising) (Crossan et al., 1999) which posits a process orientation to learning – recognising both the cognitive and situated positions – in order to delineate the processes comprising entrepreneurial opportunities. By doing so, the 4I framework builds a bridge between the fields of entrepreneurship and organisational learning research, thus providing insights into the dynamic nature of opportunities unfolding as entrepreneurs engage with them. In order to integrate the various arguments and reflections on entrepreneurial cognition and the context of entrepreneurial opportunities, a conceptual framework is developed (Figure 4.1). The aim is to advance our understanding of entrepreneurial learning through intuitive decision making by further exploring the antecedents and outcomes of the cognitive and affective processes entrepreneurs experience, and by further unpacking the social and psychological processes of the 4I framework. Therefore the intention is to demonstrate connections between emerging concepts in the context of entrepreneurial opportunities as a learning process, rather than to fully specify a model. The framework of intuitive entrepreneurial decision making is depicted in Figure 4.1.

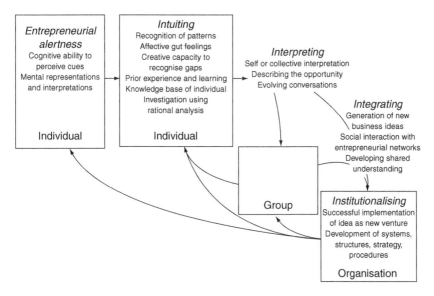

Figure 4.1 Framework of intuitive entrepreneurial decision making.

Application of the 4I framework to entrepreneurial opportunities provides a fresh perspective on how entrepreneurial opportunities may be conceptualised as a process and one which not only reconciles but also integrates conflicting elements of the two contrasting ontological positions. As discussed earlier, the emergence of entrepreneurial opportunities may be rooted in the entrepreneurs' personal dispositions (Schumpeterian view) as well as in their day-to-day knowledge (Kirznerian view). The 4I framework takes both of these perspectives as being important. Essentially the 4I framework is a process model of individual, group and organisational learning, thus incorporating within itself a dynamic interplay of knowledge flow between levels, offering useful insight into how ideas transcend from the enterprising individuals to a wider organisational system. It recognises and gives importance to the entrepreneur's previous experience and prior learning. In addition, it suggests that there is an element of preconscious intuition in the discovery of a specific opportunity at a particular instance in time. Crossan *et al.* (1999) encapsulate entrepreneurial learning through the 4I processes succinctly:

> Learning begins when individuals develop an intuition with respect to a business opportunity on the basis of their prior experience and recognition of patterns as external events unfold. The individual uses these patterns to make sense of what is going on – to interpret an insight or an idea and to put it into words. Individual interpretation can be strengthened or reinforced by sharing it with a group who can then

engage in joint exploration, interpretation, and integration of the idea, to develop it into a shared understanding of a feasible business proposition. Over time, shared understanding can be institutionalised at the organisational level in the form of systems, structures, strategy, and procedures.

(Dutta and Crossan, 2005, pp. 434–435)

The process of intuiting is an important part of the 4I framework. It recognises that any entrepreneurial action begins in an initial preconscious reflection by an individual, based on his or her intuitive patterns, about a potential business idea which the individual feels holds some potential promise and is worth pursuing. As such, Crossan *et al.* (1999) acknowledge that the driver for the intuiting process may arise in more than one form – expert intuition versus entrepreneurial intuition. Expert intuition is based on (past) pattern recognition and emphasises the complex knowledge base of the individual as being the primary means by which patterns are recognised (paralleling the Kirznerian view); on the other hand, entrepreneurial intuition relies less on the knowledge base of the individual but rather on his or her creative capacity to recognise gaps and to identify (future) possibilities (paralleling the Schumpeterian view). Irrespective of whether an idea or opportunity is discovered or is enacted by the entrepreneur, entrepreneurial intuition plays a critical role in this process of investigation, interpretation, recognition and/ or enactment. In line with previous research (Le Doux, 1996; Damasio, 1994), Crossan and colleagues point out that affect (manifested as feelings, hunches or sensations) influences cognition, and since cognition has been shown to predict opportunity identification and evaluation, it stands to reason that affect should also shape these opportunity processes (Baron and Tang, 2011; Foo, 2011).

Opportunities that have progressed from intuiting to interpreting have a higher chance of implementation compared to those that have remained at the intuiting stage. Similarly, Crossan and Berdrow (2003) find that individuals with intuitive insights need to champion those ideas in order to take them to fruition. Language is the prime means of communication; the entrepreneur must necessarily explain and defend the business concept in order for it to be developed and refined. Essentially, it is through these evolving conversations that the entrepreneur sharpens his or her interpretation. From intuiting to interpreting, conversations enable entrepreneurs to develop more coherent language to describe the opportunity. Interpreting may occur both within the minds of the individual entrepreneurs, as well as in their social interaction with the members of entrepreneurial networks and other critical stakeholders such as venture capitalists, banks, consultants and government agencies involved in the process of new venture creation.

Interpreting and integrating form the integral processes which crystallise the several interim steps arising between the generation of a new business idea in the entrepreneur's mind and its successful implementation as a new venture. Continuing innovation and change in entrepreneurial firms emerges as a constant process of interpretation and integration among members of the dominant coalition. Acknowledging the interpreting and integrating processes in the emergence of entrepreneurial opportunities suggests that the phenomenon is not only an outcome of individual intuitions but also involves other network players. Finally, incorporating institutionalising as a critical element in the process of entrepreneurial opportunities indicates that there is a greater chance of implementation and success given that the entrepreneur would engage in learning based on collective experiences.

Conclusions and recommendations

To conclude, this chapter has attempted to bring together two currently popular streams of research, entrepreneurial opportunities and intuitive decision making, based on a dual-process perspective. The field of entrepreneurship has been overly concerned with the individual to the detriment of ignoring the possibilities of entrepreneurial activities occurring at the group and organisation levels. While it is important to understand the cognitive make-up of the entrepreneurs particularly in regard to their interaction with opportunities (which inevitably exists in a social context), exploring this phenomenon outside the social context may be a limited approach.

As depicted in Figure 4.1, application of the 4I framework provides us with an improved understanding of how entrepreneurial opportunities transcend the individual entrepreneur to include other network partners and members of the organisation, offering a multi-level platform for learning. This signifies that engagement with opportunities evolves as a complex process of learning and necessarily involves a recognition of multiple perspectives and a shared view of the phenomenon. As such, the 4I framework builds a bridge between the fields of entrepreneurship and organisational learning research, thus offering insights into the dynamic nature of opportunities unfolding as entrepreneurs engage with them.

As well as highlighting the key points in this chapter, I also offer a number of recommendations for entrepreneurs and managers alike: (1) informed intuition (developed through prior learning and experience in a specific domain) is an invaluable complement to rational analysis in the skill set of the successful entrepreneur; therefore (2) intuition and analysis should be treated as complementary modes of information processing for effective decision making; (3) recognising the intuitive processes (through expertise or affectively charged judgements) has the potential to impact significantly upon entrepreneurial behaviour and outcomes, often accelerating the decision-making process; in addition, (4) affective gut feelings (e.g. positive or negative valence) play a significant role in influencing the actions of the decision maker (i.e. attraction or avoidance); and finally (5) pattern recognition through intuition is important in identifying and discovering entrepreneurial opportunities, and is a source of competitive advantage which is valuable, rare and difficult to imitate.

In terms of moving forward, there are a number of fruitful avenues in which the entrepreneurship research may evolve. At the present junction, I suggest two interesting directions for further research in order to extend our current understanding. First, there is a need to move beyond the individual entrepreneur and to explore entrepreneurial behaviour in the social environment within which the entrepreneur interacts with opportunities. Entrepreneurial intuitions are bound to be articulated and interpreted collectively; therefore in empirical studies the level of analysis should also encompass the social context (i.e. group and organisation levels including various stakeholders). The 4I organisational learning processes offer a conceptual framework as a basis for the exploration of this phenomenon. Second, serial entrepreneurs have been the focus of attention in recent research; however, it is imperative to move beyond the success stories of business venturing and direct attention to studying unsuccessful business venturing decisions that were based on intuitions. For instance, entrepreneurship researchers may use the concepts of 'intuitive hits' and 'intuitive misses' for investigating the effective and ineffective intuitive decision-making processes by using the Critical Incident Technique (Akinci, 2014b).

There appears to be much more that is yet to be learned in the study of entrepreneurship from the perspectives of dual-process theories of decision making and organisational learning. It is anticipated that entrepreneurial research and practice would benefit greatly from the insights drawn from these two fields; similarly, applying research insights from entrepreneurship would inform and advance the fields of decision making and organisational learning.

References

Adaman, F. and Devine, P. (2002) A Reconsideration of the Theory of Entrepreneurship: A Participatory Approach. *Review of Political Economy*, 14(3), pp. 329–355.

Akinci, C. (2014a) Stories of Intuition-based Decisions: Evidence for Dual Systems of Thinking. In J. Liebowitz (ed.), *Bursting the Big Data Bubble: The Case for Intuition-based Decision Making*. Abingdon, Oxon: Taylor & Francis.

—— (2014b) Capturing Intuitions in Decision Making: A Case for Critical Incident Technique. In M. Sinclair (ed.), *Handbook of Research Methods on Intuition*. Cheltenham: Edward Elgar.

Akinci, C. and Sadler-Smith, E. (2012) Intuition in Management Research: A Historical Review. *International Journal of Management Reviews*, 14(1), pp. 104–122.

Allinson, C.W., Chell, E. and Hayes, J. (2000) Intuition and Entrepreneurial

Behaviour. *European Journal of Work and Organizational Psychology*, 9(1), pp. 31–43.

Ardichvili, A., Cardozo, R. and Ray, S. (2003) A Theory of Entrepreneurial Opportunity Identification and Development. *Journal of Business Venturing*, 18(1), pp. 105–123.

Barney, J.B. (1991) Firm Resources and Sustained Competitive Advantage. *Journal of Management*, 17, pp. 99–120.

Baron, R.A. (2004) The Cognitive Perspective: A Valuable Tool for Answering Entrepreneurship's Basic 'Why' Questions. *Journal of Business Venturing*, 19, pp. 221–239.

Baron, R.A. and Ensley, M.D. (2006) Opportunity Recognition as the Detection of Meaningful Patterns: Evidence from Comparisons of Novice and Experienced Entrepreneurs. *Management Science*, 52(9), pp. 1331–1344.

Baron, R.A. and Tang, J. (2011) The Role of Entrepreneurs in Firm-level Innovation: Joint Effects of Positive Affect, Creativity, and Entrepreneurial Dynamics. *Journal of Business Venturing*, 26(1), pp. 49–60.

Baron, R.A. and Ward, T.B. (2004) Expanding Entrepreneurial Cognition's Toolbox: Potential Contributions from the Field of Cognitive Science. *Entrepreneurship Theory and Practice*, 28(6), pp. 553–518.

Bastick, T. (1982) *Intuition: How We Think and Act*. New York: Wiley.

Beach, L.R., Chi, M., Klein, G., Smith, P. and Vicente, K. (1997) Naturalistic Decision Making and Related Research Lines. In C.E. Zsambok and G. Klein (eds), *Naturalistic Decision Making*. Mahwah, NJ: Lawrence Erlbaum.

Betsch, T. (2008) The Nature of Intuition and its Neglect in Research on Judgment and Decision Making. In H. Plessner, C. Betsch and T. Betsch (eds), *Intuition in Judgment and Decision Making*. New York: Lawrence Erlbaum.

Bird, B.J. (1988) Implementing Entrepreneurial Ideas: The Case for Intention. *Academy of Management Review*, 13(3), pp. 442–453.

Bird, B.J. and Baron, R.A. (2005) Entrepreneurial Vision: Its Nature and Effects. *Academy of Management Annual Meeting*, Honolulu, Hawaii.

Blume, B.D. and Covin, J.G. (2005) Exploring Entrepreneurs' Attributions to Intuition as a Basis for the Venture Founding Decision. *Academy of Management Annual Meeting*, Honolulu, Hawaii.

—— (2011) Attributions to Intuition in the Venture Founding Process: Do Entrepreneurs Actually Use Intuition or Just Say That They Do? *Journal of Business Venturing*, 26, pp. 137–151.

Bowers, K.S., Regehr, G., Balthazard, C. and Parker, K. (1990) Intuition in the Context of Discovery. *Cognitive Psychology*, 22, pp. 72–110.

Busenitz, L.W. (1996) Research on Entrepreneurial Alertness. *Journal of Small Business Management*, 34(4), pp. 35–44.

Busenitz, L.W., West, G.P. III, Shepherd, D., Nelson, T., Chandler, G.N. and Zacharis, A. (2003) Entrepreneurship Research in Emergence: Past Trends and Future Directions. *Journal of Management*, 29(3), pp. 285–308.

Chaiken, S. and Trope, Y. (eds) (1999) *Dual Process Theories in Social Psychology*. New York: Guilford Press.

Corbett, A. (2002) Recognizing High-tech Opportunities: A Learning and Cognitive Approach. *Frontiers of Entrepreneurship Research*, 1, pp. 49–61.

Crossan, M.M. and Berdrow, I. (2003) Organizational Learning and Strategic Renewal. *Strategic Management Journal*, 24(11), pp. 1087–1105.

Crossan, M., Lane, H.W. and White, R.E. (1999) An Organizational Learning Framework: From Intuition to Institution. *Academy Management Review*, 24, pp. 522–537.

Damasio, A.R. (1994) *Descartes' Error: Emotion, Reason, and the Human Brain*. New York: G.P. Putnam & Sons.

Dane, E. and Pratt, M.G. (2007) Exploring Intuition and Its Role in Managerial Decision Making. *Academy of Management Review*, 32(1), pp. 33–54.

de Clercq, D. and Arenius, P. (2006) The Role of Knowledge in Business Start-up Activity. *International Small Business Journal*, 24(4), pp. 339–358.

Denes-Raj, V. and Epstein, S. (1994) Conflict Between Intuitive and Rational Processing: When People Behave Against Their Better Judgement. *Journal of Personality and Social Psychology*, 66(5), pp. 819–829.

Dreyfus, H.L. and Dreyfus, S.E. (1986) *Mind Over Machine: The Power of Human Intuitive Expertise in the Era of the Computer*. New York: Free Press.

—— (2005) Expertise is Real World Contexts. *Organization Studies*, 26(5), pp. 779–792.

Dutta D.K. and Crossan, M. (2005) The Nature of Entrepreneurial Opportunities: Understanding the Process Using the 4I Organizational Learning Framework. *Entrepreneurship Theory and Practice*, July, pp. 425–449.

Epstein, S. (1994) Integration of the Cognitive and the Psychodynamic Unconscious. *American Psychologist*, 49(8), pp. 709–724.

—— (1998) Cognitive-Experiential Self-Theory. In D. Barone, M. Hersen and V.B. van Hasselt (eds), *Advanced Personality*. New York: Plenum.

Ericsson, K.A. and Charness, N. (1994) Expert Performance: Its Structure and Acquisition. *American Psychologist*, 49(8), pp. 725–747.

Evans, J. St. B.T. (2003) In Two Minds: Dual-process Accounts of Reasoning. *Trends in Cognitive Sciences*, 7(10), pp. 454–459.

—— (2007) Dual-processing Accounts of Reasoning, Judgment, and Social Cognition. *Annual Review of Psychology*, 59, pp. 6.1–6.24.

Finucane, M., Alhakami, A., Slovic, P. and Johnson, S.M. (2000) The Affect Heuristic in Judgements of Risks and Benefits. *Journal of Behavioral Decision Making*, 13, pp. 1–17.

Foo, M. (2011) Emotions and Entrepreneurial Opportunity Evaluation. *Entrepreneurship Theory and Practice*, 35(2), pp. 375–393.

Gaglio, C.M. (1997) Opportunity Identification: Review, Critique and Suggested Research Directions. In J.A. Katz and R.H. Brockhaus (eds), *Advances in Entrepreneurship, Firm Emergence and Growth*. Greenwich, CT: JAI Press.

Gaglio, C.M. and Katz, J.A. (2001) The Psychological Basis of Opportunity Identification: Entrepreneurial Alertness. *Small Business Economics*, 16(2), pp. 95–111.

Gartner, W.B. (1985) A Framework for Describing and Classifying the Phenomenon of New Venture Creation. *Academy of Management Review*, 10(4), pp. 696–706.

Gartner, W.B., Bird, B.J. and Starr, J. (1992) Acting As If: Differentiating Entrepreneurial from Organizational Behavior. *Entrepreneurship Theory and Practice*, 16(3), pp. 13–32.

Gilovich, T., Griffin, D. and Kahneman, D. (eds) (2002) *Heuristics and Biases: The Psychology of Intuitive Judgment*. New York: Cambridge University Press.

Goop, A.W.A., Gopala, R. and Thakor, A.V. (2006) The Entrepreneur's Choice

Between Private and Public Ownership. *The Journal of Finance*, LXI(2), pp. 803–836.

Groves, K.S., Vance, C.M. and Choi, D.Y. (2011) Examining Entrepreneurial Cognition: An Occupational Analysis of Balanced Linear and Nonlinear Thinking and Entrepreneurship Success. *Journal of Small Business Management*, 49(3), pp. 438–466.

Groves, K.S., Vance, C.M., Choi, D.Y. and Mendez, J.L. (2008) An Examination of the Nonlinear Thinking Style Profile Stereotype of Successful Entrepreneurs. *Journal of Enterprising Culture*, 16(2), pp. 133–159.

Hill, R.C. and Levenhagen, M. (1995) Metaphors and Mental Models: Sense Making and Sense Giving in Innovative and Entrepreneurial Activities. *Journal of Management*, 21(6), pp. 1057–1074.

Hodgkinson, G.P., Langan-Fox, J. and Sadler-Smith, E. (2008) Intuition: A Fundamental Bridging Construct in the Behavioural Sciences. *British Journal of Psychology*, 99, pp. 1–27.

Hogarth, R.M. (2010) Intuition: A Challenge for Psychological Research on Decision Making. *Psychological Inquiry*, 21, pp. 338–353.

Howell, W.C. (1997) Progress, Prospects, and Problems in NDM: A Global View". In C.E. Zsambok and G. Klein (eds), *Naturalistic Decision Making*. Mahwah, NJ: Lawrence Erlbaum.

Isen, A.M. (1993) Positive Affect and Decision Making. In M. Lewis and J.M. Haviland (eds), *Handbook of Emotions*. New York: Guilford Press.

Janis, I.L. and Mann, L. (1977) *Decision Making*. New York: Free Press.

Johnson, E.J. and Tversky, A. (1983) Affect, Generalization, and the Perception of Risk. *Journal of Personality and Social Psychology*, 45, pp. 20–31.

Jung, C.G. (1933) *Modern Man in Search of a Soul*. London: Kegan Paul, Trench, Trubner.

Kahneman, D. and Klein, G. (2009) Conditions for Intuitive Expertise: A Failure to Disagree. *The American Psychologist*, 64(6), pp. 515–526.

Kahneman, D., Slovic, P. and Tversky, A. (eds) (1982) *Judgment Under Uncertainty: Heuristics and Biases*. New York: Cambridge University Press.

Kaisch, S. and Gilaad, B. (1991) Characteristics of Opportunities Search of Entrepreneurs versus Executives: Sources, Interest, and General Alertness. *Journal of Business Venturing*, 6(1), pp. 45–61.

Kirzner, I.M. (1979) *Perception, Opportunity and Profit*. Chicago, IL: University of Chicago Press.

—— (1997) Entrepreneurial Discovery and the Competitive Market Process: An Austrian Approach. *Journal of Economic Literature*, 35, pp. 60–85.

Klein, G. (1997) The Recognition-Primed Decision (RPD) Model: Looking Back, Looking Forward. In C.E. Zsambok and G. Klein (eds), *Naturalistic Decision Making*. Mahwah, NJ: Lawrence Erlbaum.

—— (1998) *Sources of Power: How People Make Decisions*. Cambridge, MA: MIT Press.

—— (2003) *Intuition at Work*. New York: Doubleday.

Krueger, N.F. (2000) The Cognitive Infrastructure of Opportunity Emergence. *Entrepreneurship Theory and Practice*, spring, pp. 5–23.

—— (2007) What Lies Beneath? The Experiential Essence of Entrepreneurial Thinking. *Entrepreneurship Theory and Practice*, January, pp. 123–138.

Le Doux, J.E. (1996) *The Emotional Brain*. New York: Simon & Schuster.

Levenhagen, M.J., Porac, J.F. and Thomas, H. (1993) Emergent Industry Leadership and the Selling of Technological Visions: A Social Constructionist View. In G. Johnson and J. Hendry (eds), *Strategic Thinking, Leadership, and the Management of Change*. New York: John Wiley.

Loewenstein, G.F., Weber, E.U., Hsee, C.K. and Welch, E.S. (2001) Risk as Feelings. *Psychological Bulletin*, 127, pp. 267–286.

Miller, C.C. and Ireland, R.D. (2005) Intuition in Strategic Decision Making: Friend or Foe in the Fast-paced 21st Century? *Academy of Management Executive*, 19(1), pp. 19–30.

Mitchell, J.R., Friga, P.N. and Mitchell, R.K. (2005) Untangling the Intuition Mess: Intuition as a Construct in Entrepreneurship Research. *Entrepreneurship Theory and Practice*, 29(6), pp. 653–679.

Polanyi, M. (1964) *Science, Faith and Society*. Chicago, IL: The University of Chicago Press.

—— (1966) *The Tacit Dimension*. Garden City, NY: Anchor Books.

Reber, A.S. (1989) Implicit Learning and Tacit Knowledge. *Journal of Experimental Psychology: General*, 118, pp. 219–235.

Rowan, R. (1986) *The Intuitive Manager*. Boston, MA: Little Brown.

Sadler-Smith, E. (2008) *Inside Intuition*. Abingdon, Oxon: Routledge.

Sadler-Smith, E. and Shefy, E. (2004) The Intuitive Executive: Understanding and Applying 'Gut Feel' in Decision-Making. *Academy of Management Executive*, 18(4), pp. 76–91.

Sadler-Smith, E., Hodgkinson, G.P. and Sinclair, M. (2008) A Matter of Feeling? The Role of Intuition in Entrepreneurial Decision-Making and Behavior. In W. Zerbe, C.J. Hartel and N.M. Ashkanasy (eds), *Research on Emotion in Organizations*, Vol. 4.

Salas, E., Rosen, M.A. and Diaz Granados, D. (2010) Expertise-based Intuition and Decision Making in Organizations. *Journal of Management*, 36(4), pp. 941–973.

Schumpeter, J.A. (1934) *The Theory of Economic Development: An Inquiry into Profits, Capital, Credit, Interest and the Business Cycle*. Cambridge, MA: Harvard University Press.

Shane, S. and Venkataraman, S. (2000) The Promise of Entrepreneurship as a Field of Research. *Academy of Management Review*, 25(1), pp. 217–226.

Shirley, D.A. and Langan-Fox, J. (1996) Intuition: A Review of the Literature. *Psychological Reports*, 79, pp. 563–584.

Simon, H.A. (1983) *Reason in Human Affairs*. Oxford: Blackwell.

—— (1987) Making Management Decisions: The Role of Intuition and Emotion. *Academy of Management Executive*, 1(1), pp. 57–64.

—— (1992) What is an 'Explanation' of Behaviour? *American Psychological Society*, 3(3), pp. 150–161.

—— (1997) *Administrative Behaviour*, 4th edn. New York: Free Press.

Sinclair, M. and Ashkanasy, N.M. (2005) Intuition: Myth or a Decision-Making Tool? *Management Learning*, 36(3), pp. 353–370.

Slovic, P., Finucane, M., Peters, E. and MacGregor, D.G. (2002) The Affect Heuristic. In T. Gilovich, D. Griffin and D Kahneman (eds), *Heuristics and Biases: The Psychology of Intuitive Judgment*. New York: Cambridge University Press.

—— (2004) Risk as Analysis and Risk as Feelings: Some Thoughts about Affect, Reason, Risk, and Rationality. *Risk Analysis*, 24(2), pp. 311–322.

—— (2007) The Affect Heuristic. *European Journal of Operational Research*, 177, pp. 1333–1352.

Smolensky, P. (1988) On the Proper Treatment of Connectionism. *Behavioral and Brain Sciences*, 11, pp. 1–74.

Stanovich, K.E. and West, R.F. (2000) Individual Differences in Reasoning: Implications for the Rationality Debate? *Behavioural and Brain Sciences*, 23, pp. 643–726.

Thorpe, R., Holt, R., Clarke, J. and Gold, J. (2006) Immaturity: The Constraining of Entrepreneurship. *International Small Business Journal*, 24(3), pp. 232–252.

Timmons, J.A. (1989) *The Entrepreneurial Mind*. Andover, MA: Brick House Publishing.

Vaughan, F.E. (1979) *Awakening Intuition*. New York: Doubleday.

Venkataraman, S. (1997) The Distinctive Domain of Entrepreneurship Research. *Advances in Entrepreneurship, Firm Emergence and Growth*, 3, pp. 119–138.

Weick, K.E. (1979) *The Social Psychology of Organizing*. New York: McGraw-Hill.

West, G.P. III (2007) Collective Cognition: When Entrepreneurial Teams, Not Individuals, Make Decisions. *Entrepreneurship Theory and Practice*, pp. 77–102.

Westcott, M.R. (1968) *Toward a Contemporary Psychology of Intuition: A Historical, Theoretical and Empirical Inquiry*. New York: Holt, Rinehart & Winston.

Zajonc, R.B. (1980) Feeling and Thinking: Preferences Need No Inferences. *American Psychologist*, 35, pp. 151–175.

5 The contribution of momentary perspectives to entrepreneurial learning and creativity

David Rae

Introduction

This chapter explores the contribution of 'the moment' in relation to processes of entrepreneurial learning and creativity. The notion of 'the Eureka' or 'lightbulb moment' of entrepreneurial creativity is prevalent at a popular level, but has been less well explored in relation to wider knowledge of human learning and creativity. However, advances in neuroscience and education are providing new understanding of these connections which may be of significant value in entrepreneurship education. These can build on deeper knowledge drawn from literature, philosophy and science, which enable us to make sense of momentary interactions in periods of complex cultural, economic and technological transition. In particular, understanding how human behaviour operates 'in the moment', and the significant role of unconscious, intuitive and emotional processes, represent an alternative stance to previous highly rational conceptualisations of entrepreneurial cognition and behaviour (e.g. Mitchell *et al.*, 2007). This chapter proposes how 'momentary perspectives' can contribute to understanding, conceptualising and using entrepreneurial behaviour in learning situations, including the roles of subconscious and serendipitous activities, which often go beyond intentional and rational working.

The aims of the chapter are as follows:

1 To explore the connections between the concept of the moment in entrepreneurship with processes of learning and creativity.
2 To develop a framework which may be used to understand momentary perspectives in entrepreneurship.
3 To explore the implications for entrepreneurial education and for practice.

The chapter summarises current and emerging knowledge on the significance of 'the moment' which originates from a range of domains of knowledge in philosophy, literature and narrative, social education, psychology and cognition, and learning. It makes conceptual connections between important themes in these disciplines with the experience of creativity and entrepreneurship. The results of two limited-scale studies of entrepreneurs and entrepreneurship educators are presented and used to develop an initial framework for momentary perspectives, which may be applied to understanding entrepreneurial behaviours such as how learning, creative thinking and decision making operate in the moment. The possible value and applications of momentary perspectives in relation to these are outlined.

What is 'the moment' and why is it significant?

The moment occurs in many aspects of everyday life, yet its definition is elusive, such as 'a turning point in a series of events' (*Shorter Oxford Dictionary*). There is a burgeoning popular literature, including Shaw (2010) and Lehrer (2009), and some studies such as Pillemer (1998) which make conceptual work available. In this chapter, the 'moment' is taken as a point in time when we experience conscious mental aware-ness of what is going on, either within the mind or around us, and are aware and able to remember our thinking and responses. Its meaning is related to the human experience and generation of meaning at a point in time. It is not a fixed time interval, such as the 'blink' identified by Glad-well (2005), but a conscious attention span of subjective duration. The experience of lived existence is a sequence of moments, expressed by Damasio's (2000) understanding of consciousness as 'the movie in the brain'.

Moments are transitory; they can bring retrospective realisation that change has occurred through an event carrying significant meaning or enduring consequences, but most are incidental and pass without signifi-cance (Bergson, 1911). Incidents and events are extrinsic phenomena which may trigger realisations with individual significance or meaning. A 'critical incident' (Cope, 2005) or 'entrepreneurial event' (Shapero and Sokol, 1982) is distinct from the cognitive meaning or emotional response it creates in the subjective moment. Concepts connected with understand-ing of the moment include extrinsic time, context and serendipity, and internal dimensions of memory, emotion, creativity and learning. As Bergson (1911) observed, the moment does not exist separately from its past, but rather there is a co-existent connection between the present, the past and the future. While the vast majority of 'endured time' is lived in moments which are neither significant at the time nor memorable in retro-spect, a tiny number of incidents are exceptions to this flow of existence, being experienced either at the time or subsequently to be 'momentous'; it is these which concern us.

Many periods in modern history have been described retrospectively as 'momentous' because they initiated disruptive shifts altering the prior direc-tion and trajectory of society. The combination of two phenomena makes the concept of the moment increasingly important to entrepreneurship in this context. One is the constantly unfolding and unpredictable economic and business context which has emerged since the financial crisis of 2008, creating a 'new era' of complexity, risk and rapid change in the entrepreneurial business environment (Rae, 2010). It is increasingly clear that the fundamental economic and social shifts in the period since 2008 will be seen as representing a momentous change in Western economies (e.g. Kaletsky, 2010; Cable, 2010). In recent history, the banking and financial crises from 2008 have demonstrated moments which had enduring consequences, such as the collapse of Lehman Bros. Bank, which brought a realisation that profound and meaningful change had occurred. This is paralleled by the rapid emergence of the digital economy, based on continually evolving technologies which are accelerating and enlarging the scale of entrepreneurial opportunities. This virtual entrepreneurial economy depends on a continuous digital media flow of messages, images and data which makes processes of momentary perception and decision making increasingly important. Together, these factors mean that processes of entrepreneurial creativity, opportunity recognition, learning and decision making which occur in the moment are increasingly important facets of entrepreneurial behaviour. These need better understanding in order to be integrated into learning and educational practices.

The entrepreneurial moment

Theories about the moment occur across numerous domains of knowledge; these include narrative, philosophy, creativity, education, psychology, neural and cognitive sciences. To understand human experience in the moment we need to consider how it connects with this range of perspectives. This chapter does not set out to systematically review these, as that is addressed elsewhere (Rae, 2015), but rather in this section to focus on the most relevant connections between entrepreneurship theory and the moment.

Philosophy, notably from the phenomenological, pragmatic and existentialist movements, provided early and illuminating insights into the 'problem' of time and past, future and present moments. While many such insights remain valid observations on the human condition, cognitive science increasingly offers understanding of neural networks, processing and how brain function operates in momentary operations which complement and to some extent supersede philosophical conclusions. Yet the moment is constructed in both subjective consciousness of experience, which may be expressed in narratives, such as life stories and reflections on learning, as well as existing scientifically as an objectively observed phenomenon, just as time may be taken to be either and both the 'flow' of the durée and of chronological Newtonian time. Neither denies the other, and both are required to understand the momentary experience. We may be closer to narrowing, but not yet bridging the gap expressed in David Lodge's novel *Thinks* (2001) between the creation of conscious understanding expressed through mindful narrative and the neural operations of the brain. How we think, feel and behave in the moment is at the centre of this debate. Based on this understanding, the concern of this chapter is with the human experience of the moment in entrepreneurial learning and creativity.

Narratives are central means of making sense of human experience within a schema or sequence of other moments. Narratives have become widely established in entrepreneurship, often related to learning and the notion of 'learning episodes' as periods of learning subsequently recognised as being significant in forming approaches to life and work as well as the production of identity (Pitt, 1998; Rae and Carswell, 2000; Rae, 2005). But narratives, as well as being retrospective, can also be prospective, building future conjecture based on past experience, such as in the presentation of a business strategy for a new venture.

In relation to creativity and recognition of entrepreneurial opportunity associated with the moment, Wallas (1926) referred to moments of 'illumination' in the four classical phases of creativity, later developed by Lumpkin *et al.* (2004) into a creativity-based model of entrepreneurial opportunity recognition, centred on a moment of 'insight'. Kneller (1965) suggested that 'first insights' precede 'the moment of creation', occurring after a period of conscious preparation and an interlude of non-conscious activity. Inspiration and opportunity recognition often stem from the insights gained by making perceptual connections between previously unassociated ideas and information: as Penaluna *et al.* (2009) concluded, 'most creative ideas are achieved through insight'.

From an educational perspective, Maslow wrote of the 'peak experience' as a revelatory moment of learning: 'these moments were of pure, positive happiness when all doubts, all fears, all inhibitions, all tensions, all weaknesses were left behind' (Maslow, 1962: 9). This idea of peak performance also relates to Carlstedt (2004) who developed a 'theory of critical moments' in sports psychology, which enabled superior athletic performance through directed thinking and repression of negative intrusive thoughts 'during critical moments of competition' (Carlstedt, 2004: 3). This has informed the use of critical moments in coaching education and practice, with awareness of doubt being identified as a recurrent factor in less experienced coaches, and the management of uncertainty, tension, emotion and doubt being essential factors in turning critical moments into 'breakthrough' moments (de Haan, 2007). This is related to the influential concept of 'flow' psychology developed by Csíkszentmihályi (1996) and applied in sports psychology, in which immersion in an activity transcends a sense of time.

Frick (1990) developed the concept of 'symbolic growth experiences' as heuristic inquiry, establishing integration and stability, and promoting change and growth in the learning experience. These experiences have a strong affinity with a momentary perspective in learning. This may also be traced in the emergence of a 'momentary turn' in thinking on teaching and learning in the United States, following Pillemer's work (1998) which identified six functional categories of personal event memories: memorable messages, symbolic messages, originating events, anchoring events, turning points and analogous events. These are useful categories which are related to memory, narrative and the development of self as well as gender and personality. This development is led by Giordano (2004, 2010) who explored the importance of serendipity and critical moments, centring on incidents such as casual comments made by educators which had transformative effects on learners' personal journeys. Giordano (2004) defines such moments as infrequent; specific in time; related to personal and emotional being; recognised only subsequently; and unnoticed by teachers. He differentiated these from 'teachable moments', making connections with dynamic systems and chaos theory (Gleick, 1987):

> Chaos theory provides a functional model for how a student's self-understanding may change dramatically over time as a result of an initial small disruption, such as a casual remark made by a professor to a student.
>
> (Giordano, 2010: 20)

Bedeian (2007) developed parallel ideas on critical moments in learning with symbolic meaning, while Baker (2004) explored the use of conversational learning in 'seizing the moment'.

The late Jason Cope conceptualised 'critical events' as a unifying theme in entrepreneurial learning, proposing that they created 'metamorphic' fundamental learning during 'dynamic temporal phases' of entrepreneurial learning (Cope, 2005). Cope acknowledged the constant adaptive and incremental learning during everyday experiences, but proposed that discontinuous, critical learning events could stimulate challenging, 'deep' reflection and create higher level entrepreneurial learning, and that proactive generative learning could enable entrepreneurs to anticipate and apply prior learning to critical events. In parallel, Rae and Carswell (2000) developed the notion of 'learning episodes' occurring within biographical narratives of entrepreneurial learning.

As in teaching, entrepreneurship can centre on serendipity, or fortunate chance events coupled with sagacity. Dew (2009) developed a conceptual framework for entrepreneurial serendipity in opportunity discovery which connected systematic exploration of extant knowledge with pre-discovery intuition, spontaneous recognition, and serendipitous discovery of something the entrepreneur was not looking for. Dew's model contributes to theories of opportunity discovery, but surprisingly did not connect with the literature or practice of entrepreneurial learning or education.

Other than these sources, the literature on entrepreneurial cognition placed less importance on 'the moment', although Mitchell *et al.* (2007) recognise the increasing evidence of emotion and affect in entrepreneurial cognition. Shapero and Sokol (1982) conceptualised the 'entrepreneurial event' as a critical point in the development of an entrepreneurial venture, such as initiative taking, consolidation, management, relative autonomy and risk taking. This was developed by Krueger and Brazeal (1994) to create a model of entrepreneurial potential which located the significance of a 'precipitating event' in shaping entrepreneurial intentions. Krueger's subsequent work showed the role of 'critical developmental experiences' in forming entrepreneurial beliefs and cognitive structures (Krueger, 2007). In relation to opportunity recognition, Grégoire *et al.* (2010) explored the role of cognitive processes, and developed a model of opportunity recognition as a cognitive process of structural alignment, finding that a range of types of mental connections and prior knowledge affect opportunity recognition. Kollmann and Kuckertz (2006) argued that the entrepreneurial event was of 'utmost importance' within the entrepreneurial process, and developed a framework for four 'archetypes' of opportunity recognition and exploitation, and a list of categories of entrepreneurial events. They suggested two classes of entrepreneurial events:

> The more confident part of the entrepreneurial population regards the starting point of the entrepreneurial process to be *the very moment* when the entrepreneur starts to *act* entrepreneurial and tries to take advantage of a certain business opportunity. However, entrepreneurs of a more sceptic nature need proof of concept provided by the market, and only start when customer interaction has happened.
>
> (Kollmann and Kuckertz, 2006: 45)

Cognitive science provides growing understanding of the moment through cognitive processing via neural networks. This is both controversial in regard to the efficacy of cognitive mapping in creating understanding of 'what is thought and felt' as distinct from showing connections between areas in the brain; and for the non-scientist much of the research is not readily understandable. Again, this chapter does not attempt a comprehensive review, but selects key contributions.

Various studies have highlighted the connected roles of identity, emotion and cognition in momentary perceptions (Sanitioso and Conway, 2006; Izard, 2009; Lewis, 2004; Damasio, 2012). Memory is a critical factor in the recall of significant moments, from Bartlett's (1932) theory of remembering, as 'imaginative reconstruction' based on attitude towards past reactions and experiences, organised through schemata. We know that memory is partial, selective, reconstructive and inferred as well as reproductive.

Cognitive neuroscience has studied episodic memory, showing connections between emotion and memory, and positive autobiographical memories containing more sensory and contextual information than negative memories (D'Argembeau *et al.*, 2003).

In relation to decision making, Banks and Isham (2009) studied the connection between action and reported decisions, finding that rather than a causal model of intuitive volition leading to consciously decided action,

> the intuitive model has it backwards; generation of responses is largely unconscious, and we infer the moment of decision from the perceived moment of action.

(Banks and Isham, 2009: 20)

This has significant implications, suggesting that subconscious mental processing resulting in decisions to act is faster and governs responses in the moment more than conscious intentionality.

There have been many studies of creativity, such as Terzis (2001) who explored the role of 'crosstalk' through visual perception in triggering creative 'eureka' moments. Damasio (2000: 315) proposed that creativity requires more mental resources of memory, reasoning ability and language than consciousness alone can provide, yet consciousness is 'ever present' in the process of creativity. Recently, Beeman and Kounios (2009) explored creative insights through monitoring brain activity, proposing that intuition and anticipation assist in creative problem solving. This demonstrated that brain activity in the temporal lobe of the anterior superior temporal gyrus is highly associated with creative work. If cognitive neuroscience has located the locus of creative insights, this has potentially broad implications for applied research on learning and creativity.

From this summary, it is suggested that three interconnected mental processes are critical in understanding the moment: perception, generation of meaning and acting. Most perception takes place at an 'unconscious' level, with selective conscious attention, awareness and memory of perception covering a much more limited span than unconscious awareness. Meaning is constantly being generated from the interconnections between perceptions and memory, with decisions to act being formed and executed. There is a complex and constant interaction between unconscious mental activity and conscious awareness, in which 'realisations' occur and conceptions of learning are generated in moments which may be remembered. These three processes of perceiving, generating meaning and acting form the framework developed later in this chapter.

The next section introduces two small studies which aim to gather perceptions of 'momentary perspectives' in entrepreneurial learning and practice. Further understanding and a conceptual framework are then developed based on exploration of these three processes.

Initial studies on entrepreneurial moments

Two small, exploratory surveys were undertaken to gather qualitative data on 'significant moments' in relation to entrepreneurship. The first was an online electronic survey of entrepreneurs and enterprise educators conducted via Surveymonkey. There was an open invitation to workshop participants to complete this. The second was a series of interviews with fifty business owners and managers who had participated in a small business development programme, and who were asked to recall any 'special moments' from their learning. This is summarised in the next section. The aim in both cases was to explore their experiences by gathering examples of the types of moment people recalled as significant. The limited number of respondents means that the results, and any conceptualisation based on them, can be no more than propositional.

The online survey used a simple framework which offered categories of commonly occurring types of entrepreneurial moments. It consisted of six questions which were developed based on selected literature and through a short workshop with enterprise educators, and the questionnaire was then tested via peer review, structured interviews with entrepreneurs and an online trial group. Respondents were asked to respond to the following questions, which focused on the recollection of a 'special moment' elicitation of responses associated with perceiving, generating meaning and acting:

1   What is your main role and activity in enterprise?
2   Think back to a 'special' or significant moment in your experience of entrepreneurial activity. Can you describe what happened in that moment? [Perceiving]
3   What made that moment 'special' or memorable for you? [Generating meaning]
4   How did the moment affect you? How did it make you feel? [Generating meaning]
5   What did you do as a result? Describe what actions it led you to take. [Acting]
6   Which of the following most closely describes your chosen moment:
    • problem or incident
    • creative inspiration
    • opportunity recognition
    • social encounter
    • discovery of new knowledge.

The survey was open to respondents who were self-selecting within three groups: entrepreneurs who had initiated new ventures; educators who helped people learn entrepreneurial skills; and advisers, mentors or researchers who worked with entrepreneurs. It was introduced in a number of learning events for both entrepreneurs and educators, in which the questions were used as an exercise and participants were then asked to record their responses through the questionnaire. A link to the survey was also circulated by 'Twitter' to enable people in these groups to respond. Of the thirty respondents who completed it, fourteen self-identified as entrepreneurs, eight as educators, six as advisers, mentors or researchers, and two did not disclose their roles. All provided textual details of their chosen moment, and categorised these as follows in response to question 6:

- Five (17%) described it as a problem or incident.
- Six (20%) described it as creative inspiration.
- Seventeen (57%) described it as opportunity recognition.
- Six (20%) described it as a social encounter.
- Seven (23%) described it as the discovery of new knowledge.

There were six cases of the same incident being described in more than one category although the question asked which *most closely* described the chosen moment; five of these cases combined opportunity recognition and discovery of new knowledge, and one combined social encounter and discovery of new knowledge.

Closer analysis of the moments and related description showed that the categories selected by the respondents could be interpreted differently; for example, most of those categorised as 'discovery of new knowledge' took place in social situations and also involved recognising new opportunities. Similarly, several of the 'creative inspirations' occurred in social situations. This small sample led to the conclusion that in considering 'the moment', even when categories are explained to respondents and simple labels provided, they are neither interpreted exclusively nor consistently, with respondents using multiple categories to describe the same moment. Hence, subjective recollection does not facilitate consistent categorisation into these groups via a remote questionnaire. However, when the same questions were used in an educational setting, respondents were able to categorise the moments, but again often used multiple categories.

Turning to the types of moment, Table 5.1 illustrates examples from the survey of each type, the effects reported and the response cited. Although the moments themselves varied quite widely in nature, there were common instances, such as gaining clients or contracts, and the decision to start a business venture or become self-employed.

It was possible from analysing the responses to Questions 2 to 5 to trace a coherent narrative for each individual of the moment, which connected why they considered it 'special', the effect and their response to it. This has also been observed in many educational settings, when the questions provide a series of 'cues' which elicit and structure a recollected account of the moment.

The questions asked people to recall a 'special' moment and their responses offer a narrative of that recollection. The recollection of past

Table 5.1 Examples of types of moments, effects and responses

Types of moment – perception	Meaning generated	Actions
Problem/incident		
Loss of dissatisfied client	Worried about losing	Initiated new client leads
Relationship breakdown	income	'Rebuilt my life and
Student issue	Experienced 'lowest of	business'
	low points'	Focused on student
	Noticed student learning	learning
	behaviour	
Creative inspiration		
Realisation of financial	Relax and take stock	Aim to double success
success	Excited at commercial	and sell out
Potential of 3D printing	potential	Acquired printer,
Chance conversation led	'Eureka!' very uplifting	promoted service
to idea	Pleased at his interest,	Brainstormed to develop
Son wanted to join my	realised business had	idea
business	independent life	Aim to grow and fulfil
		future of business
Opportunity		
Decided to start own	Realised transferable	Gained advice from
business	knowledge	ex-colleague
Client asked what they	Realised I had no idea	Worked out pricing and
owed	Felt good that I created	promoted service
Academic entrepreneur	the realisation	Supported the academic
realised commercial	Deep understanding	to exploit the idea
potential of business	became conscious	Shared with non-
I understood the 'aha'		specialists leading to
moment		new research and
		presentations
Social encounter		
Met my business partner	Found shared interest and	Conversation led to first
Meeting on trade mission	rapport	business start-up
Student clinched business	Value of networking and	Led to international
deal	serendipity	collaboration
	Surprised at student's	Student invited to give
	ability	guest lectures
Discover new knowledge		
Getting first client	Elated, confident, excited	Gave a loud 'Yeehaa'
contract	Felt trusted and confident	Set up my company
Offer of freelance work	Enlightened, lifted,	Enrolled towards MBA
Met college representative	motivated	

moments is clearly dependent on memory, and the significance of the moment selected may simply lie in it remaining 'memorable'. Two-thirds of the moments were triggered by external incidents, such as meetings, conversations or life events (such as marital breakdown or retirement), with one-third stemming from internally generated 'realisations' or ideas.

A moment may not have seemed to be significant at the time, but retro-spective sense making often triggers its memory, because it may have led to a significant outcome (Weick, 1995). Their actual experiences and feelings in the moment may have been different from those reported, and, as with any narrative research, their recollections are inevitably subject to such factors as selective recall, over-emphasis, bias, deletion or distortion rather than claiming to report with objective accuracy. There can be no 'proof' that the responses and actions they reported actually stemmed from the moment, other than their narrative attribu-tion that this was the case, nor that decisions reported were made con-sciously at the time; as Banks and Isham (2009) concluded, the decision to act may have been made intuitively with conscious judgement being attributed subsequently. However, they remained as powerful memories and in a number of the cases were recalled as 'turning points' in the lives of the respondents.

For example, the following is an example of a recollection of oppor-tunity recognition by a person who subsequently became an entrepreneur:

Q2. Think back to a 'special' or significant moment in your experience of entrepreneurial activity. Can you describe what happened in that moment?
'I was employed at the time and was asked by an old friend who was self-employed to help him out with a conference. At the time I declined, I felt that it would put my employed position at risk.'

Q3. What made that moment 'special' or memorable for you?
'That I was being asked to do something that I could be paid for as a self-employed person, that I had skills that organisations wanted.'

Q4. How did the moment affect you? How did it make you feel?
'Because I declined the offer I regretted that for about six months and thought that the opportunity could have been a break for me to become self-employed.'

Q5. What did you do as a result? Describe what actions it led you to take.
'I decided that I should look at moving to a self-employed status.'

This example illustrates a more general pattern of delayed responses; that while there was a realisation at the time and an instant response not to act on an opportunity, subsequent reflection led to an action deferred for some time after the event itself. This accords with the view from Kollmann and Kuckertz (2006) that confidence may be a differentiator between entre-preneurs who act immediately on perceived opportunities and those who take deferred action.

A number of the stories related to the decision to take entrepreneurial action, often through a social connection such as this one, which again describes a lapse of time between the moment of connection and action:

> Q2. The first time I met my business partner; on the first year of our undergraduate degree.
> Q3. We were sitting in a marketing lecture commenting on how bored we were; we started talking about computers (a shared interest) and we just clicked; after that we decided to skip university for the rest of the day and went to the pub.
> Q4. I felt great, the start of a new friendship, we were just so comfortable and shared so many interests.
> Q5. After a few months we started talking about business and the opportunities that would eventually lead to us starting our first company.

The following example is a 'classic' case of creativity:

> Q2. It was a chance 'off-the-cuff' remark, that led to a business idea.
> Q3. The fact that it was so simple, so by chance, yet seemed so obvious when later developed.
> Q4. It was like 'eureka'; it was very uplifting.
> Q5. We brainstormed further and this led to our developing the business idea.

Other examples were of incidents outside working life but which impinged heavily upon it. The following example omits the question fields to show the narrative flow:

> I was told by a consultant that medical tests showed I had only a week to live. I walked away shocked and went to see my GP down the road. He could not understand this and called the consultant. It turned out that my results had been mixed up with those for someone else with the same surname and initials. My response was obviously relief and some annoyance. It made me realise that every day after that was special, it was the rest of my life. So my attitude towards life and work has changed completely, I realised that we have a limited time and it's important to live each day in the best way you can because it could be your last.

Educators and business advisers provided several examples of significant moments recounted by learners or clients, such as the following:

> At the end of one of my courses a student made the most extraordinary announcement that she had clinched a huge deal. The moment was special, because she was such a quiet student, who was very nervous

about risk, and I was worried she would not go on to achieve very much. It really made me feel really shocked, in a good way, as she related her success to key learning points in the course. I have since invited this student back to give three guest lectures.

This accords with the critical moments described by Giordano (2010), in which the educator has no inkling of the significance of the effects of his or her teaching or other interactions with learners, whose learning and potential may exceed our expectations of them.

Question 4 aimed to elicit recollections of emotional responses and feelings generated from the moment. The language used is rich, and while diverse there are patterns within the terms people used, although for the reasons already given these are not significant in relation to the types of moments, nor the roles of respondents. Table 5.2 shows the language used to describe emotional responses, with brackets illustrating the multiple occasions on which these terms were used. Thirty-eight examples of positive language and seventeen examples of negative language suggest that the moments recalled were seen overall as emotionally positive experiences, at least in recollection. Where the terms used formed a coherent string, this is cited. In some cases, both positive and negative terms were used in the same response, suggesting the complexity of 'mixed emotions' often experienced in new situations, such as the following:

Fearful, I had that horrible sinking feeling. I was excited, buzzing with new ideas.

The results presented in Table 5.2 suggest that emotional meaning is significant, both in a moment remaining memorable and in the use of emotional language to describe it, which often show 'mixed feelings'. Rational language is used in the responses, but to a notably lesser extent than emotional discourse. The use of emotion in making sense of the moment, both at the time and subsequently, is consistent with the conclusions of Izard (2009) and Lewis (2004). There is increasing interest in the role of emotion in entrepreneurial learning and education, but surprisingly little is yet published, although Damasio (2012), and previously James (1884), have proposed the contributions of emotion in consciousness and the construction of 'the self'. The role of emotion in responses and recollections of the moment is clearly significant and requires further investigation.

It would be wrong to ascribe too much significance to what was intended to be a small and exploratory study, but it reinforces the notion that significant moments may be recalled and described through narratives in response to open questions, and that these narratives may be usefully analysed and compared to gain understanding of these reported experiences, in the context of entrepreneurship and learning. The next section adds to this through recollections from business owner/managers.

Table 5.2 Language expressing emotional effects of momentary realisations

Positive emotional language	Negative emotional language
confident (7)	exhausted (2)
excited (3), extremely excited	shocked (2)
sense of achievement (2)	bored (2)
enthusiastic (2)	lowest of low points
a lot of happiness	upset
trust	angry
comfortable	worried
relaxed	concerned
uplifting	uncomfortable
just like humour	regret
empowered	bewildered
satisfying	fearful, horrible sinking feeling
felt drive and determination to succeed	humbled
elated, proud, contented	switched off and shuddered
buzzing with ideas	
love	
respect	
admiration	
self-assured	
professional	
enlightened, lifted and motivated	
very pleased	
felt great	
very surprised	

Entrepreneurial moments in an owner/manager development programme

With the aim of furthering understanding the role of entrepreneurial moments in an educational perspective, a short session on 'special moments' was included within the 'Business Inspiration' programme for small business innovation leadership which was run by Lincoln Business School in 2010 for fifty local businesses aiming to recover from the recession. This made most participants aware of the concept which formed part of their learning experience and may have heightened their recollections of moments and the researchers' interest in the topic. The following extracts from evaluation interviews are drawn from an independent evaluation (Rae *et al.*, 2012). Participants were asked if they could recall any 'special moments' from the programme and, if so, what these moments were. The results are shown in Table 5.3, selected from this study.

The highest proportion (eight) reported that learning how to target customers was a special moment. Four said they felt learning about how to maximise use of their websites and using search engine optimisation was important. One reported, the section on segmentation by business problem rather than by location was a very significant moment.

Six reported that moments in the course had given them increased confidence or reaffirmed their existing thinking, and three specifically mentioned the enthusiasm and support provided by the tutors on the course and the project team as special moments.

A significant moment came when it was explained to me how there was more than one way to sell the same product and that I had it within me to manage this by myself. It really gave me the boost I needed.

Understanding the financial side of their business and being able to identify their break-even point was mentioned by four respondents.

The financial side was an eye-opener, it led me to ask to see the accounts.

Simply taking time out of the business and being with other business owner/managers were considered special moments by three respondents, respectively. One said rather imprecisely:

All of it [was a special moment]. I thoroughly enjoyed it and got a hell of a lot out of it. The strong thing is the diversity ... the networking opportunities were fantastic.

Table 5.3 'Special moments' in the Business Inspiration programme

Special moment	Number of occurrences
Knowing how to reach customers	8
Becoming more confident	6
Understanding finance and break-even points	4
Understanding search engine optimisation	4
Being with other interesting businesses	3
Taking time away from the business	3
The enthusiasm of the tutors/project team	3
Understanding different ways to grow the business	2
Refocusing the business	1
Developing a new area of business	1
Understanding the need to sell better	1
Total	36
Lots of special moments	6
No special moments	4

Source: From Rae et al. (2012)

Other moments that were mentioned included understanding different ways to grow, refocus and develop a new area of business. One commented:

> It gave me a total change of mindset, and made me realise that growth isn't just growth of turnover but also new products.

This reinforces the concept of moments of insight in entrepreneurial education. The respondents' recollection of these moments relates the value of the learning they gained in specific instances, interactions and content. Awareness of the significance of moments may well be helpful to learners in recalling and using learning within their business at the time and subsequently. It may also be helpful to educators in designing and evaluating programmes in which learners can derive knowledge and make a difference to running their businesses. Rae (2007) proposed five themes for owner/ manager engagement in learning, that to be accepted and effective it should be relational; relevant; authentic; useful and produce and share new learning. These themes represent practice-based criteria which are often interpreted in the moment and subsequently by learners as principles for evaluating and applying their learning.

Since such learning is as much relational as content orientated, tutor or peer interactions are significant contributors to 'special moments'. Educators may usefully intend a programme or session to include highlights or memorable instances, but there is no guarantee that these will actually be those which individual learners recall as the most valuable; as Giordano (2010) concludes, serendipity means that even casual asides may bring transformational meaning for learners. Recall is a selective process and respondents cited only one or two memorable moments which excluded other less memorable instances.

Conceptualising a momentary perspective in entrepreneurship

This section proposes a conceptual framework for a momentary perspective in entrepreneurial learning and creativity. This is based on synthesising aspects of the prior literature, combined with insights gained from the fieldwork, developed using observational thinking and inductive reasoning. These insights have also been developed and tested through interactive workshops with educators and entrepreneurs, through which a range of propositions, challenges, adaptations and re-conceptualisations occurred. Conceptualisations such as these can be no more than propositional, but are intended to assist educators and researchers to develop further the use of momentary perspectives in entrepreneurial and related learning.

A momentary perspective is a way of understanding the human experience of 'what is going on' in the moment. A single moment may be interpreted through multiple 'lenses' of knowing, such as those previously described as philosophical, narrative, educational and cognitive. This section develops a framework for a momentary perspective which may be applied in entrepreneurial creativity and learning, and possibly more generally. Figure 5.1 proposes a general framework which illustrates in a very simplified way the three essential and interdependent processes of the awareness of 'being in the moment'.

In each momentary experience, we are constantly perceiving, generating meaning, both consciously and unconsciously, and acting in response, through speech and behaviour, in interconnected ways. This occurs both consciously, with selective attention being paid to a small proportion of the sensory data being perceived in the mental 'foreground'; and unconsciously, with awareness of a much wider range of experiential data taking place as 'background'. The subconscious is 'in control' of human behaviours to a far greater extent than we may think; the subconscious governs most momentary behaviours, while the conscious mind selects 'special' moments from memory in retrospect. This conceptualises, in a simplistic way, the complex interactions which occur constantly in our experience of every moment.

The moment is an internal realisation which may be triggered by an external incident. In the moment, perceptual processes operate both consciously and unconsciously (otherwise described as 'subconsciously'), with unconscious processing being more rapid (Banks and Isham, 2009). The perceptions generate a response, which may be of verbal or physical action which is elicited at the time, and hence likely to be recalled by the person as their response 'in the moment'. An intuitive response arises from tacit knowledge not requiring conscious thought, or conditioned by experience or training, while an instinctive response results from core animal behaviour or personality. A response often expresses emotion. A conscious response, the result of 'thinking about' how to respond, will be slower, occurring subsequent to the moment. At any time following the moment there may be a conscious reflection on the meaning (new knowledge) produced from the moment.

In a creative moment, an idea, inspiration or insight occurs in conscious thought; in terms of Wallas (1926) moving from unconscious preparation

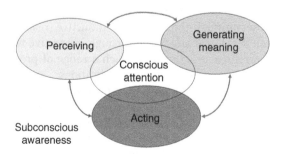

Figure 5.1 Momentary perspective of 'being' in the moment.

and incubation to illumination (the 'light bulb moment'). This may be followed by a reaction of emotion (such as joy or elation), action (moving to immediately write, draw or record the idea) and by conscious thinking about its implications: practicality (will it work? What are its applications?, etc.) or, as Wallas described, verification. The moment of revelation may be remembered by the person in its spatial or social context or location; just as Archimedes' mythical 'Eureka' moment is commonly remembered by its location in the bath. Again, conscious reflections may continue to flow long after the creative moment itself.

Awareness of time is an important aspect in the lived experience in the moment, as it connects with experiences of past recollections and anticipation of future possibilities. On a construct of narrative (also known as Kairotic) time, we subjectively and selectively perceive what is significant, rather than on an objective construct of chronological time, of which we may also be aware. Figure 5.2 suggests how meaning is generated in the moment within a perspective of narrative time.

Additional factors may be added to this diagram, but result in overcomplexity. Sensory perceiving is experienced in the physical and social context of the environment, and interactions are experienced through interpersonal dynamics of talk and non-verbal behaviour. These stimulate conscious and unconscious perceptions, and produce responses which may anticipate events, in which instinctive and intuitive perceiving is more rapid than conscious thought. Emotional states arise, with the production of 'feelings' such as happiness, sadness, companionship or alienation, joyful or fearful anticipation. Meanings of creative ideas, new learning, insights and intentions are generated as neural connections are made between experiential memory, unconscious and prospective imagination. Intentions may be decided consciously or emerge from unconscious into conscious awareness. These are all influenced and mediated by factors such as emotions,

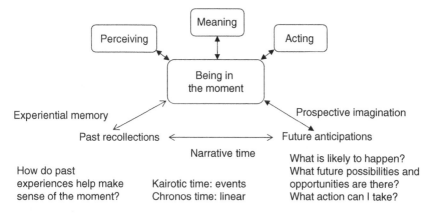

Figure 5.2 Time and the moment.

social interactions and awareness of situatedness. Behaviours result from these responses: verbally as conversation, and physical actions as both purposive acts and 'body language'.

An outcome of the moment is the decision of whether, and if so how, to act on it. The term 'decision' does not necessarily imply considered, logical or rational judgement; however, 'spur of the moment', impulsive, intuitive and conditioned responses may well precede judgement: the intention may be unconsciously rather than consciously chosen, and the moment of decision subsequently inferred from it. Such a decision may arise from a complex set of underlying factors and cognitive structures, such as personality, sense of identity, emotion, beliefs and moral sense of 'what is right', as much as rational judgement. Some responses will be conditioned by experience and learned behaviour, sometimes crudely termed the 'no-brainer'.

Implications and applications for entrepreneurial learning and creativity

It is clear that many types of moments occur in the entrepreneurial experience, although this chapter has concentrated on moments of learning and creativity. A quality of the moment is that human responses are often 'authentic', intuitive and characteristic of how people deal with moments in life more generally, rather than deliberate and planned, because there is limited control over the instantaneous response; however, learning and adaptation can quickly take place. Listed below are common types of entrepreneurial moments, drawn from the fieldwork as well as from more general experiences. This is illustrative rather than comprehensive, but provides examples of commonly experienced moments in entrepreneurial life, resulting from both externally experienced events and internal realisations.

- Innovation: recognition of how an idea may be applied to a practical situation.
- Problem: a disadvantage or setback which can or must be addressed.
- Opportunity: recognition of a potential or actual position of advantage.
- Encounter: social interaction, meeting or social connection.
- Insight: gaining a realisation of new knowledge.
- Intuition: 'knowing' at a subconscious or 'gut' level.
- Judgement: making a decision or choice.
- Resolution: intention to act.

This chapter proposes that 'momentary perspectives' can help in making sense and enhancing awareness of entrepreneurial behaviours, especially creativity and learning. This is not being advanced as a unifying and general theory of entrepreneurship in the manner that effectuation theory, for example, has been (Sarasvathy, 2001). Rather, it is positioned within the existing fields of entrepreneurial learning and creativity, where it is evident that such terms as moments, incidents, events and inspirations are used within everyday discourse, but that ways of conceptualising and using them need to be developed, both in education and in practice.

It is less important that the framework proposed, of 'being in the moment', perceiving, generating meaning and acting, is necessarily 'correct' or scientifically provable. It draws on logic offered by insights from pragmatic philosophy and recent cognitive studies, combined with limited empirical research and experience in working with entrepreneurs and learners. This is an emerging area in which propositional frameworks, which suggest how experience may be interpreted and used by educators and practitioners to heighten their awareness and understanding of momentary perspectives can play a useful role alongside more definitive frameworks being developed through in-depth research. This is a pragmatic stance, in which the value of a concept is in the practical use which can be made of it, with an implicit acceptance that it may be superseded by later work. This approach is similar to that taken in the early days of work on entrepreneurial learning in which the notions of narratives (Pitt, 1998), learning episodes (Rae and Carswell, 2000) and critical incidents (Cope and Watts, 2000) were first connected, and to which this chapter has returned.

In relation to education and learning, it is helpful for educators to be aware of the significance of moments in the learning process. As Giordano demonstrated and this study reinforces, we cannot know what other people's critical moments have been unless they tell us; they are rare and personal. But as educators we may be able to create more of them. Opening a workshop for enterprise educators I posed the unscripted question, 'Do we take risks as educators, or do we play it safe?' I had not planned to do this; it was intentionally slightly risky. Yet asking the question felt intuitively right in enabling me to engage with the participants in that moment, and whose immediate responses and interactions demonstrated the learning value through the conversation which then took place exploring the tensions they had encountered between risk taking, creativity and control in education.

In such ways, educators can be confident and creative in using their momentary insights, ideas and contextual experiences in their teaching. It may seem superfluous to propose this when excellent teachers have always done so, yet a generation of an ethos of managerial control, quality assurance and proceduralisation of education has done much to suppress educational creativity (Draycott and Rae, 2011). 'Seizing the moment' is a legitimate tactic in opportunistic education which enlivens and engages, rather than an educational strategy. However, the educator can focus on and use seminal 'teaching moments' from those which arise in the wider environment and use these as 'instant cases'; recent history provides many of these cases. Such events can provide fertile scenarios for problems, innovations and opportunities to be addressed in the educational process and to demonstrate the relevance of entrepreneurial thinking.

It has also proved useful on many occasions to share the ideas on entrepreneurial moments with learners, and to prompt them to elicit significant moments from their experiences, as described in Questions 2 to 5 of the online survey. This can be a powerful way of recalling and sharing experiences to form extemporised learning narratives. Learners can also recall and reflect on significant moments in producing learning narratives and career plans in more formal, assessable ways; this is the subject of ongoing research.

It is hoped that the momentary perspective framework may be of value in contributing to the development of entrepreneurship by educators, learners and practitioners. The idea of a momentary perspective is not new, but rather underdeveloped, and offers a way of thinking and understanding which people can understand, adapt and use intuitively for themselves. For example, recognising the interconnections between perceiving, meaning and acting can be helpful in encouraging reflection and self-awareness of how people respond momentarily. If their instinctive response to opportunities is to 'pass' and defer engagement, in the way that a reluctant football team member avoids the ball as always being associated with trouble, they need to be aware of their instincts and able to reflect on why they respond as such, and the alternative, counter-intuitive options they may develop. The powerful roles of unconscious perception and meaning, through instinct, emotion and intuition, should be appreciated and not discounted in a rationally centred educational system, so that individuals can usefully become more aware of both the value and limitations of knowing which is produced in these ways. Intuitive judgements are often the products of extensive unconscious thought and experience through the phronetic knowledge of practical and social wisdom (Baumard, 1999). Emotional engagement is critical, but may be undervalued in effective learning, momentary response, decision making and recollection. Entrepreneurship has an emotional dimension and the use of a momentary perspective can contribute to understanding, working with and applying emotional energy, intelligence and creativity as part of the learning process.

As suggested, the acceleration of digital technologies and associated business innovation is making momentary perception and judgement increasingly important in entrepreneurship. Emerging technologies rapidly become normal tools for business and learning. Through using proprietary online tools, teams of entrepreneurship students can develop new business models and trial these through both virtual simulation and real applications, gaining swift feedback on what does or does not work and either refining or scrapping their iterative models. In such ways, momentary skills in entrepreneurial innovation, decision making and trading can be practised and confidence developed. But as the modes and media of entrepreneurial commerce continue to evolve rapidly, it may be anticipated that the 'micro-skills' of momentary entrepreneurship will both become more important and intensively studied to understand them. The progress which is outlined in neural, cognitive and psychological research has significant promise in contributing to their understanding.

The insights offered in this chapter are both propositional and imperfect; they aim to draw together reflections, teaching, conversations and educational research which have occurred in a live exploration over several years to offer a momentary perspective for entrepreneurial learning. Such learning may be viewed as being formed from a stream of momentary experiences, of perceiving, meaning creation and action, occurring in a time dimension between past recollection and future anticipation. But as Polkinghorne (1988) wisely advised, we should recognise the development of such learning as a narrative over time and as the product of innumerable moments, rather than over-emphasising the significance of any single 'instantaneous now'.

> I've learned to see opportunities in the moment, and evaluate them. I just know instinctively which ones are worth exploring and which are not.
>
> (Paul, online entrepreneur)

References

Baker, A. (2004) Seizing the Moment: Talking about the 'Undiscussables'. *Journal of Management Education*, 28: 693–706.

Banks, W. and Isham, E. (2009) We Infer Rather Than Perceive the Moment We Decided to Act. *Psychological Science*, 20(1): 17–21.

Bartlett, F. (1932/1967) *Remembering*. Cambridge: Cambridge University Press.

Baumard, P. (1999) *Tacit Knowledge in Organizations*. London: Sage.

Bedeian, A. (2007) Critical Moments in Learning: A Teacher's Ultimate Reward and Glory. *Journal of Management Inquiry*, 16: 408–411.

Beeman, M. and Kounios, J. (2009) The *Aha!* Moment, The Cognitive Neuroscience of Insight. *Current Directions in Psychological Science*, 18(4): 210–216.

Bergson, H. (1911) *Creative Evolution*, trans. Arthur Mitchell. New York: Henry Holt, www.archive.org/stream/creativeevolu1st00berguoft#page/n7/mode/2up.

Cable, V. (2010) *The Storm: The World Economic Crisis and What it Means*. London: Atlantic Books.

Carlstedt, R. (2004) The Theory of Critical Moments: A Mind-Body Model of Sport Performance and Mastery of Pressure Situations. American Board of Sport Psychology, Capella University: Harold Abel School of Psychology, Integrative Psychological Services of New York City.

Cope, J. (2005) Toward a Dynamic Learning Perspective of Entrepreneurship. *Entrepreneurship: Theory and Practice*, 29(4): 373.

Cope, J. and Watts, G. (2000) Learning by Doing. An Exploration of Experience, Critical Incidents and Reflection in Entrepreneurial Learning. *International Journal of Entrepreneurial Behaviour and Research*, 6(3): 104–124.

Csíkszentmihályi, M. (1996) *Creativity: Flow and the Psychology of Discovery and Invention*. New York: Harper Perennial.

D'Argembeau, A., Comblain, C. and Van der Linden, M. (2003) Phenomenal Characteristics of Autobiographical Memories for Positive, Negative, and Neutral Events. *Applied Cognitive Psychology*, 17: 281–294.

Damasio, A. (2000) *The Feeling of What Happens: Body, Emotion and the Making of Consciousness*. London: Heinemann.

—— (2012) *Self Comes to Mind: Constructing the Conscious Brain*. London: Vintage.

de Haan, E. (2007) *I Doubt Therefore I Coach: Critical Moments in Coaching Practice*. APA Journal and Ashridge Business School.

Dew, N. (2009) Serendipity in Entrepreneurship. *Organization Studies*, 30: 735–753.

Draycott, M. and Rae, D. (2011) 'Enterprise Education in Schools and the Role of Competency Frameworks. *International Journal of Entrepreneurial Behaviour and Research*, 17(2): 127–145.

Frick, W. (1990) The Symbolic Growth Experience: A Chronicle of Heuristic Inquiry and a Quest for Synthesis. *Journal of Humanistic Psychology*, 30(1): 64–80.

Giordano, P.J. (2004) Teaching and Learning When We Least Expect It: The Role of Critical Moments in Student Development. In B.K. Saville, T.E. Zinn and V.W. Hevern (eds), *Essays from E-xcellence in Teaching*. The Society for the Teaching of Psychology website: http://teachpsych.org/resources/e-books/eit2004/index.html.

—— (2010) Serendipity in Teaching and Learning: The Importance of Critical Moments. *Journal on Excellence in College Teaching*, 21(3): 5–27.

Gladwell, M. (2005). *Blink: The Power of Thinking Without Thinking*. London: Penguin.

Gleick, J. (1987) *Chaos: Making a New Science*. New York: Penguin.

Grégoire, D., Barr, P. and Shepherd, D. (2010) Cognitive Processes of Opportunity Recognition: The Role of Structural Alignment. *Organization Science*, 21(2): 413–431.

Izard, C. (2009) Emotion Theory and Research: Highlights, Unanswered Questions, and Emerging Issues. *Annual Review of Psychology*, 60(January): 1–25.

James, W. (1884), 'What Is An Emotion? *Mind*, 9: 188–205.

Kaletsky, A. (2010). *The Birth of a New Economy*. London: Bloomsbury.

Kneller, G. (1965), *The Art and Science of Creativity*. New York: Holt Rinehart & Winston.

Knudsen, B.T., Christensen, D.R. and Blenker, P. (eds) (forthcoming) *Enterprising Initiatives in the Experience Economy Transforming Social Worlds*. Abingdon, Oxon: Routledge.

Kollmann, T. and Kuckertz, A. (2006) Venture Archetypes and the Entrepreneurial Event: Cross-cultural Empirical Evidence. *Journal of Enterprising Culture*, 4(1): 27–48.

Krueger, N. (2007), What Lies Beneath? The Experiential Essence of Entrepreneurial Thinking. *Entrepreneurship: Theory and Practice*, 31(1): 123–138.

Krueger, N. and Brazeal, D. (1994) Entrepreneurial Potential and Potential Entrepreneurs. *Entrepreneurship: Theory and Practice*, 18(3): 91–104.

Lehrer, J. (2009) *The Decisive Moment: How the Brain Makes Up Its Mind*. Edinburgh: Canongate.

Lewis, M. (2004) The Emergence of Mind in the Emotional Brain. Cambridge Studies in Cognitive and Perceptual Development. In A. Demetriou and A. Raftopoulos (eds), *Cognitive Developmental Change: Theories, Models and Measurement*. New York: Cambridge University Press.

Lodge, D. (2001) *Thinks*. London: Penguin.

Lumpkin, G.T., Hills, G.E. and Shrader, R.C. (2004) Opportunity Recognition. In H.P. Welsch (ed.), *Entrepreneurship: The Way Ahead*. London: Routledge.

Maslow, A. (1969) *Religions, Values, and Peak Experiences*, www.druglibrary.org/schaffer/lsd/maslow.htm.

Mitchell, R., Busenitz, L., Bird, B., Marie Gaglio, C., McMullen, J., Morse, E. and Smith, J. (2007) The Central Question in Entrepreneurial Cognition Research 2007. *Entrepreneurship: Theory and Practice*, 31(1): 1–27.

Penaluna, A., Coates, J. and Penaluna, K. (2009) 'Seeing Outside the Box: Creativity Based Assessment and Neural Understandings. Article presented at ISBE Conference, October, Liverpool.

Pillemer, D. (1998) *Momentous Events, Vivid Memories*. Cambridge, MA: Harvard University Press.

Pitt, M. (1998) A Tale of Two Gladiators: 'Reading' Entrepreneurs as Texts. *Organization Studies*, 19(3): 387–414.

Polkinghorne, D. (1988) *Narrative Knowing and the Human Sciences*. New York: State University Press.

Rae, D. (2005) Entrepreneurial Learning: A Narrative-based Conceptual Model. *Journal of Small Business and Enterprise Development*, 12(3): 323–335.

—— (2007) Achieving Business Focus: Promoting the Entrepreneurial Management Capabilities of Owner-managers. *Industry and Higher Education*, 21(6): 415–426.

—— (2010), Universities and Enterprise Education: Responding to the Challenges of the New Era. *Journal of Small Business and Enterprise Development*, 17(4): 591–560.

—— (2015) Towards a Momentary Perspective in Entrepreneurial Learning and creativity. In *Enterprising Initiatives. Approaches to Transformations of Social Worlds*. In press.

Rae, D. and Carswell, M. (2000) Using a Life Story Approach in Researching Entrepreneurial Learning: The Development of a Conceptual Model and its Implications in the Design of Learning Experiences. *Education and Training*, 42(4/5): 220–227.

Rae, D., Price, L., Bosworth, G. and Parkinson, P. (2012) Business Inspiration: Small Business Leadership in Recovery? *Industry and Higher Education*, 26(6): 1–17.

Sanitioso, R. and Conway, M. (2006) Autobiographical Memory, the Self, and Comparison Processes. In S. Guimond (ed.), *Social Comparison and Social Psychology: Understanding Cognition, Intergroup Relations, and Culture*. New York: Cambridge University Press.

Sarasvathy, S. (2001) Causation and Effectuation: Toward a Theoretical Shift from Economic Inevitability to Entrepreneurial Contingency. Academy of Management. *The Academy of Management Review*, 26(2): 243–264.

Shapero, A. and Sokol, I. (1982) Social Dimensions of Entrepreneurship. In C. Kent, D. Sexton and K. Vesper (eds), *The Encyclopedia of Entrepreneurship*. Englewood Cliffs, NY: Prentice Hall.

Shaw, P. (2010) *Defining Moments, Navigating Through Business and Organizational Life*. London: Palgrave Macmillan.

Terzis, G. (2001) How Crosstalk Creates Vision-related Eureka Moments. *Philosophical Psychology*, 14(4): 393–421.

Wallas, G. (1926) *The Art of Thought*. New York: Harcourt Brace.

Weick, K. (1995) *Sensemaking in Organizations*. Thousand Oaks, CA: Sage.

6 The structure and scope of entrepreneurship programs in higher education around the world

Jeff Vanevenhoven and William A. Drago

Introduction

Research and practice at the interface of education and entrepreneurship has made significant progress, fueled in large part by the dissatisfaction of students and accrediting agencies with traditional approaches to business education (Solomon and Fernald, 1991). The challenge for universities and individuals tasked with developing and delivering entrepreneurship education is to build sustainable communities of learning that balance the requirements of academic rigor with the realities of entrepreneurship. This challenge was recently considered in discussions of university-based entrepreneurship ecosystems (UBEEs), wherein analysis and conclusions were based on case studies from six universities (Fetters *et al.*, 2010). This research paper, however, reports on the entrepreneurial communities of more than 300 universities around the world, highlighting trends of where and how resources are obtained and distributed in an effort to build these sustainable communities.

Many scholars have noted the important contributions of entrepreneurs, new businesses and small businesses to the economic and social sectors of the environment through their impact on job creation, innovation and economic renewal (Chrisman *et al.*, 2003). Kuratko (2005) reported that in the USA from 1995 to 2005 approximately 600,000 new businesses were developed each year, and that firms with fewer than 500 employees employ 53 percent of the private workforce and make up 51 percent of gross domestic product. Reynolds and colleagues (1999) reported that 67 percent of all new inventions in the USA were developed by smaller firms.

There has been increasing demand to produce and deliver high-quality entrepreneurship education because entrepreneurship and innovation have been recognized as critical drivers of sustainable economic development and competitive advantage (e.g., Katz, 2003; Matlay, 2008; Solomon *et al.*, 2002). Further, it has been argued that all individuals should be exposed to entrepreneurship training and development (Gibb, 2002) because entrepreneurship graduates are three times more likely to start their own business, three times more likely to be self-employed, have annual incomes 27 percent higher, own 62 percent more assets, and be more satisfied with their jobs (Charney and Libecap, 2000). Universities have increasingly recognized the importance of these societal trends, and have instituted and expanded entrepreneurship and small business programs (Bechard and Gregoire, 2005; Katz, 2003; Solomon *et al.*, 2002).

While a few programs existed earlier, significant growth in entrepreneurship programs began in the early 1970s when the University of Southern California offered a concentration in their MBA program in entrepreneurship and then a year later offered a concentration in entrepreneurship at undergraduate level as well. In 1991, Robinson and Hayes stated that entrepreneurship programs had come a long way but several weaknesses remained. A major concern was the lack of depth in many of the programs then in existence. According to Kuratko (2005), by 2005 there were 2,200 courses being offered in some aspect of entrepreneurship at over 1,600 universities. While this explosive growth was taking place in the USA, it was also being mirrored in countries around the world (McDougall and Oviatt, 2003; Zahra *et al.*, 2001). Critical to these universities seeking to develop and implement a program of entrepreneurship education is obtaining and distributing resources in the form of human (for instance, students and faculty) and financial capital. This chapter highlights these capital trends across over 300 universities around the world.

Review

Where are entrepreneurship programs housed?

According to Vesper (1999), entrepreneurship programs have generally been developed as an add-on to business education and, as a result, tend to be housed in business schools at many universities. This is not necessarily a good fit, as business schools are often structured around increasingly specialized functional areas (i.e., marketing, finance, human resources, operations) while entrepreneurship programs more often cross functional boundaries. Zeithaml and Rice (1987) believe that education in entrepreneurship covers the entire scope of business, and because of this it is similar to the original concept and design of management education in universities. While many entrepreneurship programs remain small, some programs have developed sufficiently to be housed in their own department. This independent department may reside in the business school or elsewhere, or may be in centers of entrepreneurship or small business development. A trend toward distinct entrepreneurship program identity seems to be emerging, which may indicate an increase in the perception of importance and the sustainability of entrepreneurship in higher education (Zahra *et al.*, 2011). Entrepreneurship and small business centers are often developed to offer education and support to local entrepreneurs and small business owners, as well as to house educational programs aimed at undergraduate and graduate students.

What facilities and positions are available to entrepreneurship programs?

One important dimension to consider in determining the developing maturity of entrepreneurship programs are the types of facilities and positions provided to these programs. As noted by Zeithaml and Rice (1987), education and assistance programs for practicing small business managers and entrepreneurs are often handled by universities through entrepreneurship or small business centers established specifically for this purpose. Most centers target the local geographic region. According to Zeithaml and Rice (1987), these centers are often divorced from the university's teaching and research programs. This is perhaps unfortunate because they can provide faculty and students access to important knowledge and skill development opportunities. Research comparing US and international academically based entrepreneurship centers shows that while the USA has led in their development, there is evidence of increasing growth elsewhere (Bowers and Alon, 2010; Bowers *et al.*, 2006; Zahra *et al.*, 2011).

Positions allocated to entrepreneurship programs are also seen as an important indicator of the development of these programs. Katz (2003) found that there are 406 endowed positions in entrepreneurship at universities across the USA, reflecting a steady increase from the early 1990s. Rice and colleagues (2010) identify strong programmatic and faculty leadership as one of seven key success factors and state that it takes a team of people with skills in the full range of program development and management to create an environment that sustains successful entrepreneurship programs.

What courses are taught in these programs?

As previously noted, entrepreneurship education covers the entire range of business disciplines (Zeithaml and Rice, 1987). It is likely that highly developed programs may have entrepreneurship courses in such areas as management, marketing, finance, law and technology, and innovation. In addition, Vesper and Gartner (1997) and Solomon *et al.* (2002) found that the growth of university-level entrepreneurship programs has tended to broaden the view of entrepreneurship from one of new business entry to include other topics such as family business, managing smaller enterprises, and managing high growth businesses. The process of starting a business also introduces the possibility of starting a non-profit business or that of starting a new business within an existing business (corporate entrepreneurship). Tied closely to the process of start-up is small business management and growth management. According to the Zeithaml and Rice (1987) study, thirty-one schools (out of seventy-two) offered a single course and ten schools offered more than two courses. In their study of 240 two- and four-year colleges and universities, Solomon *et al.* (2002) found that the most predominant course offerings were small business management and entrepreneurship, but they also found consistent mention of courses focused on family business, franchising, venture capital, and technology and innovation.

What types of concentrations are offered?

It is important to explore how common entrepreneurship concentrations have become since their introduction at the MBA and undergraduate levels at the University of Southern California in the early 1970s. Equally important is how Ph.D. programs have been developed in this discipline, and whether programs are being built for students outside the business school. According to Solomon *et al.*, in 2002 among four-year colleges and universities, individual courses were the primary mechanism for delivering entrepreneurship education, with concentrations being a distant second, and minors and majors an even more distant third. Among the common elements of university-based entrepreneurship ecosystems identified by Rice *et al.* in 2010 were concentrations, minors and majors, as well as courses for non-business majors. This reflects a trend toward increased development and growth from previous studies (Gartner and Vesper, 1994; Zeithaml and Rice, 1987) that showed few universities offering entrepreneurship concentrations or degrees.

What types of collaboration and funding exist for these programs?

Collaboration and funding from outside parties are also considered to be important elements in the development and support of entrepreneurship programs. Collaboration with local business groups like Chambers of Commerce or municipal innovation centers can offer important resource funding and development opportunities. State, regional and federal agencies, like the Small Business Administration in the USA, can offer services and funding for these programs. In addition, private institutions like the Coleman Foundation and the Kauffman Foundation may provide resources for program development and growth. In the Rice *et al.* (2010) discussion of effective university-based entrepreneurship ecosystems, strong relationships at the local, national and global levels with the business community, investment community, other universities, non-governmental organizations and government agencies are considered requirements for success.

What opportunities exist for students in these programs?

Many universities offer students of entrepreneurship opportunities to learn and network outside of the classroom (Solomon *et al.*, 2002). Examples of some of these opportunities include guest speakers, onsite visits to entrepreneurial companies, business plan competitions, elevator pitch competitions, internships, small business consulting opportunities, case studies, and student organizations devoted to entrepreneurship, to name a few. The extent to which a program offers these additional experiential opportunities may be seen as a further measure of program development and potential for growth. Networking events, student clubs and business plan competitions were commonly found among the six case study institutions in the work of Rice *et al.* (2010). In their analysis of the entrepreneurial ecosystem at USC, it was noted by Allen and Lieberman (2010) that for the new generation of students who grew up with access to the internet, unstructured learning (rather than more traditional structured academic programs) and an understanding of the power of collaboration and social networking are central to the way students engage with the world. These opportunities are part of the basic lexicon of many entrepreneurship programs.

Does the university have entrepreneurship programs outside the college of business?

While most entrepreneurship programs have been add-ons to the curricula of the business school it is essential that entrepreneurship be infused in other non-business programs as well (Laukkanen, 2000; Streeter and Jaquette, 2004). There is increasing demand and interest in entrepreneurship education from beyond the business school in areas such as engineering, science, technology and the arts (Streeter and Jaquette, 2004). This may be seen in programs such as those at Millikin University and Case Western Reserve, where entrepreneurship is an integral part of students' learning process in various arts programs, and at Massachusetts Institute of Technology, where entrepreneurship is an integral part of the engineering program.

Because entrepreneurship may be thought of as a process of discovering, evaluating, and developing opportunities, students in any discipline, with any career path, could benefit from being exposed to and learning an entrepreneurial mindset and skill set (Shane and Venkataraman, 2000; Greene *et al.*, 2010). For instance, Block and Stumpf (1992) found that interdisciplinary programs are using faculty teams to develop programs for the non-business students and there is a growing trend in courses specifically designed for art, engineering and science students in entrepreneurship education in order to expose these students to the concepts, thought processes and skills related to entrepreneurship.

Methodology

As part of a larger research effort to understand the effectiveness of entrepreneurship education (The Entrepreneurship Education Project, www. entrepeduc.org), representatives from universities were solicited to complete a web-based survey examining the present state of entrepreneurship education at their universities. Representatives were identified and contacted through listservs (i.e., Academy of Management Entrepreneurship Division, United States Association for Small Business and Entrepreneurship), journal article authorship and internet searches of universities around the world offering entrepreneurship education. In total, representatives from 321 universities in over sixty countries completed the English-language survey.

Data were collected in the following general categories or dimensions relating to the scope and content of entrepreneurship programs:

- Where the program was housed in the university.
- The types of courses taught.
- Facilities and faculty positions directed at entrepreneurship or small business.
- Programs offered to students (undergraduate, graduate, Ph.D., certificate).
- Outside collaboration and funding.
- Experiential opportunities for students.
- Entrepreneurship programs outside the business college.

These variables were generally treated as dummy variables with 'yes, the university has it' equal to one and 'no, the university does not have it' equal to zero. Summary variables were also created for each major category. As an example, all variables listed under types of courses were added together to form a variable indicating the total courses offered by the program. Finally, the six summary variables were added together to provide an overall measure of program development. All analyses were conducted using SPSS 18, and descriptive statistics were used to assess the data.

Results

Entrepreneurship programs are found in various parts of the university, although the most common location is in business schools. As Table 6.1 shows, 57 percent of the entrepreneurship programs are located in a college or school of business. Based on written comments from respondents, it

Table 6.1 Where are the entrepreneurship programmes housed?

	?	Freq (%)
Entrepreneurial center	32	9.9
Department of entrepreneurship or small business	34	10.6
College or school of business	184	57.3
Other	16	5.0

appears that the most common location is in management departments. About 10 percent of the programs were found in entrepreneurial centers and another 10.6 percent had their own department of entrepreneurship or small business. Only 5 percent of the programs were housed in other colleges with no one college standing out as a clear second choice.

Table 6.2 shows the distribution of facilities and faculty positions in participating entrepreneurship programs. Entrepreneurship centers are often located outside any particular academic college and are focused exclusively on entrepreneurship courses and services. Faculty teaching courses in the entrepreneurship program may have offices there, and the center may also provide services for community members interested in entrepreneurship. Nearly 58 percent of participating universities had entrepreneurship centers or endowed entrepreneurship centers. In addition, nearly 28 percent of participating universities had centers for small business or endowed centers for small business. Chair positions at a university are given to faculty who have shown expertise in a particular academic area. Almost 26 percent of entrepreneurship programs had entrepreneurship chair positions, and an additional 16 percent had endowed entrepreneurship chair positions. The Coleman Chair is a prestigious chair directed at entrepreneurship; 3 percent of the respondents had Coleman Chair positions, and an additional 9 percent had endowed Coleman Chair positions. Approximately 14 percent of the universities had a small business chair or an endowed small business chair, 48 percent of the programs had either entrepreneurship professors or endowed entrepreneurship professors, and 24 percent of the universities had professors of small business or endowed professors of small business.

Table 6.3 shows the distribution of courses taught in participating entrepreneurship programs. The two most popular courses taught in the

Table 6.2 Entrepreneurship facilities and positions

	Yes	%
Entrepreneurship center	149	46.3
Endowed entrepreneurship center	37	11.5
Entrepreneurship Chair	85	26.4
Endowed entrepreneurship Chair	51	15.8
Coleman Chair	9	2.8
Endowed Coleman Chair	28	8.7
Entrepreneurship professor	110	34.2
Endowed entrepreneurship professor	44	13.7
Center for small business	59	18.3
Endowed center for small business	31	9.6
Small business Chair	18	5.6
Endowed small business Chair	28	8.7
Small business professor	46	14.3
Endowed small business professor	31	9.6
External grants	229	71.1

Table 6.3 Courses taught in entrepreneurship programmes

	Yes	%
Introduction to Entrepreneurship	217	67.4
New Venture Creation	132	41.0
Small Business Management	99	30.7
Practicum/Consulting/Experiential	96	29.8
Creativity and Innovation	99	30.7
Technology and Entrepreneurship	86	26.7
Strategic and Entrepreneurial Management	86	26.7
Special Topics on Entrepreneurship	85	26.4
Social Responsibility and Entrepreneurship	77	23.9
Entrepreneurial Marketing	73	22.7
Small Business Finance	58	18.0
Family Business	53	16.5
Corporate Entrepreneurship	50	15.5
Small Business Marketing	42	13.0
Law and Entrepreneurship	38	11.8
Non-profit Entrepreneurship	36	11.2
Economics of Entrepreneurs	34	10.6
Growth Management	33	10.2
Franchising	25	7.8
Sustainable Venturing	25	7.8
Minority Entrepreneurship	7	2.2

programs were Introduction to Entrepreneurship (67.4%) and New Venture Creation (41%). Also popular was Small Business Management (30.7%), practicum or consulting courses directed at entrepreneurship (30.7%), and Creativity and Innovation (39.8%). As may be seen from the list of courses, entrepreneurship spans many functional areas of a normal business school, including marketing, finance, economics and law. The average number of courses taught across all programs was between four and five, with one program indicating up to twenty-one different courses. In addition, sixty-one universities indicated that they offered no courses related to entrepreneurship, suggesting a wide variety of number of courses taught overall.

Table 6.4 identifies degree programs and other opportunities offered through the entrepreneurship program. Undergraduate degrees are fairly popular in these programs, with 25 percent indicating that they offered an undergraduate entrepreneurship major while 48 percent indicated that they either offered an undergraduate minor for business or non-business students. Graduate degrees were not uncommon but a little less popular, with 41 percent of the programs offering graduate major degrees to business or non-business students. In addition, 25 percent of the programs offered graduate minors to business or non-business students. Surprisingly, approximately 19 percent of the programs offered entrepreneurship Ph.D. programs.

Table 6.4 Degree programmes and other opportunities offered

	Yes	%
Entrepreneurship/Small Business Management Ph.D.	61	18.9
Executive Development in Courses in Entrepreneurship	73	22.7
Entrepreneurship Graduate Minor for Non-business	31	9.6
Entrepreneurship Graduate Minor for Business	51	15.8
Entrepreneurship Graduate Major	59	18.3
Entrepreneurship Undergraduate Minor for Non-business	73	22.7
Entrepreneurship Undergraduate Minor for Business	82	25.5
Entrepreneurship Undergraduate Major	80	24.8
Entrepreneurship Undergraduate Certificate	45	14.0
Continuing Education Program in Entrepreneurship	78	24.2
Distance Learning in Entrepreneurship (via the internet)	49	15.2
Internship opportunities at local companies	117	36.3
Collaboration opportunities in other countries focused on entrepreneurship	49	15.2
Entrepreneurship/creativity laboratory	62	19.3
Small business incubator	102	31.7

In terms of experiences offered to students, internship opportunities at local companies were fairly popular at 36 percent, and collaboration opportunities in other countries were somewhat less popular, with 15 percent of participants indicating availability. Small business incubators were also popular, with 32 percent indicating that this was available. The average number of offerings across all universities participating was approximately three, with the highest number of programs at fifteen. Seventy-five universities offered no programs or opportunities for students.

Table 6.5 provides participants' responses to the types of outside support opportunities available through entrepreneurship programs. Responses can be divided into two types of support, namely collaboration with outside agencies and funding from outside agencies, both at three different levels: local, state or regional, and the federal level. Most collaboration with programs came from the local (56.5 percent) or state/regional level (45 percent). Some support came from the federal level, with 28

Table 6.5 Outside support opportunities

	Yes	%
Collaboration with local agencies	182	56.5
Collaboration with state or regional agencies	145	45.0
Collaboration with Federal agencies	90	28.0
Receive support for entrepreneurship from local agencies	70	21.7
Receive support for entrepreneurship from state or regional agencies	86	26.7
Receive support for entrepreneurship from Federal agencies	77	23.9

percent of the programs indicating collaboration with federal agencies. In terms of funding, the distribution was fairly equal across all three levels, with the greatest at 27 percent directed from state/regional agencies. The average number of support opportunities for all programs was two, with a maximum of all six categories. Nearly one-third of the universities (ninety-nine) indicated no support from any of these six outside sources.

Table 6.6 identifies opportunities in addition to academic course work available for entrepreneurship students through their programs. The most popular opportunity provided is guest speakers focused on entrepreneurship or small business; 71 percent of programs offered this opportunity. The next most popular was providing a business plan competition. Student clubs or organizations focused on entrepreneurship or small business were fairly common at nearly 47 percent of the programs. Internships focused on entrepreneurship or small businesses were also popular at 40 percent. The average number of opportunities for students across programs was 3.7, with a maximum of ten. Sixty-three universities indicated that they did not make available any of the opportunities listed in Table 6.6.

While most entrepreneurship programs seem to be housed within business schools or within an entrepreneurship or small business center, they can also be found in other areas of the university. Table 6.7 provides locations of entrepreneurship programs found outside business schools. Twenty-two percent of the universities participating in this survey indicated that they had entrepreneurship programs housed in their college of engineering. Also popular were health sciences (11.5 percent), environmental sciences (10.2 percent), art/fine art (10.6 percent) and biological sciences (9.3 percent). These responses demonstrate that entrepreneurship activity extends beyond business to the sciences, engineering and other disciplines at universities as well. The mean occurrence for entrepreneurship programs outside business schools is 0.90. Two hundred and seventeen

Table 6.6 Opportunities for entrepreneurship students

	Yes	%
Guest speakers focused on entrepreneurship/small businesses	230	71.4
On-site visits focused on entrepreneurship/small businesses	120	37.3
Business plan competition	186	57.8
Elevator pitch competition	77	23.9
Internships focused on entrepreneurship/small businesses	129	40.1
Feasibility studies	110	34.2
Community development focused on entrepreneurship/small businesses	88	27.3
Student club/organization focused on entrepreneurship/small businesses	150	46.6
Kauffman Foundation FastTrac program	11	3.4
Global entrepreneurship week events	78	24.2

Table 6.7 Entrepreneurship programmes housed outside the college of business

	Yes	%
Music	18	5.6
Art/Fine Art	34	10.6
Environmental Sciences	33	10.2
Engineering	72	22.4
Health Sciences	37	11.5
Architectural/Urban Planning	16	5.0
Biological Sciences	30	9.3
Law	29	9.0
Veterinary Medicine	9	2.8
Clinical Medicine	11	3.4

(67 percent) universities had no entrepreneurship programs outside the college of business.

Table 6.8 provides descriptive statistics on summary variables created for all items in each of Tables 6.2 through 6.7. The average number of courses offered was 4.5 with a high of twenty-one. At the same time sixty-one universities had no courses and eighty-seven (27.1 percent) had one course. The average number of facilities was less than one (0.86 percent) and the average number of positions was 1.4. Thirty-seven universities reported only one facility or faculty position. The average number of programs offered was 3.15. Seventy-five schools indicated that they offered no programs for their students. Only eleven universities offered degree programs in entrepreneurship at the undergraduate, graduate and Ph.D. levels. One hundred and eighty-one schools offered no degree programs. Sixty-four schools had some collaboration at the local, state and federal levels while 102 had no collaboration at any level. In terms of funding twenty-four schools received funding from all three levels while 180 received no

Table 6.8 Descriptive statistics

	N	Minimum	Maximum	Mean	Standard deviation
Total courses	321	0.00	21.00	4.52	4.13
Total facilities	321	0.00	4.00	0.86	0.89
Total positions	321	0.00	10.00	1.4	1.81
Total programs Offered	321	0.00	15.00	3.15	2.86
Total support	321	0.00	6.00	2.02	1.87
Total opportunities	321	0.00	10.00	3.67	2.65
Total outside COBE	321	0.00	10.00	0.90	1.80
Development	274	1.00	64.00	20.4	10.17
Valid N (listwise)	274				

funding from any level. The average number of opportunities for students was 3.67. Sixty-three universities provided none of the opportunities included in the survey. Programs outside the business school existed but were not common. Two hundred and seventeen schools indicated not having a program outside of business. Development was a summary variable that totaled the scores of all items from Tables 6.2 through 6.7. As may be seen, the average score for this variable was 20.4 with a high of sixty-four. This suggests that there continues to be a wide range in the development of these programs around the world.

Discussion

The data in this study taken in the context of previous work indicate that entrepreneurship education is alive and well, and continuing to develop and grow. Trends in line with previous studies demonstrate a rise in course offerings, majors, and funding targeted at entrepreneurship education (Katz, 1994; Solomon *et al.*, 2002). While entrepreneurship education still seems to be predominantly the domain of the business disciplines, there is evidence indicating a trend toward moving entrepreneurship across the campus. As other disciplines realize the value of entrepreneurial training, this trend can help lead to beneficial results such as enhanced technology transfer and increased economic growth (Hill and Kuhns, 1994; Laukkanen, 2000).

An interesting finding in these data relates to the breadth of course topics being offered under the umbrella of entrepreneurship. Broad course offerings are available, from creativity to social responsibility to marketing to law and beyond, spanning the concepts and skills relevant to developing the next generation of entrepreneurs in many different disciplines. Significant collaboration with various agencies outside the academic institution is also evident. While the majority of this collaboration occurs naturally at the local level, significant collaboration is also taking place at both the state/regional and federal levels. This opens the door to knowledge sharing across universities, as they collaborate with the same agencies to enhance entrepreneurship education offerings. These collaborative relationships also provide an opportunity to involve constituents and policy makers in the planning and delivery of entrepreneurship education, thereby linking students into their local, state, and federal economies and governments.

One especially encouraging finding in this study was the breadth and depth of extracurricular and experiential entrepreneurial activities offered to students. From competitions to internships to student clubs, students are increasingly presented with the opportunity to enhance and apply their learning outside the classroom through many different vehicles. In order to develop effective entrepreneurs, we must expose them to learning in many different areas (McMullan and Long, 1987). Scholars have argued that for an entrepreneurship education program to be effective it must offer and emphasize actions in entrepreneurial ways and be separate from traditional hallmarks such as business plan writing (Honig, 2004). Action learning and experiential learning such as student business start-ups, live cases and simulations close the gap between academic experiences and real-world requirements (e.g., Kuratko, 2005; Revans, 1978). These experiences promote skill set diversity and authenticity in students (e.g., Grisoni, 2002; Pittaway and Cope, 2007). The results of this study provide preliminary evidence that universities are indeed enhancing programs to provide students interested in entrepreneurship with this type of learning.

Perhaps the most promising finding, however, is the substantial number of entrepreneurship degree programs. Nearly half of the more than 300 institutions offered either majors or minors of entrepreneurship, or both. This appears to support the generally accepted legitimacy of and commitment to entrepreneurship in the curriculum. Even more promising is that nearly 20 percent of the surveyed institutions had Ph.D. programs in entrepreneurship. These graduate programs support the continued development of the field and the growth of programs moving forward. One finding, however, that highlights the need for continued emphasis on entrepreneurship in higher education is that over half the universities did not have a professor of entrepreneurship and over 75 percent did not have a small business professor. This may in part be the result of entrepreneurship programs housed in a non-entrepreneurship department (e.g., management), where professors teaching entrepreneurship courses are titled as professors in their department (i.e., management professors). As evidenced in the work of Fetters *et al.* (2010), universities enhance their ability to establish strong programs by providing a distinct identity for entrepreneurship, whether by defining a major, minor, department, center, professors and/or chairs of entrepreneurship.

The implications that may be drawn from this study focus on the breadth and depth of entrepreneurship education, both within and outside the university. Entrepreneurship as an academic discipline must push beyond the cozy walls of the college of business in order to connect with a broader population of students interested in entrepreneurship. In addition, universities are increasingly connecting with various agencies and sources of funding in the community in order to enhance their entrepreneurship education program. These connections should be pursued with gusto as the increased resources enhance the students' learning experiences, and develop stronger linkages between students and their surrounding community, which can have enormous implications for local and regional economic development.

Study findings should be put in the context of several limitations. Universities from one country to another can have very different organizational structures and external environments. These variations in context may impact upon how respondents answered particular questions. Language and cultural differences may lead to varying interpretations. The survey was designed to cover a broad range of the content and scope of entrepreneurship programs but it is certainly not all-inclusive. There may be other important aspects of these programs left unexamined. The extent to which participating programs represent all programs is also unclear.

That said, a better understanding of variations in the organization, priorities, processes and economic, political and cultural environments of universities and entrepreneurship programs across countries or regions of the world could significantly enhance our understanding of entrepreneurship education. As an example, the *grande écoles de commerce* in France were set up by the regional business community and are funded in part by regional chambers of commerce and engaged area businesses. This model is veery different from most US universities, but the methods and processes for collaboration may provide ideas for improved practice here in the USA – particularly if better understood. Fetters *et al.*'s (2010) work is based on case studies of six universities, including one in Mexico, one in France and one in Singapore, but no systematic, generalizable examination has been undertaken of how political, economic and societal differences influence effective entrepreneurship education. It is possible that the identification of meaningful measures of effectiveness may be facilitated by examining differences in international contexts. Appropriate processes and structures for and outcomes from entrepreneurship education may be somewhat different in an undeveloped versus developed economy. For example, how critical or necessary is social entrepreneurship? What happens when the necessity for entrepreneurship exists but collaborative relationships and support are not readily available? How do these situations impact upon appropriate practice for the development of entrepreneurship? There is a dearth of research that examines entrepreneurship and entrepreneurship education from this type of cross-cultural perspective. Given the potential for entrepreneurship to be a powerful force driving constructive change for society, this area of future research is worthy of further pursuit.

In a similar vein, do differences exist in programs in the USA? Are there meaningful differences in entrepreneurship education practices between large research institutions and regional comprehensive universities that may influence how effective practice is understood and measured? Do effective collaborative partners vary? In addition, how might the approach to entrepreneurship education be impacted by relationships with regional economic clusters? Much is left to consider about varying contexts and impact on program development, and ultimate effectiveness and impact. Clearly, many opportunities to further examine effectiveness in entrepreneurship education remain.

Conclusion

If entrepreneurship as an academic discipline is to guide students toward productive, impactful career trajectories and contribute meaningfully to economic development, it must move beyond the walls of the business discipline, shed the traditional pedagogical approach, and develop strong connections in the local, regional, national, and even global community. In recent years, entrepreneurship education has received the zealous attention of academic and economic communities across the globe. This study adds to the conversation begun in the late 1970s by examining the state of entrepreneurship education and providing some evidence that it is changing for the better for students, academic institutions and communities around the world

Acknowledgments

This chapter is based on an article which first appeared in the *Journal of Entrepreneurship Education*, which is owned and published by Jordan Whitney Enterprises, Inc.

References

Allen, K. and Lieberman, M. (2010) University of Southern California. In M.L. Fetters, P.G. Greene, M.P. Rice and J. Sibly Butler (eds), *The Development of University-based Entrepreneurship Ecosystems*. Northampton, MA: Edward Elgar Publishing, pp. 76–95.

Bechard, J.-P. and Gregoire, D. (2005) Entrepreneurship education research revisited: The case of higher education. *Academy of Management Learning and Education*, 4(1): 22–43.

Block, Z. and Stumpf, S.A. (1992) Entrepreneurship education research: Experience and challenge. In D.L. Sexton and J.D. Kasarda (eds), *The State of the Art of Entrepreneurship*. Boston, MA: PWS/Kent Publishers, pp. 17–45.

Bowers, M. and Alon, I. (2010) An exploratory comparison of U.S. and international academically based entrepreneurship centers. *International Journal of Business and Globalisation*, 5(2): 115–134.

Bowers, M.R., Bowers, C.M. and Ivan, G. (2006) Academically based entrepreneurship centers: An exploration of structure and function. *Journal of Entrepreneurship Education*, 9: 1–14.

Charney, A. and Libecap, G. (2000) The Impact of Entrepreneurship Education: An Evaluation of the Berger Entrepreneurship Program at the University of Arizona, 1985–1999. May Report to the Kauffman Centre for Entrepreneurial Leadership, Kansas City, MO.

Chrisman, J.J., Chua, J.H. and Sharma, P. (2003) Current trends and future directions in family business management studies: Toward a theory of the family firm. *Coleman White Paper Series*, 4: 1–63.

Fetters, M.L., Greene, P.G., Rice, M.P. and Sibly Butler, J. (eds) (2010) *The Development of University-based Entrepreneurship Ecosystems*. Northampton, MA: Edward Elgar.

Gartner, W.B. and Vesper, K.H. (1994) Experiments in entrepreneurship education: Success and failures. *Journal of Business Venturing*, 9: 179–187.

Greene, P.G., Rice, M.P. and Fetters, M.L. (2010) University-based entrepreneurship ecosystems: Framing the discussion. In M.L. Fetters, P.G. Greene, M.P. Rice and J. Sibly Butler (eds), *The Development of University-based Entrepreneurship Ecosystems*. Northampton, MA: Edward Elgar, pp. 1–11.

Grisoni, L. (2002) Theory and practice in experiential learning in higher education. *International Journal of Management Education*, 2(2): 40–52.

Hill, R.C. and Kuhns, B.A. (1994) Experiential learning through cross-campus cooperation: Simulating and initiating technology transfer. *Simulation and Gaming*, 25(3): 368–382.

Honig, B. (2004) Entrepreneurship education: Towards a model of contingency based business planning. *Academy of Management Learning and Education*, 3(3): 258–273.

Katz, J.A. (1994) Modelling entrepreneurial career progressions: Concepts and considerations. *Entrepreneurship, Theory and Practice*, 19(2): 23–39.

—— (2003) The chronology and intellectual trajectory of American entrepreneurship education 1876–1999. *Journal of Business Venturing*, 18(2): 283–300.

Kuratko, D.F. (2005) The emergence of entrepreneurship education: Development, trends, and challenges. *Entrepreneurship Theory and Practice*, 29(5): 577–598.

Laukkanen, M. (2000) Exploring alternative approaches in high-level entrepreneurship education: Creating micro-mechanisms for endogenous regional growth. *Entrepreneurship and Regional Development*, 12: 25–47.

Matley, H. (2008) The impact of entrepreneurship education on entrepreneurial outcomes. *Journal of Small Business and Enterprise Development*, 15(2): 382–396.

McDougall, P.P. and Oviatt, B.M. (2003) Some fundamental issues in international entrepreneurship. *Coleman White Paper Series*, 2: 1–27.

McMullan, W.E. and Long, W.A. (1987) Entrepreneurship education in the nineties. *Journal of Business Venturing*, 2: 261–275.

Revans, R.W. (1978) *The A.B.C. of Action Learning: A Review of 25 Years of Experience*. Salford: The Revans Centre for Action Learning and Research.

Reynolds, P.D., Hay, M. and Camp, S.M. (1999) *Global Entrepreneurship Monitor*. Kansas City, MO: Kauffman Center for Entrepreneurial Leadership.

Rice, M.P., Fetters, M.L. and Greene, P.G. (2010) University-based entrepreneurship ecosystems: Key success factors and recommendations. In M.L. Fetters, P.G. Greene, M.P. Rice and J. Sibly Butler (eds), *The Development of University-based Entrepreneurship Ecosystems*. Northampton, MA: Edward Elgar, pp. 177–196.

Robinson, P. and Hayes, M. (1991) Entrepreneurship education in America's major universities. *Entrepreneurship Theory and Practice*, 15(3): 41–52.

Solomon, G.T. and Fernald, L.W. (1991) Trends in small business and entrepreneurship education in the United States. *Entrepreneurship: Theory and Practice*, 15(3): 25–40.

Solomon, G.T., Duffy, S. and Tarabishy, A. (2002) The state of entrepreneurship education in the United States: A nationwide survey and analysis. *International Journal of Entrepreneurship Education*, 1(1): 65–86.

Streeter, D.H. and Jaquette, J.P. Jr. (2004) University-wide entrepreneurship and education: Alternative models and current trends. *Southern Rural Sociology*, 20(2): 44–71.

Upton, N., Teal, E.J. and Felan, J.T. (2001) Strategic and business planning practices of fast-growing family firms. *Journal of Small Business Management*, 39(4): 60–72.

Vesper, K.H. (1999) Unfinished business (entrepreneurship) of the 20th century. Coleman White Paper. USASBE National Conference, January.

Vesper, K.H. and Gartner, W.B. (1997) Measuring progress in entrepreneurship education. *Journal of Business Venturing,* 12(5): 403–421.

Zahra, S., Newey, L. and Shaver, J. (2011) Academic Advisory Boards' contributions to education and learning: Lessons from entrepreneurship centers. *Academy of Management Learning and Education,* 10(1): 113–129.

Zahra, S.A., Hayton, J., Marcel, J. and O'Neill, H. (2001) Fostering entrepreneurship during international expansion: Managing key challenges. *European Management Journal,* 19(4), 359–369.

Zeithaml, C.P. and Rice, G.H. (1987) Entrepreneurship/small business education in American universities. *Journal of Small Business Management,* 25(1): 44–50.

7 Progression and coherence in enterprise education

An overall framework supporting diversity

Per Blenker, Sarah Robinson and Claus Thrane

Introduction

The domain of enterprise education has expanded with respect to who designs the courses and teaches them, who the students are and what is being taught. With respect to the latter, the scale and scope of the courses has expanded significantly from a narrow definition of 'about' entrepreneurship often centred around traditional business school competences – to include training 'for' entrepreneurship – and finally to encompass experiential and existential aspects of enterprise education by a focus on 'learning through' entrepreneurship.

Parallel to this shift in learning philosophy there has been a significant transformation in how we educate, from the cognitive, teacher-centred to the experiential student-centred. In other words, moving from a simplistic toolbox of business competences towards a diverse learner-centred entrepreneurial pedagogy. The increase in entrepreneurship centres, student incubators and growth houses are some examples of the diverse sites where non-curricular training is blossoming. Other examples may be found in the spread of curricular education within the business schools extending to a broad range of faculties including science and technology, arts and humanities, health and medicine (Hindle, 2007). Furthermore, the delivery of enterprise education has trickled down from universities to other higher educational institutions, such as teaching and nursing colleges and technical institutions, as well as high schools and even primary school education.

A range of educational institutions delivering many different activities using a number of pedagogies now offer enterprise education. However, the diversification of content and pedagogy within the discipline has not been adequately articulated either in course descriptions or in the academic literature. More often than not these distinctions are ignored and enterprise education is framed as a homogeneous entity, and an acknowledgement of the diversity, variety and potential of the field seems to have become lost or disregarded (Blenker *et al.*, 2012). As educators and researchers in the field the heterogeneity of purpose and range of target groups must be acknowledged. Therefore we challenge entrepreneurship educators to reflect on what they do, how they do it and who they are doing it for.

Overview and aim of this chapter

This chapter develops a framework that allows us to decide when to use different pedagogies for different learning activities related to enterprise education (Fayolle, 2008; Jones and Matlay, 2011; Draycott and Rae, 2011; Wang and Chugh, 2013). A well-established distinction between learning about (entrepreneurship theory), for (entrepreneurial methods) or through (enterprising learning processes) entrepreneurship (Hannon, 2005; Pittaway and Cope, 2007; Fayolle, 2008) is used. The distinction of about, for and through is often described as competing or conflicting approaches that the educator has to choose between or as a development process where the field has progressed from the traditional and conservative philosophy of teaching 'about' entrepreneurship, via the training of methods 'for' enterprising behaviour, to the focus on experiential learning 'through' enterprise. In this chapter we use the distinction pragmatically, meaning that we see the three approaches as complementary to each other and therefore as mutually supporting parts that may be used both to distinguish between essential pedagogical tasks in a course, and to combine these parts into a coherent and progressive learning process. To demonstrate this we organize the three pedagogical approaches of about, for and through in a matrix together with the six competences that comprise fundamental elements of progression in enterprise education. Within the matrix specific enterprise learning activities are positioned for each approach, allowing a comprehensive and coherent framework for enterprise education to be portrayed in detail.

The proposed model has evolved through four years of experimenting with two different Master's courses at Aarhus University. The learning philosophy and the progression has been thoroughly described by the educators over the years (Bager *et al.*, 2011; Blenker *et al.*, 2011, 2012), and, as they have been implemented in curricular course activities, they have been further studied by two anthropologists (Frederiksen, 2013; Robinson and Blenker, 2014). Based on the observations and input from the anthropologists the course activities have been further systematically revised and compressed into a two-week full-time summer school, where the participants' changes in self-efficacy, ways of thinking, acting and learning have been empirically studied. The results of this education-based research are twofold. First, the conceptual work of organizing learning activities along pedagogical approaches and enterprise education elements carried out by the educators is valuable in itself as a tool for course development. Furthermore, the empirical results from the anthropologists' study of the summer school inform us with deep and thick knowledge about the students' perception of the different enterprise learning activities.

Therefore this chapter makes two contributions. The first offers a research-based model of enterprise learning activities built on an explicit learning philosophy and organized with emphasis on progression and differentiated pedagogy. The second contribution is methodological, demonstrating how different research methods may be used in combination to develop entrepreneurial course content and pedagogy.

Background: the diffusion and diversity of entrepreneurship education

The understanding of enterprise education at our institutions of higher education has broadened in several ways over the past twenty-five years. Among these are the following:

1   The development away from the business school monopoly into a broader range of higher educational institutions (Hynes, 1996; Kirby, 2004; Hindle, 2007). This may be seen as a broadening of *who is providing* and *who is receiving* the enterprise education.
2   The labelling has been broadened from teaching entrepreneurship as the start-up of new ventures to entrepreneurial learning or enterprise education (Gibb, 2002). This may be seen as a broadening of *what* is taught and learned.
3   The scope of activities has broadened from single entrepreneurship modules and courses to whole entrepreneurship programmes and a wide range of extracurricular activities (Hytti and O'Gorman, 2004). This may be seen as an increase in *scale* and a change of the *scope* of enterprise education.
4   The purpose of enterprise education has broadened from a focus on building particular enterprise competences towards the development of a general entrepreneurial pedagogy (Hjort, 2003; Hannon, 2005; Grüner and Neuberger, 2006; Gelderen, 2010). This may be seen as a change in pedagogy away from the focus on what is taught towards a focus on *how* enterprise behaviour is learned (Blenker *et al.*, 2012).

From this point of view the positioning of enterprise education can today be characterized as taking place in a wide range of educational institutions, which perform a complex system of activities with enterprise connotations involving several pedagogical approaches.

This is in many ways a fruitful development, but often the price of broadening the understanding of a phenomenon is a lack of precision in understanding it. With a variety of enterprise education activities taking place in a number of different ways, we need a nuanced vocabulary of didactics and pedagogy that is able to distinguish between central enterprise education elements and ways of learning these elements.

Delivering this vocabulary and a useful set of conceptual distinctions that can assist educators in positioning their education with respect to who, what and how, and inclusion of the scale and scope of these decisions, is an essential role of enterprise education research.

Research consequences and methodological challenges

The increase and spread of enterprise education has fostered a growing interest also in enterprise education research. A number of journals (*Education + Training, Industry and Higher Education, Journal of Small Business and Enterprise Development*) now regularly have special issues which focus on enterprise education; the major conferences in entrepreneurship (ISBE, RENT) usually have one or two parallel sessions on enterprise education, and recently a new annual conference (3EC–ECSB European Entrepreneurship Education Conference) focusing solely on enterprise education research has been established.

It therefore seems that the area of enterprise education research is positively influenced from two sides. On the supply side there is a growing and broader array of teacher/researchers with hands-on experiences from teaching and facilitating entrepreneurship education, and on the demand side there is a growing number of relevant outlets through conferences and journals interested in publishing this research.

It is, however, a challenge to ensure that this increase in the quantity of enterprise education research is supported by similar improvements in the quality of the research. In addition, research in enterprise education faces particular problems that challenge its methodological rigour; problems that relate to the fact that often the object studied (modules, courses and programmes) is strongly linked to the subjects (teachers, researchers and educational institutions) studying them. To examine these challenges further we must look more deeply into the reasons for doing enterprise education research.

There are many reasons to do enterprise education research (Pittaway and Cope, 2007) but it is possible to condense these purposes into two broad categories:

- The first of these are output studies which seek to measure the effect of enterprise education in order to test the legitimacy of entrepreneurship education (e.g. Gorman *et al.*, 1997). This category understands entrepreneurship education as the independent variable and the effects or consequences of education, for example, in terms of number of start-ups, job creation or growth, as the dependent variable. The primary purpose of this kind of research is typically to inform politicians whether or not to invest further resources in enterprise education, or for an educational institution to legitimize that their enterprise education activities have relevant impact on society in terms of firm creation, job creation and economic growth.

- The second category are process studies which seek to build insight into the dynamics and mechanism of learning entrepreneurship (e.g. Löbler, 2006), and therefore make a contribution to the dissemination of best practice and experiences of entrepreneurship courses and programmes (Bager *et al.*, 2010). This approach understands different approaches to entrepreneurship education (philosophy, theories, didactics and pedagogy) as the independent variable – and different types of modules, courses and programmes as the dependent variable (Bécard and Gregoire, 2005; Blenker *et al.*, 2014). The primary purpose of this kind of research is to serve as input for the development of enterprise education's modules, courses and programmes.

The research presented in this chapter does not contribute to the first of these categories, but only to the second. In this category of entrepreneurship education research, the researchers and the research subjects are, however, often closely related institutionally, if not the same people. Entrepreneurship scholars often also teach entrepreneurship. In that way they often do research on themselves or other entrepreneurship educator's teaching. Often research takes place as single case studies, where the researcher studies courses or programs he has taught himself.

This holds some advantages with respect to deep insight and thick knowledge, but there are certainly methodological problems related to this double role. To overcome this problem it is important to apply an appropriate methodological framework, both with respect to being explicit about what is being studied in terms of learning outcome, teaching method, institutional settings or student diversity (Biggs and Tang, 2007) and with respect to combining several different research methods that can supplement each other (Blenker *et al.*, 2014).

One of the possible solutions to this problem is to use research teams consisting of researchers-as-educators who are directly involved with the education activities together with other researchers who are not involved in the education activities studied. In this way the researchers-as-educators as 'insiders' or 'natives' would embrace an engaged and embedded sensitivity and loyalty. The insiders may be expected to be sensitive and true to the purposes and meaning of the education studied. To balance the research, the researchers who are not involved in the education can as 'outsiders' or 'foreigners' provide a detached and objectified stance to the research and make sure the questions studied are of general interest (Blenker *et al.*, 2014).

The research method used in the PACE project and in this chapter

The PACE (Promoting a Culture of Entrepreneurship) project is a four-year research project that aims to study what works and what does not work in enterprise education, and to test the teaching content and methodologies on an interdisciplinary group of national Master's students in four separate countries: Denmark, Finland, France and the United States.[1]

To do this, the PACE project uses a rather advanced methodological set-up of a controlled experiment combined with deep ethnographic studies of both the teaching and the students' learning processes.

The controlled experiment part of the project is constructed in the way that the students' level of self-efficacy is measured through a survey questionnaire before intervening with them and measured in the same way following the intervention (Karlson and Moberg, 2013). As the students are not exposed to other courses during this period this resembles the logic of a controlled experiment. The intervention is an intense two-week summer school for training enterprising behaviour in each of the four countries using the same course content, pedagogy and teachers.

The before-and-after self-efficacy measurement only document whether the summer school has produced *any changes* in the students' self-efficacy, but it does not explain in detail *what changes* in the students' way of thinking have caused a change in self-efficacy. The students' preferred mode of thinking is therefore also studied by using think-aloud protocols (Dew *et al.*, 2009; Hannibal, 2012) before and after the course, in order to identify if the summer school has created changes in whether students are using primarily causation or effectuation as their preferred decision-making modes.

Together, the questionnaire and the think-aloud protocol document whether something has changed in self-efficacy and explain what has changed in terms of causation and effectuation. These two methods are, however, unable to identify *why* and *how* these changes have been produced. To gain this insight into how the teaching and the learning processes may create changes in the students' mode of thinking and in their self-efficacy, a number of more qualitative research methods are used. Some of these qualitative methods relate to the development of the didactics in terms of target group, learning goals and content of course and development of the pedagogy in terms of designing the learning process. Other qualitative research methods are used to study the learning process of the students. These involve analysis of documents such as assignments and learning journals produced by the students through the course, and analysis of the expectations, experiences and learning processes of the students through qualitative interviews pre and post summer school as well as observations of behaviour and conversations of the students during the course period.

This chapter draws largely from the PACE project described above, but is focused on only two elements of the qualitative research methods: (1) the systematic design of the course content and pedagogy; and (2) the study of the learning process as experienced by the students during the summer school.

The course design process has been longitudinal and systematically structured through a research-based development process. Many of the elements in the new course have drawn extensively from two established courses. There has been a systematic sharing and reflection among the teachers about the elements of the two established courses throughout the process. These courses were studied by two anthropologists who gleaned knowledge of the discipline from observations of day-to-day teaching throughout the courses, reflective interviews with the teachers after each teaching session and participation in all the meetings pertaining to planning of the teaching in order to identify what elements of the course had a direct effect on the students' learning. These data were gathered over a period of two years.

There are three authors in this chapter, deliberately seeking to split the roles of insiders and outsiders as described above. Two of us therefore have the insider's role of involved teachers and researchers, the other the outsider's role of an anthropologist researcher. The combination of two distinct roles and perspectives strengthens the analysis of enterprise education content, pedagogics and outcomes.

The teachers (Per and Claus), who are also researchers, have fifteen to thirty years' experience in teaching and research – fifteen of those in entrepreneurship education. During this period their courses have gradually developed away from being primarily theory courses *about* entrepreneurship, towards courses that train *for* entrepreneurship and courses where the students learn elements of entrepreneurship *through* enterprising behaviour. Their primary role in the research process has been, together with two other teachers, to design a summer school course that focuses on combining academic knowledge and value creation.

The researcher (Sarah) has over ten years' experience researching in educational contexts. Prior to this project however, she had no experience of entrepreneurship education and was therefore a real outsider. She spent the best part of a year focusing on two separate courses in which she used participant observation, combining observations of teaching and reflective interview techniques with the teachers to gain a deep understanding of their learning goals and definition(s) of the concept of entrepreneurship as a discipline and as a method in preparation for the summer school.

Teaching approach

Entrepreneurship teaching is often focused on starting a business. However this particular course had a broader goal. The course entitled 'Combining academic curiosity with value creation; a process course in innovation and entrepreneurship' aimed to make students aware of opportunities to create value through a purposeful focus on the individual opportunities they face in their everyday practice and by using effectuation.

The students represented a broad spectrum of disciplines and this interdisciplinary element of the course was described as a strength. The course description emphasized the early pre-idea phases of entrepreneurship where eventual opportunities do not yet belong to a particular discipline.

The design of the course is based on entrepreneurship theory as input for inspiring and forming *what the students are going to learn*, the learning goals and the content – and a combination of learning theory and entrepreneurship theory as input for inspiring and structuring *how the students are going to learn*, the process and progression of the course.

Broadly speaking, entrepreneurship is understood as the rather mundane enterprising activity where individuals transform problems in their everyday life into opportunities for themselves. Education must facilitate the students' processes in a way where they learn about themselves as enterprising individuals who are able to enact opportunities through the process. There are three approaches that are significant in this course.

First, the content of the course is most fundamentally based on Shane and Venkataraman's (2000) understanding of entrepreneurship as an individual–opportunity nexus. Opportunities are however not understood as existing independently of entrepreneurial individuals, but as potential social constructs that individuals are able to enact (Korsgaard, 2013). In the course the focus of the learning therefore deliberately switches between having the students look inside themselves as opportunity-creating individuals and outside themselves as opportunities that are specific to them as individuals. Furthermore, the understanding of both individuals and opportunities as social constructs emphasizes a pedagogy where the students are to be trained in constructing opportunities socially and in constructing themselves as entrepreneurs.

The course is based on Spinosa *et al.*'s (1997) perspective of entrepreneurship as everyday practice, meaning that performing enterprising behaviour is not an elitist phenomenon but a possibility for everyone, and that opportunities stem from the everyday practice of individuals as they disclose personal disharmonies or problems in their own everyday practices and transform these into opportunities. In the course the students are therefore trained to be sensitive towards their personal disharmonies as a valuable source and analytical in the examination of whether their personal disharmonies are also general anomalies of relevance for a number of other people, and therefore an opportunity for acting entrepreneurially.

Finally, the course is based on the idea that opportunities can be socially enacted through effectuation processes (Sarasvathy and Venkataraman, 2011). Students are trained to analyse their own competences and social resources, and to seek interaction with relevant stakeholders in order to jointly construct and realize opportunities.

Other theories on prototyping (Ries, 2011) and business models (Osterwalder and Pigneur, 2010) are used to construct the content of the course, but the three lines of thought described above form the basic skeleton and the basis of didactic progression throughout the two weeks.

In a similar way the process and progression of the course rest on particular learning theories. The classic distinction of learning about, for and through is used as the fundamental pedagogical framework. About, for and through is however not used as approaches we should choose between, but rather as elements that must always be present in enterprise education. The logic is that the deepest learning is created when students learn *through* the creation of their own entrepreneurial project. In order to be able to learn *through*, students must however be trained *for* each particular element of the process, and before they can be trained they must be taught *about* the specifics of that element.

The particular understanding of entrepreneurship as a social construction process accentuates a need to train students in social construction processes. This involves not only strengthening their understanding of themselves and opportunities as social constructs, but also training their actual ability to participate in the social construction of new worlds. For this purpose inspiration has been found in appreciative ways to listen and talk (Cooperrider and Whitney, 2005; Kahane, 2004). An appreciative approach to communication serves two purposes. Open communication with peers increases both the understanding of yourself as an individual and the understanding of the opportunities you can engage in; and it is an important element in bringing stakeholders into an entrepreneurial project. Students are therefore continuously trained in sharing with each other through peer-to-peer forms of listening and talking together.

The programme structure

Following the presentation of the didactics and pedagogy behind the summer school, this section seeks to present the actual activities and progression of the two weeks in more detail. The course was structured to move the students from a focus on themselves as individuals and the analysis of their particular opportunities (first week) towards a deliberate social constructionist approach of creating their joint entrepreneurial opportunities (second week), concluding with an entrepreneurial project (prototype and business model) which each group presented at the conclusion of the course. (See Figure 7.1). In this process the students shifted between primarily divergent phases where they were examining interpretations of themselves, opportunities and ideas, and convergent phases where they where narrowing down, analysing and closing in on decisions.

Each day contained elements that deliberately incorporated about, for and through. A typical day would begin with a debriefing of the previous day, followed by a traditional lecture (about) introducing and legitimizing the theoretical rationale behind the activities of the day, then classroom exercises (for) activating the students for training, either individually, in pairs or groups, and the last part of the day would be devoted to formulating, analysing and bringing forward the specific project (through) of each

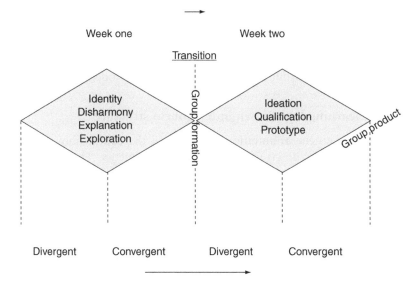

Figure 7.1 Model of summer school progression.

student or student group. A minimum of two hours were then spent allow-ing the students to interact in groups giving peer-to-peer feedback on a given task without any interference from the teacher. Bringing the students back to the classroom the next task was to write an individual learning journal. This important element should ensure that learning was internal-ized by reflecting upon the learning process. Finally the teacher summed up the work for the day and encouraged the students to take part in an open discussion about the learning, the concepts and the process progression.

The course began by focusing first on the students' experience, know-ledge and skills and building awareness of these. Throughout the first week the students became more aware of their own identity and potential, and their identity was constructed in a number of settings: first through diver-gent work and then convergent processes. By the end of the first week all the students had identified a personal disharmony and had carried out research that qualified it into a general anomaly of relevance for other people. The turning point for the course and the critical moment came at the end of the first week when the individual process reached a climax. The students were each asked to present their anomaly in poster form and to examine the anomalies of others. The goal was to identify commonalities either between anomalies or to find an anomaly that stimulated interest by a number of students so that a group could be formed to develop the ideas further in week two. The teachers were most anxious about this day. It was crucial for the outcome of the course that no student was left isolated and unable to find connections of some sort to others. Much time was allocated to this exercise and care was taken to ensure that connections were made and that each student was part of a group. Having achieved this goal the students followed the same structural pattern in the following week, now working in groups to open up the process again, identify and qualify opportunities, and finally to close down the process through examining and prototyping possible solutions into a business model.

Breaking the learning logic down into a course structure

Having outlined the general ambition and logic of the course above, this section breaks this logic down into specific course elements. The essential enterprise education elements are divided into a few fundamental competences argued, from the didactic considerations above, to be essential in this particular broad form of enterprise education:

These competences are as follows:

1   *Entrepreneurial identity construction.* Students must work with their initial understanding of what and who an entrepreneur is, in order to able to construct themselves as entrepreneurs.
2   *Effectuation from everyday practice.* Students must learn to construct opportunities on the basis of the resources to which they have access in their everyday practice.
3   *Opportunity formation from personal disharmonies.* Students must learn to be sensitive towards disharmonies and problems that can serve as the foundation of their entrepreneurial opportunity.
4   *Validating opportunities.* Students must learn to examine whether the particular disharmonies they sense in their everyday practice are of general relevance to others.
5   *Mobilizing stakeholders around opportunities.* Students must learn to involve stakeholders with relevant resources that can assist them in co-constructing opportunities.
6   *Prototyping and business modelling.* Students must learn ways to explore, describe and model their opportunity in ways that enable communication and learning between themselves and other stakeholders.

In Table 7.1 the six competences are positioned against the classic distinction of learning about, for and through entrepreneurship. The table may be read in two ways that have to do with different aspects of the pedagogical process. One way is a chronological reading from left to right, indicting how the students meet the learning activities: first they have lectures; then they have training exercises and finally they learn more deeply by using the new knowledge on their own project. The table may also be read from right to left, as a course planning framework. In this case the teachers must begin with the question of what assignment the students should work

Table 7.1 Entrepreneurial competences and pedagogies

	Learning through entrepreneurship *Assignments where students work with their entrepreneurial project*	Training for entrepreneurship *Exercises training students to work with this aspect of entrepreneurship*	Teaching about entrepreneurship *Lectures introducing and legitimizing the activity*
Entrepreneurial identity construction	Students describe themselves through activities; what they do in terms of education, jobs, hobbies, network or family	Students are asked to 'draw' an entrepreneur Further students exchange drawings and interview each other on their drawings	The teacher presents alternative theories of entrepreneurship trying to raise awareness of some of the 'figures' and myths associated with being an entrepreneur
Effectuation from everyday practice	Students describe when they use effectual and causal logic in their everyday practice Students are asked to describe who they know and what key resources they have access to	Students go out in pairs for two hours to earn an income on the basis of the resources they have brought with them to class today	The teacher introduces Sarasvathy's theory of causation and effectuation Students discuss in groups the difference between causal and effectual logic
Opportunity formation from personal disharmonies	Students describe a particular part of their everyday practice with respect to what, where and when this practice exists; they describe the dominating forms of behaviour and seek to be sensitive towards eventual disharmonies or conflicts in this behaviour	Students are given examples of real-life businesses and asked to construct a narrative of how these opportunities could have emerged from personal disharmonies of the entrepreneur	The teacher introduces the distinction between the discovery and creation of opportunities – and the idea of how opportunities emerge from disharmonies in the everyday practice of the entrepreneur

continued

Table 7.1 Continued

	Learning through entrepreneurship Assignments where students work with their entrepreneurial project	*Training for entrepreneurship* Exercises training students to work with this aspect of entrepreneurship	*Teaching about entrepreneurship* Lectures introducing and legitimizing the activity
Validating opportunities	Students must develop an analytical strategy: how are they going to analyse whether their personal disharmonies are of relevance for others? What do they know already? What do they not know? How are they going to find out? Students examine critically if others share their disharmony: Who experiences this anomaly? Where do they experience the anomaly? How do they experience the anomaly? Why do they experience this anomaly?	This is rather traditional analytical thinking, which most students know well – therefore no extra exercises are needed	The teacher introduces the logic that if a personal disharmony is to serve as the foundation for creating an opportunity it must be shared by a number of other persons. It is therefore important to qualify whether their personal disharmonies are also more general anomalies of relevance to others

Mobilizing stakeholders around opportunities	Students should articulate their anomalies and projects to other students in order to form groups around joint anomalies Students should communicate their anomalies and projects with external stakeholders in order to get buy-in from actors with relevant resources	Students are trained in the pitching of ideas, such as elevator speeches In groups students formulate the worst business idea they can come up with – afterwards they switch ideas and seek to improve them Students are trained in appreciative peer-to-peer communication	The teacher introduce the importance of involving stakeholders with relevant resources that can assist them in co-constructing opportunities The teacher introduces the importance of being able to give up parts of their projects (affordable loss) in order to create buy-ins from stakeholders
Prototyping and business modeling	Students should specify their learning needs and build a prototype that facilitates this learning need Students should build a preliminary business model and collect data to test the two to three selected elements Students should develop a second version business model	Students study early prototypes from successful companies and identify the learning purpose these are made for Students analyse a few given start-up cases and reconstruct their business models Students should analyse the business models cases for strengths and weaknesses	The teacher introduces the role of prototypes in the entrepreneurial process: Why prototype? What to look for? What to achieve? The teacher introduces and explains the business model canvas as a learning tool to be used with several iterations

on in order to gain deep-level learning; next teachers should consider which exercises can train students for the deeper learning, and finally teachers should specify what the students need to be presented with in lectures in order to be prepared for the exercises and assignments. The lectures have the role of legitimizing these two more important learning activities.

The insight shown in Table 7.1 may be used by educators in two different ways. The learning goals behind the course and the six competences elaborated in the table differ only marginally from what many teachers seek to teach their students. Some educators may therefore use the model, or parts of it, for inspiration on how to integrate the three aspects of learning about, for and through entrepreneurship into their course.

Other educators may however face other target groups and have quite different learning goals, and thus disagree with the six competences described above. These educators may nevertheless be able to use the model by replacing the described competences with other competences, but use the systematic progression of theory lectures, training exercises and project assignments to pedagogically restructure the learning processes for their students.

The students' perspectives

Making an assessment in teaching is always a challenge (Hattie, 2009). It is not unreasonable to assume that what is taught is seldom what is learned. There can be a large difference between what teachers write into a course description, try to support and expect to happen – and what students actually take with them from a course.

In this final section we examine this phenomenon by using some of the ethnographic results from the PACE project. We will briefly present the students' expectations about the course from interviews a few weeks before the course – and we will examine central aspects of the learning with respect to the six competences that the course tried to teach on the basis of our ethnographic observations through the course and demonstrated in the interviews shortly after the course completion.

The students had been heavily influenced in their choice of course by the course description, but by the time they were interviewed a week before the summer school their recollection of the course description was not clear. Instead they suggested a number of different reasons for choosing this particular course:

- to start a business;
- getting and working with 'tools' for business (e.g. business plan);
- establishing connections with other people from different disciplines (new networks);
- self-efficacy and developing a clearer vision of their future;
- increasing their learning potential.

The diversity in expectations ranging from quite instrumental reasons for choosing the course – such as 'starting a business' or 'getting tools' – to softer motivations – like getting a 'vision of the future' or broad 'learning' – is not particularly surprising. Most teachers meet a heterogeneity of student motivations when they start a course.

The same diversity may be found with respect to the students' pre-understanding of what entrepreneurship is about. They expressed a number of different understandings of what entrepreneurship means in practice. Before they started the course entrepreneurship was about the following:

- creating value (for self and society) from 'something not there';
- becoming aware of the potential of 'new' ideas;
- starting their own company and being the boss;
- moving from creativity to commercialism, but then 'getting people to follow you is more important than the money';
- having a passion and a goal;
- being in a team and testing ideas.

Given this heterogeneity of student expectations and pre-understandings, the actual content and processes of the course came as a surprise to the students, as the citations below illustrate:

> Well I have had some experience with entrepreneurship and it is very much about this blank idea of just getting out there with it and we can afterwards look at what has happened, did it work? This was really my take on entrepreneurship and I hadn't thought of other ways of doing it. And the class took a totally different entry point to entrepreneurship, therefore I didn't expect that.

> I really feel at the end of the summer course that something has changed. You have to believe that things will change with a course but I can really feel myself approaching the problems in another way. And team work, definitely. And it was only ten days but I can really feel the change. And I was very positive about the course. Of course I understand that some of the others maybe had a bad experience, or not as good as mine, but that is to do with expectations.

Good learning processes need to some extent to be in alignment with student expectations (Biggs and Tang, 2007) – but they must also confront existing expectations with something different for deep learning to emerge. Therefore, it is important to identify which parts of the course confronted and challenged the students and created deep learning. The interviews performed after the course were systematically analysed in order to identify how each of the six competences presented earlier has influenced the students.

1   One of the major outcomes of this course was a clearer understanding of self. This relates to the first competence, *entrepreneurial identity construction*. Students talked about personal growth, a new understanding of self and an increased awareness of their creative potential:

> I am going to use the thing that I am capable of being a creative, entrepreneurial individual and actually that I am a creative individual. The way I thought of being creative obviously were wrong. You can be creative in many ways also in your approach to other people, to motivate other people. So I really learned a lot about myself. But I don't think I will use any of the techniques but that was not my goal.

Working with yourself through an enterprising learning process could also be regarded as a liberating project or even an emancipatory activity. One student expresses this self-realization:

> That there are always many ways to do stuff and again there is not a correct one. But also for the different people they need the freedom to work differently. So it is about this. Enabling people to work in their ways and, at least for the course, it ended up with really great results. So it is about allowing people to be themselves.

2   Some students articulated an ability to approach problems in a new and different way, where they work closely with other peers in teams and learn to engage and motivate others. This learning relates closely to the second competence, *effectuation from everyday practice*. These parts of the course seemed to move the students from an elitist and business-oriented understanding towards a mundane approach to entrepreneurship. Students made the following comments:

> I thought this was only for special people. I would categorize these people as ... I don't know whether to say brave or stupid or maybe not thinking about the risks. But now I see that everyone has the opportunity but I still think that you need to be in a certain position in order to be an entrepreneur;

and that it is

> 'not about starting a business but about creating/generating ideas' and seeing 'problems as possibilities.

Related to the effectuation part of the second competence there is also acknowledgement among the students that like-minded people work in similar ways, whereas people with different perspectives and backgrounds may bring a different perspective not only on problems but on the extent of the opportunities.

> It might not sound like a big surprise but it was to me that people can work on the same problem but from totally different starting points.

Many referred to the learning that came through working with people outside of their own disciplines as well as an awareness of the complexity and diversity of their own network as a resource. This was regarded as a strength and, rather than seeking out like-minded people for their projects, many expressed a desire to be more open to interdisciplinary teams in the future.

3 Students expressed surprise at the particular interpretation of the individual opportunity nexus on which the course was built, where opportunities are seen as arising from the students' own personal disharmonies. This relates to the third competence: *Opportunity formation from personal disharmonies.* One student explained how their understanding of motivation for a project had changed: '*Exactly what the entrepreneur does to find solutions is different from before the class started.*' Another student said it '*gave me a method for thinking about opportunities rather than ideas*'. Talking about the future, students articulated that they would act on the basis of a stronger awareness of opportunities created by disharmonies.

4, 5, 6 The first three competences seem to have had the deepest impact on the students. These are the broadest competences, whereas the last three competences – *validating opportunities, mobilizing stakeholders around opportunities* and *prototyping and business modelling* – are more in line with traditional academic thinking, business thinking and more tools oriented. The students emphasized the importance of tools for communication, networking or generating ideas as well as for working with prototyping and business planning. For some students the course did not go far enough in this respect. There was, as shown earlier in the chapter, an expectation for more tools that would equip them to find funding and to present their projects for future stakeholders.

Coming close to realizing their projects in any deep way over a ten-day intensive course could not be realized even by the most enthusiastic students. An exploration of value, the connections to stakeholders and mobilization of resources were not achieved in the time frame. Even though the students all talked about the importance of prototyping and business modelling and were enthusiastic to learn and use these tools, they were never able to utilize, experiment and grasp their full potential in the few hours allotted to this work.

More generally, it may be said that the students got a taste of learning through entrepreneurship but that it was not completely realized in the course by any of the students, even though there was a willingness to do so. What this kind of enterprising behaviour course does is rather to make it possible for the students themselves to recognize their own entrepreneurial competences and create insight in themselves that enables them actively to build self-efficacy in ways where they combine their personal and academic background to make changes for themselves and society. One student expressed this process as a feeling of *'day by day, we got more and more sucked in'*. Another student, from political science, linked her academic competences with an opportunity to make a positive change in society, which is unmet in practical terms in the academic discipline she comes from.

> I think it is also not entrepreneurship in 'now we are starting up a firm' but more like the broader way, as creating new ideas with value for the society. That point of view I think is very valuable for my study especially because political science people are very interested in society and learning a lot about the society, but you don't get any tools to try to make the society better, or improve it, so the students really want to do this. So it is kind of clashing. My experience with this course, and some other experiences, is that it is possible and there are simple tools and if you get to know these tools and get to know this way of thinking, it is possible to get a better understanding of the society and how to maybe make it better in a way. So yes. I will try to do this.

Discussion and contributions

Teaching and learning are distinct elements. In this research project we have the opportunity to examine the many facets of teaching goals and learning outcomes. The teachers had particular perspectives on entrepreneurship as a process and had specific learning goals for the course. An examination of the course using the tables and models above attests to the importance of the combination and integration of about, for and through elements, and that although the course planning has a directional flow in one direction learning processes take place through an oppositional flow.

The results from this chapter are threefold.

First, the conceptual work of organizing learning activities along pedagogical approaches and enterprise education elements is valuable in itself as a tool for future course development, and in particular how we combine elements of about, for and through into our teaching. Educators can use the model, or parts of it, when they seek to integrate the aspects of learning about, for and through entrepreneurship into their own courses. Even educators who face quite different target groups and learning goals may use the model, by replacing the described competences with the specific competences they seek to build, but still use the pedagogical progression of theory lectures, training exercises and project assignments to restructure the learning process.

Second, the chapter contributes methodologically to one of the general research problems within enterprise education research that often the object of study (modules, courses and programmes) is tightly knitted to the subjects studying them (teachers, researchers and educational institutions). The researcher studies courses or programmes he has taught him/herself. The chapter shows how it is possible to combine the use of 'insider' teacher/researchers with 'outsider' researchers bringing the two perspectives – teacher formulated didactics, values and beliefs, and student learning processes, expectations and motivation – together for analysis. When these two roles are brought together it is possible to make the course design process a systematically structured and research-based development process as it enables a systematical sharing and reflection among the teachers and researches about the elements and learning processes of courses.

Finally, the empirical results from the summer school inform us with deep and thick knowledge about students' reception of enterprise learning activities and how their reception often differs from teacher expectations. There is still much work to be done. However, the framework provided here may at least be a starting point for a productive discussion among teachers and researchers for improvement in the quality of enterprise education.

Acknowledgement

This project is generously sponsored by the Danish Council for Strategic Research and is carried out within the PACE (Promoting a Culture of Entrepreneurship) project. The usual disclaimers apply.

Note

1 For more information about the PACE project see http://badm.au.dk/research/research-groups/icare/pace/.

References

Bager, L.T., Blenker, P., Rasmussen, P. and Thrane, C. (2010) Entreprenørskabsundervisning: Process, refleksion og handling. Århus Entrepreneurship Center, Århus Universitet.

Bécard, J-P. and Gregoire, D. (2005) Entrepreneurship education research revisited: The case of higher education. *Academy of Management Learning and Education*, 4(1): 22–43.

Biggs, J. and Tang, C. (2007) *Teaching for Quality Learning at University*. Maidenhead: Open University Press.

Blenker, P., Korsgaard, S., Neergaard, H. and Thrane, C. (2011) The questions we care about: Paradigms and progression in entrepreneurship education. *Industry and Higher Education*, 25(6): 417–427.

Blenker, P., Elmholt, S.T., Frederiksen, S.H., Korsgaard, S. and Wagner, K. (2014) How do we improve the methodological quality of enterprise education research. *Education + Training* (forthcoming).

Blenker, P., Freeriksen, S.H., Korsgaard, S., Müller, S., Neergaard, H. and Thrane, C. (2012) Entrepreneurship as everyday practice: Towards a personalized pedagogy of enterprise education. *Industry and Higher Education*, 26(6): 417–430.

Cooperrider, D. and Whitney, D.D. (2005) *Appreciative Inquiry: A positive revolution in change.* San Francisco, CA: Berrett-Koehler Publishers.

Dew, N., Read, S., Sarasvathy, S.D. and Wiltbank, R. (2009) Effectual versus predictive logics in entrepreneurial decision-making: Differences between experts and novices. *Journal of Business Venturing*, 24(4): 287–309.

Draycott, M. and Rae, D. (2011) Enterprise education in schools and the role of competency frameworks. *International Journal of Entrepreneurial Behaviour and Research*, 17(2): 127–145.

Fayolle, A. (2008) Entrepreneurship education at a crossroads: Towards a more mature teaching field. *Journal of Enterprising Culture (JEC)*, 16(4): 325–337.

Frederiksen, S.H. (2013) Identity Matters in Entrepreneurship Education. Figuring the Entrepreneurial Self in the Classroom. Paper presented at the RENT XXVII Conference in Vilnius, November.

Gelderen, M. Van (2010) Autonomy as the guiding aim of entrepreneurship education. *Education + Training*, 52(8/9): 710–721.

Gibb, A. (2002) In pursuit of a new 'enterprise' and 'entrepreneurship' paradigm for learning: Creative destruction, new values, new ways of doing things and new combinations of knowledge. *International Journal of Management Reviews*, 4(3): 233–269. doi:10.1111/1468–2370.00086.

Gorman, G., Hanlon, D. and King, W. (1997) Some research perspectives on entrepreneurship education, enterprise education and education for small business management: A ten-year literature review. *International Small Business Journal*, 15(3): 56–77.

Grüner, H. and Neuberger, L. (2006) Entrepreneurs' education: Critical areas for the pedagogic-didactic agenda and beyond. *Journal of Business Economics and Management*, 7(4): 163–170.

Hattie, J. (2009) The black box of tertiary assessment: An impending revolution. In L.H. Meyer, S. Davidson, H. Anderson, R. Fletcher, P.M. Johnston and M. Rees (eds), *Tertiary Assessment and Higher Education Student Outcomes: Policy, practice and research* (pp. 259–275). Wellington, NZ: Ako Aoteraroa.

Hannibal, M. (2012) *Sensemaking of the Entrepreneur in the University Spin-off.* Ph.D. thesis, Southern Denmark University.

Hannon, P.D. (2005) Philosophies of enterprise and entrepreneurship education and challenges for higher education in the UK. *The International Journal of Entrepreneurship and Innovation*, 6(2): 105–114.

Hindle, K. (2007) Teaching entrepreneurship at university: From the wrong building to the right philosophy. *Handbook of Research in Entrepreneurship Education*, 104–126.

Hjorth, D. (2003) In the tribe of Sisyphus: Rethinking management education from an 'entrepreneurial' perspective. *Journal of Management Education*, 27(6): 637–653.

Hynes, B. (1996) Entrepreneurship education and training – introducing entrepreneurship into non-business disciplines. *Journal of European Industrial Training*, 20(8): 10–17.

Hytti, U. and O'Gorman, C. (2004) What is 'enterprise education'? An analysis of the objectives and methods of enterprise education programmes in four European countries. *Education+ Training*, 46(1): 11–23.

Jones, C. and Matlay, H. (2011) Understanding the heterogeneity of entrepreneurship education: Going beyond Gartner. *Education + Training*, 53(8/9): 692–703.

Kahane, A. (2004) *Solving Tough Problems: An open way of talking, listening, and creating new realities*. San Francisco, CA: Berrett-Koehler Publishers.

Karlson, T. and Moberg, K. (2013) Improving perceived entrepreneurial abilities through education: Exploratory testing of an entrepreneurial self efficacy scale in pre-post setting. *The International Journal of Management Education*, 11: 1–11.

Kirby, D.A. (2004) Entrepreneurship education: Can business schools meet the challenge? *Education + Training*, 46(8/9): 510–519.

Korsgaard, S. (2013) It's really out there: A review of the critique of the discovery view of opportunities. *International Journal of Entrepreneurial Behaviour and Research*, 19(2): 130–148.

Löbler, H. (2006) Learning entrepreneurship from a constructivist perspective. *Technology Analysis and and Strategic Management*, 18(1): 19–38.

Osterwalder, A. and Pigneur, Y. (2010) *Business Model Generation: A handbook for visionaries, game changers, and challengers*. New York: John Wiley & Sons.

Pittaway, L. and Cope, J. (2007) Simulating entrepreneurial learning: Integrating experiential and collaborative approaches to learning. *Management Learning*, 38(2): 211–233.

Ries, E. (2011) *The Lean Startup: How today's entrepreneurs use continuous innovation to create radically successful businesses*. New York: Crown Publishing.

Robinson, S. and Blenker, P. (2014) Tensions between rhetoric and practice in entrepreneurship education: An ethnography from Danish higher education. *European Journal of Higher Education*, 14(1): 80–93.

Sarasvathy, S.D. and Venkataraman, S. (2011) Entrepreneurship as method: Open questions for an entrepreneurial future. *Entrepreneurship Theory and Practice*, 35(1): 113–135.

Shane, S. and Venkataraman, S. (2000) The promise of entrepreneurship as a field of research. *Academy of Management Review*, 25(1): 217–226.

Spinosa, C., Flores, F. and Dreyfus, H.L. (1997) *Disclosing New Worlds: Entrepreneurship, democratic action, and the cultivation of solidarity*. Cambridge, MA: MIT Press.

Wang, C.L. and Chugh, H. (2013) Entrepreneurial learning: Past research and future challenges. *International Journal of Management Reviews*, 16(1): 24–61.

8 A Gestalt model of entrepreneurial learning

Rita G. Klapper and Deema Refai

Introduction

Aware of the economic and social significance of entrepreneurial activity, and responding to student demand, universities train entrepreneurship students on every continent. Policy makers too are showing an increasing interest in entrepreneurial education, with a recent European report (EC 2013) seeking to bolster activity in this area. Entrepreneurial educators are experimenting with innovative pedagogical approaches that use different ways of learning to create entrepreneurial and enterprising mindsets among a variety of student populations (see e.g. Béchard and Grégoire 2007, Istance and Shadoian 2009, Klapper and Neergaard 2012, Klapper and Tegtmeier 2011, Robinson 1996, Verzat *et al.* 2009). This is in many ways a response to a growing dissatisfaction among learners and educators with the classical way of teaching entrepreneurship in Europe and the USA, namely through lectures and case studies. In addition, it reflects an increasing recognition of the need to equip students with a mindset that is open to entrepreneurial action (Hytti and Kuopusjärvi 2004).

As Klapper (2004: 8) and Klapper and Neergaard (2012) have argued, most higher education institutions teach students to become employees for either the public or private sector, but not to become enterprising and potential entrepreneurs themselves. Moreover, higher education institutions rarely offer personalised, life cycle-, motivation- and context-appropriate entrepreneurship teaching programmes, but instead deliver large-scale, off-the-shelf teaching content tailored only to broad cohorts of undergraduate and postgraduate students. This teaching material ignores the specificities of the learners in terms of their particular motivation for studying enterprise, as well as their varied personalities and life stages. While this appears to reflect the need to reach a large number of students, we would argue that there remains scope for more personalised approaches. Indeed and to some extent ironically, the internet and digital advances simultaneously offer the potential for more personalised teaching delivery while at the same time offering the potential to reach much larger audiences. The emerging MOOC (Massive Open Online Courses) are a clear case in point.

In this chapter we propose and illustrate a learner-focused teaching model appropriate for entrepreneurship and enterprise that aims to trigger change in the way educators and senior managers in further and higher education and government departments think about enterprise and entrepreneurship. For this purpose we use Wenger's (2009) social theory of learning, which consists of four dimensions: learning as doing; learning as experiencing; learning as becoming; and learning as belonging. We combine these dimensions with seven guiding educational design principles: who learns what, how, why, with whom, where and when. We draw upon our teaching experience in different cultural contexts, in which we have experimented with ways in which alternative learning initiatives may enhance entrepreneurial and enterprising thinking among students. We propose that it is necessary to consider the seven guiding principles which influence the impact and quality of entrepreneurship education and also students' motivation for studying and learning. Our approach is comprehensive in that we consider both entrepreneurship and enterprise. We follow Gartner (1988: 11) who proposed that entrepreneurship is 'the creation of organizations, the process by which new organizations come into existence'. In comparison, we understand enterprise and enterprising behaviour as activities outside the domain of venture creation; intrapreneurship is one form of such enterprising behaviour.

Underlying our approach is the premise that entrepreneurial learning needs to be considered from a holistic perspective in which each dimension contributes to the others to create a sense-giving Gestalt, a concept that may be translated as organisation or configuration (Koehler 1947; Phillips and Soltis 2009). By bringing Gestalt theory and Wenger's social theory of learning together, we advocate a more comprehensive way of designing entrepreneurial teaching programmes than is the norm, intended to bring the learner closer to the realities of entrepreneurial practice. Our aim is to render learners and ultimately society as more entrepreneurial and enterprising.

In advocating a comprehensive approach to entrepreneurial learning we acknowledge the multi-dimensional nature of entrepreneurship as an inherently dynamic phenomenon that goes beyond a sole focus on new venture creation. Following Rae (2000), Cope (2005: 374) expressed this as 'a contextual process of becoming', focusing on what entrepreneurs do and with whom, but also who they are (Gartner 1988). We argue for the person (i.e. the one who learns) to be considered in his or her holistic nature, as a multi-faceted being, as part of a collectivity, a context, a location, motivated by different objectives. We consider the importance of context in entrepreneurship education, a topic which has more recently been emphasised by researchers such as Klapper (2008, 2011), Welter (2011), but under-estimated in education despite earliest work by Lavand and Wenger (1991) and Lave (2009) on situated learning.

Seeking to communicate this in a less abstract way, we use interrogative descriptors to draw attention to the specificities that need to be attended to in course design. Students learn in context with others – hence we integrate and consider the notion of *With whom?* We examine the motivation for learning (*Why?*) as well as the *When*, referring to the learner's life cycle. The contents dimension (*What*) covers a spectrum reaching from learning about entrepreneurship, learning for entrepreneurship and learning 'into' entrepreneurship (Gibb 1999), to learning through 'withness', i.e. from within (Klapper and Neergaard 2012; Shotter 2006). The *How* dimension considers alternative ways of learning and teaching such as through lectures, running a new venture and role play and simulation (Gibson *et al.* 2009), as well as through innovative pedagogy involving art, music, theatre, dance and collage (Adler 2006; Klapper and Tegtmeier 2011; Shrivastava 2010). While there is some overlap between our seven guiding design principles, this interrelatedness is indeed important to fully grasp the Gestalt of entrepreneurial learning and allow for more holistic educational approaches to emerge.

Theoretical underpinnings

The Gestalt theory of learning

As Bluckert (2012: 81) notes, the German word 'Gestalt' is difficult to translate and approximate to pattern, shape, configuration or meaningful organised whole. Gestalt, which is a 'needs-based approach to understanding human functioning and behaviour' (Bluckert 2012: 81) draws upon a variety of influences coming from psychoanalysis, Gestalt psychology, Gestalt therapy, field theory, existential philosophy and the humanistic therapy movement (Bluckert 2012), and one of its earliest written manifestations is by Perls, Goodman and Hefferline (1951) and their seminal paper on Gestalt therapy, which Latner described (1992: 15) as 'the cornerstone of the Gestalt approach'. Early Gestalt psychologists such as Max Wertheimer, Wolfgang and Kurt Koffka sought to understand how humans make sense of their experience, moment by moment, 'against the background of the field which includes our current mental models and historical experience' (Bluckert 2012: 81). To be clear, in Gestalt thinking, 'field' includes the local physical environment of a person as well as his or her cognitive and emotional reality.

Hence Kurt Lewin's work on interconnectedness proposed that human beings are part of an environmental field and that their behaviour can only be understood in relation to that field (Bluckert 2012). As part of this field, human beings actively seek to impose order and perceive meaningful wholes in what they see and experience. Gestalt theory also draws on philosophical roots provided by Kierkeggard, Sartre and Heidegger, and in particular the themes of personal responsibility, freedom and authenticity have enriched the theory. Gestalt thinking implies looking for balance in human functioning through effective self-regulation to eliminate tensions in an individual's personal and professional life. The notion of balance is very important in entrepreneurship teaching. In fact achieving a balance between theory and practice (*What*) in a practice-oriented subject such as entrepreneurship is demanding, and considering the *Who*, with *Whom*, *Where*, *Why*, *How* and *When* is even more challenging.

A definition of learning

As Phillips and Soltis (2009) comment, there is more than one type of learning, and attempts to establish a single comprehensive learning theory have not met with great success. Beach (1980: 22) defined learning as 'the human process by which skills, knowledge, habits and attitudes are acquired and altered in such a way that behaviour is modified'. Honey and Mumford (2006: 1) proposed that learning happens 'when people can demonstrate that they know something that they did not know before (insights and realisation as well as facts) and/or when they can do something they could not do before (skills)'. These definitions of learning emphasise a subsequent and consequent change in behaviour, highlighting the social aspects of learning rather than viewing it merely as a cognitive process (Wenger 2009). As a result, in addition to knowing something cognitively and understanding it, the learning process is associated with a change in actions (Guirdham and Tyler 1992; Gibb 1993a, b, c). We follow these definitions as we seek to trigger more entrepreneurial and more enterprising mindsets in our learners, with consequent change in behaviour.

Our conceptual framework

Building on this ontological base, for our conceptual framework we draw in particular upon the work of Etienne Wenger (2009) who developed an initial inventory of a social theory of learning. For Wenger the concept of learning consisted of: (1) learning as doing, which represents the notion of practice; (2) learning as experience, which relates to students making meaning through experience; (3) learning as becoming, which relates to the learner's identity; and (4) learning as belonging, i.e. a learner belongs to a community. We relate these four dimensions to our guiding questions of who learns, what, why, when, how, with whom and where, in the context of entrepreneurship/enterprise education.

We also acknowledge the importance of prior work by, for instance, Rae (2005) who suggested a triadic model of entrepreneurial learning, consisting of three major themes – personal and social emergence, contextual learning, and negotiated enterprise – to be applied, both in entrepreneurial practice and by educators. Seikhula-Leino *et al.* (2009) also applied Shulman and Shulman's (2004) model, which aimed to develop a new frame for conceptualising teacher learning and development within

Table 8.1 A conceptual framework of different learning styles and associated guiding design principles based on Wenger (2009)

Learning dimensions	Learning as doing	Learning as experience	Learning as becoming	Learning as belonging
Design principles	What to learn?	How to learn?	Who learns why and when?	With whom?
Represented as	Practice	Meaning	Identity	Community

communities and context in Finland. The latter's model illustrates the ongoing interaction among individual student and teacher learning, institutional or programme learning, as well as the characteristics of the critical policy environment in which the educational programme is occurring. Cope's (2005) work on a dynamic learning perspective of entrepreneurship, which acknowledges the processual nature of learning, the entrepreneurial learning task orientation as well as the social side of learning, has also informed our work (Table 8.1).

Educating and learning as doing: practice

We associate Wenger's (2009) dimension of learning as doing with the 'What to learn' guiding learning principle. In this we follow Gartner (1988), who suggested that research should concentrate on what entrepreneurs do rather than who they are. The 'What' perspective deals with the need to tailor the contents of our courses/programmes in entrepreneurship. What we teach needs to be in alignment with the context and the stage of the life cycle of the individual, but also in line with the societal aim of creating entrepreneurial awareness/preparedness in our student population (Cope 2005; European Commission 2013). In most universities, 'fact-learning' is still the predominant approach (Klapper and Neergaard 2012), which involves a detached learning of theories about the phenomenon of entrepreneurship (Krueger 2007). Cope (2005) made some practical recommendations as to what the what dimension should embrace. He mentioned in particular learning about oneself, about the business, about the environment and entrepreneurial networks, but also about small business management. Rae's (2005) triadic model of entrepreneurial learning with its focus on personal and social emergence, contextualisation of learning and negotiated enterprise provides further inspiration as to what contents an entrepreneurial learning programme would comprise.

Education and learning 'about' entrepreneurship is of a predominantly theoretical nature and aims to develop awareness of the concept of entrepreneurship and the role that entrepreneurs and entrepreneurship play in the development of economies and societies (Gibb 1999; Carter and Jones-Evans 2000; Glancey and McQuaid 2000; Swedberg 2000). Learning 'about' is usually provided through business schools to those interested in this type of learning (Jamieson 1984). Such 'formal learning' aims to develop theory and conceptual frameworks (Broad 2007) and learning takes place through structured systems and organised programmes (Conner 2009). Much of this learning focuses mainly on developing left-brain processing of data, numbers, logic and symbols (Lewis 1987; Ornstein 1986), where educators focus initially on acquiring, arranging and instructing information to learners who then absorb that information passively (Barrows 2000; Wee and Kek 2002; Wee *et al.* 2003). The functional skills developed through formal learning include writing business plans, understanding and managing finance, managing legal and statutory requirements, product and service development, understanding marketing and sales strategies, setting standards for operational performance and understanding business environments (Broad 2007). However, education 'about' entrepreneurship does not equip students with the necessary entrepreneurial skills to become successful businesspeople (Solomon and Fernald 1991); neither does it add to their creativity or their ability to act strategically in changing environments (Kirby 2004). Therefore, education 'about' entrepreneurship is not seen to be capable – by itself – of 'producing' students who can handle real-life entrepreneurial problems since they would lack the necessary skills to integrate and relate their knowledge (Berry 1993; Doyle 1995).

Educating and learning 'for' entrepreneurship

In comparison, education '*for*' entrepreneurship and learning for entrepreneurship are about preparing learners to become self-employed, with the specific objective of developing practices and motivation supportive of start-up and running one's own business (Jamieson 1984; Rae 1997; Jack and Anderson 1999; Solomon *et al.* 2002; Henry *et al.* 2005; Edwards and Muir 2005). Newby (1998) advocated that education '*for*' entrepreneurship should be delivered in balance with education '*about*' entrepreneurship. He argued that the development of business and management skills through education '*for*' entrepreneurship should enable individuals to effectively manage the different functional skills developed through education '*about*' entrepreneurship, and, thus, should be combined so that individuals could ultimately attain the skills and personal qualities that would allow for behaving entrepreneurially.

Education '*for*' entrepreneurship which makes the student learn for entrepreneurship is basically achieved by training the various managerial aspects with a focus on how to ensure growth and the future development of the business (Henry *et al.* 2005) through a learning process that acts as a 'push into entrepreneurship' (Jamieson 1984; Hjorth and Johannisson 2006). Gibb (1999) described this objective as '*learning to become entrepreneurial*' which is concerned with developing individuals who are capable of holding responsibility of their own learning, lives and careers. Learning '*for*' entrepreneurship is expected to develop in learners a sense of responsibility, initiative, creativity, organisation, as well as motivation and commitment, which are necessary for the success of enterprise (Broad 2007).

Very often the development of business and managerial skills in education '*for*' entrepreneurship is associated with business plans. However, Gibb (1997) suggested that this approach does not expose students to hidden or indirect knowledge. Wan (1989) identifies a number of other criteria besides the business plan that practitioners consider when evaluating new business proposals, particularly the entrepreneurial skills and abilities of a person. However, in many entrepreneurial learning initiatives we find that the development of business plans is the predominant part. Timmons *et al.* (1987) also argued that entrepreneurship training programmes can only pass on limited knowledge and skills, and that real personal experience is the only way to learn. Drawing upon Rae (2004), we conclude that entrepreneurship learning as a dynamic and changing process needs more experimental and experiential, potentially innovative teaching methods.

Educating and learning 'into' entrepreneurship

Education '*into*' entrepreneurship, also referred to as education or learning '*through*' entrepreneurship, deals more with helping individuals adopt an enterprising approach throughout their lives, by stressing the importance of effective student engagement at all stages of learning. Education '*into*' entrepreneurship is linked to the development of business understanding and enterprise skills through new venture creation processes (Fayolle and Gailly 2008) which support adopting lifelong enterprising approaches. In addition to this value of education '*into*' enterprise in business disciplines, Refai (2012) emphasised the value of this learning in non-business, and more specifically science-related disciplines. Here, education '*into*' entrepreneurship is applied by embedding experiential learning approaches within the curricula in ways that lead to developing a range of transferable enterprise skills and personal traits that are valuable to all people, whether employed or self-employed (Refai 2012).

The skills developed through education '*for*' and '*into*' entrepreneurship are referred to as 'behavioural skills', since they affect the ways in which different tasks are carried out; these skills are developed through means of 'informal learning' (Broad 2007), with informal learning understood as a continuous lifelong learning process that is self-directed usually within a social context, and may be adapted to fit certain needs and interests (Falk 2001, Dierking *et al.* 2003). Such learning provides individuals with the experience and drive for lifelong self-learning and activity (NSF, 2006). According to Broad (2007) and Conner (2009), informal learning is the means by which skills, attitudes, values and knowledge are built daily through experiences, educational impacts and the surrounding environment, including people, resources and media.

In addition to these three ways of educating and learning entrepreneurship we add a fourth dimension which is very much based in practice. In particular we refer to Shotter's (2006) work on 'aboutness' and 'withness' thinking. Shotter's withness thinking suggests that the learner learns from 'inside the entrepreneur's mind' or through 'withness' thinking. The aim of such teaching is for the student to experience the 'lived experience' of entrepreneurs to acquire 'a second kind of knowledge' (Shotter 2006: 585), a 'subsidiary awareness of certain felt experiences as they occur to us from within our engaged involvement' (Shotter 2006: 586) in order to combat the prevailing 'aboutness' thinking. As Reid *et al.* (2005) argue, 'lived experience' offers a subjective and reflective process of interpretation, which allows a deeper understanding than traditional approaches to learning entrepreneurship. However, what entrepreneurs do has so far been interpreted largely as writing business plans or making decisions using various business management tools and marketing approaches. Such thinking overlooks, however, that what makes an entrepreneur is the mindset, and you cannot learn how entrepreneurs think through business plans and the like (Klapper and Neergaard 2012; Krueger 2007).

This withness approach brings us to the important topic of 'work-placed learning' (Hoyrup 2004) and extends the notion of practice. Wenger (2009: 211), for instance, relates learning as doing to practice, defining this as 'a way of talking about the shared historical and social resources, frameworks and perspectives that can sustain mutual engagement in action'. At about a similar time as Wenger, the French sociologist Bourdieu (1977) developed his vision of practice and his concept of *practice* in the broad sense (as compared to a specific practice), with practice denoting routinised behaviour comprised of elements that include physical, cognitive, knowledge, affect and motivation-related aspects (Reckwitz 2002, in Warde 2004). The term *practice* is thus integrated and composite relative to contemporary psychological analytical constructs such as attitude, behaviour, values and norms. Schatzki (1996) adds to this the distinction between integrated and dispersed practices, with the former being relatively domain specific (e.g. cooking) and the latter being relatively generic (e.g. describing) (Warde 2004). Practices may also come to be socially nurtured, protected and institutionalised (ibid.). Significantly, practices necessarily involve shared understandings and templates of organisation and behaviour; they take place in fields but are not synonymous with fields (ibid.).

Learning as experience: how to learn?

This learning dimension focuses on the way learners create meaning. Hence the key question is how to learn from the learner's point of view and how to teach from the educator's perspective. As Wenger (2009) suggested, meaning is a way of talking about a learner's ability, albeit changing, on his own, but also as part of a collectivity, to experience life and the world as meaningful. Arguably, we obtain meaning through different ways of learning. Hence the question of how different types of learning trigger meaning is important.

While recognition is growing that entrepreneurship is vital to the well-being of economies and many teaching initiatives exist worldwide, there has been inadequate research conducted on the efficacy of programmes and their effectiveness in instilling entrepreneurial skills and aptitudes, and as a consequence while educators have preferred approaches we do not really know what works or why it works (Klapper and Neergaard 2012). Entrepreneurship education does require different approaches to do justice to the heterogeneity of entrepreneurship and entrepreneurs but, as Fletcher and Watson (2006) emphasise, entrepreneurship is about processes of creativity and innovation that ask entrepreneurs to conduct their work in innovative and sometimes unorthodox ways, which is very different from the way that educators traditionally educate students.

As Fiet (2000) notes, there is a growing shift from tutor-centred to learning to student/learner-centred approaches. Tutor-centred approaches are widely practised and are referred to as passive or reactive, since learning is based on acquiring information without empowering learners or enhancing their skills to adopt a continuous lifelong learning process. Learner-centred approaches, on the other hand, suggest learning through methods which provoke thoughts such as projects, presentations, videos and case studies that encourage learning about both the 'subject' and 'process'. Dolmans and Schmidt (2000) argued that learning should be an active process of constructing knowledge rather than a passive process of memorising information; they also argued that involving learners in the learning process helps them relate their knowledge and to structure new over existing knowledge. Students have to get their hands dirty, so to speak; they need to 'work with the autonomy of self-reward' (Bruner 1971: 88). Thus, learning is approached as a task of discovery, and students are taught something that touches their lives in some fundamental sense (Frick 1987).

Little is known, however, about which type of innovative pedagogy could enhance students' 'entrepreneurial action' and students' ability to introduce creative solutions to 'real-world' problems (DeTienne and Chandler 2004). Klapper (see in European Commission 2013) and Klapper and Neergaard (2012) have, over a number of years, experimented with the integration of art, music, theatre and collage into their course design, aiming to encourage out-of-the box thinking and bridge the practice/theory divide. We also take inspiration again from Cope (2005) who suggested that entrepreneurs are very action oriented and hence the question of how to learn needs to respond to this need. More research is, however, necessary to establish whether such action learning approaches are more effective and efficient than traditional approaches – and, if yes, why. We suggest that a traditional lecture theatre is not amenable to the type of entrepreneurial learning in line with Shotter's (2006) witthess approach, and the question is what type of classroom *will* facilitate entrepreneurial learning and whether such learning should be classroom bound at all. The requirements may well change from class to class and hence from learner to learner, from age to age, from context to context, from motivation to motivation.

Learning as becoming: who learns, why and when?

The who dimension – the who of the learner, the who of the entrepreneur, the who of the educator

Arguably, the *who* dimension of our teaching model incorporates three dimensions: the who of the learner, the who of the educator and the who of the entrepreneur. We argue that both dimensions are intimately inter-related when teaching entrepreneurial as well as enterprising thinking and behaviour. The learners, their pre-understanding (Gummesson 2000) and their habitus (Bourdieu 1986), determine who they are and what they want to know about the entrepreneur and enterprise and what they want to experience in the classroom. Is the person sitting in front of the educator a fledgling entrepreneur already? Does he or she have the innate abilities to become one? Is he or she an undergraduate, postgraduate student, with or without professional experience? In terms of the educator, we need to consider this person, in this particular context. Is the educator also a practitioner, i.e. an entrepreneur, a pure academic or an educator who has the benefits of both academia and practice?

The nature of the educator and his or her background and experience will make a difference to the way in which this person educates about entrepreneurship and enterprise. In understanding the roles of both learner and educator, the notion of their *habitus* is also useful in relation to practice. Shulman and Shulman (2004) and Seikhula-Leino *et al.* (2009), for instance, focused on developing new frames for conceptualising teacher learning and development within communities and contexts. Bourdieu's (1986) work about habitus, which he defined as a system of dispositions (i.e. lasting, acquired schemes of perception, thought and action) seems to be particularly appropriate in this context. Bourdieu argued that the individual agent develops these dispositions in response to the objective conditions (e.g. through family life and education). Bourdieu aimed to relate objective social structures to the subjective, mental experience of agents. Bourdieu's (1986) 'habitus' is, according to Lizardo (2004: 375), a 'useful and flexible way to conceptualise agency and the former's ability to transform social structure'. Bourdieu (1989: 1) observed that there is a close relationship between 'social structures and mental structures, between the objective divisions of the social world ... and the principles of vision and division that agents apply to them' (Bourdieu 1996, quoted in Lizardo 2004: 376).

Equally important as the learner and educator identity is the *who*; that is, the identity of the entrepreneur with his or her characteristics and traits as presented in seminars/courses, etc. Learning about the entrepreneurial nature and what it takes to be enterprising is essential, as pointed out by Rae (2005). Hence the nature of the entrepreneurial character is of key interest. In the literature we find the entrepreneurial personality to be a continuing theme, and a range of different models have aimed to shed light on the entrepreneurial personality such as Kets de Vries' (1977) psychodynamic model, Gibb and Ritchie's (1981) social development model and the trait approach which all aim to discover the traits or cluster of traits that distinguish the entrepreneur from other groups. Indeed, much research into entrepreneurship has endeavoured to discover a single trait or constellation of traits which would distinguish the entrepreneur from other groups in society (Gartner 1988), which, to some extent, has been a futile attempt not resulting in one single model of the entrepreneur, but in a long list of entrepreneurial traits and characteristics associated with entrepreneurs. We find, for instance, that much attention has focused on the 'need for achievement (nAch), locus of control, desire for autonomy, deviancy, creativity and opportunism, risk-taking ability and intuition' (Kirby 2004), with the most commonly applied theories being McClelland's (1961) theory of the need to achieve, and Rotter's (1966) locus of control (Littunen 2000). Shane *et al.* (2003) identified similar concepts, yet also added tolerance for ambiguity, self-efficacy, goal-setting, independence, drive and egoistic passion.

There are also researchers such as Casson (1982) who included the ability to take risks, innovativeness, and knowledge of how the market functions, manufacturing know-how, marketing skills, business management skills, and the ability to cooperate. In addition, Caird (1993) put forward aspects such as a good nose for business, and the ability to identify and grasp business opportunities as well as correct errors effectively. Given this vast literature on the entrepreneurial character the important question remains, however, how this is translated in our actual teaching practices and to what extent this theory relates to the learner and his existing characteristics/traits but also those he wishes to achieve. For us as educators the challenge is now to bring the learner's predispositions for entrepreneurship and enterprise together with what the literature suggests an entrepreneur is about, in alignment with actual entrepreneurial practice.

Why learn?

Much research has endeavoured to establish entrepreneurial intentions of different audiences of learners (e.g. Klapper and Jarniou 2006), as intentions are understood as a precursor for entrepreneurial action. In addition, research such as that by Hedegaard (1999) and Herzberg (1966: 87) have focused on motivation, as motives are generally related to goals and this is no different in the entrepreneurial classroom. Goal-oriented learning assumes, however, that the educator is aware of the student's goals. Whereas the individual traits of the individual learner will play a role in his or her intention to create an entrepreneurial venture, Frederick Herzberg's (1966, 1987) motivation theory takes Maslow's ideas and his hierarchy of needs further by identifying the job or work itself as the source of motivation. Herzberg's motivation belongs to the category of the content theory of motivation (Bassett-Jones and Lloyd 2005).

Herzberg's theory is based on research which aimed to establish the different factors that lead to greater employee satisfaction. Herzberg identified certain characteristics, also called *intrinsic factors*, such as achievement, recognition, work itself and responsibility, as consistently associated with job satisfaction; and *extrinsic factors* such as supervision, company policy, relationship with supervisor, working conditions, salary, relationship with peers as the source of job dissatisfaction (DeCenzo and Robbins 2008). In addition, he distinguished between two classes of factors: first, *hygiene factors* which make up a continuum ranging from dissatisfaction to no dissatisfaction. The relevant factors could be pay, interpersonal relations, supervision, company policy, working conditions and job security (Fulop and Linstead 2004, based on Herzberg 1966: 71–91). Whereas these factors do not promote job satisfaction their absence can create job dissatisfaction. If these factors are present they only eliminate dissatisfaction. These hygiene factors are also referred to as 'context of work' (Fulop and Linstead 2004: 285). The second types of factors, the so-called *motivation factors*, which are internally generated drives, may be found on a continuum from no satisfaction to satisfaction. Examples are the job itself being challenging, gaining recognition and scope for achievement, with the possibility for growth, advancement and greater responsibility (Fulop and Linstead 2004: 85). For an employee to be truly motivated the job itself must be the source of that motivation, i.e. the job content. Herzberg recommended emphasising '*motivators*' that increase job satisfaction, as a mentally healthy person is a motivation seeker who requires a balance of both motivation and hygiene factors. One of the aspects Herzberg underlined is the idea of developing the job content of motivation seekers and he emphasised the need for job enrichment. This would imply an increase in basic skills such as giving whole tasks to individuals requiring more complex skills and greater expertise on the horizontal level (DeCenzo and Robbins 2008). For most entrepreneurship courses in the UK the intrinsic motivation of students is the pursuit of a degree, not necessarily in entrepreneurship, very often as a means to becoming an employee. There are presently three degree programmes in the UK – one at the University of Huddersfield, one at the University of Coventry and a third at the University of Buckinghamshire – which are different, as they require students to create their own business from the first day they join the university. These degree programmes are very demanding, as they carry a very strong practical dimension but also require students to build a sound theoretical foundation related to their ventures. One of the authors was the former head of the BSC in Enterprise Development at one of those universities and was thus involved in the development and running of the programme. A driving motivator for the students is the intrinsic motivation of being in charge of one's own entrepreneurial venture, gaining financial rewards and external recognition for one's own venture, creating one's own workplace, and being in charge of one's own destiny.

When to learn?

Following Wenger (2009), the notion of identity is intimately linked to the idea of the becoming of the learner in the context of a community. Such thinking implies a process of learning, which arguably may be different at different stages of the learner's life cycle. The 'When' guiding principle we propose addresses the question of age and career stage at which the learning is taking place. For this purpose we draw upon Super (1957, 1980) and Super *et al.*'s (1996) research into chronological age and life cycles (the 'life career rainbow'). Super indicated the parallels between an individual's chronological age, his or her state of development and his or her career stage. The stages include: (1) childhood growth (up to the age of fourteen), (2) search and inquiry (up to the age of twenty-five), establishment (up to the age of forty-five) and continuity or maintenance – up to the age of fifty-six, followed by decline or disengagement for the rest of life.

In the life career rainbow, the growth stage (1) deals with becoming concerned about the future, increasing control over one's own life, committing to school and work, and acquiring competent work habits and attitudes (Super *et al.* 1996). During the exploration stage (2) individuals encounter crystallising, specifying and implementing occupational choice. The establishment phase (3) follows at the beginning of one's career and the associated tasks are stabilising, consolidating and progressing in one's chosen professional orientation. The final phase – disengagement (4) – is about phasing out. In Europe, entrepreneurship education generally starts at the university level, but there are also an increasing number of initiatives at secondary schools in France (see e.g. Byrne and Fayolle 2008). This begs the question of how early students should learn entrepreneurship and be encouraged to think in an enterprising way. And, of course, what should we teach in different life cycles of the learner? According to Super (1957, 1980), at university, educators have a unique opportunity to influence the career choices of their students. They are in what he calls the 'search and inquiry phase or exploration stage' up until the age of twenty-five, and during this period they start 'crystallizing, specifying and implementing their occupational choice, (Super *et al.* 1996). Consequently educators as well as higher and further education institutions should benefit from this opportunity to integrate entrepreneurial and enterprising courses across the different disciplines in their organisations.

Learning as belonging: where and with whom to learn?

Wenger (2009) proposed the fourth dimension of his learning paradigm, i.e. learning as belonging, which considers in particular the idea of community. We take this further and argue that we need to consider where and with whom an individual learns, and for this we need to look at the wider term of context. The consideration of context is relatively recent in entrepreneurship literature (Zahra and Wright 2011; Welter 2011; Klapper *et al.* 2012; Klapper 2008). In the learning literature it was in the 1990s that Lave (2009: 201) emphasised the importance of context, and that 'learning is ubiquitous in ongoing activity though often unrecognised as such'. Lave was particularly concerned with the context of socially situated activity and the role of learning as socially situated activity. The context in which we learn and the social configurations of which the learner is part are essential to the way an individual learns, his or her motivation to learn and the meaning he or she gives to learning. For this purpose, Bourdieu's notion of habitus is useful, as it represents: 'the store of cultural and sub-cultural knowledge that people carry around in their heads and which condition their everyday practices' (Morrison 2005: 314). Habitus is also about with whom people learn, in their family, with their friends, in kindergartens, schools, in universities, in their home country and so on.

The 'where' dimension proposed here as part of our learning paradigm may be understood both from a macro and micro dimension. Macro refers to locality of learning in terms of countries, the north and south of a country, cities (small and large as well as rural), as well as learning in countries which are not part of the learner's home country, i.e. part of his or her usual habitus. The micro dimension of the where is about learning in classrooms, but also out there in 'real-world' places such as companies through work-placed learning and in unexpected places such as museums, art galleries, sport halls and kitchens. Gibb (1987) argues that it is impossible to impart entrepreneurial, present-oriented, dynamic, 'real-world' learning in a static, past-oriented classroom teaching context. Thus, in Gibb's interpretation it is not possible to re-create or enact entrepreneurial situations unless students are exposed to real-world situations. Starting their own venture may be one situation to acquire such knowledge, but not the only one.

In the light of the above discussion that combines Wenger's learning theory with seven interrogative words and pro-adverbs – who, when, why, where, with whom, how and what – we propose a learning model that is learner focused, but which also represents a multi-perspective, Gestalt view of learning (Figure 8.1).

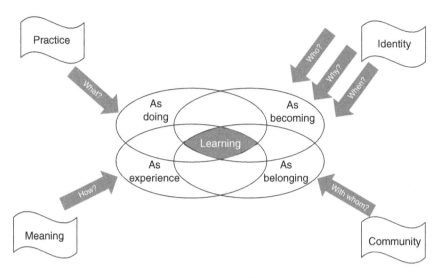

Figure 8.1 A multi-perspective, Gestalt view of learning.

Conclusions and further work

In this chapter we have developed and justified a Gestalt learning model intended to support educators engaged in entrepreneurial and enterprising education development. The model provides a rationale for a holistic approach that is based in the German Gestalt thinking. It aims to achieve a balance between theory and practice, between the learner, the educator and their context. As such it has potential for practical applications both in the educational and business practitioner's habitus, as a conceptual basis for developing teaching/training programmes and related research.

In terms of further research, there is a need to put this model into practice, i.e. to relate the theoretical approach to learning to teaching interventions, both in terms of understanding processes and in terms of evaluation research focused on assessing appropriateness and effectiveness. This need has been partially fulfilled by Klapper (2014) who investigated the impact of an innovative learning tool – repertory grids from George Kelly's (1955) Personal Construct Theory (PCT) – on two postgraduate student audiences, one in France and one in Poland. As part of this work, the author investigated some of the model's aspects as part of a cross-national research project. Given the model's complexity, it is suggested, however, that a more comprehensive research programme is necessary to investigate *all* aspects of the model, an endeavour the authors are presently envisaging. Such a comprehensive approach would also take a critical look at the contemporary appropriateness of the theories underpinning the model, given that in some cases these may be viewed as normatively structural in their epistemology (e.g. Maslow's and Super's approaches).

We believe that the comprehensive approach we propose has the potential to support more appropriate and effective learning strategies, learners and educators, and that this potential is applicable across disciplines. Ultimately, a Gestalt learning model is a highly specific one that takes close account of the learner's particular situation. While we allude only briefly to the role of digital advances in facilitating this style of learning and teaching, there is surely much work to be done in this area. Structured learning programmes that allow the learner to proceed at his or her own pace fit well with the bespoke approach we advocate. At the same time, it is 'real' experience that students need. There are limits to the role that digital learning can play in this regard, but even here, computer-based gaming, role playing and visualisation all have the potential to assist in an experiential approach. In many ways, despite the many and varied pressures on learners, educators and their institutions in an increasingly globalised and competitive educational environment, this is also a very interesting time for the educational researcher. Furthermore, as Rae (2005) has suggested, no theory of entrepreneurial learning presently exists that is based on social constructionist thinking. Given that both authors have a research competence in the latter there is potential to develop the said theoretical underpinnings.

Acknowledgements

Special thanks for constructive criticism and support to Paul Upham and Denis Feather; also thanks to the editors for their comments.

References

Adler, N. (2006) The arts and leadership: Now that we can do anything, what will we do? *Academy of Management Learning and Education*, 5(4), 486–499.

Barrows, H.S. (2000) *Problem-based Learning Applied to Medical Education.* Springfield, IL: Southern Illinois University School of Medicine.

Basset-Jones, N. and Lloyd, G.F. (2005) Does Herzberg's motivation theory have staying power? *Journal of Management Development*, 24, 929–943.

Beach, D. (1980) *Personnel: The management of people at work*. New York: Macmillan.

Béchard, J.P. and Grégoire, P. (2007) Achetypes of pedagogical innovations in entrepreneurship in French higher education (Archétypes d'innovations pédagogiques dans l'Enseignement Supérieure de l'entrepreneuriat: modèles et illustrations). *Revue de l'Entrepreneuriat*, 8(2), 35–57.

Berry, L.L. (1993) Our roles as educators: Present and future. *Journal of Marketing Education*, 15(fall), 3–8.

Bluckert, P. (2012) The Gestalt approach to coaching. In E. Cox, T. Bachkirova and D. Clutterbuck, *The Complete Handbook of Coaching* (pp. 80–94). Los Angeles, CA: Sage.

Bourdieu, P. (1977) *Outline of a Theory of Practice*. Cambridge: Cambridge University Press.

―― (1986) The forms of capital. In J. Richardson (ed.), *Handbook of Theory and Research for the Sociology of Education* (pp. 241–258). New York: Greenwood. Available at: www.marxists.org/reference/subject/philosophy/works/fr/bourdieu-forms-capital.htm (accessed 28 July 2013).

―― (1996) *The State Nobility*. Stanford, CA: Stanford University Press.

Broad, J. (2007) *Enterprising Skills: A literature review*. White Rose Centre for Excellence in Teaching and Learning (CETL) Enterprise Research Report, coordinated by The University of Sheffield.

Bruner, J. (1971) *On Knowing: Essays for the left hand*. New York: Atheneum.

Byrne, J. and Fayolle, A. (2008) *Global University Entrepreneurial Spirit Students' Survey (GUESS 2008)*. National Report France, EM Lyon.

Caird, S.P. (1993) What do psychological tests suggest about entrepreneurs? *Journal of Managerial Psychology*, 8(6), 11–20.

Carter, S. and Jones-Evans, D. (2000) *Enterprise and Small Business: Principles, practice and policy*. New York: Pearson Education.

Casson, M. (1982) *The Entrepreneur: An entrepreneur theory*. Oxford: Martin Robertson.

Conner, M. (2009) *Informal Learning* [online]. Available at: www.marciaconner.com/intros/informal.html (accessed 13 October 2011).

Cope, J. (2005) Toward a dynamic learning perspective of entrepreneurship. *ET&P*, 29(4), 373–397.

DeCenzo, D.A. and Robbins, S.A. (2008) *Fundamentals of Management Mixed Media*. New Delhi: Prentice Hall.

DeTienne, D.R. and Chandler, G. (2004) Opportunity identification and its role in the entrepreneurial classroom: A pedagogical approach and empirical test. *Academy of Management Learning and Education*, 3(3), 242–257. Reprinted in *The International Library of Entrepreneurship*, Vol. 9 (2006), ed. P. Greene and M. Rice. Cheltenham: Elgar Reference Collection.

Dierking, L.D., Falk, J.H., Rennie, L., Anderson, D. and Ellenbogen, K. (2003) Policy statement of the 'Informal Science Education' Ad hoc Committee. *Journal of Research in Science Teaching*, 40(2), 108–111.

Dolmans, D. and Schmidt, H. (2000) What directs self-directed learning in a problem based curriculum? In D. Evenson and C. Hmelo (eds) *Problem Based Learning: A research perspective on learning interactions* (pp. 251–262) Mahwah, NJ: Lawrence Earlbaum.

Doyle, P. (1995) Marketing in the new millennium. *European Journal of Marketing*, 29 (13), 23–41.

Edwards, L.J. and Muir, E.J. (2005) Promoting entrepreneurship at the University of Glamorgan through formal and informal learning. *Journal of Small Business and Enterprise Development*, 12(4), 613–626.

European Commission (2013) *A Guide for Educators*. Brussels: European Commission.

Falk, J.H. (2001) *Free-choice Science Education: How we learn science outside of school*. New York: Teachers College Press.

Fayolle, A. and Gailly, B. (2008) From craft to science: Teaching models and learning processes in entrepreneurship education. *Journal of European Industrial Training*, 32(7), 569–593.

Fiet, J.O. (2000) The pedagogical side of entrepreneurship theory. *Journal of Business Venturing*, 16(2), 101–117.

Fletcher, D.E. and Watson, T.J. (2006) Social change in the countryside: The role of entrepreneurship and shifting life orientations in processes of counter-urbanisation. In C. Steyaert and D. Hjorth (eds), *Entrepreneurship as Social Change: Third Movements in Entrepreneurship book* (pp. 145–164). Cheltenham: Edward Elgar.

Frick, W.B. (1987) The symbolic growth experience: Paradigm for a humanistic-existential learning theory. *Journal of Humanistic Psychology*, 27(4), 406–423.

Fulop, L. and Linstead, S. (2004) Motivation and meaning. In S. Linstead, L. Fulop and S. Lilley (eds), *Management and Organization: A critical text* (pp. 411–473). Basingstoke: Palgrave.

Gartner, W.B. (1988) Who is an entrepreneur? is the wrong question. *American Journal of Small Business*, 12(4), 11–31.

Gibb, A.A. (1987) Enterprise culture – its meaning and implications for education and training. *Journal of European Industrial Training*, 11(2), 1–38.

—— (1993a) The enterprise culture and education. Understanding enterprise education and its links with small business, entrepreneurship and wider educational goals. *International Small Business Journal*, 11(3), 11–34.

—— (1993b) Key factors in the design of policy support for the small and medium enterprise (SME) development process: An overview. *Entrepreneurship and Regional Development*, 5, 1–24.

—— (1997) Small firms' training and competitiveness: Building upon the small business as a learning organisation. *International Small Business Journal*, 15(3), 13–29.

—— (1999) Can we build 'effective' entrepreneurship through management development? *Journal of General Management*, 24(4), 1–22.

Gibb, A. and Ritchie, J. (1981) Influences on Entrepreneurship: A study over time. In Bolton Ten Years On – Proceeding of the UK Small Business Research Conference, 20–21 November. Polytechnic of Central London.

Gibson, D., Harkin, A. and Scott, J.M. (2009) Towards a pedagogical model of new venture based learning. Paper presented at the efmd Entrepreneurship Conference.

Glancey, K.S. and McQuaid, R.W. (2000) *Entrepreneurial Economics*. Basingstoke: Macmillan.

Guirdham, M. and Tyler, K. (1992). *Enterprise Skills for Students*. London: Butterworth Heinemann.

Gummesson, E. (2000) *Qualitative Methods in Management Research* (2nd edn). London: Sage.

Hedegaard, M. (1999) The influence of societal knowledge traditions on children's thinking and conceptual development. In M. Hedegaard and J. Lompscher, *Learning Activity and Development* (pp. 21–50). Aarhus: Aarhus University Press.

Henry, C., Hill, F. and Leitch, C. (2005) Entrepreneurship education and training: Can entrepreneurship be taught? Part I. *Education + Training*, 47(2), 98–111.

Herzberg, F. (1966) *The Work and the Nature of Men*. Cleveland: The World Publishing Company.

—— (1987) One more time: How do you motivate employees? *Harvard Business Review*, 65(5), 109–120.

Hjorth, D. and Johannisson, B. (2006) Learning as an entrepreneurial process. In A. Fayolle (eds), *Handbook of Research in Entrepreneurship Education*. Cheltenham: Edward Elgar.

Honey, P. and Mumford, A. (2006) *The Learning Styles Questionnaire, 80-item Version*. Maidenhead: Peter Honey Publications.

Høyrup, S. (2004) Reflection as a core process in organisational learning. *Journal of Workplace Learning*, 16(8), 442–454.

Hytti, U. and Kuopusjärvi, P. (2004) *Evaluating and Measuring Entrepreneurship and Enterprise Education: Methods, tools and practices*. Small Business Institute Business Research and Development Centre, Turku School of Economics and Business Administration.

Istance, D. and Shadoian, V. (2009) *Innovative Pedagogy* (Education innovante). OECD Observatory (l'Observateur de l'OCDE), 270/271, December 2008 to January 2009.

Jack, S.L. and Anderson, A.R. (1999) Entrepreneurship education within the enterprise culture. Producing reflective practitioners. *International Journal of Entrepreneurship Behaviour and Research*, 5(3), 110–125.

Jamieson, I. (1984) *Education for Enterprise*. In A.G. Watts and P. Moran, CRAC. Cambridge: Ballinger, pp. 19–27.

Kelly, G.A. (1955) *The Psychology of Personal Constructs*, Vol. I. New York: Norton.

Kirby, D. (2004) Entrepreneurship education: Can business schools meet the challenge? *Education + Training*, 6(8/9), 510–519.

Klapper, R. (2004) Government goals and entrepreneurship education – an investigation at a Grande Ecole in France. *Education and Training*, 46(3), 127–137.

—— (2008) *The Role of Social Capital in French Entrepreneurial Networks*. Unpublished Ph.D. thesis, Leeds University.

—— (2011) *The Role of Social Capital in French Entrepreneurial Networks: Using contacts for successful start-ups*. Germany: Lambert Academic Publishing.

—— (2014) A role for George Kelly's repertory grids in entrepreneurship education? Evidence from the French and Polish context. *International Journal of Management Education*, in press.

Klapper, R. and Léger-Jarniou, C. (2006) Entrepreneurship intention among French Grande Ecole and University students: An application of Shapero's model. *Industry and Higher Education*, 20(2), 97–110.

Klapper, R. and Neergaard, H. (2012) Five steps to heaven: From student to entrepreneur – an agenda for innovative pedagogy. European Summer University conference paper, Kolding, Denmark, 19 to 25 August.

Klapper, R. and Tegtmeier, S. (2010) Innovating entrepreneurial pedagogy: Examples from France and Germany. *Journal of Small Business Enterprise and Development*, 17(4), 552–568.

Klapper, R., Biga, M. and Lahti, A. (2012) Small business support and enterprise promotion: The case of France. In R. Blackburn and M. Schaper (eds), *Entrepreneurship, Small Business and Government Support* (pp. 123–137). London: Gower Publications.

Koehler, W. (1947) *Gestalt Psychology: An introduction to new concepts in modern psychology*. New York: Liveright, a revised edition of the 1929 book. Norton 1992 reprint.

—— (1969) *The Task of Gestalt Psychology*. Englewood Cliffs, NJ: Princeton University Press.

Krueger, N.F. (2007) What lies beneath? The experiential essence of entrepreneurial thinking. *Entrepreneurship Theory and Practice*, 31(1), 1540–6520.

Latner, J. (1992) The theory of Gestalt therapy. In E.C. Nevis, *Gestalt Therapy: Applications and perspectives*. New York: Garden Press.

Lave, J. (2009) The practice of learning. In D.C. Philips and J.F. and Soltis, *Perspectives on Learning*. London: Teachers' College Press, pp. 200–208.

Lave, J. and Wenger, E. (1991) *Situated Learning: Legitimate peripheral participation*. Cambridge: Cambridge University Press.

Lewin, K. (1997) Field theory and learning. In D. Cartwright (ed.), *Field Theory in Social Science and Selected Theoretical Papers*. Washington, DC: American Psychological Association, pp. 212–230. (Original work published 1942.)

Lewis, D. (1987) *Mind Skills: Giving your child a brighter future*. London: Souvenir Press.

Linstead, L., Fulop, S. and Lilley, L. (2004) *Management and Organisation: A critical text*. Basingstoke: Palgrave Macmillan.

Littunen, H. (2000) Networks and local environmental characteristics in the survival of new firms. *Small Business Economics*, 15, 59–71.

Lizardo, O. (2004) The cognitive origins of Bourdieu's habitus. *Journal for the Theory of Social Behaviour*, 34(4), 375–401.

McClelland, D.C. (1961) *The Achieving Society*. Princeton, NJ: Van Nostrand.

Morrison, K. (2005) Structuration theory, habitus and complexity theory: Elective affinities or old wine in new bottles? *British Journal of Sociological Education*, 26(3), 311–326.

National Science Foundation (NSF) (2006) *Informal Science* education programme solicitation (NSF 06–520). Retrieved from www.nsf.gov/pubs/2006/nsf06520/nsf06520.htm (accessed 29 December 2011).

Newby, P. (1998) After enterprise in higher education – holding the ground or sustaining the momentum? *Education + Training*, 40(6/7), 307.

Ornstein, R. (1986) *The Psychology of Consciousness*. Harmondsworth: Penguin.

Perls, F.S., Hefferline, R. and Goodman, P. (1951) *Gestalt Therapy: Excitement and growth in the human personality*. Gestalt Journal Press (new edition 1994).

Peterman, N.E and Kennedy, J. (2003) Enterprise education: Influencing students' perceptions of entrepreneurship. *Entrepreneurship and Theory and Practice*, 28 (2), 129–144.

Philips, D.C. and Soltis, J.F. (2009) *Perspectives on Learning*. London: Teachers' College Press.

Rae, D.M. (1997) Teaching entrepreneurship in Asia: Impact of a pedagogical innovation. *Entrepreneurship Innovation and Change*, 6(3), 193–227.

—— (2000) Understanding entrepreneurial learning: A question of How. *International Journals of Entrepreneurial Behaviour and Research*, 6(3), 145–159.

—— (2004) Entrepreneurial learning: A narrative-based conceptual model. Paper presented at the Institute for Small Business Affairs 27th National Conference, Newcastle, 2–4 November.

—— (2005) Entrepreneurial learning: A narrative-based conceptual model. *Journal of Small Business Enterprise and Development*, 12(3), 323–335.

Reckwitz, A. (2002) Toward a theory of social practices: A development in culturalist theorizing. *European Journal of Social Theory*, 5(2), 243–263.

Refai, D. (2009) The significance of problem-based learning in developing enterprise skills for pharmacy students in UK HEI. In *Business and Organisational*

Survival and Sustainability – Papers from the Northern Leadership Academy Fellows 2009 Conference, pp. 73–84.

—— (2012) *Developing Enterprise Skills Through Enterprise Education: The significance of the contribution of experiential learning approaches in the pharmacy education context in the UK HEIs.* Unpublished Ph.D., University of Huddersfield.

Reid, K., Flowers, P. and Larkin, M. (2005) Exploring lived experience. *The Psychologist*, 18(1), 20–24.

Robinson, P.B. (1996) The MINEFIELD Exercise: The challenge. *Entrepreneurship Education Simulation and Gaming*, 350–363.

Rotter, J.B. (1966) Generalised expectancies for internal versus external control of reinforcement. *Psychological Monographs*, Vol. 609.

Schatzki, T. (1996) *Social Practices: A Wittgensteinian approach to human activity and the social.* Cambridge: Cambridge University Press.

Seikhula-Leino, J., Ruskovaara, E., Ikavalko, F., Mattila, J. and Rytkola, T. (2009) Teachers as learners promoting entrepreneurship education. Paper presented at the 20th Biannual NFF Conference 'Business as Usual', Turku/Abo, Finland, 19–21 August.

Shane, S., Locke, E. and Collins, C. (2003) Entrepreneurial motivation. *Human Resource Management Review*, 13(2), 257–279.

Shotter, J. (2006) From minds hidden in the heads of individuals to the use of mind-talk between us: Wittgensteinian developmental investigations. *Journal for the Theory of Social Behaviour*, 36(3), 279–297.

Shrivastava, P.A. (2010) Pedagogy of passion for sustainability. *Academy of Management Learning and Education*, 9(3), 443–455.

Shulman, L.S. and Shulman, J.H. (2004) How and what teachers learn: A shifting perspective. *Journal of Curriculum Studies*, 36(2), 257–271.

Solomon, G.T. and Fernald Jr., L.W. (1991) Trends in small business management and entrepreneurship education in the United States. *Entrepreneurship Theory and Practice*, 15(3), 25–40.

Solomon, G.T., Duffy, S. and Tarabishy, A. (2002) The state of entrepreneurship education in the United States: A nationwide survey and analysis. *International Journal of Entrepreneurship Education*, 1(1), 65–86.

Super, D. E. (1957) *The Psycholology of Careers.* New York: Harper and Row.

—— (1980) A life-span, life-space approach to career development. *Journal of Vocational Behavior*, 16, 282–298.

Super, D.E., Savickas, M.L. and Super, C.M. (1996) The life-span, life-space approach to careers. In D. Brown, L. Brooks & Associates (eds), *Career Choice & Development* (3rd edn). San Francisco, CA: Jossey-Bass, pp. 121–178.

Swedberg, R. (2000) *Entrepreneurship: The social science view.* Oxford: Oxford University Press.

Timmons, J.A., Muzyka, D.F., Stevenson, H.M. and Bygrave, W.D. (1987) Opportunity recognition: The core of entrepreneurship. In N. Churchill (ed.), *Frontiers of Entrepreneurial Research*. Babson College, Babson Park, MA, pp. 42–49.

Verzat, C., Byrne, J. and Fayolle, A. (2009) Tangling with spaghetti: Pedagogical lessons from games. *Academy of Management of Learning and Education*, 8(3), 356–369.

Vries de, K. (1977) The entrepreneurial personality: A person at the crossroads. *Journal of Management Studies*, 14(1), 34–57.

Wan, V. (1989) The enterprise workshop programme in Australia. *International Small Business Journal*, 7(2), 23–34.

Warde, A. (2004) *Practice and Field: Revising Bourdieusian concepts*. CRIC discussion paper 65. University of Manchester. Available at: www.cric.ac.uk/cric/Pdfs/dp65.pdf.

Wee, K.N.L. and Kek, Y.C. (2002) *Authentic Problem-based Learning: Rewriting business education*. New York: Prentice Hall, Pearson Publications.

Wee, K.N.L., Kek, Y.C. and Kelley, C. (2003) Transforming the marketing curriculum using problem-based learning: A case study. *Journal of Marketing Education*, August.

Welter, F. (2011) Contextualizing entrepreneurship – Conceptual challenges and ways forward. *ET&P*, 165–184.

Wenger, E. (2009) A social theory of learning. In D.C. Philips and J.F. Soltis, *Perspectives on Learning*. London: Teachers' College Press, pp. 209–218.

Zahra. S.A. and Wright, M. (2011) Entrepreneurship's next act. *Academy of Management Perspectives*, 25(4), 67–83.

9 Entrepreneurial learning in small firm management teams

Ian McKeown

Introduction

The lived experience and real world of the entrepreneur is often a volatile, lonely, disjointed and opportunistic place, more often than not driven by events and frequently punctuated by crises from which lessons are sometimes learned.

However, it is in this context that entrepreneurs develop their understanding of both who they are becoming (Rae, 2005) and how they will navigate the changing environment, in which future opportunities are made or discovered usually through myriad experiences, encounters and relationships with others, and that for good or bad shape their learning and subsequent behaviour.

Historically and perhaps understandably, research into the field of entrepreneurial learning has predominantly focused on the level of the individual. However, while this has provided valuable insights into the nature of individual learning, it has also, unfortunately, only helped reinforce the myth of the entrepreneurial lone ranger; one person singularly responsible for the development and growth of a venture or business.

This distorted perspective is unwittingly or deliberately perpetuated in the media by programmes such as *The Apprentice* or *Dragons' Den*, thereby affirming the theory of the 'great man or woman', which makes for great viewing but is not particularly helpful in understanding how entrepreneurs learn. What appear to be missing in much of the literature are conceptualisations of entrepreneurial learning from a collective perspective involving multiple actors in the process. However, there is increasingly a turn in the literature that challenges individualistic perceptions of entrepreneurial learning (Cooney, 2005; Devins and Gold, 2004; Jones *et al.*, 2010; Kempster and Cope, 2010; McKeown, 2010; Rae, 2007; Thorpe *et al.*, 2006)

Studying how entrepreneurs learn to negotiate the growth and development of small firms has also become an increasingly important area of academic study (Cope, 2005; Pittaway and Thorpe, 2012; Rae, 2005).

The purpose of this chapter is to explore entrepreneurial learning within the context of the small firm management team and the difficulties they collectively face in trying to share their experiences to co-construct knowledge and an understanding of their environment that subsequently creates or reveals opportunities for the small firm.

The insights this chapter makes are drawn on both existing literature and empirical research undertaken in the field of entrepreneurial learning in small firms (McKeown, 2010, 2012a, 2012b). These studies were based on an in-depth, longitudinal qualitative case study of an entrepreneurial small firm management team involved in manufacturing in the West Midlands. The model of entrepreneurial learning in Figure 9.1 was developed from this.

The picture of entrepreneurial learning that emerges from this is a complex and often messy one, involving a dynamic interplay between three core issues. First, the opportunity and nature of team participation in entrepreneurial learning; second, the forms of shared practice they collectively exercise; and third, the influence of situated power on team learning, often determining what gets valued as learning and what does not.

What we find is that a positive, shared learning climate is characterised by trust, transparent leadership, shared reflective practice, and a willingness to challenge assumptions, learn from mistakes and engage in networks beyond the team. There is strong task cohesion, engagement and interdependence among the team members. However, there are, as we will see, many barriers in nurturing or creating this type of learning climate.

Perspectives on entrepreneurial learning

Entrepreneurial learning has been variously described by different authors as the study of how entrepreneurs negotiate the successful growth of a small business and as 'Learning to recognise and act on opportunities and interact socially to initiate, organise and manage ventures' (Rae, 2005, p. 324).

Within the context of the small firm management team, entrepreneurial learning is taken to mean how the team learn to act in entrepreneurial ways. How do they recognise and enact opportunities, manage and grow the business and learn about themselves? How do they cooperate or collaborate in learning? How are existing ideas and practices challenged and new ideas and behaviour adopted? How does the team learn to engage with external networks and contacts? And how do they learn – if they do – from mistakes?

There are three predominant theoretical perspectives on learning which are worth briefly exploring to understand what contribution they make in helping us frame and develop our understanding.

Learning as knowledge

The first of these may be best described as cognitive based; that is, learning is essentially an intellectual endeavour in which the continual assimilation of new knowledge allows for individuals to construct and modify mental schemas or models of their perceived world. This perspective emphasises the importance of acquiring, integrating and exploiting new knowledge in the small firm (Jones *et al.*, 2010) pointing to the significance of creating appropriate knowledge-sharing systems, capitalising on social capital and embedding knowledge into the organisational memory (Jones and Macpherson, 2006).

The accumulated stocks of knowledge developed within the firm build on previous experience that enables individuals to recognise patterns from the past and act accordingly. However, these also have the potential to constrain learning to known and familiar paths or patterns – known as path dependency (Tripsas and Gavetti, 2000).

Stocks of knowledge are not necessarily synonymous with learning; viewing entrepreneurial learning predominantly in terms of knowledge accumulation is a static interpretation of learning in which the term *learning* simply refers to establishing a causal relationship between an entrepreneur's previous experiences and the subsequent successful performance of the firm. This assumes of course that more knowledge means better learning or better performance, though there is little empirical evidence to suggest that this is the case. A further problem with this perspective is that it assumes that learning is simply the sum cognition of the individual members of the team, which fails to acknowledge the shared, participative and socially situated nature of learning within the context of a team.

Learning by doing

A second and widely accepted perspective of entrepreneurial learning shifts the focus away from knowledge accumulation, focusing instead on learning as a more dynamic and experiential process; learning by doing. Rae (2007) conceptualises this as negotiated and contextual learning involving an ongoing process of skills development, knowledge, know-how and experience through social interaction. This knowledge of what works, why, how and with whom, gained from experience and intuition, constitutes what has been described as practical theories of action that enable entrepreneurs to develop contextualised forms of knowing and perceiving connections between different aspects of their lives and practices (Shotter, 1993).

From this perspective learning is complex and iterative; experiences are transformed into knowledge in numerous different ways. The nature of the learning environment for small firms is one in which the ongoing formation of subjective and contextual knowledge is favoured over more objective but often decontextualised forms of learning, for example, in the classroom (Gibb, 1997).

However, although this experiential and highly contextualised form of learning is often very meaningful and relevant to the entrepreneur, it is often ad hoc and frequently not explicitly recognised or acknowledged as learning (Devins and Gold, 2004). The implication of this for the small firm management team is that the team may very well fail to recognise or understand the significance of team members' individual and shared learning. Cope (2005) observes that while much of the learning of entrepreneurs is action oriented, it is essential that they are not only capable as 'doers of action', but also capable of reflecting on these actions. Critical reflection brings meaning to experiences and holds the potential to move learning beyond simply following incremental, adaptive patterns into the possibility of transformative learning; namely developing new frames of reference.

Learning as socially situated

A third perspective of entrepreneurial learning shifts the focus on to the social, collective, situated and provisional nature of learning within a particular context, in which learning is located within a specific community and inseparable from everyday practice (Lave and Wenger, 1991). This perspective recognises that conversations and stories provide the means by which the team share experiences and construct a shared 'reality'. These shared discourses often shape what are acceptable ways to think, talk and act in the group and are influenced by an array of different issues such as identity, leadership, power, trust, legitimacy and cohesion, among other factors.

The notion of a community of practice is a useful one here, though exactly what this means is still ambiguous (Lindkvist, 2005). In the context of a small firm management team one might assume that this represents a group with common goals that have been practising together long enough to develop into a cohesive community with relationships of mutuality and shared understanding. From this perspective entrepreneurial learning not only resides within an individual but is dispersed among the team. Theoretically at least, new ideas or opportunities emerge via participation in the practices of the team which are institutionalised into the social structures and maintained in the tacit knowledge, customs and rituals of the management team.

What this suggests is that team members develop preferences and predispositions which strongly influence their learning. As collective perceptions and behaviours become embedded into the routines and practices of the team, they usually act to support and maintain the identity of the group. Consequently ideas, knowledge and practices that support rather than challenge the group are more likely to be adopted. This has been described as a 'dominant logic' (Prahalad and Bettis, 1986), a shared mental schema that is taken for granted by those within the community, in which learning usually becomes a self-reinforcing process of existing knowledge and perspectives. The possibility of moving away from existing patterns of thinking, unlearning, or generating new insights that radically challenge existing practices is therefore very difficult to bring about. Janis (1982) coined the phrase 'groupthink' to describe how individual thought and behaviour usually conform to the group norms, rendering new insights very difficult.

Alongside this are also the issues of conflict, politics and the use of power within the community. Roberts (2006) usefully highlights issues of power, trust and the predisposition of learners within the community as potential barriers to learning. Equally, it is argued that learning practices are fundamentally shaped, enabled and constrained within relations of power (Contu and Willmot, 2003)

The research that underpins the development of the model for this chapter is based on an in-depth qualitative case study of a small firm management team in a manufacturing business based in the West Midlands. This is explored from the lens of socially situated learning theory, looking at the contextual experiences of the team to offer some rich insights into their lived experience

The model in Figure 9.1 is taken from McKeown (2012b) and identifies three core themes that frame entrepreneurial learning within the context of the management team. These are: the nature and opportunity for participa-

Figure 9.1 Entrepreneurial learning in the small firm management team.

tion within the team; the forms of shared practice adopted, and finally the influence of power on team learning. From these three core themes, nine associated dimensions are identified which have the potential to either enable or constrain entrepreneurial learning in the small firm management team. The three core themes and associated dimensions are now discussed in more depth.

Learning and the nature of participation

The nature of participation relates to the extent to which members of the management team are both willing and able to engage and learn from both one another, external networks and contacts in order to develop the business and explore future opportunities. Participation is usually an iterative process of co-creating meaning and connections with others in the team, developing ideas and drawing on each other's skills and experience, but without necessarily explicitly realising that this is happening. The nature of participation in learning is often at a tacit level; understanding among different members of the team is primarily contextual and relates to experience and knowledge held informally in the team. Participation is characterised by three related dimensions: commitment/task cohesion, opportunity and motivation to engage, and boundary spanning inside and outside the firm.

Not surprisingly, levels of commitment and task cohesion within the entrepreneurial management team can be mixed and are often linked to issues of leadership and power. High levels of interdependence, trust, transparency in decision making and a willingness to engage, share ideas, knowledge and experience usually characterise a healthy learning climate. This environment enables team members to cross their functional areas of expertise to develop a more holistic and connected understanding of the business. In practice this is often fairly localised among particular team members rather than shared within the whole team. Conversely, the lack of opportunities to engage meaningfully can be a source of tension and frustration, demotivating members of the team and leading to relational conflict which can fractionalise the team and act as a barrier to learning. It is important to differentiate between what may be described as mere engagement in the practices of the community, at a relatively superficial level and full participation (Wenger, 1998). Full participation involves a more enduring form of commitment and a deeper sense of belonging, group identity and mutual responsibility to fellow team members.

The inequality of opportunity to fully participate or contribute to learning within the team can arise because of the status and influence of particular individuals, in which legitimacy is often ascribed on the basis of perceived credibility and local forms of tacit knowledge or ways of understanding and getting things done within the firm. More often than not this acts as a filtering process, in which new ideas, knowledge or ways of looking at problems in the business must successfully pass through the ascribed gatekeepers. In effect what this does is create a self-reinforcing dominant narrative affirming tried and trusted knowledge and marginalising whatever falls outside of this. This phenomenon was described by Edmondson (1999) as the concept of psychological safety; that is, the reluctance of team members to share certain ideas or knowledge which do not reinforce the dominant narrative or logic of the firm for fear of embarrassment or loss of credibility.

The importance of participation in external networks is also widely recognised in the literature as an essential part of the learning processes of small firms (Baron and Markman, 2000; Taylor and Thorpe, 2004; Shaw and Conway, 2000). These networks act as an important conduit for bringing new knowledge and experience into the firm and also as a valuable source of social capital to build networks and exploit opportunities. External contacts also hold the potential to act as catalysts that are able to question and challenge the existing assumptions prevalent in the firm.

Learning and forms of shared practice

Shared practices are usually deeply ingrained in the way things get done in the firm; very often they are not immediately explicit or even spoken, but are the taken-for-granted assumptions that underpin the collective thinking and consequent actions of team members. Practices usually develop out of a process of trial and error – discovering what works and what doesn't, practical theories for entrepreneurship, often intuitive involving tacit know-how and know-who (Rae, 2004).

An interesting conceptualisation of how small firms might learn through shared practice may be understood in terms of 'strategic space'; that is, the processes by which small firms are able to access the necessary resources, social capital and absorptive capacity, and have the motivation and capability to reflect upon existing practices (Jones *et al.*, 2010). However, a common problem in small firm management teams is the lack of time and appropriate space or opportunity to properly engage in reflection on actions either individually or as a team. When this does happen in small firms it is usually on an informal basis between individuals rather than a conscious effort to reflect and draw lessons from experience; consequently it does not become part of the shared memory or learning of the team. Unfortunately when mistakes or poor decisions are made they are often rationalised, defended or accompanied with a muddying of the waters to divert blame away from particular individuals rather than making any purposeful attempt to critically reflect on why things went wrong and what might be learned.

Although opportunities for critical reflection are limited, individuals do champion internal conversations or dialogues to affect change. However, sharing new ideas, insights or the recognition of potential opportunities with team members is often a difficult and slow process, particularly if this is a 'disruptive' discourse attempting to enact a different path or future opportunity for the business that moves it away from the underlying dominant narrative.

What is required is a sustained and reflective dialogue within the team that allows understanding to emerge and be collectively understood, adopted and integrated as part of the teams' new practices.

However, this reveals the difficulties associated with sharing an emerging understanding of what opportunities might represent and how different team members interpret and understand this. If opportunities are viewed as essentially socially constructed, they emerge as a result of what individuals do, rather than just as a result of what they see (Gartner *et al.*, 2003). In this sense, opportunities are made rather than found. Shane and Venkataraman (2000) reiterate that this stance, asserting the reason why certain individuals recognise opportunities while others don't, rests on two factors: 'firstly the possession of the prior information necessary to identify an opportunity and secondly the cognitive properties necessary to value it' (2000, p. 222). While different individuals possess different fragments of knowledge, they also reason with this knowledge in different ways and therefore reach different understandings.

For the small firm management team, this means communication, and in particular the art of listening and reflection as they attempt to make sense and recognise possible opportunities is extremely important. The concept of sense making developed by Weick (1995) argues that this is an ongoing process that has no beginning or end, but is in a continual state of transition and co-construction. Sense making is often a retrospective process in which lived experiences and past interactions with others are examined and ideally reflected upon to create a sense of meaning. It is also a process of enactment, to the extent that it attempts to create a link between interpretation and action. This is an important concept because it suggests that individuals construct, as part of their learned behaviour, realities which are then enacted or possibly imposed upon the small firm. This is particularly relevant in terms of the power relationship between the lead entrepreneur and other members of the management team, not least in terms of how opportunities are made, interpreted or recognised.

The practices of the small firm are usually deeply embedded in the social structure of the team and, given the self-reinforcing nature of practice coupled with weak critical reflection, it is perhaps not surprising that this pushes thinking and learning towards known and familiar paths. This is also combined with individual team members' own entrenched knowledge, experience and beliefs that they have acquired and nurtured over a considerable period of time and which are closely linked with their sense of identity, self-worth and often emotional commitment. It is not difficult to understand why the team struggles to learn or adopt new ideas, perspectives or innovative/experimental ways of doing things. Abandoning even part of these deeply ingrained mental schemas can be a painful and disturbing experience with the potential loss of perceived expertise and/or power within the firm.

This then leaves the question of how the management team learns to go beyond simply incremental or adaptive ways of doing things that are aligned in the dominant narrative within the firm. Cope (2005) explores this in terms of critical learning episodes, crisis events that challenge the existing thinking and assumptions of the entrepreneur. These are often painful and discontinuous episodes in the life of the entrepreneur that act as a catalyst to much deeper reflection and higher level learning.

Another way to conceptualise this is to consider the process of unlearning: letting go of existing knowledge or beliefs that limit or impede new learning. Newstrom (1983, p. 36) defines unlearning as 'reducing or eliminating pre-existing knowledge or habits that would otherwise present a formidable barrier to new learning'. What this acknowledges is that it is not necessarily the absence of knowledge, but the presence of prior and now limiting knowledge that necessitates unlearning. There is then a difference between learning and unlearning, and although unlearning usually precedes learning they frequently occur simultaneously. Unlearning is not simply attempting to wipe away past thinking, which is unrealistic, but a deliberate and conscious shift of an individual's underlying frame of reference. Rather than simply learning to replace one course of action with another, unlearning enables the emergence of new ways of thinking and behaving. However, as has already been discussed, letting go or releasing prior knowledge, practices and learning within the team is much easier said than done.

Challenging the taken-for-granted assumptions and practices of the firm is often beyond the capability of the team itself. McKeown (2012a) argues that what this often requires is the intervention of external actors in the form of either mentors or coaches to create the necessary reflective space in the team; drawing on their skills, credibility and trust within the team to legitimise new ways of thinking and behaving that enable them to break with the past. These essentially act as action learning interventions; the external actor as a credible and legitimate outsider challenging and destabilising the taken-for-granted assumptions of the firm. Drawing upon their perceived credibility, knowledge and experience they are able to foster strong conditions of trust and consequently open up opportunities for internal dialogue and reflection, introducing new knowledge, practices and most importantly permission for the team to reframe their thinking and learning.

The influence of power on learning

Power, in this context, may be understood as the capacity or ability of members of the team to assert influence or control over decision making and the legitimacy of particular knowledge, ideas or learning within the firm. Power is used as a key part of the filtering process of what gets valued and learned and what does not. The credibility and equality of different team members to exert power and influence is of course not necessarily equal among different members of the management team. It has been argued that learning is often shaped, enabled and constrained within relations of power, and that all learning in organisations is probably best understood through the lens of power (Contu and Willmot, 2003).

The first dimension explored in relation to power in Figure 9.1 is the style of leadership present in the small firm management team and in particular the lead entrepreneur. Many small firms fail to achieve their full potential because the lead entrepreneur does not have the necessary management and/or leadership skills to motivate or effectively lead others in the business as it grows (Leach and Kenny, 2000). This is commonly characterised by autocratic and hierarchical styles of leadership in which the management team have a more transactional relationship with the lead entrepreneur. This often undermines interdependency and a genuinely collaborative approach to developing the business. It can also erode mutual trust between team members and the lead entrepreneur and create factions within the management team with a perceived or real lack of legitimacy or equality in the learning process and recognition of contribution. Over the longer term this can dissipate the management teams' sense of shared vision and purpose for the business.

One particularly interesting perspective of leadership receiving increasing attention in the small firm literature is authentic entrepreneurial leadership (Jones and Crompton, 2009; Kempster and Cope, 2010). This makes a noticeable shift away from 'vertical' notions of the entrepreneurial leader as charismatic hero. These more distributed forms of leadership emphasise the importance of shared responsibility, accountability and participation in decision making, in which one of the key roles of leadership is to create the right conditions for learning; fostering high levels of trust, transparency, mutual respect, greater interdependency and team cohesion. This cultivates a learning climate that creates and encourages space and time for reflection and opportunities to challenge the dominant narratives and assumptions of the firm; enabling interdependent learning and creative ideas to flourish. This perspective to entrepreneurial leadership is not without its critics of course; Collinson and Collinson (2009) argue that there is a necessary ebb and flow between vertical and horizontal or shared forms of entrepreneurial leadership, particularly with regard to decision making.

The second dimension identified in the model is the importance of trust and mutual respect among members of the team. Roberts (2006) argues that trust is an essential prerequisite for creating a favourable learning environment that is open and willing to collaborate. Trust manifests itself within the team in terms of competency, intention and integrity.

Competency-based trust is the extent to which others feel confident in the skills, experience and ability of others as credible and worth listening to and learning from. Competency and credibility is an essential precursor for learning within the management team, both in terms of a willingness to learn from the expertise that different members of the team can contribute to, and in highlighting the boundaries to their knowledge.

Intentions-based trust refers to the extent to which members of the management team believe that their interests and well-being are valued and represented. Behavioural characteristics that influence the degree of intentions-based trust include acting with discretion, consistency in word and deed, fairness and transparency, and frequency and richness of communication (Abrams *et al.*, 2003).

From a learning perspective trust is important in enabling individuals to willingly share their thoughts or challenge one another without fear of rejection, embarrassment or damage to their reputation and self-esteem. Edmondson's notion of psychological safety within the team highlights the role trust and mutual respect play in promoting attentive listening, interpersonal support and an openness to learning. High levels of psychological safety also help to reduce individuals resorting to known and familiar paths of behaviour and falling back on defensive routines. Arygris and Schon's (1996) investigation of top management teams found that senior managers often created defensive barriers to rationalise poor decisions, unwilling to admit mistakes, seeking to blame others rather than solve problems. By contrast, adopting a problem-solving mentality helps the team become more willing to purposefully learn from mistakes; transparency within the firm allows the team to honestly reflect on what went wrong and why. By sharing experiences the team can collectively address the reasons for failure and reduce the likelihood of repeating the same mistakes (Edmondson, 1999). However, this is almost always dependent on the capability of the leader to inculcate a healthy and open climate for learning, building strong internal relationships of trust with members of the team.

Finally, integrity-based trust is concerned with consistently adhering to a set of principles that the trustee finds acceptable. While perhaps not as influential on learning as the previous two attributes of trust, integrity is important within the context of practice; for example, team members relying on the consistency of behaviour and motives in relation to the development of the business, honesty of actions or the completion of particular tasks.

As the model reveals, entrepreneurial learning within the context of the small firm management team is a complex and interrelated process that cannot be neatly partitioned. It is not solely concerned with the learning of a single entrepreneur, but rather a process of co-participation embedded in the shared practices of the management team, though this is often fractured and locally developed between particular members of the team rather than collectively shared. Learning is not simply the sum cognition of the individual members of the team, but the emergence of a shared understanding of how to develop the business and influenced by issues such as the degree of motivation and legitimacy/opportunity to engage and contribute to learning, the degree of commitment and task cohesion, opportunities for reflection and dialogue, the involvement or intervention of external actors, the style of leadership, and the degree of trust and transparency in the small firm. Significantly, the model highlights the centrality of embedded power relations in influencing opportunities for entrepreneurial learning; in particular the role of leadership and the conditions of trust, legitimacy and credibility in shaping what is learned.

Conclusions

The importance of learning and knowledge transfer in small firms is consistently stressed by successive governments as a mechanism by which to enhance the competitiveness of the UK economy. However, the track record of the numerous support programmes tasked with promoting, transferring and embedding new knowledge is questionable. This may be partly attributable to the unwanted bureaucracy that such programmes impose upon small firms, but in large part, it is argued, reflects a failure to acknowledge the complexity and contextual nature of learning in small firm management teams. Generic, one-size-fits-all approaches to assisting small firms are very unlikely to succeed. Instead, support interventions should aim to nurture appropriate learning spaces for the entrepreneur and management team, reflecting how management teams actually learn, and engaging with them in their specific context and lived world experience. This must be based on a relationship of trust and credibility, nurturing interdependency, transparency and an openness to change.

Many of the different support programmes designed to enhance the learning capability of small firms and transfer or embed knowledge and skills centre, understandably, on the content issues of knowledge and skills. However, in order to create a climate more conducive to learning itself, it may be more helpful to first focus on the relational dynamics of learning within the team itself. The model presented in this chapter suggests that developing a better understanding of the conditions that facilitate team learning is an important antecedent to the content of support programmes and subsequent learning itself. This should mark a shift in focus on to issues of team dynamics, creating more opportunities for reflection and a wider reflective dialogue within the team, as well as on how practice is shared and learning co-constructed, the significance of boundary spanning both within and beyond the business, and the role of entrepreneurial leadership and power and its impact on team learning.

Leadership training programmes in small firms have in the past been criticised as overly formalised, prescriptive and ultimately ineffectual (Devins *et al.*, 2005.) More effective interventions need to recognise the contextually sensitive and situated nature of learning in small firms, encouraging collaboration in the learning process with peers through learning networks. These networks can offer informal opportunities for knowledge and skill exchanges that are experiential and located within their particular contexts. This may involve peer learning through observation, shadowing entrepreneurial leaders and developing collaborative leadership learning relationships.

One interesting model of this type of engagement is the Leading Enterprise and Development Programme (LEAD) developed at Lancaster University. The programme, piloted in 2004, is a leadership development programme lasting ten months that is aimed at small businesses, usually involving cohorts of between fifteen and twenty-five business owners that demonstrate a strong growth orientation. The purpose of the programme is to create relational learning among participant entrepreneurs using a mixture of master classes, coaching, situated learning, shadowing, exchanges, and observational learning through action learning sets. The learning model of LEAD acknowledges the significance of creating reflective space from the routine working environment of the entrepreneur and the value of interacting with peers in high trust networks, inculcating openness in the development of new perspectives.

A quantitative evaluation of the programme by Wren and Jones (2012) revealed that it had a significant impact on developing leadership attributes among participants, self-efficacy, reflective practice and strategic vision. In terms of the outcomes for the business, turnover, profit and employment also showed significant improvements for participating small firms.

Interventions can of course come in many different shapes and sizes, but one particularly effective form, it is argued, is the role of mentors and coaches acting as catalysts to learning and unlearning. Their independence and perceived credibility, free from the historical baggage of the firm itself, can, as this chapter has revealed, act as a powerful legitimising influence for breaking with the past, in which assumptions and beliefs may, at least temporarily, be suspended, loosening their grip. In effect, this opens up the reflective space that is an essential antecedent to enable the small firm management team to rejoin the dots together in new patterns, as it reframes and enacts new ways of seeing its external environment and consequently new ways of behaving. This of course is dependent on establishing a high level of trust with these mentors and coaches, both in terms of their credibility, breadth of experience, knowledge and their ability to 'join' the entrepreneur and senior management team in understanding the real lived experience of the small firm.

Successful mentoring/coaching interventions are usually characterised by individuals who are empathetic listeners, sensitive to the particular context of the firm, but equally undaunted by the prospect of challenging existing ideas and practices. Building the trust relationship is essential and opens the door to legitimately raising concerns or doubts which in turn initiates the prospect of a wider dialogue and the emergence of the necessary reflective space to develop new perspectives and explore opportunities for experimentation. Coaching and mentoring programmes offer the opportunity to engage small firms in action-learning interventions with the whole team. However, while there is a growing interest in the value of these interventions to support entrepreneurial learning in small firms (NESTA, 2009) there is relatively little research in the small firm sector on the nature of these mentoring and coaching interventions, the interpersonal relationship developed, the value gained through these interventions and in what ways and to what extent learning is affected or new capabilities developed.

In environments that are increasingly characterised by economic uncertainty, volatility and discontinuous change, entrepreneurial learning in small firms becomes increasingly important. This chapter has explored this from a socially situated and participative learning perspective, developing a collaborative model for entrepreneurial learning in the small firm. It is hoped that this helps move others beyond the owner-centric perspectives that dominate the literature and acts as a platform for further discussion and future research into the nature of learning within the relational and lived experiences of the small firm management team.

References

Abrams, L.C., Cross, R., Lesser, E. and Levin, D.Z. (2003) Nurturing interpersonal trust in knowledge-sharing networks. *Academy of Management Executive*, 17(4), pp. 64–77.

Arygris, C. and Schon, D.A. (1996) *Organizational Learning II: Theory, method, and practice*. Reading, MA: Addison-Wesley.

Baron, R. and Markman, G. (2000) Beyond social capital: How social skills can enhance entrepreneurs' success. *Academy of Management Executive*, 14(1), pp. 106–116.

Collinson, D. and Collinson, M. (2009) Blended leadership: Employee perspectives on effective leadership in the UK further education sector. *Leadership*, 5(3), pp. 365–380.

Contu, A. and Willmott, H. (2003) Re-embedding situatedness: The importance of power relations in learning theory. *Organization Science*, 14(3), pp. 283–296.

Cooney, T.M. (2005) Editorial; What is an entrepreneurial team? *International Small Business Journal*, 23, pp. 226–235.

Cope, J. (2003) Entrepreneurial learning and critical reflection: Discontinuous events as triggers for higher level learning. *Management Learning*, 34(4), pp. 429–450.

—— (2005) Toward a dynamic learning perspective of entrepreneurship. *Entrepreneurship Theory and Practice*, 29(4), pp. 373–398.

Devins, D. and Gold, J. (2004) The value of HRD in small owner manager organisations. In J. Stewart and G. Beaver (ed.), *HRD in Small Organisations: Research and practice*. London: Routledge.

Devins, D., Gold, J., Johnson, S. and Holden, R. (2005) A conceptual model of management learning in micro businesses. *Education and Training*, 47(8/9), pp. 540–551.

Edmondson, A. (1999) Psychological safety and learning behaviour in work teams. *Administrative Science Quarterly*, 44, pp. 350–383.

Gartner, W.B., Carter, N. and Hills, G. (2003) The language of opportunity. In C. Steyaert and D. Hjorth (eds), *New Movements in Entrepreneurship*. Cheltenham: Edward Elgar, pp. 103–124.

Gherardi, S. (2001) From organizational learning to practice-based knowing. *Human Relations*, 54(1), pp. 131–139.

Gibb, A. (1997) Small firms training and competitiveness: Building on the small organisation as a learning organisation. *International Small Business Journal*, 15(3), pp. 13–29.

Janis, I.L. (1982) Groupthink (2nd edn). Boston, MA: Houghton Mifflin.

Jones, O. and Crompton, H. (2009) Enterprise logic and small firms: A model of authentic entrepreneurial leadership. *Journal of Strategy and Management*, 2(4), pp. 329–351.

Jones, O. and Macpherson, A. (2006) Inter-organizational learning and strategic renewal in SMEs: Extending the 4i network. *Long Range Planning*, 39(2), pp. 155–175.

Jones, O., Macpherson, A. and Thorpe, R. (2010) Learning in owner-managed small firms: Mediating artefacts and strategic space. *Entrepreneurship and Regional Development*, 22, pp. 649–673.

Kempster, S.J. and Cope, J. (2010) Learning to lead in the entrepreneurial context. *International Journal of Entrepreneurial Behaviour and Research*, 16(1), pp. 6–35.

Lave, J. and Wenger, E. (1991) *Situated Learning: Legitimate peripheral participation*. Cambridge: Cambridge University Press.

Leach, T. and Kenny, B. (2000) The role of professional development in stimulating changes in small growing business. *Continuing Professional Development Journal*, 3, pp. 7–22.

Lindkvist, L. (2005) Knowledge communities and knowledge collectivities: A typology of knowledge work in groups. *Journal of Management Review*, 42(6), pp. 1189–1210.

McKeown, I. (2010) No More Heroes: entrepreneurial learning in the SME management team, *Industry & Higher Education*, 24(6) pp. 429–441.

—— (2012a) Teaching old dogs new tricks: Why unlearning matters in SMEs. *The International Journal of Entrepreneurship and Innovation*, 13(1), pp. 25–34.

—— (2012b) Team learning in SMEs: Learning the lessons. *Industry and Higher Education*, 26(6), pp. 491–503.

NESTA (2009) *A Review of Mentoring Literature and Best Practice: Creative business mentor pilot report*. London: NESTA.

Newstrom, J.W. (1983) The management of unlearning: Exploding the 'clean slate' fallacy. *Training and Development Journal*, 37(8), p. 36.

Pittaway, L. and Thorpe, R. (2012) A framework for entrepreneurial learning: A tribute to Jason Cope. *Entrepreneurship and Regional Development*, 24, pp. 837–859.

Prahalad, C.K. and Bettis, R.A. (1986) The dominant logic: A new linkage between diversity and performance. *Strategic Management Journal (1986–1998)*, 7(6), p. 485.

Rae, D. (2004) Practical theories from entrepreneur's stories: Discursive approaches to entrepreneurial learning. *Journal of Small Business and Enterprise Development*, 11(2), pp. 195–202.

—— (2005) Entrepreneurial learning: A narrative based conceptual model. *Journal of Small Business and Enterprise Development*, 12(3), pp. 323–335.

—— (2007) *Entrepreneurship, from Opportunity to Action*. London: Palgrave Macmillan.

Roberts, J. (2006) Limits to communities of practice. *Journal of Management Studies*, 43(3), pp. 623–639.

Shane, S. and Venkataraman, S. (2000) The promise of entrepreneurship as a field of research. *Academy of Management Review*, 25(1), pp. 217–226.

Shaw, E. and Conway, S. (2000) Networking and the small firm. In S. Carter and D. Jones-Evans, *Enterprise and Small Business*. London: Routledge.

Shotter, J. (1993) *Conversational Realities*. London: Sage.

Taylor, D.W. and Thorpe, R. (2004) Entrepreneurial learning: A process of co-participation. *Journal of Small Business and Enterprise Development*, 11(2), pp. 203–211.

Thorpe, D., Anderson, L. and Gold, J. (2006) It's all action, it's all learning: Action learning in SMEs. *Journal of European Industrial Training*, 30(6), pp. 441–455.

Tripsas, M. and Gavetti, G. (2000) Capabilities, cognition and inertia: Evidence from digital imaging. *Strategic Management Journal*, 21, pp. 1147–1161.

Weick, K. (1995) *Sensemaking in Organisations*. Thousand Oaks, CA: Sage.

Wenger, E. (1998) *Communities of Practice: Learning, meaning, and identity*. Cambridge: Cambridge University Press.

Wren, C. and Jones, J. (2012) *Quantitative Evaluation of the LEAD Programme, 2004–11*. Newcastle: Newcastle University.

10 The struggle for product development and innovation in a family-owned business

A knowledge transfer partnership approach

Mark D'Souza-Mathew, Robert Pickard, Howard Pickard and Jeff Gold

Introduction

Entrepreneurial learning (EL) is concerned with both creating new ventures and how existing businesses are managed and sustained (Wang and Chugh 2014). Given that in the UK there are approximately three million family businesses, mostly small and medium-sized enterprises (SMEs), forming two-thirds of private sector firms (IFB 2011), there is an interest in how they can grow and provide a sustainable future for their owners and staff (Foreman-Peck 2012). Product development and innovation (PDI) therefore becomes crucial. However, if official figures are used to measure investment in such processes, it would suggest that such firms do proportionately less and as a consequence innovate less (Harris 2009). This may be partly explained by the relatively informal processes used leading to under-reporting of research and development (Lev 2001). However, a reliance on informality may just as easily result in PDI becoming a second or third order consideration as the business copes with the vagaries of resource limitations and is forced into a reactive strategic orientation (Qian and Li 2003). In EL terms, learning is adaptive by working within existing constraints and processes, and responding incrementally to any requirements for change. By contrast, for PDI to become significant, learning must become more generative, allowing key assumptions about the firm to be strategically surfaced and challenged (Slater and Narver 1995). Existing entrepreneurial business therefore face somewhat of a PDI conundrum. While studies suggest that formality of structure and strategy, just like larger firms, are likely to improve performance (Terziovski 2010), informality and adaptive learning provides a business with the ability to respond flexibly to customers – their nimbleness – and develop niche markets which provide a degree of competitive advantage over larger organisations in that niche (Fuchs *et al.* 2000). But such informality can, through resource constraints, pressures on meeting customer deadlines and restrictive performance measurement systems (Garengo *et al.* 2005), squeeze out the ability to innovate, even if there is a desire to do so.

Our aim in this chapter is to consider how a family-based business in West Yorkshire sought to make learning more generative by providing more recognition and action for PDI. Such an effort may be seen as crucial for an existing business, since it sustains the EL process and the development of the organisation (Rae 2000; Cope 2005). Therefore, in seeking to develop more PDI, the company formed a Knowledge Transfer Partnership (KTP) with the University of Leeds, leading to the appointment of a highly qualified chemical engineer. The chapter has been co-written with members of the KTP and is based on the idea that PDI in a mature family business is a disturbance to existing routines but a very necessary EL process to ensure sustainability. However, learning does become a struggle. We will report on the results of this struggle, drawing key lessons for PDI in family businesses. First, we will consider some of the key ideas of PDI in small family businesses and our view of EL.

Product development and innovation and EL

Much of the activity in a small family business is focused on dealing with present demands, solving problems as they occur or through making mistakes (Deakins 1996). Such processes are inherently reactive and give an impression that managers are consistently in fire-fighting mode. Thus even when managers do have time to take a more strategic view of activities, the return to everyday life soon prompts normal ways of working (Hudson *et al.* 2003), and that normality means that activities such as PDI become sidelined and informal.

Informality is a well-recognised feature of family business life (Goffee 1996), which has even been understood to some extent in policy making (CBI 2003; BIS 2012). It is argued that this informality provides a business with significant benefits, such as an ability to focus on niche markets based on a more limited variety of products and services. Furthermore, as a result of informal systems and structures, SMEs are more flexible and responsive to customers, and so acquire a competitive advantage in niche areas of their markets (Terziovski 2010). Interaction with customers and an understanding of their needs can result in the generation of new ideas, which may well result in innovation (Konsti-Laakso *et al.* 2012). However, informality also has its downsides for PDI, resulting in its relegation to a second or third order consideration through the failure to plan and devote sufficient resources. Even if new ideas can be generated, many businesses have faced a variety of obstacles to PDI such as limited resources and qualified expertise, and the ability to manage the innovation process (Mohen and Roller 2005). It is argued therefore that there is a need to formalise approaches to PDI and this will facilitate implementation (Prakash and Gupta 2008). Formalisation of PDI allows for a more considered approach, providing clarity and even responsibility within roles with sufficient time provided and accepted as necessary for new ideas to be generated and developed for feasibility. However, there are also downsides to formality with PDI through the risks attached to what may be uncertain outcomes and waste of resources entailed. Furthermore, family firms in particular may be averse to more formality, associating such a move with greater 'professionalism', which may be interpreted as a threat to valued beliefs about personal responsibility, family ownership and management, and succession (Stewart and Hitt 2011).

To avoid the pitfalls of either formality or informality in PDI, it is therefore suggested that attention needs to be paid to how innovation occurs, with particular emphasis on how implementation is managed. There is a need for an ongoing effort and commitment to PDI (Humphreys *et al.* 2005). However, this has to be done and seen to be done by managers, who signify the values, attitudes and behaviours that are preferred. In this way, a culture of support for PDI becomes possible and provides the context for PDI activities since so much of the relationship between innovation and performance is context dependent (Rosenbusch *et al.* 2011). Further, a crucial factor in context making is the innovation orientation of the SME, defined by Lumpkin and Dess (1996: 142) as a 'tendency to engage in and support new ideas, novelty, experimentation, and creative processes that may result in new products, services, technological processes'. This further allows for the learning and development of the necessary skills and capabilities, receptiveness to information from different sources, acceptance of risk taking and involvement in making decisions, all part of a learning orientation and the development of organisation learning capabilities which can play a key part in the link between an entrepreneurial orientation and enhancing organisation performance (Wang 2008; Alegre and Chiva 2013).

In addition, an innovation orientation is more likely to help attract specialised staff and encourage more commitment among existing employees (Zhou *et al.* 2005). A crucial finding from Rosenbusch *et al.*'s (2011) analysis is that an innovation orientation has to be strategic rather than just focusing on delivering products and services that are innovative. A strategic approach is also a more formal approach through the attention given to setting goals and consideration of how budgets and resources are allocated, which also indicate the firm's intentions to both internal and external stakeholders. For more mature organisations, such as the firm considered in this chapter, PDI can become restrained by past successes which justify engrained routines (Schreyögg and Kliesch-Eberl 2007). Innovation in such firms may be restricted to responding to problems within existing routines, with little time or ability to step back and reconsider the appropriateness of the routine.

PDI therefore represents quite a challenge to many family-based firms, where on the basis of a cherished culture and history there is a fear that resources could be wasted if PDI becomes too prominent. Even if market conditions suggest the need for PDI, the uncertain time lags inherent in the innovation process may prove too much of a risk for the commitment required for such decisions (Virtanen and Heimonen 2011). This can often lead to a retreat to the safety of reactive and informal PDI. Of course, even small changes through PDI may be seen as disturbances to existing ways of working. Learning will therefore be a requirement (Humphreys *et al.* 2005). Given that existing ways of working can become highly valued by staff, and protected if challenged, PDI has the strong potential to become a disturbance which can just as easily be dismissed as well as accepted. Support may therefore be needed to help managers become ambidextrous (O'Reilly and Tushman 2004), where managers can embrace both exploration for new products, structures and configurations, while also maintaining an exploitation of existing products and services, and ways of working and organising. Chang *et al.* (2011: 1671) argue, based on a survey of Scottish organisations, that smaller firms are in a good position to embrace what they call 'innovation ambidexterity' through their greater responsiveness internally to external changes. What is needed are 'appropriate organizational structures'. This requires a both/and approach to considering PDI and current working; if achieved, it can help a business to strategically align PDI processes with its culture (Narayanan 2001).

While seen as a crucial area of understanding for EL (Wang and Chugh 2014), the integration of exploitation and exploration in entrepreneurial firms is relatively under-researched. However, one study by Laforet (2011) was based on fifteen in-depth interviews with board members of SMEs. Each was considered to have an innovation orientation or was seeking to move in this direction. The results were indicative of the challenge and the struggle for PDI. There were positive outcomes from innovation such as better operations and efficiency, market advantage, employee satisfaction, and improved skills of the workforce and ways of working. Interestingly, Knowledge Transfer Partnerships featured in two of these interviews. There was also recognition of negative possibilities, such as financial risk through failure, uncontrollable growth, damage to reputation and loss of skilled staff through added pressure on work conditions. Such outcomes could sap the energy for PDI and prevent the development of innovation orientation. PDI is a risk and there are consequences, some of which are unintended or cannot be foreseen, which highlights the challenge and the struggle of PDI, and the disturbance it inevitably brings. Therefore, given the dilemmatic conditions for PDI decision making, it would be suggested that the pursuit of a path for PDI would involve attention to finding innovation possibilities in existing products and services. This may be achieved through modification and improvement but also through the introduction of external expertise to provoke the disturbance required (Autio 2009; Heimonen 2012).

Of course, even small changes through PDI may be seen as disturbances to existing ways of working. Learning therefore will be a requirement

(Humphreys *et al.* 2005). Given that existing ways of working can become highly valued by staff, and protected if challenged, it requires a strategic reconsideration of the direction of the company, involving a coordinated effort to adjust structures and systems so that new practices can be developed to allow innovation (Van de Ven 1986). PDI therefore has the strong potential to become a disturbance which can just as easily be dismissed as well as accepted. EL can become single-loop dependent with little chance for double-loop learning (Argyris 1993), which becomes necessary when competition and change challenge existing routines.

EL usually takes place in the midst of action that entrepreneurs learn; therefore such learning is based on their experiences (Rae and Carswell 2000). While most learning will be informal and hardly recognised as learning, there will also be occasions where such experiences become recognised as personally significant or critical events, creating insights that facilitate transformative learning (Cope and Watts 2000). Furthermore, this process can be enhanced through critical reflection (Cope 2003). These views of EL are augmented by ideas and frameworks which include the importance of an entrepreneur's identity, their career experiences, their relationship with the family (Rae 2004; Politis 2005), the influence of significant others as role models (Kempster 2009) and the networks of relationships that are maintained as crucial features of context (Taylor and Thorpe 2004).

Crucially, it is recognised that any understanding of EL has to take account of the situated experiences of practice within a community of practice, which closely aligns with the requirements, context, and indeed the history of the firm. This would suggest a need to consider EL in more collective terms, as an aspect of organisation learning by working with the metaphor of the organisation as a community, or, better, communities of practice (Lave and Wenger 1991). This considers learning as situated, which occurs through practice obtained from work. Situated learning, which is usually informal and incidental, would suggest that it is through participation in everyday practice, by watching, doing, talking and sharing stories, that a community develops. These processes allow members of a community to make meaning and sense of the ideas, and, through practice, they learn what is acceptable or not. Taking this view of learning, and with consideration for PDI, we can see how any attempt to interfere with what is acceptable to a community or communities may be considered as a disturbance. EL needs to be contextual and relational if it is to be accepted. Anyone outside the communities seeking to disturb the practice of communities may find difficulties in doing so; hence our view of PDI in a family business as a struggle. For the remainder of this chapter we will consider the case of Mark as the outsider and the business, LBBC.

The case

The business considered in this chapter is LBBC Technologies in Pudsey, West Yorkshire. LBBC began in 1876 as the Leeds Bradford Boiler Company, a manufacturer of boilers for local crane suppliers, tar stills and brewing pans for local pubs. Since 1892 it has remained connected to the same family and is now managed by their fifth generation. The company has become a leading designer and manufacturer of pressure vessels and autoclaves through precision engineering. It is a niche which has seen the company survive and sometimes prosper, but it has been recognised that, for long-term sustainability, there is a need for a more formal approach to PDI, through restructuring and the introduction of new routines. While LBBC has to some degree sought PDI through a number of collaborations with other organisations, including universities, it was recognised that a more stable and formalised approach was needed, because 'so many opportunities for product improvement and development' were being missed. Therefore a decision was taken by the owners to form a Knowledge Transfer Partnership (KTP) with the University of Leeds. KTPs are relationships formed between a company, an academic institution and a qualified person (Associate). The purpose is to allow the transfer of knowledge, technology or skills to the company from the academic institution, via the Associate (TSB 2013).

In the case of LBBC, once approval for the project was obtained, recruitment began for a qualified postgraduate in engineering. In November 2012, Mark was appointed as the Associate. Mark has an Honours degree in Nanotechnology, and, soon after joining the KTP, he gained his Ph.D. in the field of chemical engineering related to nanoparticles and functional surfaces. The aim of the KTP was double-edged. Specifically, there was a focus on surface engineering related to the dewaxing stage of the investment casting process. Through its deliverables, the primary goal of the KTP was to seek and implement a cost-effective resolution to what we will call *the deposition problem*. The secondary goal related more generically to PDI. LBBC had recently undergone restructuring to create a team committed to PDI. The goal was to complement the restructuring with an organised approach towards the collection and collation of new and existing knowledge.

Our approach to the study is based on the sociology of translation (Latour 1987; Callon 1986), which provided a framework for considering how the project worked. Sometimes referred to as actor network theory (ANT), the sociology of translation is concerned with the progression of knowledge towards its status of a truth or fact through a focus on the concerns of human interests. It is a method that is recognised as appropriate for the study of innovation (Miettinen 1999). Further, Fox (2000) argued that ANT, combined with a communities of practice perspective, can strengthen our understanding of organisation learning.

According to Latour (2005: 12), it is necessary 'to follow the actors themselves ... in order to learn from them'. The explanation of facts can then be discerned by working backwards to consider how various aspects of knowledge are 'assembled' to form a pattern which, through elaboration, repetition and possibly a great deal of argument, becomes accepted or appears to be accepted as a reality or truth. If we consider the move to a more formal PDI in LBBC, it may be seen as a knowledge progression and a flow of learning, which needs to be accepted as a new reality; therefore it can also be accepted as a process that may be rejected, disbelieved or, at the very least, greeted with scepticism; learning is interrupted or distorted.

In this chapter, the actor followed is Mark but the business owners Howard and Robert were fully supportive of his project and this research. Thus access to key interests and artefacts such as documents, emails and texts was gained. In addition, regular meetings with Mark were held, as were a number of meetings with Howard and Robert. It became possible to construct a view of the struggle of the moves being made and how PDI was embraced.

Struggle 1: Mark as a fact builder

KTPs always involve an agreed project plan with goals set and a quarterly monitoring process involving all partners, including a representative from the Technology Strategy Board, a government agency. To begin with, the pattern for PDI was set in motion through the proposal for a KTP, which in November 2012 resulted in Mark's appointment as the Associate. The proposal had a sufficiently solid status in this process, such that it became the baseline for the way the project unfolds and is used to review progress, although there is some degree of flexibility to allow deviation. The terms 'road map' and 'work plan' are used to set the direction around the project's objectives.

Mark's task was to continue the work of the project plan by constructing a pattern that lined up all the key factors in favour of what he wanted to achieve, referred to in the sociology of translation as enrolment (Callon 1986). Crucially this has to involve others but not just people; enrolment also involves other elements – both organic and non-organic – that are needed to form a pattern and to sustain it. Law (1992: 381) refers to this combination as a network of 'bits and pieces'. The test for Mark would be how far he could enrol the key factors in his favour. However, even if this can be achieved, he could not be certain that the pattern will hold together as he would desire, since the elements can take actions according to their own interests rather than Mark's. As an initial outsider to the various communities of practice, he lacked a certain legitimacy to practise. Despite his obvious academic credentials, he had not yet met the correct conditions for legitimacy to practise (Holland and Lave 2001). His efforts to enrol also faced a counter-enrolment (Callon and Law 1982); hence the struggle.

Mark faces what Latour (1987: 103) called the 'quandary of the fact-builder', in that in his quest to follow the road map as set out in the project plan, he cannot rely with certainty on the actions of others to stick to the map; they may just as easily follow their own 'interest maps' (Callon and Law 1982: 617). In an SME, very often such interest maps highlight values and desires of communities, developed over time through practise. To achieve translation requires skills of argumentation, negotiation, persuasion and justification, occurring principally through conversations in which fact building can be made meaningful. If this can work, Mark would become 'indispensable' within the company (Callon 1986: 6).

When Mark was appointed, the first translation was of the project plan by Mark so that he could decide how to allocate his time. While significance was given to the first part, the deposition problem, he quickly found that insufficient attention had been given to the second, the development of product development methodologies. In particular, he could see how he could add value to the project by aligning himself with the newly created product development team in LBBC. His interest map was adjusted accordingly to work with this emerging community of practice. Initial efforts to participate with the time highlighted his position on the periphery; he 'felt out of my depth in understanding the topics and motives at play'. This was his first struggle. Clearly as a novice in this particular community, he had still to find a way to legitimise his participation (Lave and Wenger 1991). Mark understood this and that the apparent disinterest in his work was 'due to my not having penetrated the inner circle yet, and therefore I felt only time would help settle'. As his attendance at the meetings became more regular, a sense of urgency was generated around a 'functional design idea generation structure'. Working with the team, Mark was able to focus discussion by recording minutes, thus creating a 'bit' for the pattern. Finding that the team were struggling to make progress on their interests due to lack of paperwork and manpower for processing data, he proposed an automated system that would integrate within LBBC's network, manage the collection of data and allow sorting so that design decisions could be made. He could even add further 'bits' to the pattern by setting up a server that hosted a dedicated website for the storage and automation of idea evaluation.

Latour (1987: 110) saw such moves as one of the easiest ways to enrol others in the creation of facts; translation one is a process of showing how what Mark wanted was also what the team wanted. In this way, while the team had goals for PDI, they were struggling to find a way forward. By focusing on their interests, Mark could move his forward too in what is referred to as a 'piggy-back' strategy. For the idea of the automated system to become more real, Mark needed to repeat his claims and elaborate further, allowing the emergence of what was quickly called the 'LBBC Technologies Portal'. He created an image in a map of possibilities for the portal, still rhetorical but yet sufficiently powerful for others to be enrolled as supporters. Through display, discussion and adjustment, the value of the proposed portal is an effect of the energy given to the claims by Mark, the product development team and others. Such others had to include Howard and Robert, and in turn other members of the KTP. Howard in particular could see that the portal could help 'service engineers', who operated close to customers and therefore could be a source of ideas for PDI, but who had 'expressed their frustration at being unable to register and capture ideas in real time'. The portal therefore would apparently solve the problem. Crucially, the portal, even though it was not yet operating, was sufficiently real, and through translation an association was forming that made it appear durable (Grint and Woolgar 1997), but would need ongoing and continuous persuasive talk to keep it moving (Bardini 2003). The first struggle was over.

The 'piggy-back strategy' continued. Mark could cite how LBBC:

> seems inundated by internal requests for change, even though processes have been put in place to address them. The product development methodology is part of an initiative to standardize these processes and to ensure all change is monitored, recorded and approved in a centralized and accessible location.

The *Portal* (Mark's emphasis) was an indication of the network becoming more concrete. With the help of an online learning resource (buildamodule.com), a content management system was installed and tailor-made for its application at LBBC. The 'alpha form' was soon ready, and Mark saw the need for further development prior to 'roll out'. Howard suggested that it didn't need to be fully developed before being rolled out to a selected group for testing. This presented an apparent dilemma for Mark between the need for 'fast' and 'slow' movement of the project. The second struggle was now beginning.

Mark did meet counter-enrolment efforts to 'park this work and pick it up again at an agreed time in the future'. However, he injected further energy into the translation with the result of a working *Portal*, shown as Figure 10.1.

At a demonstration of the *Portal* to the KTP, Mark could point to 118 ideas logged and the inclusion of the stages of uploading an idea, reviewing these ideas, through to effecting design changes based on the outcomes; this helps provide accountability. Robert, in-company supervisor in the KTP and a family owner of LBBC, could immediately see how this could replace the current process where ideas could get lost or cold; the *Portal* could help centralise all ideas and ensure they are dealt with as priorities dictate. However, others saw the need for adjustment, where only the high-value meaningful issues and significant ideas are logged. Furthermore, it was argued that it was not just the receipt of ideas that they wished to log, but the ability to see that they were being taken through to fruition. There

Figure 10.1 The *Portal* (source: ©LBBC).

was a need for 'a good evaluation process of which issues to deal with and which are most important would be useful, as well as an idea of how many times people should log in to check the Portal for new and existing projects'. For the KTP at least, the reality of the *Portal* was now more visible but its progress was still to be tested, or a trial of strength (Callon 1986), and this would need action. For Mark at this stage, this meant agreement to draw up a how-to guide for users. Nevertheless, the demonstration provided a situation for EL, and a proto-community of practice was now emerging.

While seeking to advance the *Portal*, Mark was also working on the first objective of the project – developing solutions for high-temperature fouling by organic compounds or *the deposition problem*. As LBBC's principal product which is widely used in the dewaxing stage of the investment casting process, the problem represented Mark's main struggle for PDI. Wax buildup reportedly impaired its efficient operation. Furthermore, a newly commissioned dewaxing autoclave had recently suffered from undesirable reactive processes occurring within the vessel which also warranted further investigation. Mark could see that in combination, a study of these reactions would also contribute to a consideration of the *deposition problem*. The KTP recognised that understanding the problem was a key issue, with a lot of work to do before this could be achieved and solutions proposed. Through recording in the project plan, the various actors came to define the story and enable the actions that followed. It also supports the view that PDI should initially consider innovation possibilities in existing products, and that external experts can provide the possibilities for action (Autio 2009; Heimonen 2012).

As Mark began this third struggle, he had certainly proven his expertise elsewhere as a highly academically qualified chemical engineer. While not averse to an academic slant, Howard was concerned to strike a balance between academic analysis and practical problem solving. However, Mark was quickly able to dispel any doubts by applying expertise to two small projects:

- Research, design and development of a standardised risk management document for the Boilerclave® in response to a customer requirement.
- Improving the efficiency of the alkaline hydrolysis processes of another product.

From both cases, Howard and Robert had evidence of the value of such expertise. In particular, the risk management documentation had never been previously supplied with an order. However, it would now be routinely supplied, and the process of producing it was embedded in the product development team – product development was now alive! Mark had gained some power through the translation of Howard and Robert's interest into his world and thereby began a degree of shift in the innovation culture (Burgess *et al.* 2000). Enrolling Howard and Robert allowed Mark some time and space to advance work on the *deposition problem*. He could devote energy to working carefully and *slowly* on the following:

- A literature review on the mechanism of wax deposition.
- A literature review on engineering solutions for preventing wax deposition.
- Analysis of wax blend components responsible for deposition.
- Isolation of asphaltenes in the anti-corrosive paint as a likely cause.
- Offering potential solutions to the problem.
- Construction of an experimental rig to test the effectiveness of coatings.

This list represents how Mark assembled a variety of 'heterogeneous' elements (Law 1992; Mol 2002) to make progress on the *deposition problem*. While much of this work took place either in the university or through visits to external sites, it required assembling by Mark for it to become available for making associations. However, there would need to be more attention to the relations that would be necessary for further facts to emerge and be considered as real or as a solution to the problem. Without such relations a solution could not exist and PDI would flounder (Alcadipani and Hassard 2010). This was also sensed by members of the KTP, who suggested that Mark 'should consider structuring his time spent at LBBC and to arrange short presentations to interested groups within the business, as appropriate'. The struggle for PDI moved to a new stage.

Struggle 2: Building relationships to make the facts

Having begun to develop sufficient claims for expertise, Mark needed to enrol others into the network of the *deposition problem*. His association of the literature, analytical results from the lab and representation in a 2D model formed the resource needed to persuade others to enrol. However, this would also require others, without any strong degree of certainty, to accept identities and roles, and to make choices in conformance to the direction set by Mark (Callon 1986). Latour's (1987: 111) translation two suggests that some might be prepared to follow Mark because their interests are best served by doing this, although this may be 'rare'. More possible is translation three or 'if you must make a short detour…', which would represent the solution to the *deposition problem* as something that could not be achieved quickly, but if others could follow Mark, even for a short time, it would enable their interests to be served. To do this, Mark would need to show that:

- the very quick route is not solely recommended;
- the slower route is clearly laid out;
- the slower route does not look too slow.

However, it is not sufficient to just show this; Mark must enact through conversations that build relationships (Mol 2002). The facts that already exist for Mark are still to be made with others, so he can expect contests, controversy and alternative views (Law 2008). As part of this struggle for acceptance, Mark needed to begin the process of persuasion, or rhetoric, defined by Latour (1987: 30) as 'the name of the discipline that has for millennia, studied how people are made to believe and behave and taught people how to persuade others'. Figure 10.2 highlights this process.

Through the conversations and relationships built with peers, it became apparent to Mark that there are significant differences in the problem-solving/innovation methodology employed by academia and a businesslike LBBC, where the former is generally focused on obtaining quantitative and unbiased data, and the latter is generally concerned with qualitative information regarding potential avenues. With a view to managing expectations, Mark's initial foray into project planning therefore led him to divide his antifouling research to tackle the *deposition problem* with a fast and slow route to cater to the qualitative and immediate industrial expectations, and the quantitative, systematic academic approach respectively. The marketing and communication phases would follow from completion of the fast track.

While aware that he was a disruptive force for PDI at LBBC, Mark struggled with the concept of his identity. This confusion had mostly to do with the difficulties peers have in accepting and understanding the nature of his job, and the outcome this has for their relationships. His membership of the varied communities of practice was still not regarded as fully

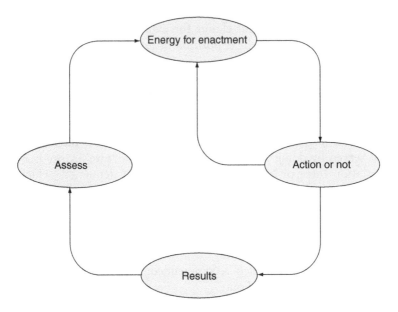

Figure 10.2 The cycle of rhetoric.

legitimate and so his identity was not yet shaped by them (Wenger 2000). Other issues such as an unclassified employment grade, and being exempt from companywide bonuses due to his status as a KTP Associate, added to his identity struggle. Due to the ingrained practices from his academic background, Mark was initially reluctant to give the qualitative pathways much emphasis, but he realised that the restructuring of his research would go a long way towards creating allies and supporters of his work so that the innovation culture could be nurtured. Initial results were well received. The fast-track methodology improved on the knee-jerk investigations common to LBBC, and introduced the concepts and principles of systematic studies. As several key employees would need to be involved in the design and operation of the test rig, it is expected that the methodology might see adoption within the innovation-minded workforce, and with careful guidance could improve the quality of collective conclusions. There had already been a surge in this type of thinking, as Mark had been inundated with requests for studies relating to process within various other product vessels.

Enrolment of others centred on the construction of the test rig, initially by finding the person to produce a CAD diagram. This involved what seemed to be an easy persuasion of Kyle, who was willing to produce a new version of the 2D model as 3D, a clear enhancement of the reality of the emerging solution. However, as translation theory would suggest, nothing can be so easy, and no sooner had Kyle agreed to become enrolled than he had diverted his energies elsewhere for the time being. Thus, as Mark was starting to understand, assembling the parts of the test rig for finding a solution to the deposition problem would be both uncertain and sometimes contested (Elbanna 2008). As the energiser for the enactment for the test rig to solve the *deposition problem*, the proxy for PDI in LBBC, Mark must attempt to build a set of relations with both people and materials such as 2D and 3D diagrams, but this is a difficult process and translations can fail, causing delays and setbacks (Law 2009).

Nevertheless, it was still possible for Mark to continue to appreciate the importance of relationships, both human and non-human. For example, he could order the panels for the rig, arrange for coatings with others outside the company, and he could attend a social event with staff at a greyhound track! In such ways, his job – nature or otherwise – PDI and the innovation culture are being enacted as a result of the relational effects that combine the social and the technical (Law 2009). He could also select the position of the test rig on the workshop floor, allocating the space to conduct the test and collect data through measurement, a necessary trial of strength (Callon 1986). Mark's proposed route was still controversial, so he needed to make the case for his representation stronger through measurement (Martin 2005), which would enable further strengthening through inscription devices such as figures and graphs (Smith *et al.* 2000).

While progress on the *deposition problem* was being made, and its translation was speeding up, Mark was able to question some fundamental aspects of the operation of the dewaxing autoclave. Speculation was in progress, and through conversation with his community at the university, some different and more radical possibilities surfaced. Such speculation in science has long been recognised as an essential part of reasoning, referred to as abduction, and seen as prior to induction and deduction. As Charles Sanders Peirce (1903) argued:

> Deduction proves that something must be; Induction shows that something actually is operative; Abduction … suggests that something may be.

Mark's speculation on the *deposition problem* led him to consider other possibilities, such as:

- Could wax deposition be the symptom of another reaction rather than a stand-alone problem?
- Was the geometry of the jacket more significant in creating temperature differences?

Such questions are abductive in the sense that they are a tentative presentation of possible truths and are new ideas that may work. In the words of Peirce, they become hypotheses 'on probation'. In this way, abductive reasoning has also been linked to creativity (Dyer 1986). Of course, to pursue these new ideas required the setting up of another road map, and one that would need a relatively slower journey. However, such hypotheses on probation carry 'contextual meaning' (Shotter 2008: 33) with a high possibility of a radical change in the design of the dewaxing autoclave that would represent a form of double-loop learning for LBBC (Argyris 1993).

In effect, the new possibilities represented a significant challenge to the way the dewaxing autoclave had been designed for the past forty years and therefore a very challenging struggle. He was suggesting a need to open the 'black box' (Latour 1987), but in doing so he was also setting up a slower route, the *internal jacket problem*, as well as continuing with the relatively quicker route, the *deposition problem*. He now had two detours for translation available: one relatively fast and the other relatively slow.

Working on what he now saw as a 'two-pronged attack', Mark knew he would have to assemble 'bits and pieces' for the translation of both routes. For the faster route a pattern was already discernible, but he could now argue that the benefits of the solution were likely to be 'short-lived'; sufficient for commerciality and even the requirements of the KTP, but fraught with uncertainty about eventual deterioration due to competing reactions and restrictive geometry. The slower route with its focus on the *jacket design* would require more time and resources, but with the prospect of an enduring solution to the problem. He regarded this route as a potential 'game-changer'.

Mark began to build the argument for the slower route, first, by doing a literature review on research into fouling within heat exchangers, so that he could build a model to explain what was happening within the Boilerclave®. He informally began the enrolment of Howard and then began sketching the process. To the sketches, he could add calculations and information from the support of specialists, before presentation to Howard and Robert.

Mark now injected energy into the cycle of rhetoric to persuade others about the importance of the slower route (Latour 1987). Mark assembled key elements of his own expertise, expressed in meanings to persuade others, initially Howard and Robert, but also non-human elements such as diagrams with coloured patterns, graphs and photographs, to be displayed on screen. Having established sufficient grounds for enrolling interests for the *deposition problem*, he now sought to repeat this for the slower route, the internal *jacket problem* (Callon and Latour 1982). However, as a challenge to a long-established feature of Boilerclave®, he was proposing generative learning (Senge 1990) which could easily provoke defensive responses from others (Argyris 1991).

In the presentation to Howard and Robert, the initial move was to revert to the faster route of wax deposition, but to place it alongside the revelation of a new participant, *scaling*, where thick deposits were observed on the heating elements. The problem was the behaviour of *scaling* related to surface roughness and concentration of contaminants in the boiler section – this was part of the internal *jacket* – which produced 'steady and self-increasing growth', along with other effects of corrosion and 'foaming', recognised immediately by Howard as having 'happened before'. Furthermore, there were the effects of increased operating costs as a consequence of *scaling*. It was easy to establish some fast routes:

1   Increase the frequency of boiler blow-downs.
2   Flush the boiler sections.
3   Add anti-*scaling* solutions.

Both Howard and Robert were enrolled in what appears to be a sensible change and, having secured this step, Mark showed how *scaling* in the internal *jacket* and the *deposition problem* were linked. *Scaling* was shown to be likely, but not yet proven, to be acting as a buffer to lower heat; it was Mark's theory or, better, a theory on probation in abductive terminology (Peirce 1903), so more testing was needed. Howard, possibly accepting the fact rather than a fact being made, considered that a 'double whammy' had been found with links to recent stories of undesirable reactions in the dewaxing autoclave. The first part of the struggle was complete, and Mark could now suggest the testing of wax-repellent solutions to line the interior of the vessel.

Were Howard and Robert still interested? Yes, 'super-interested'. This enabled Mark to present a final 'trick'. He produced four vials, each containing pellets of wax in various states of dissolution, and related these to high-definition electron microscope images of the same, which he used to raise doubts about the predominance of wax in the *deposition problem*. It was not just *wax*, but more so *the filler material*, leading Mark to conclude that *filler* becomes 'trapped' in the wax and causes *the deposition problem*. There were two possible options to proceed, both requiring testing and reviewing:

1   Surface coatings that enable both the wax and filling to be removed.
2   Reshaping the geometry of the dewaxing autoclave to enable wax and filler material to discharge more effectively.

On conclusion to the presentation, both Howard and Robert were enrolled in the faster and slower routes of translation three (Latour 1987). Wax was still the problem but now it was also seen as a *wax and filler deposition problem*. Mark could:

1   Conduct practical trials in real situations.
2   Complete further tests on coatings, depositions and *scaling*.
3   Prepare guidance on water treatment for customers.
4   Enrol the design engineers in both routes.

In agreeing to both routes, Howard and Robert were also agreeing as owners of LBBC to extend PDI to others, both within LBBC but also beyond, so becoming part of this network. They could also, along with Mark, enrol others to adopt roles within the network and play a part in the projects of *scaling, wax deposition and filling*, and even *jacket design* (Mahring et al., 2004). PDI was now becoming more stable and durable within LBBC as more participants were willing to join his community of practice to explore and exploit the opportunities emerging (Wang and Chugh 2014).

Conclusion

We began this chapter by pointing to the importance of family-owned businesses to the UK economy but how, due to the predominance of informal processes of EL, PDI in such firms seemed to be of less importance. It was also argued in much of the literature that the route to PDI lay in becoming more like large organisations. However, this would present something of a conundrum in that advantages could be gained by not aping PDI processes of larger organisations.

In the case of LBBC, a long-established family business, EL is mostly about sustaining the business into the future. Indeed, as a family with parents and sister also board members, sustainability was considered essential and PDI had been highly desired. However, the conundrum had played in a number of ventures for PDI with other organisations, but also a series of missed opportunities. There was a sense of being caught on the horns of an exploration/exploitation dilemma but in the light of a recent strategic review, from which the values of long-term security and sustainability emerged, the decision was made to tilt the position towards PDI through the KTP with Leeds University. This led to the appointment of Mark who, with his doctorate qualification in chemical engineering, was bound to create a disturbance to LBBC's life composed of different but long-standing communities of practice, requiring an ability to engage with a struggle for the making of PDI.

Dictionary meanings of the term *struggle* point to verbs and verbal phrases such as:

- Contend with an adversary or opposing force.
- Contend with a task, difficulty or problem.
- Strive for existence and identity.
- Advance with violent effort (e.g. through the snow).

From such a list of terms, we can point to the various ways by which Mark sought to enhance PDI and thereby influence EL. One of the main conclusions of this chapter is for the necessity of disturbance and struggle in EL to shift the balance towards PDI as exploration while retaining the importance of incremental learning in exploitation.

The struggle began from the moment Mark arrived when his very presence, for some, became the source of confusion or ambiguity, or, even worse, as non-person. That is, despite being very well qualified for PDI, he was an outsider who had not yet established a legitimacy to practise. There were adverse and opposing forces at work and Mark's first struggle, as a fact builder, was to find a way of arguing not only for the importance of the project but also for his own existence.

A crucial move in this first phase was to find ways of working with others' interests to advance his own. This enabled Mark to learn about the lives and problems of others so that they could learn what he could do for them. The pattern which followed, in the form of a server to host a website for the storage and evaluation of ideas for PDI, made visible to all how EL was occurring. Although relatively small, such learning with a real presence could then be shared with others. Struggling with a problem to be solved to help others was a quick way of creating interest in PDI. Therefore, we conclude that the foundation for PDI has been built on the establishment of a mutuality of interests and EL which works with current issues and problems.

Mark eventually demonstrated enough expertise to move the project forward. However, it was not enough to work with problems; he also had to redefine problems in new ways. In order to do this, he could not just expect the project to work without his efforts. However, such efforts need a response from others so that they also make efforts. As the case suggests, an innovation culture has to be constructed through a relational process in conversations requiring rhetoric, argument and the energy of a good story. EL is situated in such conversations and those seeking to make advances for PDI need to see themselves as relational leaders (Cunliffe 2011).

Of course, working in and with relationships cannot be guaranteed to secure results quickly or as desired. At times Mark's struggle was for his identity, which challenged his understanding of his own expertise and traditions. However, part of the way of dealing with the tensions was to offer a both/and approach in the form of fast and slow tracks. This became an important source of personal learning for Mark which eventually enabled him to offer both incremental and generative possibilities to Howard and Robert. A crucial skill and way of talking in shifting the culture was to offer dual tracks and reconcile dilemmas. The arguments had to be two-sided (Billig 1996). In this way, Mark was able to avoid the possible defensive behaviour in the face of double-loop learning, embracing positive attitudes that made radical innovations more possible (Hage 1980).

Finally, in unfolding this story of EL, we have shown the value of 'following the actors' in LBBC. While the principal actor may have been Mark, the story had to involve learning by others, including Howard, Robert and other staff at LBBC but also the 'bits and pieces' (Law 1992) which could all make a difference in PDI (Latour 2005). This had to include his pictures, notes, university, sample vials and so on. All played their part in assembling the elements of PDI, but continued energy would be needed to sustain its further progress. By creating the disturbance through Mark's project, Howard and Robert had set off a dynamic, that was not without difficulty but carried the prospect and opportunities for a more ongoing and continuous EL (Voudouris *et al.* 2011).

References

Alcadipani, R. and Hassard, J. (2010) Actor-network theory, organizations and critique: Towards a politics of organizing. *Organization* 17(4): 419–435.

Alegre, J. and Chiva, R. (2013) Linking entrepreneurial orientation and firm performance: The role of organizational learning capability and innovation performance. *Journal of Small Business Management* 51(4): 491–507.

Argyris, C. (1991) Teaching smart people how to learn. *Harvard Business Review*, May–June: 99–109.

—— (1993) *On Organizational Learning*. Cambridge, MA: Blackwell.

Autio, E. (2009) The Finnish paradox: The curious absence of high-growth entrepreneurship in Finland. ETLA, The Research Institute of the Finnish Economy, Helsinki, discussion papers no. 1197.

Bardini, T. (2003) What is actor-network theory? Available from http://carbon. cudenver.edu/~mryder/itc_data/ant_dff.html (accessed 2 October 2013).

Billig, M. (1996) *Arguing and Thinking: A rhetorical approach to social psychology*. Cambridge: Cambridge University Press.

BIS (2012) *Growth Accelerator*. London: Department of Business Innovation and Skills.

Burgess, J., Clark, J. and Harrison, K. (2000) Knowledges in action: An actor network analysis of a wetland agri-environment scheme. *Ecological Economics* 35: 119–132.

Callon, M. (1986) Some elements of a sociology of translation: Domestication of the scallops and the fishermen of St Brieuc Bay. In J. Law (ed.), *Power, Action and Belief: A new sociology of knowledge?* (pp. 196–233). London: Routledge.

Callon, M. and Law, J. (1982) On interests and their transformation: Enrolment and counter-enrolment. *Social Studies of Science* 12: 615–625.

CBI (2003) *Informality Works: A new approach to training for SMEs*. London: Confederation of British Industry.

Chang, Y-Y., Hughes, M. and Hotho, S. (2011) Internal and external antecedents of SMEs' innovation ambidexterity outcomes. *Management Decision* 49(10): 1658–1676.

Cope, J. (2003) Entrepreneurial learning and critical reflection. Discontinuous events as triggers for 'higher-level' learning. *Management Learning* 34(4): 429–450.

—— (2005) Toward a dynamic learning perspective of entrepreneurship. *Entrepreneurship Theory and Practice* 29(4): 373–397.

Cope, J. and Watts, G. (2000) Learning by doing: An exploration of experience, critical incidents and reflection in entrepreneurial learning. *International Journal of Entrepreneurial Behaviour and Research* 6(3): 104–124.

Cunliffe, A. (2011) Relational leadership. *Human Relations* 64(11): 1425–1449.

Deakins, D. (1996) *Entrepreneurship and Small Firms*. London: McGraw-Hill.

Dyer, A. (1986) Veblen on scientific creativity: The influence of Charles S. Peirce. *Journal of Economic Issues* 20(1): 21–41.

Eisenhardt, K.M. and Martin, J.A. (2000) Dynamic capabilities: What are they? *Strategic Management Journal* 21(10/11): 1105–1121.

Elbanna, A. (2008) Strategic systems implementation: Diffusion through drift. *Journal of Information Technology* 23(2): 89–96.

Foreman-Peck, J. (2012) Effectiveness and efficiency of SME innovation policy. Cardiff Economic Working Papers, Cardiff.

Fox, S. (2000) Communities of practice, Foucault and actor-network theory. *Journal of Management Studies* 37(6): 853–868.

Fuchs, P.H., Mifflin, K.E., Miller, D. and Whitney, D.O. (2000) Strategic integration: Competing in the age of capability. *California Management Review* 42: 118–147.

Garengo, P., Biazzo, S. and Bititc, U.S. (2005) Performance measurement systems in SMEs: A review for a research agenda. *International Journal of Management Reviews* 7(1): 25–47.

Goffee, R. (1996) Understanding family businesses: Issues for further research. *International Journal of Entrepreneurial Behaviour and Research* 2(1): 36–48.

Gray, C. (2002) Entrepreneurship resistance to change and growth in small firms. *Journal of Small Business and Enterprise Development* 9(1): 61–72.

Grint, K. and Woolgar, S. (1997) *The Machine at Work*. Cambridge: Polity Press.

Hage, J. (1980) *Theories of Organizations: Form, process, and transformation*. New York: John Wiley & Sons.

Harris, R. (2008) An Empirical Study of the Respective Contributions of Exporting and Foreign Direct Investment to UK R&D. UK Trade and Industry, November.

Heimonen, T. (2012) What are the factors that affect innovation in growing SMEs? *European Journal of Innovation Management* 15(1): 122–144.

Holland, D. and Lave, J. (2001) History in person: An introduction. In D. Holland and J. Lave (eds), *History in Person: Enduring struggles, contentious practice, intimate identities* (pp. 3–33). Santa Fe and Oxford: School of American Research Press and James Currey.

Hudson M.A., Smart, A. and Bourne, M. (2001) Theory and practice in SME performance measurement systems. *International Journal of Operations and Production Management* 21(8): 1096–1115.

Humphreys, P., McAdam, R. and Leckey, J. (2005) Longitudinal evaluation of innovation implementation in SMEs. *European Journal of Innovation Management* 8(3): 283–304.

IFB (2011) *The UK Family Business Sector*. London: Institute for Family Business.

Kempster, S. (2009) Observing the invisible. *Journal of Management Development* 28(5): 439–456.

Konsti-Laakso, S., Pihkala, T. and Kraus, S. (2012) Facilitating SME innovation capability through business networking. *Innovation Capacity and Business Networking* 21(1): 93–106.

Laforet, S. (2011) A framework of organisational innovation and outcomes in SMEs. *International Journal of Entrepreneurial Behaviour and Research* 17(4): 380–408.

Latour, B. (1986) The powers of association. In J. Law (ed.), *Power, Action and Belief*. (pp. 264–280). London: Routledge.

—— (1987) *Science in Action*. Cambridge, MA: Harvard University Press.

—— (1991) Technology is society made durable. In J. Law (ed.), *A Sociology of Monstors: Essays on power, technology and domination* (pp. 103–131). London: Routledge.

—— (2005) *Reassembling the Social*. Oxford: Oxford University Press.

Lave, J. and Wenger, E. (1991) *Situated Learning: Legitimate peripheral participation*. Cambridge: Cambridge University Press.

Law, J. (1992) Notes on the theory of the actor-network: Ordering, strategy and heterogeneity. *Systems Practice* 5(4): 379–393.

—— (2008) On sociology and STS. *Sociological Review* 56(4): 623–649.

—— (2009) Actor network theory and material semiotics. In B. Turner (ed.), *The New Blackwell Companion to Social Theory* (pp. 141–158). Oxford: Blackwell.

Lev, B. (2001) *Intangibles: Management, measurement, and reporting*. Washington, DC: Brookings Institution Press.

Lumpkin, G.T. and Dess, G.G. (1996) Clarifying the entrepreneurial orientation construct and linking it to performance. *Academy of Management Review* 21(1): 135–172.

Mahring, M., Holmstrom, J., Keil, M. and Montealegre, R. (2004) Trojan actor-networks and swift translation: Bringing actor-network theory to IT project escalation studies. *Information Technology and People* 17(2): 210–238.

Martin, A. (2005) Agents in inter-action: Bruno Latour and agency. *Journal of Archaeological Method and Theory* 12(4): 283–310.

Miettinen, R. (1999) The riddle of things: Activity theory and actor network theory as approaches to studying innovations. *Mind, Culture and Society* 6(3): 170–195.

Miller, D. and Friesen, P.H. (1983) Strategy-making and environment: The third link. *Strategic Management Journal* 4(3): 221–235.

Mohen, P. and Roller, L. (2005) Complementarities in innovation policy. *European Economic Review* 46: 1431–1450.

Mol, A. (2002) *The Body Multiple: Atherosclerosis in practice*. Durham, NC: Duke University Press.

Narayanan, V.K. (2001) *Managing Technology and Innovation for Competitive Advantage*. Upper Saddle River, NJ: Prentice-Hall.

O'Reilly, C.A. and Tushman, M.L. (2004) The Ambidextrous Organization. *Harvard Business Review* 82(4): 74–81.

Peirce, C.S. (1903) Harvard Lectures on Pragmatism, *CP* 5(1): 71–172.

Politis, D. (2005) The process of entrepreneurial learning: A conceptual framework. *Entrpreneurship, Theory and Practice*, July: 399–424.

Prakash, Y. and Gupta, M. (2008) Exploring the relationship between organisation structure and perceived innovation in the manufacturing sector of India. *Singapore Management Review* 30(1): 55–76.

Qian, G. and Li, L. (2003) Profitability of small- and medium-sized enterprises in high-tech industries: The case of the biotechnology industry. *Strategic Management Journal* 24(9): 881–887.

Rae, D. (2000) Understanding entrepreneurial learning: A question of how? *International Journal of Entrepreneurial Behaviour and Research* 6(3): 145–159.

—— (2004) Entrepreneurial learning: A practical model from the creative industries. *Education and Training* 46(8/9): 492–500.

—— (2005) Entrepreneurial learning: A narrative-based conceptual model. *Journal of Small Business and Enterprise Development* 12(3): 323–335.

Rae, D. and Carswell, M. (2000) Using a life-story approach in researching entrepreneurial learning: The development of a conceptual model and its implications in the design of learning experiences. *Education and Training* 42(4/5): 220–227.

Rosenbusch, N., Brinckmann, J. and Bausch, A. (2011) Is innovation always beneficial? A meta-analysis of the relationship between innovation and performance in SMEs. *Journal of Business Venturing* 26: 441–457.

Schreyögg, G. and Kliesch-Eberl, M. (2007) How dynamic can organizational capabilities be? Towards a dual-process model of capability dynamization. *Strategic Management Journal* 28(9): 913–933.

Senge, P.M. (1990) *The Fifth Discipline: The art and practice of the learning organisation.* New York: Currency Doubleday.

Slater, S.F. and Narver, J.C. (1995) Market orientation and the learning organization. *Journal of Marketing* 59(3): 63–74.

Shotter, J. (2008) Embodiment, abduction and difficulties of orientation: On coming to feel 'at home' in the world. *History and Philosophy of Psychology* 10(2): 27–38.

Smith, L., Best, L., Stubbs, D.A., Johnston, J. and Archibald, A. (2000) Survey of inscription practices scientific graphs and the hierarchy of the sciences: A Latourian survey of inscription practices. *Social Studies of Science* 30(1): 73–94.

Stewart, A. and Hitt, M. (2011) Why can't a family business be more like a non-family business? Modes of professionalization in family firms. *Family Business Review* 25(1): 58–86.

Taylor, D.W. and Thorpe, R. (2004) Entrpreneurial learning: A process of co-participation. *Journal of Small Business and Enterprise Development* 11(2): 203–211.

Terziovski, M. (2010) Innovation practice and its performance implications in small and medium enterprises (SMEs) in the manufacturing sector: A resource-based view. *Strategic Management Journal* 31: 892–902.

TSB (2013) *Knowledge Transfer Partnerships: Achievements and outcomes 2011/12.* Swindon: Technology Strategy Board.

Virtanen, M. and Heimonen, T. (2011) The development of high growth and highly successful SMEs: Cases from Eastern Finland. *International Journal of Technology Transfer and Commercialisation* 10(3/4): 411–432.

Van de Ven, A.H. (1986) Central problems in the management of innovation. *Management Science* 32(5): 590–607.

Voudouris, I., Dimitratos, P. and Salavou, H. (2011). Entrepreneurial learning in the international new hightechnology venture. *International Small Business Journal* 29(3): 238–258.

Wang, C. (2008) Entrepreneurial orientation, learning orientation, and firm performance. *Entrepreneurship, Theory and Practice* 32(4): 635–657.

Wang, C. and Chugh, H. (2014) Entrepreneurial learning: Past research and future challenges. *International Journal of Management Reviews* 16(1): 24–61.

Weick, K., Sutcliffe, K. and Obstfeld, D. (2005) Organizing and the process of sensemaking. *Organization Science* 16(4): 409–421.

Wenger, E. (2000) Communities of practice and social learning systems. *Organization* 7(2): 225–246.

Zhou, K.Z., Gao, G.Y., Yang, Z. and Zhou, N. (2005) Developing strategic orientation in China: Antecedents and consequences of market and innovation orientations. *Journal of Business Research* 58(8): 1049–1058.

11 Learning to evolve

Developing a practice-based evolutionary language of entrepreneurial learning

Dermot Breslin

Introduction

A core theme running through this text is the importance of entrepreneurial learning and adaptation as businesses struggle for survival. This metaphor of a struggle for survival which pervades the literature in entrepreneurship is derived from Herbert Spencer (1864) first coining the term to describe biological evolution, following a reading of Darwin's *Origin of Species* (1859). This heuristic relationship between the biological evolution of organisms and the socio-economic evolution of organisations has indeed attracted much attention before, during and since the time of Darwin. Scholars have thus wondered whether lessons may be learned from the living world around us. One hundred and fifty years years after Darwin wrote his seminal book on the origin of species, science has shown how nature's survivors learn to adapt to the tumultuous changes in the Earth's history, with some microscopic organisms adapting to change over the millennia. Might small and growing organisations likewise adapt to the increasingly competitive, global and hostile economic environments facing them in the twenty-first century? To this end, a group of social scientists have been searching for clues in this evolutionary story, with a view towards understanding the wider 'evolution' of culture, politics, technology, and more recently organisations (Aldrich and Ruef 2006; Arthur 2009; Boschma and Frenken 2011; Boschma and Martin 2007; Breslin 2008a; Cavalli-Sforza 2001; Dawkins 1983; Dennett 1995; Dobson 2012; Durham 1991; Essletzbichler and Rigby 2005; Nelson and Winter 1982; Plotkin 1994; Richerson and Boyd 2005; Tooby and Cosmides 1992). In light of the need for nascent and growing organisations to learn to adapt in the face of such socio-economic and political challenges, an evolutionary language is emerging which offers entrepreneurs the opportunity to draw from nature's survivors. In this chapter, this practice-based language in which individuals learn to evolve will be explored.

Entrepreneurial learning and evolving components of knowledge

Entrepreneurial learning is a core process in the birth, growth and ultimately survival of small businesses. Given the centrality of the founding entrepreneur in such enterprises, this study of learning has focused on the individual as a level of analysis, as the behaviour of the organisation becomes inseparable from learning at the level of the entrepreneur (Deakins and Freel 1998; Kim 1993). In terms of the emerging behaviour of entrepreneurs, attention has centred on evolving components of knowledge, including heuristics, cognitive frameworks and entrepreneurial skills (Breslin 2008b; Forbes 1999; Grégoire *et al.* 2011; Loasby 2007). Many have stressed the importance of entrepreneurial heuristics when completing both novelty-generating activities such as the discovery of opportunities, and more routine functional activities associated with the exploitation of these opportunities (Busenitz and Barney 1997; Forbes 1999; Loasby 2007; Shane and Venkataraman 2000; Ucbasaran *et al.* 2001). These cognitive heuristics refer to simplified rules of thumb or strategies which entrepreneurs employ as they make decisions in the face of uncertainties, and which they develop to assist in the perception and interpretation of changes in the marketplace (Daft and Weick 1984; Forbes 1999). Others highlight the role played by cognitive frameworks which entrepreneurs use to model the world around them and help them make sense of an uncertain landscape (Busenitz and Lau 1996; Cope 2005; Dutta and Crossan 2005; Kirzner 1997). In some instances these mental models can help entrepreneurs identify new means–ends relationships in the discovery of opportunities (Baron 2007; Shane and Venkataraman 2000), and serve as a basis for making predictions about how to exploit these opportunities (Busenitz and Lau 1996; Gaglio and Katz 2001). In this way, entrepreneurs might develop unique ways of viewing the world around them and in so doing spot under-exploited opportunities. Thus, in addition to entrepreneurial heuristics, cognitive frameworks clearly have a role to play in explaining how entrepreneurs learn and adapt to uncertainties associated with the start-up process. In terms of the process of entrepreneurial learning, some argue that entrepreneurs learn through a process of 'learning by doing' as they launch a new venture (Cope 2005; Deakins and Freel 1998; Gartner 1984; Politis 2005), with more successful entrepreneurial learning resulting in better adapted skills, heuristics and frameworks. Similarly, others refer to entrepreneurs acquiring *entrepreneurial knowledge* through the experiences of start-up (Deakins and Freel 1998; Politis 2005) as they discover and exploit opportunities. In this way, entrepreneurs learn through trial and error, learning from mistakes and interpreting feedback from the environment (Gibb 1997). Thus entrepreneurs develop skills and competences to complete tasks in the production and delivery of products and services (Aldrich and Ruef 2006) as they exploit opportunities over time

(Shane and Venkataraman 2000), and the entrepreneur acquires and develops these various knowledge components as the needs of the business dictate.

However, a key element in the development and survival of small businesses relates to learning within the fledgling team of individuals and not just the entrepreneur, as growth brings with it an increasing need to routinise knowledge and behaviours within the growing group of employees (Aldrich and Ruef 2006; Churchill and Lewis 1983; Greiner 1972; Politis 2005; Scott and Bruce 1987). Wang and Chugh (2014) recently point to the paucity of research on collective learning in entrepreneurial firms, and with this the process of opportunity exploitation. In this way, successful skills developed by the entrepreneur need to be 'transferred' to others within the company (Dutta and Crossan 2005; Jones and Macpherson 2006; Macpherson and Holt 2007), and this process is again typically shown to involve a process of action learning. In this sense individuals work closely together, sharing and interpreting collective experiences as they develop a distinct group identity through participation and socialisation (Jones and Macpherson 2006; Lave and Wenger 1990).However, the entrepreneur is a central figure in this process and the collectivisation of practices at the very birth of organisations (Clarysse and Moray 2002; Forbes *et al.* 2006) can have a profound, long-lasting impact on the future development of the business (Aldrich and Ruef 2006; Baron *et al.* 2001). In these models, growth is thus viewed largely as a one-way transfer of knowledge between the entrepreneur and the group of employees, through the routinisation of existing behaviours and, where these routines are recurring, collective patterns of behaviours which develop within the growing organisation (Nelson and Winter 1982). Unlike the 'entrepreneurial heuristics' discussed above, these concepts are often associated with mindless, automatic behaviours more familiar to large, established organisations. Indeed, many scholars have highlighted how the entrenchment of such routinised behaviours can result in the subsequent ossification of behaviours within the growing firm, undermining the continuing adaptive learning of the entrepreneur (Churchill and Lewis 1983; Greiner 1972; Scott and Bruce 1987). As a result there can be a move away from the exploration of knowledge towards the exploitation of what is already known and fine-tuning of routines (Cyert and March 1963; Levitt and March 1988; Nelson and Winter 1982; Politis 2005) as small firms grow. Thus, on the one hand entrepreneurs need to develop skills and knowledge within this team in order to free up valuable cognitive resources, but on the other they need to retain the flexibility and adaptivity which underpins learning in the early stages of the firm's existence. As a result, many have searched for ways in which organisations can balance the ongoing need for both the exploitation of existing knowledge and exploration of new sources of knowledge as the firm grows (Breslin 2010; Macpherson and Holt 2007; March 1991; Phelps *et al.* 2007).

In summary, a narrative emerges in which entrepreneurial learning is seen as the acquisition and development of entrepreneurial skills, heuristics and frameworks to meet the demands of the business, with research largely focusing on the entrepreneur as a level of analysis. Furthermore, this process is practice-based, involving 'learning by doing', socialisation and participation (Cope 2005; Deakins and Freel 1998; Gartner 1984; Lave and Wenger 1990; Politis 2005). Given the importance of these knowledge components to the survival of the business, one might argue that surely they should become the focus of attention rather than the entrepreneur. Moreover, others are involved in the process, including the entrepreneurial team, employees and wider network (Dobson *et al.* 2013; Dutta and Crossan 2005; Gibb 1997; Jack *et al.* 2008; Jones and Macpherson 2006; Macpherson and Holt 2007). Therefore some of this knowledge assumes a *collective nature*, and a study of the entrepreneur alone would fail to capture its evolving nature and development over time. Each evolving element of knowledge is uniquely adapted for its role in the exploration and exploitation of opportunities, and for the organisation and industry in which it operates.

The evolutionary approach and what evolves

This narrative of components of knowledge at first emerging within the nascent small business, and later becoming selectively retained within the growing organisation, shares many parallels with studies of cultural evolution (Breslin 2008b, 2010). In the biological world evolution occurs over time through the mechanisms of variation (of genotypes), selection (of the consequent phenotype) and retention (of the underlying genotype), where the genotype is defined as the information inherited by an individual from its parents (i.e. genes), which has the potential to be transmitted to future generations. The phenotype on the other hand is the developmental expression of the genotype in a particular environment, as manifest through the physical characteristics of the organism. Abstracting from the specifics of biology and genes, one can likewise conceptualise the evolution of heuristics, frameworks and routines through the mechanisms of variation–selection–retention, and a number of scholars have adopted this approach to study organisational change and learning (Aldrich and Ruef 2006; Breslin 2008a; Burgelman 1991; Jones 2005; Loasby 2003; Murmann 2003). However, care must be taken in transferring concepts across disciplines through the use of analogies given the clear differences between biological and 'organisational evolution' (Breslin 2011). This relates in particular to the question of the unit of evolution, or 'what is evolving?' (Breslin forthcoming). In the past few decades a number of different candidates have been put forward depending on the level of analysis. Population ecologists propose organisational forms (Hannan and Freeman 1977) given their focus on populations of organisations. Others focusing on the level of the organisation have proposed a number of concepts for the genotype, including routines and competences (Aldrich and Ruef 2006), comps (McKelvey 1982), routines (Nelson and Winter 1982), strategic initiatives (Burgelman 1991), ideas/knowledge (Murmann 2003) and techniques (Mokyr 2000).

When studying entrepreneurship, identifying this evolving unit becomes more difficult. Does the entrepreneur evolve? Clearly the entrepreneur evolves in a biological sense, as a member of a society passing on key genes to successive generations. In this way researchers may seek to unpick aspects of behaviour which are 'linked' to the genetic make-up of the entrepreneur, in a manner similar to how evolutionary psychologists and sociobiologists seek to explain the evolution of an individual's behaviour (Shane 2010; Tooby and Cosmides 1992). In this approach, genes are clearly the focus of attention, alongside their phenotypic expression in behaviour. However, if one is focusing on the evolution of knowledge itself, a knowledge equivalent of the genotype and phenotype is needed. For instance, in many of these accounts, the 'organisation' has been treated as some organism-like, bounded entity, which acts as a vehicle for bundles of knowledge. In this sense, the organisation is the phenotype carrying bundles of knowledge (or routines) in much the same way that our bodies act as vehicles for our genes (Dawkins 1976, 1982). As a result these 'bounded entities', organisations, 'carry' the routines, which are in turn 'kept alive within the boundaries of organizations' (Aldrich and Ruef 2006: 140). As a consequence, the fate of both the routine and the organisation are bound together (Aldrich and Ruef 2006; Hodgson and Knudsen 2010). In these organisation-as-vehicle accounts, learning occurs through the selective retention of routines based on their fit with the needs of the environment.

However, if one assumes that entrepreneurial learning occurs through action and practice, as noted above, these accounts become problematic. First, knowledge cannot be seen to be accumulated or indeed separated from the specific activity or practice involved (Orlikowski 2002). Therefore to link heuristics or routines with the socially constructed concept of the organisation becomes problematic. For instance, routines can pass between organisations and through spin-outs (Cordes 2006; Szulanski 2000; Szulanski and Winter 2002). Moreover, routines are frequently discontinued within organisations, as groups innovate, change and improvise behaviours (Feldman and Pentland 2003) and the cognitive reasoning underlying these behaviours. As a consequence the 'life' of the routine is not always tied to the 'life' of one particular group or organisation. Knowledge-in-practice on the other hand is tied to the fate of the practice and not the organization. Second, it cannot be assumed that this continually evolving knowledge-in-practice is a static entity, subject to forces acting beyond the boundaries of the group or even the organisation. Its maintenance or variation occurs through the continual interrelationship between local performances and abstracted cognitive structures (Feldman and Orlikowski 2011). Third, it is through the individuals enacting and participating in the activity that the dynamics of these evolving components of knowledge are played out, and not only through the actions of some distant customers or other selective forces in the environment. As Miner (1994) notes, many of these accounts treat knowledge as entities independent of the individuals enacting them, thus ignoring social interaction. As a result key critics have thus focused on the lack of agency, intentionality and creativity in related evolutionary accounts (Cordes 2006; Witt 2004).

Developing an evolutionary account of entrepreneurial learning thus involves searching deeper for an understanding of what evolves in small businesses, and crucially how this occurs over time (Breslin and Jones 2012). As noted above, the process is subsumed within practice or learning through action. Some have thus distanced themselves from the organisation-as-vehicle assumption, and put forward candidates for the genotype–phenotype which they argue better reflects the process and practice of socio-cultural evolution. For instance, some propose a genotypic–phenotypic duality, including the 'stored information' of the knowledge, and its behavioural 'expression' or enacted 'manifestation' (Galunic and Weeks 2002; Plotkin 1994; Warglien 2002). In this manner the routine, for instance, would be represented as a duality of actual performances (the phenotype) and underlying cognitive understandings (the genotype) (Breslin 2008a; Pentland *et al.* 2010, 2012). This 'practice' move marks a conceptual shift in emphasis in the story of evolving knowledge. In the 'organisation-as-vehicle' approach noted above, change is seen to occur through the variation–selection–retention of knowledge, through the selection 'of' organisations or groups which act as vehicles 'for' the underlying components of knowledge (Hodgson and Knudsen 2010). In this sense, the routine represents the genotype and the organisation the phenotype (Aldrich and Ruef 2006; Baum and Singh 1994; Hodgson and Knudsen 2010; Murmann 2003; Nelson and Winter 1982). In the practice view, change is seen to occur through practice, with variation–selection–retention acting on the mutually constitutive duality of performances and associated cognitive structures (Giddens 1984). Clearly, the latter conceptualisation better lends itself to the process of learning-by-doing which as noted above characterises small business survival and growth (Cope 2005; Deakins and Freel 1998; Gartner 1984; Politis 2005).

The evolution of entrepreneurial knowledge

Thus evolution describes the development over time of key components of knowledge through the mechanisms of variation, selection and retention. Some of this knowledge is retained within the head of the entrepreneur, given the latter's dominance of the new venture creation process. However, collective knowledge will also emerge within the fledgling organisation and wider network. While a learning approach focuses its attention on the entrepreneur and individuals within the team, an evolutionary approach focuses on the development of these knowledge components. In this way it tries to identify the emergence of evolving entities at a lower level of analysis (some of which may develop a *life* of their own, as noted above (Baron *et al.* 2001)). The entrepreneur and team are still relevant in the study of this evolutionary process, not as units of analysis, but through their evolving behaviour and practice as manifest through the mechanisms of variation, selection and retention. A simple illustration is given as follows:

- *Variation:* During the entrepreneurial process entrepreneurs continually adapt to changes in the external world by *varying* skills, heuristics and frameworks. This variation may be orientated towards the exploration and/or exploitation of opportunities and underpins the process of action learning. Thus in some instances this may result in new means–ends relationships being created in response to a changing world or indeed in anticipation of a changing world (Gartner 1989; Kirzner 1997; Shane and Venkataraman 2000). By continually varying the firm's knowledge the entrepreneur generates more options for selection, and in so doing the chances of finding an effective strategy in a changing business environment are increased.
- *Selection:* While selective forces in the environment will ultimately select the business's offering of products and services, at a micro-level the entrepreneur *selects* particular skills, heuristics and frameworks when completing key entrepreneurial activities. The enactment of these components of knowledge results in behaviours, and ultimately products and services, which are presented to the external world to be selected for or against. Selection is thus both anticipatory based on expected results, and retrospective based on the interpretation of resultant behaviours (Dewey 1922; Daft and Weick 1984; Weick 1995). However, choices made by the entrepreneur during the selection of skills, heuristics and frameworks are complicated by a number of factors, including the misinterpretation of environmental feedback as a result of cognitive bias, where positive outcomes are attributed to the actions of the entrepreneur and negative outcomes to external factors beyond their control (Baron 1998; Busenitz and Barney 1997).
- *Retention:* The entrepreneur *retains* chosen skills, heuristics and frameworks over time based on the interpretation of this environmental feedback. The retention of knowledge allows the entrepreneur to free up scarce cognitive resources for generating new knowledge needed to meet the demands of a changing world (Loasby 2007). In this way, as the firm grows the individual skills of the entrepreneur must be transformed into collective 'routines' within the fledgling team (Loasby 2007). Indeed, it may be argued that an entrepreneur's failure to establish

a 'library of knowledge' can overload these scarce cognitive resources (Breslin 2008b, 2010). As Loasby (2007) argues, 'entrepreneurship defies routine; but it requires routine and results in routine' (Loasby 2007: 1104), and a failure to achieve a balance between routinisation and creativity is a major difficulty which few entrepreneurial ventures overcome.

While these three mechanisms are described above in a sequential fashion, they are continually and contemporaneously enacted through practice. In this way, the entrepreneur both preselects knowledge variants in thought in an anticipatory fashion (Dewey 1922), and selectively retains knowledge based on the post-hoc sense making of enacted behaviours (Daft and Weick 1984; Weick 1995). There are many similarities between the conceptualisation of evolution through the mechanisms of variation, selection and retention, and different models of learning (Jones 2005; Miner 1994). Both approaches study the process in which knowledge develops over time in response to endogenous and exogenous changes. Both approaches also consider the directional, path-dependant nature of this development and incorporate multiple levels of analysis, including the entrepreneur, team and organisation (Crossan *et al.* 1999; Dixon 1999; Kim 1993). Both also put socio-political, behavioural and cognitive dimensions at the core of this process, in which individuals are viewed as boundedly rational (Simon 1991). Thus it may be seen that the process of knowledge evolving through the actions of individuals as they learn from mistakes, anticipate futures and interpret feedback from the environment shares many features with the learning-based narratives outlined above (Cope 2005; Deakins and Freel 1998; Gartner 1984; Gibb 1997; Politis 2005). In sum, entrepreneurs learn on the job as they develop skills, heuristics and frameworks to meet the changing needs of the business (Aldrich and Tang 2014).

The shift in emphasis away from the entrepreneur towards evolving components of knowledge has important consequences for both research and practice. In research terms it requires scholars to delve deeper into the small business, and to identify and study the development of knowledge vis-à-vis skills, heuristics and frameworks that are themselves modified and inherited over time. Researchers also need to develop a rich picture of the context surrounding the development of these knowledge components. The evolutionary approach thus offers researchers the opportunity to develop theory using the same key mechanisms of variation, selection and retention regardless of the level of analysis, unit of analysis, or contextual circumstances surrounding the phenomena under investigation. Essentially, an evolutionary approach focuses on what evolves and how this evolves over time in relation to changes in the environment, with the key question being fitness between the evolving entity and the particular environment at that time. Ultimately the performance of a small business is determined by this matching of the firm's knowledge with the changing demands of the external environment. This potential to harmonise and unify the conceptu-alisation of phenomena across levels and disciplines offers significant opportunities for scholars. In terms of practice, the approach views the entrepreneurial process as an emergence and development of key know-ledge components to suit the changing demands of the external world. This has different implications depending on the perspective one takes on the evolution of the organisation, as discussed next.

Implications for practice

'Learning to evolve'

If changing behaviour within small and growing businesses is conceptual-ised as a multi-level struggle for survival among competing knowledge components, then this may have some interesting implications for the way in which entrepreneurs behave and make decisions. In this perspective the entrepreneur must manage the evolution of skills, heuristics and frame-works through the evolutionary practice of variation, selection and reten-tion, as shown in Table 11.1.

- *Variation:* The entrepreneur must first create an environment in which skills, heuristics and frameworks are continually varied, as these vari-ants become the raw material for future competences. Entrepreneurs at start-up may rely heavily on previously learned heuristics, frameworks and skills for two key reasons: first, such acquired knowledge becomes increasingly enacted in an automatic sense over time (Cyert and March 1963; Nelson and Winter 1982); and second, entrepreneurs lack the time and resources to invest in learning new ways of behaving and thinking (Aldrich and Tang 2014). Aldrich and Tang (2014) argue that acquiring knowledge is a lifelong process for entrepreneurs that can constrain their ability to create 'blueprints' to meet the needs of the business. As a result, innovative behaviours may become severely con-strained. To counteract these pressures, the entrepreneur must untap and encourage sources of variation throughout the organisation and extended entrepreneurial network (Jack *et al.* 2008; Neergaard 2005).
- *Selection:* Having introduced new variations, the entrepreneurial team must then correctly select skills, heuristics and frameworks for enact-ment over time. The alignment between this 'internal' selection mecha-nism and the 'external' selection of the company's products and services becomes critical to the firm's longer term survival (Aldrich and Ruef 2006). However, the interpretation of feedback from the external world is fraught with difficulties due to interpretation biases (Baron 1998; Busenitz and Barney 1997) and the tendency of individuals (such as the entrepreneur) to dominate collective choices. In this sense the entrepreneur must strive to put in place processes that act to improve

Table 11.1 Learning to evolve

	'Learning to evolve'
Variation	The generation of new skills, heuristics and frameworks is the raw material of any evolutionary process Variation can be dominated by powerful individuals, such as the entrepreneur Individuals differ in their levels of creativity and experience • Are resources and processes in place to encourage the generation of ideas for the needs of the business? • Are all voices within the team heard to maximise the process of generation?
Selection	Choices made by individuals are subject to interpretation biases, and assumptions about the marketplace Past experience can both enable and constrain choices made Selections within the group can be dominated by powerful or influential individuals • Has sufficient market research been carried out to develop an accurate understanding of the marketplace based on customer feedback? • Are measures taken to identify and overcoming interpretation biases? • Who are the sources of power and how are they influencing choices made?
Retention	Retention of knowledge within the team may involve a process of individual to collective learning The past experience of individuals may facilitate or hinder this process of learning 'Learning to evolve' involves the accumulation of knowledge to free up scarce resources needed for continued variation • Have enough resources and time been committed to ensure copy fidelity of routines within the team? • Is the balance between the continued exploration of knowledge and the exploitation of routines appropriate for the changing needs of the business?

the 'accuracy' of his or her understanding of the marketplace, and the interpretation of feedback from that environment. While detailed market research is clearly critical in this endeavour, overcoming socio-political and interpretive biases is a more challenging proposition. Efforts therefore need to be focused on ensuring that all voices are included in the selection process, and most importantly those critical of the accepted consensus view. This clearly presents a challenge for organisations which tend to be dominated by the founding entrepreneur.

- *Retention:* Finally, the entrepreneur must ensure that 'successful' competences are retained and collectivised within the team (Breslin and Jones 2011).The replication of skills, heuristics and frameworks cannot be taken for granted as, in the absence of continual efforts by the entrepreneur, copied routines can quickly fall apart and lose their replicative fidelity (Argote *et al.* 1990). This retention of knowledge involves a process of individual to collective learning (Dutta and Crossan 2005), in which the experiences of those learning impact upon their ability to accumulate new skills (Cohen and Levinthal 1990; Zahra and Gerard 2002). At the same time, the entrepreneur needs to ensure that the collectivisation of practices does not result in the premature ossification of the firm, undermining the continuing need to adapt and explore new opportunities (Churchill and Lewis 1983; Greiner 1972; Scott and Bruce 1987).

Gartner (1989) argued that successful entrepreneurs develop the skill of 'learning to learn'. This is an interesting argument, with the successful entrepreneur becoming a more powerful learner or faster adaptor than other business leaders. This notion of 'learning to learn' reflects aspects of absorptive capacity (Cohen and Levinthal 1990), which is defined as the set of practices by which firms acquire, assimilate, transform and exploit knowledge to produce a dynamic organisational capability (Zahra and Gerard 2002). Thus as the entrepreneur learns key entrepreneurial skills or knowledge through experience, he or she also begins to learn the 'skills' of learning itself. However, these higher level skills are clearly also context specific, and while the ability of the entrepreneur to evaluate and utilise knowledge is a function of prior related knowledge (Cohen and Levinthal 1990), learning becomes more difficult in novel domains. In this way even serial entrepreneurs tend to specialise in a limited number of industrial sectors.

It is argued here that the evolutionary language of variation–selection–retention can represent this dynamic entrepreneurial capability. 'Learning to evolve' thus becomes a higher level entrepreneurial skill or heuristic underpinning the practice, and ultimately the success, of entrepreneurial learning. 'Learning to evolve' is thus an extension of the notion of 'learning to learn', in that the entrepreneur through practice becomes a more effective explorer and exploiter of knowledge. However, in viewing this process as an evolutionary one, embedded within a wider ecology of customers and competitors, the 'learning to evolve' heuristic forces the entrepreneur to take a broader, externally focused perspective. Rosen (1975) argued that the appropriateness of actions can only be determined by adopting the perspective of an 'outside observer', as selection acts on aggregate externally focused behaviours and not on the complexity of micro-level actions. The problem, however, is that the heuristics and frameworks held by individuals reflect the world local to them and not that which is representative of the selection environment external to the organisation as a whole, or as Rosen (1975) argued, individuals respond to each other rather than to the forces imposed upon the company by the external world. Therefore, while individuals make local choices which they believe offer local improvement, the resultant behaviour may detrimentally affect the group's longer term survival. If the process of making choices within an organisation is thus made entirely on the basis of local models, 'there is very little chance that these decisions will result in appropriate behaviour' (Rosen 1975: 148). By 'learning to evolve', the entrepreneur views the learning process from this external perspective, as discussed further below.

'Artificial breeders'

While the evolution of skills, heuristics and frameworks is placed at the core of the evolutionary process in small businesses, the mechanisms of variation, selection and retention are nonetheless enacted through the individuals concerned. Individuals thus become the means through which this knowledge evolves. Taking a step back, the entrepreneur must therefore consider how individuals within the growing team of employees influence this practice of 'learning to evolve'. So how do new recruits facilitate or hinder the process of variation, selection and retention? The experiences of individuals can have a profound impact on the pace and direction of learning. For instance, while existing practices can provide stability, they can also act to resist change, and in this sense the exploration of new practices might be resisted by the experiences of individuals within the organisation. In this way, the group can become tied to historical, collective and localised practices as exploration, and indeed continuing evolution through variation is suppressed. The entrepreneur must therefore ensure that knowledge accumulated through this past experience is appropriate for the needs of the business, and crucially the evolutionary demands of the business. Closely connected with the notion of path dependence is power, with individuals exerting different degrees of socio-political influence on the collective learning experience. This influence can affect the generation of ideas and/or their selective retention. As a result, the exploration of new practices may be resisted by the socio-political status quo directly associated with key individuals within the organisation. Equally, this exploration may be driven by key players within the emerging team, pushing those around them to challenge existing ways of working. This discussion clearly points to the importance of people in the wider evolutionary processes within the growing firm, as shown in Table 11.2. Are the right individuals put together in the right way to match the needs of the emerging evolutionary process?

If one adopts an evolutionary perspective on learning it may be argued that practices are not inextricably tied to the past, as the group can overcome inertia, break with past interpretations, untap variations from individuals and broaden their understandings of the external challenges they face. In this manner, groups can explore new futures through variation. However, some individuals are more adaptable and less resistant to change than others (Shane 2010). If we put forward the notion that knowledge

Table 11.2 The entrepreneur as the 'artificial breeder'

	The entrepreneur as the 'artificial breeder'
People	The process of 'learning to evolve' is influenced by past experience
	Different individuals have different levels of power and influence
	Different individuals have different degrees of evolutionary potential (EP)
	• Are the right individuals in place for the changing needs of the process/group in question?
	• Is the recruitment procedure selecting individuals with the right evolutionary potential (EP) for the needs of the group?
Process	Different groups/parts of the organisation face different learning challenges
	Some groups face the need to exploit skills and develop consistent and high-quality processes
	Some groups need to continue to explore knowledge and emerging opportunities
	• Have salient selective forces been identified for each group within the organisation?
	• If the emphasis shifts towards exploitation, are variations suppressed, and are individual voices brought into the collective fold?
	• If the emphasis shifts towards exploration, are sources of variation unlocked from within the organisational hierarchy?

evolves through individuals, then clearly having the right people in the right places to meet the evolutionary needs of that business are key. This may involve changing the evolutionary behaviours of individuals within the group itself or introducing it through new arrivals. Entrepreneurs therefore need to know their employees, and their evolutionary potential (EP), with recruitment becoming a key process. Bird (1989) notes how entrepreneurs recruit employees with the right 'chemistry' in terms of personality and synergy with the team, as they look for employees whom they can trust, with look-alike groups becoming formed. Nicholls-Nixon (2005) goes further, arguing that the entrepreneur seeks to develop shared sets of cognitive rules which guide behaviour in the absence of formal structures in the growing firm. Thus by selectively recruiting individuals with similar perspectives, the founder can directly influence the adaptation of behaviours over time. It is argued here that by assessing the evolutionary potential of employees, the entrepreneur can ensure the right fit with the changing needs of the growing business.

Once the right people are in place, the attention of the entrepreneur 'as artificial breeder' shifts towards managing the wider evolutionary process of learning (see Table 11.2). This involves ensuring that different processes of learning within different groups or parts of the organisation match the needs of the environment. Thus, while an emerging production team may focus their attention on producing goods and services, and improving the quality and efficiency of this process, an emerging marketing group need to continue to explore opportunities and develop new ways of meeting customer needs. While the emphasis of the former tends towards the exploitation of skills within the growing team, the latter seek to continue to explore new frameworks and heuristics to meet emerging opportunities in the marketplace. Indeed, balancing these competing needs for exploration and exploitation is a key challenge of business growth (Breslin 2010; Macpherson and Holt 2007; March 1991; Phelps *et al.* 2007), and one which to date has been underexplored in research (Wang and Chugh 2014). In evolutionary terms the entrepreneur needs to carefully consider the selective forces that are salient to the group in question. When selective forces shift towards the need to exploit knowledge and develop consistent group practices, then *variations* need to be suppressed. Thus, for example, *variations* introduced by individuals or subgroups are inhibited because they disagree with the emerging routines and/or because they challenge the existing status quo. This pressure to exploit knowledge thus involves bringing individuals into the collective fold and modifying their individual behaviour to that of the group. A focus on exploration on the other hand involves unlocking sources of *variation* through individual creativity and learning. In particular this involves untapping sources of *variation* from individuals within the group, as well as exploring different practices used by other groups and individuals both within the organisations and beyond. From the entrepreneur's perspective, managing this process to meet the competing needs of different groups within the organisation involves ensuring that the right individuals with the right evolutionary potential are in the right place at the right time.

In this sense, while the focus in our evolutionary narrative shifts towards evolving knowledge, individuals and groups do matter and cannot be divorced from the evolutionary processes which define the development of that knowledge over time. It is the job of the entrepreneur to manage this process, not only at the first level of order by 'learning to evolve' (see Table 11.1), but in terms of the wider process itself (see Table 11.2). The entrepreneur thus acts as an artificial breeder, continually varying, selecting and retaining desired knowledge within the organisation to meet the changing needs of the marketplace in much the same manner as Darwin's pigeon fanciers vary, select and retain desired characteristics in their prize pigeons (Darwin 1859). Taking a step back, entrepreneurs thus need to consider the influence of different actors in this process, adding or removing key individuals, or retraining or developing capabilities within the team. In this manner they manage the higher level process through which knowledge evolves, without directly becoming an acquirer of that knowledge itself.

Conclusion

A number of researchers have viewed the evolutionary approach as a useful tool or language when informing entrepreneurial management practices. In this way Burgelman (1991) developed the variation–selection–retention framework to guide and inform the development of strategic management practice within Intel, as the organisation adapted to meet the changing needs of their external environment. Likewise Murmann (2003) saw an evolutionary approach as influencing managerial practice in organisations, as managers establish and maintain internal selection criteria guiding the actions of individuals and groups to meet the challenges of the external world. Indeed, Murmann (2003) argued that the organisation's CEO might be viewed as the Chief Evolutionary Officer! Reinterpreting change in terms of variation–selection–retention puts the focus on co-evolving components of knowledge which underpin competitive advantage within companies. This knowledge evolves through the actions of groups, but is retained within the organisation despite the arrival or removal of key individuals. If knowledge evolves through a process of variation, selection and retention, and more importantly if entrepreneurs become aware of this evolution, they may then use that understanding to inform their actions, and in the process influence these same evolutionary mechanisms. Clearly parallels may be drawn with the notion of 'learning to learn' (Gartner 1989), or in this case 'learning to evolve'. As a result the entrepreneurial team develops a set of 'evolutionary heuristics' which can inform their actions, and in the process influence these same evolutionary mechanisms, and the wider evolutionary environment. The continued conceptual and empirical development of the approach thus offers the future prospect of using an evolutionary language as a constructive tool for practising entrepreneurs, as they reinterpret their understanding of the evolution of their business.

References

Aldrich, H.E. and M. Ruef (2006) *Organizations Evolving* (2nd edn). London: Sage.

Aldrich, H. and T. Yang (2014) How do entrepreneurs know what to do? Learning and organizing in new ventures. *Journal of Evolutionary Economics*, DOI: 10.1007/s00191–013–0320-x.

Aldrich, H., G. Hodgson, D. Hull, T. Knudsen, J. Mokyr and V. Vanberg (2008) In defence of generalized Darwinism. *Journal of Evolutionary Economics* 18, 577–596.

Argote, L., S.L. Beckman and D. Epple (1990) The persistence and transfer of learning in industrial settings. *Management Science* 36, 140–154.

Arthur, B. (2009) *The Nature of Technology: What it is and how it evolves.* London: Penguin.

Baron, J.N., M.T. Hannan and M.D. Burton (2001) Labor pains: Change in organizational models and employee turnover in young, high-tech firms. *American Journal of Sociology* 106, 960–1012.

Baron, R. (1998) Cognitive mechanisms in entrepreneurship: Why and when entrepreneurs think differently than other people. *Journal of Business Venturing* 13, 275–294.

Baum, J. and J. Singh (1994) Organizational hierarchies and evolutionary processes: Some reflections on a theory of organizational evolution. In J. Baum and J. Singh (eds), *Evolutionary Dynamics of Organizations*. New York: Oxford University Press, pp. 3–22.

Bird, B. (1989) *Entrepreneurial Behavior*. Glenview, IL: Scott, Foresman.

Boschma, R. and K. Frenken (2011) The emerging empirics of evolutionary economic geography. *Journal of Economic Geography* 11, 295–307.

Boschma, R. and R. Martin (2007) Constructing an evolutionary economic geography. *Journal of Economic Geography* 7, 537–548.

Breslin, D. (2008a) A review of the evolutionary approach to the study of entrepreneurship. *International Journal of Management Reviews* 10, 399–423.

—— (2008b) The nascent small business: An evolutionary approach. *International Journal of Entrepreneurship and Innovation* 9, 177–186.

—— (2010) Broadening the management team: An evolutionary approach. *International Journal of Entrepreneurial Behaviour and Research* 16, 130–148.

—— (2011) Reviewing a generalized Darwinist approach to studying socio-economic change. *International Journal of Management Reviews* 13, 218–235.

—— (forthcoming) What evolves in organizational co-evolution? *Journal of Management and Governance*.

Breslin, D. and C. Jones (2012) The Evolution of Entrepreneurial Learning. *International Journal of Organizational Analysis* 20, 294–308.

Burgelman, R.A. (1991) Intraorganizational ecology of strategy making and organizational adaptation: Theory and field research. *Organization Science* 2, 239–262.

Busenitz, L.W. and J. Barney (1997) Differences between entrepreneurs and managers in large organizations: Biases and heuristics in strategic decision-making. *Journal of Business Venturing* 12, 9–30.

Busenitz, L.W. and C.M. Lau (1996) A cross-cultural cognitive model of new venture creation. *Entrepreneurship, Theory and Practice* 20, 25–39.

Cavalli-Sforza, L. (2001) *Genes, Peoples and Languages*. London: Penguin.

Churchill, N. and V. Lewis (1983) The five stages of business growth. *Harvard Business Review* May/June, 30–50.

Clarysse, B. and N. Moray (2002) A process study of entrepreneurial team formation: The case of a research-based spin-off. *Journal of Business Venturing* 19, 55–79.

Cohen, W. and D. Levinthal (1990) Absorptive capacity: A new perspective on learning and innovation. *Administrative Science Quarterly* 35, 128–152.

Cope, J. (2005) Towards a dynamic learning perspective of entrepreneurship. *Entrepreneurship Theory and Practice* 29, 373–397.

Cordes, C. (2006) Darwinism in economics: From analogy to continuity. *Journal of Evolutionary Economics* 16, 529–541.

Crossan, M., H. Lane and R. White (1999) An organizational learning framework: From intuition to institution. *Academy of Management Review* 24, 522–537.

Cyert, R.M. and J.G. March (1963) *A Behavioural View of the Firm* (2nd edn). Oxford: Blackwell.

Daft, R.L. and K.E. Weick (1984) Toward a model of organizations as interpretation systems. *Academy of Management Review* 9, 284–295.

Darwin, C.R. (1859) *On the Origin of Species By Means of Natural Selection or the Preservation of Favoured Races in the Struggle for Life* (1st edn). London: Murray.

Dawkins, R. (1976) *The Selfish Gene*. New York: Oxford University Press.

—— (1982) *The Extended Phenotype*. New York: Oxford University Press.

—— (1983) Universal Darwinism. In D.S. Bendall (ed.), *Evolution from Molecules to Man*. Cambridge: Cambridge University Press, pp. 403–425.

Deakins, D. and M. Freel (1998) Entrepreneurial learning and the growth process in SMEs. *The Learning Organization* 5, 144–155.

Dennett, D. (1995) *Darwin's Dangerous Idea*. New York: Simon & Schuster.

Dewey, J. (1922) *Human Nature and Conduct*. New York: Henry Holt.

Dixon, N. (1999) *The Organisational Learning Cycle: How we can learn collectively*. Aldershot: Gower.

Dobson, S. (2012) Characterizing the evolution of commercial organizational spaces. *International Journal of Organizational Analysis* 20, 309–322.

Dobson, S., D. Breslin, L. Suckley, R. Barton and L. Rodriguez (2013) Small firm growth and innovation: An evolutionary approach. *International Journal of Entrepreneurship and Innovation* 14, 69–80.

Durham, W.H. (1991) *Coevolution: Genes, Culture and Human Diversity*. Stanford, CA: Stanford University Press.

Dutta, D.R. and M. Crossan (2005) The nature of entrepreneurial opportunities: Understanding the process using the 4I organizational learning framework. *Entrepreneurship Theory and Practice* 29, 425–449.

Essletzbichler, J. and D. Rigby (2005) Competition, variety and the geography of technology evolution. *Tijdschriftvoor Economische en Sociale Geografie* 96, 48–62.

Feldman, M.S. and W.J. Orlikowski (2011) Theorizing practice and practicing theory. *Organization Science* 22, 1240–1253.

Feldman, M. and B. Pentland (2003) Reconceptualizing organizational routines as a source of flexibility and change. *Administrative Science Quarterly* 48, 94–118.

Forbes, D.P. (1999) Cognitive approaches to new venture creation. *International Journal of Management Reviews* 1, 415–439.

Forbes, D.P., P.S. Borchert, M.E. Zellmer-Bruhn and H. Sapienza (2006) Entrepreneurial team formation: An exploration of new member addition. *Entrepreneurship Theory and Practice* March, 225–248.

Gaglio, C. and J. Katz (2001) The psychological basis of opportunity identification: Entrepreneurial alertness. *Small Business Economics* 16, 95–111.

Galunic, D.C. and D.R. Weeks (2002) Intraorganizational ecology. In J.A.C. Baum (ed.), *The Blackwell Companion to Organizations*. Oxford: Blackwell, pp. 75–97.

Gartner, W.B. (1984) 'Problems in business startup: The relationships among entrepreneurial skills and problem identification for different types of new ventures. In J.A. Hornaday, F. Tarpley, J.A. Timmons and K.H. Vesper (eds), *Frontiers of Entrepreneurship Research: The Proceedings of the Babson Conference on Entrepreneurship Research*. Wellesley, MA: Babson College, pp. 496–512.

—— (1989) Who is an entrepreneur? Is the wrong question. *Entrepreneurship Theory and Practice* 13, 47–68.

Gibb, A. (1997) Small firms' training and competitiveness. Building upon small business as a learning organisation. *International Small Business Journal* 15, 13–29.

Giddens, A. (1984) *The Constitution of Society: Outline of the Theory of Structuration*. Berkeley: University of California Press.

Grégoire, D.A., A.C. Corbett and J.S. McMullen (2011) The cognitive perspective in entrepreneurship: An agenda for future research. *Journal of Management Studies* 48, 1443–1477.

Greiner, L.E. (1972) Evolution and revolution as organizations grow. *Harvard Business Review* July–August, 37–46.

Hannan, M.T. and J. Freeman (1977) The population of ecology of organization. *American Journal of Sociology* 82, 929–964.

Hodgson, G.M. and T. Knudsen (2010) *Darwin's Conjecture: The search for general principles of social and economic evolution*. Chicago, IL: The University of Chicago Press.

Jack, S., S. Drakopoulou Dodd and A.R. Anderson (2008) Change and the development of entrepreneurial networks over time: A processual perspective. *Entrepreneurship and Regional Development: An International Journal* 20, 125–159.

Jones, C. (2005) Firm transformation: Advancing a Darwinian perspective. *Management Decision* 43, 13–25.

Jones, O. and A. Macpherson (2006) Inter-organizational learning and strategic renewal in SMEs. *Long Range Planning* 39, 155–175.

Kim, D. (1993) The link between individual and organizational learning. *Sloan Management Review* 35, 37–50.

Kirzner, I.M. (1997) Entrepreneurial discovery and the competitive market process: An Austrian approach. *Journal of Economic Literature* 35, 60–85.

Lave, J. and E. Wenger (1990) *Situated Learning: Legitimate peripheral participation*. Cambridge: Cambridge University Press.

Levitt, B. and J. March (1988) Organizational learning. *Annual Review of Sociology* 14, 319–340.

Loasby, B.J. (2003) *Knowledge, Institutions and Evolution in Economics*. London: Routledge.

—— (2007) A cognitive perspective on entrepreneurship and the firm. *Journal of Management Studies* 44, 1078–1106.

Macpherson, A. and R. Holt (2007) Knowledge, learning and small firm growth: A systematic review of the evidence. *Research Policy* 36, 172–192.

McKelvey, B. (1982) *Organizational Systematics: Taxonomy, evolution, classification*. Berkeley, CA: University of California Press.

March, J.G. (1991) Exploration and exploitation in organizational learning. *Organization Science* 2, 71–87.

Miner, A.S. (1994) Seeking adaptive advantage: Evolutionary theory and managerial action. In J. Baum and J. Singh (eds), *Evolutionary Dynamics of Organisations*. New York: Oxford University Press, pp. 76–89.

Mokyr, J. (2000) Evolutionary phenomena in technological change. In J. Ziman (ed.), *Technological Innovation as an Evolutionary Process*. Cambridge: Cambridge University Press, pp. 52–65.

Murmann, J.P. (2003) *Knowledge and Competitive Advantage: The co-evolution of firms, technology and national institutions*. New York: Cambridge University Press.

Neergaard, H. (2005) Networking activities in technology-based entrepreneurial teams. *International Small Business Journal* 23, 257–278.

Nelson, R. and S. Winter (1982) *Evolutionary Theory of Economic Change*. Cambridge, MA: Bellknap Press.

Nicholls-Nixon, C.L. (2005) Rapid growth and high performance: The entrepreneur's 'impossible dream'. *Academy of Management Executive* 19, 77–89.

Nonaka, I. (1994) A dynamic theory of organizational knowledge creation. *Organization Science* 5, 14–37.

Orlikowski, W.J. (2002) Knowing in practice: Enacting a collective capability in distributed organizing. *Organization Science* 13, 249–273.

Phelps, R., R. Adams and J. Bessant (2007) Life cycles of growing organizations: A review with implications for knowledge and learning. *International Journal of Management Reviews* 9, 1–30.

Pentland, B.T., T. Hærem and D. Hillison (2010) Comparing organizational routines as recurrent patterns of action. *Organization Studies* 31, 917–940.

Pentland, B.T., M.S. Feldman, M.C. Becker and P. Liu (2012) Dynamics of organizational routines: A generative model. *Journal of Management Studies* 49, 1484–1508.

Plotkin, H. (1994) *Darwin Machines and the Nature of Knowledge*. Cambridge, MA: Harvard University Press.

Politis, D. (2005) The process of entrepreneurial learning: A conceptual framework. *Entrepreneurship Theory and Practice* 29, 399–424.

Richerson, P.J. and R. Boyd (2005) *Not by Genes Alone: How culture transformed human evolution*. Chicago, IL: The University of Chicago Press.

Rosen, R. (1975) Complexity and error in social dynamics. *International Journal of General Systems* 2, 145–148.

Scott, M. and R. Bruce (1987) Five stages of growth in small business. *Long Range Planning* 20, 45–52.

Shane, S. (2010) *Born Leaders, Born Entrepreneurs: How your genes affect your work life*. Oxford: Oxford University Press.

Shane, S. and S. Venkataraman (2000) The promise of entrepreneurship as a field of research. *Academy of Management Review* 25, 217–226.

Simon, H. (1991) Bounded rationality and organizational learning. *Organization Science* 2, 125–134.

Spencer, H. (1864) *Principles of Biology*. London: Williams and Norgate.

Szulanski, G. (2000) Appropriability and the challenge of scope: Banc One routinizes replication. In G. Dosi, R.R. Nelson and S.G. Winter (eds), *The Nature and Dynamics of Organizational Capabilities*. Oxford: Oxford University Press, pp. 69–97.

Szulanski, G. and S.G. Winter (2002) Getting it right the second time. *Harvard Business Review* 80, 62–69.

Tooby, J. and L. Cosmides (1992) The psychological foundations of culture. In J.H. Barkow, L. Cosmides and J. Tooby (eds), *The Adapted Mind: Evolutionary psychology and the generation of culture*. Oxford: Oxford University Press, pp. 19–136.

Ucbasaran, D., P. Westhead and M. Wright (2001) The focus of entrepreneurial research: Contextual and process issues. *Entrepreneurship Theory and Practice* 25, 57–80.

Wang, C.L. and H. Chugh (2014) Entrepreneurial learning: Past research and future challenges. *International Journal of Management Reviews* 16, 24–61.

Warglien, M. (2002) Intraorganizational evolution. In J.A.C. Baum (ed.), *The Blackwell Companion to Organizations*. Oxford: Blackwell, pp. 98–118.

Weick, K.E. (1995) *Sensemaking in Organizations*, Thousand Oaks, CA: Sage.

Witt, U. (2004) On the proper interpretation of 'evolution' in economics and its implications for production theory. *Journal of Economic Methodology* 11, 125–146.

Zahra, S. and G. Gerard (2002) Absorptive capacity: A review, reconceptualisation and extension. *Academy of Management Reviews* 27, 185–203.

12 Entrepreneurial preparedness

An exploratory case study of Chinese private enterprises

Catherine L. Wang, Mohammed Rafiq, Xiaoqing Li and Yu Zheng

Introduction

Entrepreneurial preparedness (EP) is an emerging concept within the entrepreneurial learning (EL) literature. It is broadly defined as 'a cumulative learning process' (Cope 2005: 378), emphasising the developmental nature of entrepreneurs. The concept may be traced back to Scherer *et al.* (1989), which argues that entrepreneurial (career) preparedness among business administration students consists of two dimensions: entrepreneurial task self-efficacy (i.e. confidence in entrepreneurial skills) and entrepreneurial education and training aspirations. Furthermore, Festervand and Forrest (1993) develop a multi-stage model of EP by which an entrepreneurial aspirant can better prepare for an entrepreneurial career. Since then, while a handful of studies have touched on the concept (Harvey and Evans 1995; Jones and Tullous 2002; Johnsen and McMahon 2005; Dimov 2007; Lee and Jones 2008; Cooper and Park 2008), it is Cope (2005) who brings it to the forefront of the EL literature and places EP as a core concept within the EL literature (Pittaway and Thorpe 2012). However, Cope's (2005) work only focuses on the cumulative nature of EP: 'learning history' that shapes EL, rather than a systematic development of the EP concept. Moreover, it is conceptual without empirical support. Therefore, more research is required to advance EP's conceptual and empirical development.

EP deserves more attention for two main reasons. First, entrepreneurship research recognises that the traditional traits approach focusing on entrepreneurs' psychological characteristics and personality traits has failed to address why some individuals are more likely than others to start their own businesses (Brockhaus and Horwitz 1986; Sexton 1987; Wortman 1987). More attention is drawn to the role of a stock of experiences and skills individuals possess in their decisions to enter the start-up process (Reuber and Fischer 1999). Accordingly, how individuals acquire and accumulate knowledge, skills and experience to prepare for entrepreneurship – that is, the learning and developmental process – has stimulated a great deal of scholarly interest (Wang and Chugh 2014). The fact that during the recession an increasing number of white-collar employees turn into 'accidental entrepreneurs' – entrepreneurs by chance (Aldrich and Kenworthy 1999; Haynes *et al.* 1999; Shah and Tripsas 2007) – is a testimony to the limitation of the traits approach, and to the importance of the changing entrepreneurial context as well as learning and development in entrepreneurial careers. EP, essentially a learning process in which prior accumulated knowledge, skills and experience shape individuals' attitudes, beliefs and abilities, and prepare them for an entrepreneurial career (Harvey and Evans 1995; Starr and Fondas 1992), offers a better scope to understand entrepreneurial behaviours and processes. However, more research is required to understand the processes by which individuals prepare themselves for entrepreneurial endeavours, and the context in which learning takes place.

Second, early work on EP is largely based on empirical evidence from student samples, examining students' entrepreneurial career choice (e.g. Scherer *et al.* 1989; Harvey and Evans 1995; Thandi and Sharma 2004). While it offers insight into certain aspects of learning, such as vicarious learning from role models (Scherer *et al.* 1989) and prior education (Thandi and Sharma 2004), such research cannot offer insight into how real-life entrepreneurs learn as a 'lived experience' involving a cumulative series of independent events (Morris *et al.* 2012) or how learning occurs from moments in which an entrepreneur is situated (Rae 2013a). The lived experience is deeply rooted in Cope's (2005) work, providing a critical understanding of how entrepreneurs make of their 'here-and-now' (Pittaway and Thorpe 2012: 840). Following Rae's (2013b) argument that EP is dependent on the specific situation that confronts the entrepreneur and the social groups to which the entrepreneur relates, more research is needed to understand how real-life entrepreneurs learn and prepare themselves for entrepreneurial challenges, and hence the human and social dynamics of entrepreneurship.

Given the importance of EP and its lack of conceptual and empirical development, our first objective is to advance the conceptualisation of EP with a particular emphasis on its role in EL theory. Our conceptualisation goes beyond the cumulative nature of EP as defined by Cope (2005). Our second objective is to study the process of EP in new venture creation and management, and especially what entrepreneurs learn, and how and under what conditions they learn to prepare themselves, drawing on evidence from an exploratory case study of two Chinese high-tech private enterprises founded and run by three Chinese entrepreneurs. This will illustrate the process of EP, taking into account the unique learning context (e.g. industrial and organisational factors in Chinese private enterprises) and personal characteristics of Chinese entrepreneurs. By pursuing these objectives, we intend to contribute to EL theory through advancing the conceptualisation of EP and its role in the EL literature and providing empirical evidence of EP based on a micro-level contextual analysis, rather than generalised findings, of two Chinese high-tech private enterprises. Hence, we contribute to the understanding of human and social dynamics of entrepreneurship, as called for by scholars (Rae 2013b; Bygrave and Minniti 2000). Our findings have practical implications for entrepreneurs and "would-be" entrepreneurs to better understand the learning needs of entrepreneurs and how they prepare themselves for entrepreneurial challenges.

Theoretical background

EP is an emerging concept within the EL literature. EL is referred to as learning in the entrepreneurial process in general (Ravasi and Turati 2005; Politis 2005; Holcomb *et al.* 2009; Wang and Chugh 2014), while EP emphasises the cumulative nature of the learning process in prior literature (Cope 2005). Currently, there are only a handful of articles focusing on EP specifically (e.g. Scherer *et al.* 1989; Festervand and Forrest 1993), although a large body of EL literature exists to provide insight into how entrepreneurs learn from their own experience and the experience of others, and from not only successes but also failures (Cope 2011; Minniti and Bygrave 2000).

Within the limited EP literature, research has largely focused on how students learn to be more entrepreneurial and prepare themselves for an entrepreneurial career (e.g. Scherer *et al.* 1989; Harvey and Evans 1995; Thandi and Sharma 2004). In particular, Festervand and Forrest (1993) propose that EP builds on education, experience and planning, and its outcome is 'entrepreneurial readiness' when the actual entrepreneurial activity takes place. Building on prior work, Cope (2005: 378) articulates EP as 'a cumulative learning process' – 'a concept that encapsulates the immense complexity of accumulated learning that individuals bring to the new venture creation process'. By this definition, Cope (2005) discerns the importance of 'learning history' (Mezirow 1991; Boud *et al.* 1993): the way in which entrepreneurs perceive new situations and thereby experience learning is inextricably linked to their prior learning. Learning history defines the unique path and level of EP brought to start-up (Cope 2005). This follows Harvey and Evans' (1995) call for entrepreneurs to actively assess their learned skills and abilities. Cope (2005) emphasises that in order to assess skills and abilities, entrepreneurs must look backward (i.e. reflecting on the relevance of past experience), inward (i.e. assessing how ready they are to enter into entrepreneurship), outward (i.e. interacting with, and learning about, the wider environment) and forward (i.e. visualising how to make their business survive and succeed).

Despite the above contribution, EP in the existing literature is limited in three ways: first, its conceptual development focuses on its cumulative nature, without a deeper understanding of other important aspects of EP; second, prior work focuses largely on how students prepare themselves for an entrepreneurial career, rather than how entrepreneurs learn; and third, EP is restricted to conceptual work with little empirical evidence on how and under what conditions EP takes place in new venture creation and management. Our study aims to help fill this research gap. To advance the conceptualisation of EP, we further articulate the mechanism that underpins the cumulative nature of EP defined by Cope (2005). More importantly, we go beyond Cope (2005), and articulate two other key dimensions of EP – the social and purposeful nature of EP – the missing link in the conceptualisation of EP.

First, the cumulative nature of EP implies that experiential learning (Kolb 1984) is an important mechanism for entrepreneurs to accumulate knowledge and prepare themselves for entrepreneurship. Experiential learning theory considers learning as 'the process whereby knowledge is created through the transformation of experience. Knowledge results from the combination of grasping and transforming experience' (Kolb 1984: 41). Entrepreneurs discover opportunities related to the knowledge they already possess; such prior knowledge creates a 'knowledge corridor' which allows the entrepreneur to immediately get interested in certain kinds of information (Busenitz 1996), and to recognise certain opportunities (Venkataraman 1997). Shane (2000) identifies three major dimensions of prior knowledge that are important to the process of entrepreneurial discovery: prior knowledge of markets, of ways to serve markets, and of customer problems. Further, West and Noel (2009) argue that business-related knowledge has a positive impact on high-tech venture performance, whereas industry knowledge gained from prior experience does not have a significant impact, suggesting that industry knowledge erodes very quickly in technology industries (Newbert 2005). The experiential nature of EP determines that preparedness is path dependent. The learning history of each entrepreneur defines the unique process of EP brought to the creation and management of new ventures (Cope 2005). Empirical evidence supports the fact that experienced entrepreneurs, such as serial and portfolio entrepreneurs, are more likely to learn over time leading to the identification of opportunities, compared with nascent entrepreneurs (Westhead *et al.* 2005).

Second, EP involves social learning – an important mechanism for individuals to prepare themselves for entrepreneurial endeavours (Scherer *et al.* 1988). Social learning theory posits that learning occurs through close contact with other people and observation and imitation of role model behaviours (Bandura 1977; Williams 2001). Behaviour is a function of both personal and environmental factors and in turn influences environment (Kreitner and Luthans 1984). Entrepreneurs' self-efficacy, managerial experience, business skills and education levels are all influenced by the socialisation process (Jones and Tullous 2002), and hence affected by the social groups to which the entrepreneur is related and the specific situation that confronts the entrepreneur (Cope 2005). This sentiment is echoed by Dimov (2007: 578): "[entrepreneurial] preparedness is not universally instrumental, but is situated – it is effective only when the "right" context comes along'. Within the wider organisational learning literature, situated learning, which positions the learner within social, historical and cultural contexts (Lave and Wenger 1991; Taylor and Thorpe 2004; Wenger 1998; Hamilton 2011), additional insights are offered to understand the context-dependent nature of EP. Recently, research has gone a step further by arguing that learning occurs from moments in which an entrepreneur is situated (Rae 2013a). In other words, learning is a lived experience involving a cumulative series of independent events (Morris *et al.* 2012). In particular, critical events – significant, discontinuous events – during the entrepreneurial process could trigger learning (Cope 2003). Critical events could well be dissatisfaction from past employment (Haynes *et al.* 1999) or venture failure (Cope 2011). Such critical events may trigger both double-loop learning (Argyris and Schön 1978) and transformative learning (Mezirow 1991); the former generates a renewed understanding or redefinition of organisational processes, while the latter has the capacity to trigger considerable personal changes in the entrepreneur's self-awareness (Cope 2003, 2005). Entrepreneurs may learn not only about themselves but also about the nature of networks and relationships which can increase their preparedness (Westhead and Wright 2011). However, little empirical research exists to reveal the different contexts in which entrepreneurs learn and prepare themselves for entrepreneurship.

Finally, EP involves purposeful or goal-oriented learning, emphasising the role of an entrepreneurial goal or aspiration in the learning process (Scherer *et al.* 1989). The knowledge accumulation process is directed by an entrepreneurial goal, and the cumulative learning process builds up to the point of entrepreneurial readiness to realise that goal (Festervand and Forrest 1993). Generally, a goal helps individuals to direct attention towards actions that are relevant to the goal, adjust their effort to the difficulty level of the goal, and motivate them to persist in their effort until that goal is reached (Seijts and Latham 2005). However, attention should be paid to the effects of two different types of goals: learning goals that identify needs for skills and knowledge acquisition, and performance goals that specify outcomes (Seijts and Latham 2005). On a simple and straightforward task, a performance goal is associated with better outcomes, while a learning goal works better in a complex task situation (Winters and Latham 1996) and is particularly important for individuals to develop competences (Leonard 2008). Indeed, setting a specific challenging performance goal has a negative effect on an individual's effectiveness in the early stage of learning in a complex task situation (Kanfer and Ackerman 1989), where skills and knowledge acquisition and development is instrumental. Entrepreneurial activity by nature involves a high degree of uncertainty and risk-taking for individuals taking on entrepreneurial endeavours. Under such conditions, establishing learning goals would help individuals to identify needs for knowledge and skills development, as well as develop strategies to implement learning. In contrast, performance goals allow individuals to stay focused on the anticipated entrepreneurial outcomes without being overly distracted in the process of pursuing such endeavours. Therefore, a balance between learning and performance goals, depending on the individuals' prior knowledge, skills and experience and the complexity of the entrepreneurial task, is required for entrepreneurship.

We have further articulated experiential learning as a mechanism that underpins the cumulative learning process of EP as defined by Cope (2005). Moreover, we have identified and conceptualised social learning and purposeful learning as two other important dimensions of EP, going beyond Cope's (2005) work. Accordingly, we define EP as a cumulative, social and purposeful learning process in preparing for, and undertaking, entrepreneurial activity (see Table 12.1). EP has a clear bearing on entrepreneurial goals in addition to its cumulative and social nature, differentiating the concept from the general concept of EL. In the empirical study below, we aim to explore how the cumulative, social and purposeful learning process of EP takes place in new venture creation and management.

Research method

Because EP as an emerging concept lacks theoretical and empirical development, our research used an exploratory case study approach recommended by Yin (2009) to extend our understanding of the concept of EP and reveal the idiosyncrasies of EP and its contexts in Chinese high-tech private enterprises. Our case study is based on data collected from two Chinese private high-tech ventures (hereafter SpinalFixture and LiverPharma to ensure anonymity) in the healthcare industry sector. Specifically, SpinalFixture designed, developed and manufactured bone fixtures (Class III medical devices); LiverPharma primarily researched in and developed liver disease diagnosis and treatment (pharmaceutical).

Background

Both the medical devices and pharmaceutical markets have experienced tremendous growth in recent years (e.g. 21.1 per cent and 13.6 per cent annual growth respectively: Datamonitor 2008a, 2008b), due to the huge and increasingly ageing population, improved living standards, and swift urbanisation leading to improved consumer affordability and increased demand for drugs and medical treatment (Hu *et al.* 2007). The markets are characterised by their huge sizes, wide geographical span, immature regulatory regimes, and regional protection under the old state-controlled system that continues to shadow the development of national innovation systems and distribution channels. Consequently, the pharmaceutical market is fragmented, with the four leading pharmaceutical companies accounting for only about 10 per cent of the market share (Datamonitor 2008a). The medical devices market is polarised: high concentration in the high-end market dominated by leading multinational companies; low concentration at the low-end market with a

Table 12.1 A conceptualisation of entrepreneurial preparedness

Key dimension	Definition	Implications
The cumulative nature	The process of EP is experiential in nature, building on prior knowledge.	• Entrepreneurs discover opportunities related to knowledge they already possess (Busenitz 1996). • Different knowledge, such as business or industry knowledge (West and Noel 2009) and knowledge of markets, ways to serve markets and customer problems (Shane 2000) may have different impact on how entrepreneurs learn. • EP is *path dependent*; the learning history of each entrepreneur defines the unique process of EP (Cope 2005).
The social nature	The process of EP is situated in the learning context (i.e. peer groups, social, historical, cultural context, and critical events).	• What and how an entrepreneur learns is influenced by both personal and environmental factors (Kreitner and Luthans 1984). • Vicarious learning through observing and imitating others is interwoven in the EP process (Bandura 1977; Williams 2001). • Learning is a lived experience involving a cumulative series of independent events (Morris *et al.* 2012); such critical events could well be dissatisfaction from employment (Haynes *et al.* 1999) or venture failure (Cope 2011). • EP is *context dependent*, and takes place in social, historical and cultural contexts (Lave and Wenger 1991).
The purposeful nature	The process of EP is inspired and directed by entrepreneurial goals.	• Entrepreneurial goals help individuals to accumulate knowledge related to the goals, and the cumulative learning process builds up to the point of entrepreneurial readiness to realise the goal (Festervand and Forrest 1993); the cumulative nature and the purposeful nature support each other in the EP process. • Learning and performance goals play different roles: the former helps to identify needs for skills and knowledge acquisition, and the latter specifies performance outcomes (Seijts and Latham 2005). A balance between learning performance goals is required, as the former works better in a complex task situation, while the latter helps to improve performance on a simple and straightforward task (Winter and Latham 1996). • EP is *goal dependent*, and is influenced by the complexity of the entrepreneurial task.

large number of domestic companies competing on price. While such market conditions offer tremendous opportunities for new entrants, they also pose major challenges for incumbent firms to learn from external sources (including new start-ups) and upgrade their own technology, knowledge and skills.

State-owned organisations traditionally lacking incentives to invest in Research and Development (R&D) are increasingly under pressure to reform; consequently, many employees are encouraged or forced to take early retirement to make room for young talent. The Chinese government also encourages Chinese overseas scholars and students to return to set up high-tech private ventures or take up senior positions in existing high-tech ventures. Under such institutional environments, retiree entrepreneurs and overseas returnee entrepreneurs (Wright *et al.* 2008) are idiosyncratic phenomena in China. Nevertheless, the immature financial market, the lack of support systems for private enterprises and intense competition constrain the growth of private enterprises. Chinese private entrepreneurs have to demonstrate their entrepreneurial flair by constantly looking for new opportunities and developing new skills and competences. Therefore, Chinese private healthcare firms provide an interesting context to study EP.

Case selection, data collection and analysis

Our chosen case study companies are located in Beijing, one of the most highly concentrated high-tech areas in China (Yam *et al.* 2004). A key challenge for researching in China is to gain research access, which can be time consuming, complex and extremely difficult (Zhao *et al.* 2006). In addition to cultural issues (Easterby-Smith and Malina 1999) and sensitivity and confidentiality issues, managers may not have the time or see the value of academic research (Hirsch 1995). Using personal contacts and social networks is often the main way of gaining full cooperative access to Chinese firms (Liang and Lu 2006). Once initial access is granted, continued access allowing the researcher to interact with the interviewees long enough in order to collect relevant and sufficient data poses another challenge (Gummesson 2000).

To overcome these challenges, we adopted a two-stage case selection process to conduct the case study in 2008 and 2009. The first stage, informal sampling, started with broad selection criteria: high-tech private enterprises operating in the healthcare sector located in Beijing. We followed personal recommendations, an efficient way of gaining access to Chinese firms (Liang and Lu 2006), and also used cold calls to a number of companies. As a result, four healthcare companies (including one in pharmaceutical and three in medical devices) agreed to take part. We conducted one to two initial interviews with all four companies in order to fully assess their suitability.

In the second stage, formal sampling, we selected two firms (SpinalFixture and LiverPharma) from the four initial cases based on Yin's (2009) 'two-case' case study design. We believe that findings independently emerging from these two cases are more powerful than a single case study alone (Yin 2009), although we are fully aware that our findings, while useful to reveal some idiosyncrasies of EP in Chinese private enterprises, may not be generalisable to other firms or research contexts. We applied theoretical sampling at this stage based on the following rationales. (1) Given the vastly diverse nature of Chinese new ventures, we held the geographical location and the year of start-up constant when selecting case studies to allow us to control the effect of regional policy on enterprises and improve between-case comparability; SpinalFixture and LiverPharma were both located in Beijing and were founded around the same time (Table 12.2). (2) Since EP is inextricably linked to the 'learning history' involving personal and interactive dimensions (Cope 2005), and transformative learning (Mezirow 1991) requires time for individuals to engage in critical reflection on their entrepreneurial experience (Pittaway and Thorpe 2012), we selected two established firms, SpinalFixture and LiverPharma, to provide rich historical and cultural contexts to study EP. (3) Given that our aim is to understand the idiosyncrasies of EP within the context of Chinese high-tech private enterprises, we chose two typical cases (akin to Yin's (2009) concept of the 'average case' in a single case study design) to illustrate the typical learning challenges faced by the Chinese private ventures. (4) SpinalFixture and LiverPharma offered contrasting situations in terms of the different personal backgrounds of the founding entrepreneurs and the different organisational contexts (see the case study firms below). In addition, ensuring continued access was a practical concern of our second-stage sampling; the founders of both firms were not only personally willing to participate in the interviews but also allowed or even encouraged employees to participate; such continued access was crucial for us to gain insights (Gummesson 2000).

Within each firm, we used purposive sampling (Lincoln and Guba 1985) to identify and select key informants who were most knowledgeable about the topical area (Saunders *et al.* 2009). Specifically, we selected the founder(s) (i.e. entrepreneurs who created the new ventures and continued to seek and pursue entrepreneurial opportunities), who had knowledge about the new venture creation and management. Wherever appropriate, we also selected an R&D manager, production manager and marketing manager (see Table 12.2). These people were considered to have specific knowledge about entrepreneurial activity within the firms. For example, an R&D manager and production manager had specific knowledge about product development – the inward-looking part of pursuing an entrepreneurial opportunity, while a marketing manager had specific knowledge about taking the product to market – the outward-looking part of pursuing an entrepreneurial opportunity. Interviewing people other than the founders provided (1) rich information on the organisational contexts, especially at the operational level where the founders might not be directly involved, and (2) triangulation of the data from the founders' interviews.

We conducted seven (including two follow-up) interviews with selected informants in SpinalFixture, and five (including one follow-up) in Liver-Pharma; each interview was conducted by at least one researcher of the research team with an individual informant on the respective sites of the firms. The follow-up interviews were conducted when the particular interviewees offered especially relevant and useful insights that deserved further attention. Once we had conducted five interviews with SpinalFixture and four interviews with LiverPharma, additional insights from further interviews were marginal, indicating a point of diminishing returns (Strauss and Corbin 1998). This suggested that the number of interviews we conducted in each firm was sufficient to reveal the contexts and processes of EP. These interviews were semi-structured and conducted face to face, each lasting from one to one-and-a-half hours. All the interviews were recorded and transcribed for data coding and analysis.

Our case study is based on retrospective interview data (i.e. the new venture creation process), concurrent interview data (i.e. the new venture management process) and secondary published data. This data triangulation approach helps mitigate risks involved in using only retrospective interview data. First, although researchers have warned that informants' recall of brief, episodic interactions may be inaccurate (Bernard *et al.* 1984), they are remarkably accurate in recalling typical interactions and important events (Freeman *et al.* 1987). Since this study focuses on the key milestones of the new venture creation process and critical events influencing learning, rather than trivial, insignificant matters, it is therefore reasonable to believe that the founders were able to accurately recall key events in new venture creation. In the case of LiverPharma, we interviewed both founders to triangulate their accounts of key events in new venture creation. In addition, the founders' account of the impact of external contexts on firm development was consistent with the secondary data on the industry context. This provides additional support for the validity of the founders' recall of the new venture creation process. Second, data on the new venture management process are based on concurrent interviews with multiple informants from each firm. The consistency among interviewees from each firm strengthens the validity of the data. In addition, the interviewees' account of the impact of external contexts on firm development was consistent with the secondary data on the industry development. This supports the validity of the data regarding the new venture management process.

Triangulating data are often used by researchers (e.g. Gardet and Fraiha 2012) to improve the research validity. In particular, combining concurrent and retrospective data is valuable, because the concurrent data provide real-time understanding of events and retrospective data enable efficient data collection (Bingham and Davis 2012) as compared with the concurrent longitudinal case study approach. For instance, the high failure rate of start-ups means that any chosen case study firm could have failed, making it impossible to continue concurrent longitudinal case study data. Moreover, the difficulty of continued access means that any chosen case study firm could have withdrawn its cooperation, resulting in incomplete concurrent longitudinal case study data. Exceptionally, research may employ a longitudinal case study, but the data collected are often from a small number of venture team members over a short period of time. For example, Karataş-Özkan (2011) collected data from participant observation and in-depth interviews with five new venture team members over ten months. Therefore, combining concurrent and retrospective data is an efficient and effective way of data collection.

The interview questions covered five broad categories in order to capture the complex context and process of EP: (1) the entrepreneur: the background, skills, knowledge, experience, personal values, motivations, personal events prior to setting up the new venture, and perception of the environment and the organisation; (2) the entrepreneurial opportunity: how it was discovered, what and how learning occurred, and the key events leading to the new venture creation; (3) the organisational developmental process: the

Table 12.2 The profiles of the case study firms

	SpinalFixture	*LiverPharma*
Industry sector	Medical devices (developing and manufacturing internal and external spinal fixture)	Primarily pharmaceutical (development of liver disease diagnosis and treatment)
Start-up year	1996	1994
Ownership	Independent, private	Independent, private
Founder(s)	One founder (a retiree entrepreneur and ex-employee from a state-owned organisation)	Two founders (both overseas returnees and ex-employees from a state-owned hospital)
No. of employees in 2009	About 150 employees; 20 in R&D; self-perceived as a small business	About 50 employees; 9–10 employees in R&D; self-perceived as a small business
Sales turnover in 2009	About RMB¥30 million	About RMB¥20 million
R&D intensity ratio and R&D staff ratio	10%; 13%	50%; 20%
Interviewees	1. Founder (also President) (first interview) 2. R&D Manager (first interview) 3. Production Manager 4. Quality Control Manager 5. Marketing Manager 6. R&D Manager (second interview) 7. Founder (also President) (second interview)	1. Founder A (also General Manager) 2. Founder B 3. R&D Manager (first interview) 4. Production Manager 5. R&D Manager (second interview)

firm's historical account, key milestones of learning, current skills and competences; (4) the organisational context: ownership, structure, strategic orientation, management and leadership style, organisational values, and key entrepreneurial activity, etc.; and (5) the business environment: the firm's strategic position in the industry, target markets, perceived competition, approaches to dealing with competition, and ways to acquire new information and knowledge from external sources. In addition, secondary data (e.g. company websites, industry reports, newspaper and magazine publications, and academic publications) were also gathered to understand the country-, industry-, market- and firm-specific information. Information on the individual entrepreneurs, the entrepreneurial firms, and the wider environment in which they operated allowed us to study the multi-level relations involved in entrepreneurial learning and preparedness (Karataş-Özkan 2011).

A thematic content analysis was performed based on a preliminary analytical framework – a two-by-three matrix encompassing two key entrepreneurial stages (i.e. new venture creation and new venture management) as one axis and the three dimensions of EP (i.e. cumulative, social and purposeful) as the other axis. Within each case, data obtained from each informant were analysed using the matrix to identify the emerging themes of what was learned and how and under what conditions (i.e. personal characteristics, organisational contexts and external environment) EP occurred at different stages of new venture creation and management. The themes that emerged in each individual interview were compared across different interviews to build insights into the three dimensions of EP, namely cumulative, social and purposeful learning in the two key stages of new venture creation and management. Building on individual case analysis, we conducted between-case comparisons, using the standard cross-case comparison techniques (e.g. Eisenhardt 1989; Miles and Huberman 1994). We not only looked for similar, but also different concepts and relationships between the two cases in order to understand EP in different contexts. This was then used to extend the theory of EP.

Research findings

Case study firms

SpinalFixture was founded in 1996 in Beijing (see Table 12.2) by a retiree entrepreneur who took early retirement from a state-owned aerospace organisation with secure pension and benefits. SpinalFixture focused on adapting foreign bone fixture technology to the requirements of Chinese patients. Since its start-up, SpinalFixture has pursued organic growth through self-finance. In the early 2000s, facing increasing market pressure due to price-based competition, SpinalFixture focused on increasing efficiency and capacity. To achieve this, it moved into a large rural site in 2005, and transformed its ad-hoc workshop-style management to a formal, functional management structure to achieve efficiency and standardisation. However, since 2009 SpinalFixture has faced intensified domestic competition in the low-end market and international competition in the high-end market, and the founder realised that opportunities lay in the mid-range domestic market. However, SpinalFixture needed to improve its R&D capability, change the employee mindset and break down 'organisational silos' caused by functional management in order to create an innovative culture. The founder wanted to transform SpinalFixture into an employee-owned organisation with effective reward systems for innovation.

LiverPharma was founded in 1994 in Beijing (see Table 12.2) by two overseas returnees, Founder A and Founder B, who had been doctor colleagues in a state-owned hospital. Founder A returned to China after obtaining a Master's degree in Public Administration in the USA, while Founder B returned to China from Indonesia with family relocation. Founder A quit her secure medical profession due to dissatisfaction caused by control in state-owned hospitals, and set up LiverPharma with the help of her husband, a renowned doctor specialising in Hepatitis B. Subsequently, Founder B left his secure job due to infighting and the lack of intellectual freedom in the state-owned hospital where he worked, taking his research on Hepatitis B diagnosis and treatment to join LiverPharma. Unlike SpinalFixture, LiverPharma could not pursue organic growth due to high R&D investment (about 50 per cent of sales annually) required for developing its technology. This was exacerbated by the lack of external finance due to the financial crisis, the immature capital market, and the lack of government support for private enterprises in China. Consequently, LiverPharma in parallel developed over-the-counter skincare products through licensing-in technology from a state-owned hospital; its revenue was reinvested in the R&D of Hepatitis B. Compared with its peers, LiverPharma had strong R&D capability and a culture that respected learning. Founder A aspires to build a vertically integrated pharmaceutical company in the future, with a better R&D centre and more scientists working on new drugs, manufacturing facilities, and a hospital for training and clinical trials.

EP during venture creation

First, there was clear evidence of the cumulative nature of EP during venture creation. We found that prior knowledge, skills and experience of the founders/entrepreneurs was instrumental to EP in both firms. For example, the Founder of SpinalFixture commented:

> I have expertise in designing aerospace products using titanium, the same material for bone fixtures.... However, I didn't have medical knowledge, so I informally learnt medical knowledge from experts, and combined such knowledge with my engineering knowledge of aerospace design with titanium accumulated over the past thirty years.

In LiverPharma, the two founders' prior knowledge, skills and experience complemented each other: Founder A gained clinical trial expertise through working in a state-owned hospital and management knowledge and skills through an MPA study in the USA; Founder B developed expertise in basic medical research while working in a state-owned hospital and subsequently gained an international reputation. This provides evidence to support the importance of a stock of experience and skills that entrepreneurs possess in their decisions to enter the start-up process (Reuber and Fischer 1999), and hence the experiential nature of EP (Kolb 1984). Moreover, our findings go a step further to suggest that, although the founders' different personal characteristics and background alone (i.e. a retiree entrepreneur in Spinal-Fixture, who perceived himself as 'conservative', and the two returnee entrepreneurs in LiverPharma, who portrayed themselves as 'unconventional thinkers') are not the determining factors in entrepreneurial start-ups, they are associated with the different learning paths and processes which entrepreneurs take. Entrepreneurs' prior knowledge and personal characteristics interact to shape their learning paths leading to the identification of business opportunities (McMullen and Shepherd 2006).

Second, the social nature of EP was evidence. For instance, there was clear evidence that the founders' family members and close social groups (e.g. friends and ex-colleagues) played a major role in new venture creation. For example, close social groups were instrumental to the founder of SpinalFixture in identifying the business opportunity: 'After I took early retirement, I talked to the Head of a [state-owned] hospital, who is a friend of mine. He told me that there was a good opportunity to develop bone fixtures.' Similarly, Founder A of LiverPharma received crucial support from her husband and formed a business partnership with an ex-colleague: 'My husband was a famous doctor in Hepatitis. He said, "we [I] really should establish a research company and do better research" [as he felt that the control in state-owned hospitals was stifling research]. In fact, both of us were doctors, and also did clinical trials.' In LiverPharma, Founder B's passion for, and expertise in, Hepatitis B diagnosis and treatment helped to acquire new knowledge through networking among the wider expert community, as Founder A recounted: 'He [Founder B] travels a lot, giving lectures and seminars, attending conferences, and training people and doctors.... He could always find new information from internet, books, or other sources.... He is my teacher providing us information.' Our findings support the idea that the social groups with which entrepreneurs are associated are influential factors, and EP is embedded in socialisation (Cope 2005; Scherer *et al.* 1989). Moreover, our findings go a step further by suggesting that entrepreneurs' prior knowledge helps define the parameters of socialisation, which in turn provides opportunities for knowledge acquisition and upgrade. This mutually reinforcing process of prior knowledge and socialisation shapes the learning history of each entrepreneur, which defines the unique process of preparedness brought to new venture creation and management (Cope 2005).

Third, we found that the purposeful nature of EP evolved over time, as noticeably marked by critical events. In SpinalFixture, the founder's early retirement guaranteeing him a secure pension and benefit package was an important turning point of preparedness. Conversely, both founders of LiverPharma were dissatisfied with the lack of intellectual freedom and respect for research under the state-controlled system and disheartened by internal conflicts and infighting. Subsequently, both founders of LiverPharma quit secure jobs and took risks in setting up their own enterprise. For example, Founder B recalled his frustration in a state-owned hospital:

> I presented a paper on Hepatitis at a US conference [in 1983], and it was very well received.... During the coffee break, someone [a leading international expert] approached me and asked me to carry on with my research.... He also invited me to collaborate with him on his [Hepatitis] technology.... I promised to work on it. However, when I got back to work, the Head of the Hospital did not allow me to work on it. I was furious and hurt, shouting at him and also banging the table.... Later on, I informally and secretly worked with a colleague on the project.

Dissatisfaction with employment could provide a major motivation for entrepreneurship (Haynes *et al.* 1999).

Before these critical events, the entrepreneurs were explicitly driven by learning goals, which were instrumental in the accumulation of knowledge, skills and experience, while the pursuit of performance goals (i.e. setting up a new venture) was implicit. The critical events were turning points where performance goals were brought to the fore and learning became driven by performance goals. Our findings revealed that it was after the critical events that the entrepreneurs' networking activities were characterised by deliberate socialisation with a particular purpose in mind (i.e. looking for an opportunity) accompanied by active information seeking. These findings go beyond Cope (2005) by explicating the important role played by critical events in prioritising and balancing entrepreneurial goals (between learning and performance goals) and triggering deliberate socialisation with entrepreneurial goals in mind.

EP during venture management

Throughout venture management, although the founders continued to play a major role in EP, the organisational context under the founders' leadership was vital. SpinalFixture and LiverPharma experienced different growth patterns and hence had different strategic priorities. SpinalFixture went through fast, organic growth based on their core technology of spinal fixtures. Therefore, the Founder was not particularly looking for new opportunities in order to concentrate on the existing technology to achieve efficiency and scale. Conversely, suffering from financial constraints, Liver-Pharma could not stay focused on its core technology; instead, while Founder B carried on working on the Hepatitis B research, Founder A constantly sought other opportunities to quickly gain much-needed revenues to reinvest in Hepatitis B research. The different organisational contexts affected learning priorities.

First, the nature of experiential learning was manifested differently in the firms. To achieve efficiency and scale, SpinalFixture adopted functional management and focused on employees' learning to comply with regulations and practices: 'Our employees tend to stay with the company. When someone joins our company, she or he must learn the procedures and regulations, and the manufacturing requirements.... Everyone must comply with the industry and company standards' (the founder). In line with the functional management that promoted standardisation, SpinalFixture instilled a culture that favoured consensus seeking: 'our company focuses on convergent thinking that promotes harmony and consistency' (R&D manager). The marketing manager echoed this sentiment: 'I place a great emphasis on developing group spirit. Our sales and marketing staff are all recent university graduates. It is important to imbue the company's management mindset among them and develop the group spirit of a marketing and sales team.' Such traditional functional management and organisational culture was associated with the founder's personal characteristics and hence his management mindset, as the production manager commented:

> Many new enterprises have expanded very fast and overtook our company, and their bold management style is a key contributing factor to fast expansion. Our President [the founder] is old and conservative, which explains why our company prefers a steady growth. If our President were younger, we might have a more aggressive expansion plan.

Conversely, Founder A of LiverPharma championed and facilitated a team-based approach to learning, based on her experience of management training in the USA. Its focus was to develop unconventional thinking and learn from international management practice, as Founder A commented:

> I don't want to follow tradition just because our managers are not happy with certain decisions; I am using the [Harvard Business School] material to organise seminars for managers to discuss the case studies, initially monthly and subsequently every fortnight.... I hope that they can train their own departmental staff too in the future.

In addition, the R&D manager commented on LiverPharma's culture:

> First, as a pharmaceutical company, our priority is to save people's lives. Second, we encourage due diligence despite limited resources and

hardship. Third, regardless of our size and resources, our key motivation is to advance technology. We invest a lot in R&D, and have just built a new R&D lab.

The production manager added to LiverPharma's organisational culture: 'Our organisational culture is influenced by our General Manager [Founder A] who read an MPA at a US university…. She encourages all the employees to come up with more and better ideas.' Our findings suggest that, while organisational contexts define learning and hence EP, it is founders' background, knowledge and skills that help shape organisational contexts. The interaction between founders' personal background, knowledge and skills and the organisational contexts shapes EP during the venture management. Founders who are also owner-managers are often involved in all the key dimensions of entrepreneurial decision making (Wang and Altinay 2012); hence their conspicuous influence on the organisational contexts and what and how employees learn.

We also found that while LiverPharma was still pursuing growth in its core technology, SpinalFixture realised the need for a strategic transition towards becoming an innovative company in the light of intensified domestic and international competition. The founder identified the problem with the current functional management and employee mindset:

> [Over time] these functions have become isolated, each blaming the other functions whenever problems occur … we need to develop 'team spirit' among top management who are responsible for making decisions, planning for implementation and actually executing the plan…. We also need to have effective reward systems in place to encourage employees to contribute their new ideas … I also want to turn this to an employee-owned company, but this is not possible at the moment. Some people are selfish; they want dividends from profits rather than investing profits for future growth.

These findings suggest that learning history could well hinder new learning in the face of new challenges. EP is effective only when the 'right' context comes along; organisational contexts may well impede EP (Dimov 2007).

Second, what and how social learning took place differed between the firms. SpinalFixture focused on learning from doctors and foreign companies to adapt existing technology to the requirements of Chinese patients, as its founder stated:

> Our sales people discuss with the doctors in hospitals about the disease and the device required to treat the disease. They will then bring the information back into the company. We will then look at what new technology is available in foreign countries.

In stark contrast, LiverPharma faced financial constraints, as Founder B commented:

> We are so constrained by finance. If we were given resources similar to those of a stated-own research institute, we would have achieved much more than a state-owned research institute would with the same resources.

To cope with the constraints, LiverPharma focused on learning to develop creative solutions to problems and developed 'ambidextrous' capability: on the one hand developing Hepatitis B diagnosis and treatment, and on the other hand working with a reputable medical university to jointly develop skincare products to generate much-needed revenues to reinvest into research on the liver disease treatment: 'We always work with this university to find new ideas. We buy the technology [from the university], develop it and then share the profit together.' Our findings suggest that organisational contexts (especially strategic priorities) play a key role in shaping what to learn, how to learn and from whom to learn. The findings highlight the importance of studying EP in a real-life situated context (Cope 2005; Dimov 2007; Morris *et al.* 2012; Rae 2013a).

Moreover, both firms had different learning experiences about developing social capital in the wider community. SpinalFixture had a positive experience, according to the Founder:

> Our social capital is a resource advantage. We are approved by the government; we have received many awards including Harmonious Labour Relationship Award; we have the Union, the Communist Party Unit, and Communist Party Youth Unit in place.... Provincial and city-level project bidding often requires a statement of social capital. For example, in our last bidding in Inner Mongolia, our Harmonious Labour Relationship Award earned us extra points.

In contrast, LiverPharma learned from negative experience according to Founder A:

> Corruption puts extra financial constraints on small businesses. We have to use connections with people.... We have a third partner since four years ago; he used to work in a government body and has strong connections with government agents.... Even with his help, we could not obtain a patent for our treatment, as we did not have enough money to pay [for corruption].

Interestingly, the Founders' personal characteristics and background appeared to be associated with their experience of learning. In particular, the founder of SpinalFixture was more willing to conform to traditions and the existing norms, while the founders of LiverPharma endeavoured to break away from traditions and norms.

In addition, both firms learned vicariously from the failures of other companies. For example, the founder of SpinalFixture said:

> Everyone knows about San Lu [a milk powder manufacturer]; this company's reputation is ruined, domestically and internationally. We have learned [from San Lu's mistake] that customers are always first and quality is fundamental.

Similarly, Founder A of LiverPharma stated:

> A hospital accidently transferred their technology with their trademark to a company in Jiangsu Province. Now the hospital is not allowed to use their own trademark. We have learnt to protect our own brand.

These findings provide evidence of vicarious learning (Bandura 1977; Scherer *et al.* 1989), and move on to highlight the effect of negative role models in positive learning.

Third, it was evident that goals were established in both firms. However, performance goals (e.g. efficiency and scale) took priority in SpinalFixture. Accordingly, SpinalFixture focused on learning to improve efficiency through putting in place functional management, and to improve quality through complying with different trading standards: 'We comply with ISO9001 as part of our effort to improve product quality and management processes and to establish our brand reputation' (the quality control manager). In contrast, performance (e.g. revenue generation) and learning goals (e.g. developing unconventional thinking and creative problem-solving solutions) were both given priority in LiverPharma. For example, to overcome the problem of the lack of R&D investment, LiverPharma learned from Boeing in self-financing R&D:

> Boeing was trying to develop a new aerospace technology. They spent a huge amount of money and nearly went bankrupt. They had to stop [developing this technology] and started to design furniture to make some money and then went back to continue the aerospace technology. This inspired us. If we cannot afford something, we can do something else instead to make money and reinvest in what we really want to do.
>
> (Founder A)

These findings are consistent with Winters and Latham (1996), who argue that a performance goal is associated with better outcomes in a simple and standardised organisational context (e.g. SpinalFixture), and a learning goal is more effective in a complex and innovative environment (e.g. Liver-Pharma). Table 12.3 summarises the key findings.

Table 12.3 Main research findings

Key dimensions of EP	New venture creation	New venture management
The cumulative nature	• The founders' prior knowledge, skills and experience were instrumental to the discovery of opportunities and hence EP in both firms. In particular, the co-founders' complementary knowledge, skills and experience were instrumental to LiverPharma. • The founders' different personal characteristics and background are not the determining factor in entrepreneurial start-ups, but are associated with the different learning paths and hence the process of EP.	• Experiential learning was manifested differently in the two firms due to their different growth patterns and strategic priorities, although team and organisational learning took priority in both firms: SpinalFixture focused on learning best practices to comply with regulations and product quality standards through functional management, while LiverPharma adopted a team-based approach to learn from international management practice and develop unconventional thinking. • The founders' personal background, knowledge and skills shape the organisational contexts, which in turn shape the way employees learn. • Learning history could well hinder new learning in the face of new challenges.
The social nature	• The founders' family members and close social groups (e.g. friends and ex-colleagues) played a major role in identifying the business opportunities (in SpinalFixture), and in forming a business partnership (in LiverPharma). • Furthermore, the founders' prior knowledge helps to define the parameters of socialisation, which in turn shapes knowledge acquisition and upgrade in both firms. • Critical events, such as the founder's early retirement and the founders' dissatisfaction with employment and infighting within a state-owned organisation, provided a major motivation for the entrepreneurial start-ups.	• Social learning differed in the firms due to their different growth patterns and strategic priorities: SpinalFixture focused on learning from doctors and foreign companies to adapt existing technology to the requirements of Chinese patients, while LiverPharma focused on learning from a reputable medical university to develop new products and identify creative solutions to problems. • The founders' different personal backgrounds, knowledge and skills shape the focus of social learning in their firms: the founder of SpinalFixture encouraged employees to conform with traditions and norms, while the founders of LiverPharma endeavoured to break away from traditions and norms.

| The purposeful nature | • The purposeful nature of EP evolved over time, rather than being constant and unchanging.
• The critical events (i.e. the founder's early retirement in SpinalFixture and the founders' dissatisfaction with employment and infighting within a state-owned organisation) were turning points for EP: learning goals dominated prior to the critical events, and performance goals (i.e. creating a new venture) overtook the learning goals after the critical event.
• Different goals as marked by the critical events influenced the way in which the founders socialised with others. In particular, the performance goal was associated with the founders' deliberate socialisation and active information seeking with a particular goal in mind. | • Vicarious learning took place in both firms, and negative role models have a strong positive effect on learning in both firms.
• Learning and performance goals were given different levels of attention in the firms due to their different growth patterns and strategic priorities: SpinalFixture focused on performance goals – learning to improve efficiency and improve quality standards, while LiverPharma balanced learning and performance goals – learning to develop unconventional thinking and creative solutions and learning to be 'ambidextrous' in order to generate income for reinvestment in R&D.
• The emphasis of learning and performance goals was constrained by organisational contexts, such as organisational culture, structure and employee mindset. In particular, SpinalFixture's vision to transform into a more innovative company was constrained by its organisational contexts. |

Discussion

Prior literature focusing specifically on EP, either conceptually or empirically, is few and far between. Our study contributes to the EL literature by advancing the conceptualisation of EP and providing much-needed empirical evidence on how EP takes place in real-life entrepreneurial contexts. Specifically, we go beyond Cope's (2005) conceptualisation of EP as a cumulative process of learning, and articulate the social and purposeful learning process of EP. These three dimensions of EP deepen our understanding of how EP takes place and the mechanisms that enable it. Moreover, prior EP research focuses on career preparedness of entrepreneurial students (e.g. Scherer *et al.* 1989; Harvey and Evans 1995; Thandi and Sharma 2004), providing little insight into how real-life entrepreneurs learn and prepare themselves for entrepreneurial endeavours. In this study, we illustrate how a cumulative, social and purposeful learning process takes place in real-life learning contexts through a case study of two Chinese private enterprises. In particular, our study has the following theoretical implications (also summarised in Table 12.3).

First, in terms of the cumulative nature, our findings show that experiential learning is ongoing, and builds on prior knowledge, skills and experience gained well before and leading up to start-ups in our case study. These findings provide evidence for the conceptual work on the cumulative nature of EP (Cope 2005). Entrepreneurs' personal characteristics and prior knowledge, skills and experience shape the learning history and paths of EP, although personal characteristics alone are not the sole determinants of entrepreneurial start-ups. This broadly supports the view that interaction between prior knowledge and the personal characteristics enables entrepreneurs to identify opportunities (McMullen and Shepherd 2006). More importantly, our findings warn that the unique learning history could well hinder new learning in the light of environmental change. How firms can break away from outdated learning history and embracing a new learning path deserves further attention in future research.

Second, with regard to the social nature, although the extant literature argues that preparedness is 'situated' (Dimov 2007: 578), little empirical evidence exists to illustrate how learning contexts influence EP. We found that family members and close social groups to which entrepreneurs are associated are vital in shaping EP. These findings are broadly in line with the situated nature of EP (Dimov 2007) and the theory of situated learning in general (Lave and Wenger 1991; Taylor and Thorpe 2004). Most importantly, we found that it is entrepreneurs' prior knowledge, experience and background that helps define the parameters of socialisation and general networking in new venture creation. This suggests that the cumulative and social nature of EP interact and mutually support each other in the EP process, and that the cumulative nature of EP cannot be fully understood without taking into account its social context.

The interaction between the cumulative and social nature not only occurs in new venture creation but continues throughout the venture management where the accumulation of knowledge is dependent upon a range of organisational factors. For example, different growth patterns, strategic directions and management approaches are associated with different learning priorities. Moreover, as the owner-managers, the founders' personal characteristics, knowledge, skills and experiences influence their approaches to managing the firms and hence continue to shape the organisational contexts. Such findings are consistent with the argument that entrepreneurs are instrumental to firms' decision making and hence influence the entrepreneurial behaviours and practice of their firms (Wang and Altinay 2012). Finally, our findings highlight that negative role models have a strong impact on positive learning. This finding deserves further attention as prior vicarious learning has largely overlooked this aspect. Overall, these findings support the view that preparedness is dependent on the specific situations (Cope 2005; Dimov 2007). Our findings add new insight into the real-life learning contexts (Morris *et al.* 2012), complementing prior EP literature that focuses on how entrepreneurial students learn and prepare themselves for an entrepreneurial career (e.g. Scherer *et al.* 1989; Harvey and Evans 1995; Thandi and Sharma 2004).

Third, our findings highlight the importance of entrepreneurial goals, and hence the purposeful nature of EP. Although EP builds on prior knowledge well before the new venture creation, the early stage learning is primarily driven by learning goals to acquire knowledge and skills, which could be implicit in the performance goal (e.g. setting up a new venture). It is at the moment of critical events that experiential and social learning becomes explicitly driven by the performance goal. Moreover, while the entrepreneurs' prior knowledge helps define the parameters of socialisation in general, it is after the critical events that the entrepreneurs' networking activities are characterised by deliberate socialisation with a particular business focus in mind and a deliberate search for information relevant to the identified opportunities. Therefore, our findings have gone a step further to highlight the role of critical events in transforming entrepreneurs' experiential and social learning with an entrepreneurial goal. The presence of such a goal motivates the entrepreneurs to concentrate on the tasks at hand and persist in their efforts (Seijts and Latham 2005).

Conclusion

Our study advances the conceptualisation of EP as a cumulative, social and purposeful learning process. Accordingly, we articulate how experiential and social learning as well as entrepreneurial goals can act as a mechanism to enable EP. More importantly, our findings reveal that the social and purposeful nature of EP is an integral part of EP that is interwoven into the cumulative learning process. The three dimensions of EP deepen our understanding of how and under what conditions EP takes place in new venture creation and management. Practically, our findings alert entrepreneurs to pay attention to the double-edged role (positive and negative) of prior experience, especially when the context has changed; to reflect on the extent to which their personal background influences their firm's development and to break away from their own constraints in the changing business environment; and to keep a balanced approach to learning and performance goals, taking into account the needs of firm development.

Our study is exploratory in nature, based on qualitative data from two Chinese high-tech private enterprises. While our findings reveal idiosyncrasies of EP in this particular context (involving one retiree entrepreneur and two overseas returnee entrepreneurs), future research may investigate different types of entrepreneurial firms (e.g. non-high-tech private enterprises or state-owned organisations) or different types of entrepreneurs in China (e.g. the rising middle-class entrepreneurs with high formal education and prior professional experience often in multinational companies, second-generation entrepreneurs, and entrepreneurs running a management buyout or spin-off of a state-owned organisation). Given that EP is specific to personal, organisational, institutional and socio-cultural contexts, another fruitful avenue would be for future research to study how the changing market, socio-cultural and institutional environment affects EP over time, especially in an international comparative setting. Finally, our study uses triangulation of retrospective interview data with concurrent interview and secondary data to mitigate the risks involved in retrospective interview data only. Future research may pursue concurrent longitudinal case study data to unpack real-time events in the new venture creation and management processes.

Acknowledgements

We thank the Economic and Social Research Council, UK for their funding support for the project (Award No. RES-061–25–0023). This chapter was previously published in *International Journal of Entrepreneurial Behaviour and Research*, 2014, Volume No. 20, Issue No. 4, pp. 351–374.

References

Aldrich, H.E. and Kenworthy, A. (1999) The accidental entrepreneur: Cambellian antinomies and organizational foundings. In J.A.C. Baum and B. McKelvey (eds), *Variations in Organizational Science: In Honor of Donald T. Campbell.* Newbury Park, CA: Sage, pp. 19–33.

Argyris, C. and Schön, D.A. (1978) *Organisational Learning: A theory of action perspective.* Reading, MA: Addison-Wesley.

Bandura, A. (1977) *Social Learning Theory.* Englewood Cliffs, NJ: Prentice Hall.

Bernard, R.H., Killworth. P., Kronenfeld, D. and Sailer, L. (1984. The problem of informant accuracy: The validity of retrospective data. In B.J. Siegel (ed.), A.R. Beals and S.A. Tyler (Associate eds), *Annual Review of Anthropology*, Vol. 13. Palo Alto, CA: Annual Review, pp. 495–517.

Bingham, C.B. and Davis, J.P. (2012) Learning sequences: Their existence, effect, and evolution. *Academy of Management Journal*, 55(3), pp. 611–641.

Boud, D., Cohen, R. and Walker, D. (1993) Introduction: Understanding learning from experience. In D. Boud, R. Cohen and D. Walker (eds), *Using Experience for Learning*. Buckingham: SRHE and Open University Press, pp. 1–18.

Brockhaus, R.H. and Horwitz, P.S. (1986) The psychology of the entrepreneur. In D.L. Sexton and R.W. Smilor (eds), *The Art and Science of Entrepreneurship*. Cambridge, MA: Ballinger, pp. 25–48.

Busenitz, L.W. (1996) Research on entrepreneurial alertness: Sampling, measurement, and theoretical issues. *Journal of Small Business Management*, 34, pp. 35–44.

Bygrave, W. and Minniti, M. (2000) The social dynamics of entrepreneurship. *Entrepreneurship Theory and Practice*, 24(3), pp. 25–36.

Cooper, S.Y. and Park, J.S. (2008) The impact of 'incubator' organizations on opportunity recognition and technology innovation in new, entrepreneurial high-technology ventures. *International Small Business Journal*, 26(1), pp. 27–56.

Cope, J. (2003) Entrepreneurial learning and critical reflection: Discontinuous events as triggers for 'higher-level' learning. *Management Learning*, 34(4), pp. 429–450.

—— (2005) Toward a dynamic learning perspective of entrepreneurship. *Entrepreneurship Theory and Practice*, 29(4), pp. 373–397.

—— (2011) Entrepreneurial learning from failure: An interpretative phenomenological analysis. *Journal of Business Venturing*, 16(6), pp. 604–623.

Datamonitor (2008a) *Industry Profile: Pharmaceutical industry in China*. London: Datamonitor.

—— (2008b) *Industry Profile: Healthcare devices in China*. London: Datamonitor.

Deakins, D. (1996) *Entrepreneurship and Small Firms*. Maidenhead: McGraw-Hill.

Dimov, D. (2007) From opportunity insight to opportunity intention: The importance of person–situation learning match. *Entrepreneurship Theory and Practice*, 31(4), pp. 561–583.

Easterby-Smith, M. and Malina, D. (1999) Cross-cultural collaborative research: Toward reflexivity. *Academy of Management Journal*, 42(1), pp. 76–86.

Eisenhardt, K.M. (1989) Building theories from case study research. *Academy of Management Review*, 14, pp. 532–550.

Festervand, T.A. and Forrest, J.E. (1993) Entrepreneurial preparedness: A multi-stage model. *Journal of Business and Entrepreneurship*, 5(3), pp. 65–77.

Freeman, L.C., Romney, A.K. and Freeman, S.C. (1987) Cognitive structure and informant accuracy. *American Anthropologist*, 89, pp. 310–325.

Gardet, E. and Fraiha, S. (2012) Coordination modes established by the hub firm of an innovation network: The case of an SME bearer. *Journal of Small Business Management*, 50(2), pp. 216–238.

Gummesson, E. (2000) *Qualitative Methods in Management Research*. London: Sage.

Hamilton, E. (2011) Entrepreneurial learning in family business: A situated learning perspective. *Journal of Small Business and Enterprise Development*, 18(1), pp. 8–26.

Harvey, M. and Evans, R. (1995) Strategic windows in the entrepreneurial process. *Journal of Business Venturing*, 10, pp. 331–347.

Haynes, P.J., Becherer, R.C., Helms, M.M. and Jones, M.A. (1999) The accidental entrepreneur: When dissatisfaction is the primary motivation for entrepreneurship. *Journal of Business & Entrepreneurship*, 11(2), pp. 89–104.

Hirsch, P.M. (1995) Tales from the field: Learning from researchers' accounts. In R. Hertz and J.B. Imber (eds), *Studying Elites Using Qualitative Research*. London: Sage, pp. 72–79.

Holcomb, T.R., Ireland, R.D., Holmes Jr., R.M. and Hitt, M.A. (2009) Architecture of entrepreneurial learning: Exploring the link among heuristics, knowledge, and action. *Entrepreneurship Theory and Practice*, 33(1), pp. 167–192.

Hu, Y., Geng, F., Bian, Y. and Wang, Y. (2007) The Chinese pharmaceutical market: Perspectives of the health consumer. *Journal of Medical Marketing*, 7(4), pp. 295–300.

Johnsen, G.J. and McMahon, R.G.P. (2005) Owner-manager gender, financial performance and business growth amongst SMEs from Australia's business longitudinal survey. *International Small Business Journal*, 23(2), pp. 115–142.

Jones, K. and Tullous, R. (2002) Behaviors of pre-venture entrepreneurs and perceptions of their financial needs. *Journal of Small Business Management*, 40, pp. 233–249.

Kanfer, R. and Ackerman, P.L. (1989) Motivation and cognitive abilities: An integrative/aptitude-treatment interaction approach to skill acquisition. *Journal of Applied Psychology*, 74, pp. 657–690.

Karataş-Özkan, M. (2011) Understanding relational qualities of entrepreneurial learning: Towards a multi-layered approach. *Entrepreneurship and Regional Development: An International Journal*, 23, pp. 9–10, 877–906.

Kolb, D.A. (1984) *Experiential Learning: Experience as the source of learning and development*. Englewood Cliffs, NJ: Prentice Hall.

Kreitner, R. and Luthans, F. (1984) A social learning approach to behavioral management: Radical behaviorists 'mellowing out'. *Organizational Dynamics*, 13(2), pp. 47–65.

Lave, J. and Wenger, E. (1991) *Situated Learning: Legitimate peripheral participation*. New York: Cambridge University Press.

Lee, R. and Jones, O. (2008) Networks, communication and learning during business start-up: The creation of cognitive social capital. *International Small Business Journal*, 26, pp. 559–591.

Leonard, D.C. (2008) The impact of learning goals on emotional, social and cognitive intelligence competency development. *Journal of Management Development*, 27 (1), pp. 109–128.

Liang, B. and Lu, H. (2006) Conducting fieldwork in China: Observations on collecting primary data regarding crime, law, and the criminal justice system. *Journal of Contemporary Criminal Justice*, 22(2), pp. 157–172.

Lincoln, Y. and Guba, E. (1985) *Naturalistic Inquiry*. Beverly Hills, CA: Sage.

McMullen, J.S. and Shepherd, D.A. (2006) Entrepreneurial action and the role of uncertainty in the theory of the entrepreneur. *Academy of Management Review*, 31(1), pp. 132–152.

Mezirow, J. (1991) *Transformative Dimensions of Adult Learning*. San Francisco, CA: Jossey-Bass.

Miles, M.B. and Huberman, A.M. (1994) *Qualitative Data Analysis*. Thousand Oaks, CA: Sage.

Minniti, M. and Bygrave, W. (2001) A dynamic model of entrepreneurial learning. *Entrepreneurship Theory and Practice*, 25(3), pp. 5–16.

Morris, M.H., Kuratko, D.F., Schindehutte, M. and Spivack, A.J. (2012) Framing the entrepreneurial experience. *Entrepreneurship: Theory and Practice*, 36(1), pp. 11–40.

Newbert, S.L. (2005) New firm formation: A dynamic capability perspective. *Journal of Small Business Management*, 43(1), pp. 55–77.

Pittaway, L. and Thorpe, R. (2012) A framework for entrepreneurial learning: A tribute to Jason Cope. *Entrepreneurship and Regional Development: An International Journal*, 24(9–10), pp. 837–859.

Politis, D. (2005) The process of entrepreneurial learning: A conceptual framework. *Entrepreneurship Theory and Practice*, 29(4), pp. 399–424.

Rae, D. (2013a) The contribution of momentary perspectives to entrepreneurial learning and creativity. *Industry and Higher Education*, 27(6), pp. 407–420.

—— (2013b) Editorial. *International Journal of Entrepreneurial Behaviour and Research*, 19(1).

Ravasi, D. and Turati, C. (2005) Exploring entrepreneurial learning: A comparative study of technology development projects. *Journal of Business Venturing*, 20(1), pp. 137–164.

Reuber, A.R. and Fischer, E. (1999) Understanding the consequences of founders' experience. *Journal of Small Business Management*, 37(2), pp. 30–45.

Saunders, M.N.K., Lewis, P. and Thornhill, A. (2009) *Research Methods for Business Students* (5th edn). Harlow, FT: Prentice Hall.

Scherer, R.F., Adams, J.S. and Wiebe, F.A. (1988) Social learning theory as a conceptual framework for entrepreneurship research: The role of observational learning. In G.B. Roberts, H. Lasher and E. Maliche (eds), *Entrepreneurship: New direction for a global economy. Proceedings of the International Council for Small Business*, pp. 243–249.

Scherer, R.F., Adams, J.S., Carley, S.S. and Wiebe, F.A. (1989) Role model performance effects on development of entrepreneurial career preference. *Entrepreneurship Theory and Practice*, 13(3), pp. 53–71.

Seijts, G.H. and Latham, G.P. (2005) Learning versus performance goals: When should each be used. *Academy of Management Executive*, 19(1), pp. 124–131.

Sexton, D.L. (1987) Advancing small business research: Utilizing research from other areas. *American Journal of Small Business*, 11, pp. 25–30.

Shah, S.K. and Tripsas, M. (2007) The accidental entrepreneur: The emergent and collective process of user entrepreneurship. *Strategic Entrepreneurship Journal*, 1(1–2), pp. 123–140.

Shane, S. (2000) Prior knowledge and the discovery of entrepreneurial opportunity. *Organization Science*, 11, pp. 448–469.

Starr, J.A. and Fondas, N. (1992) A model of entrepreneurial socialization and organization formation. *Entrepreneurship Theory and Practice*, 17(1), pp. 67–76.

Strauss, A. and Corbin, J. (1998) *Basics of Qualitative Research: Techniques and procedures for developing grounded theory* (2nd edn). Thousand Oaks, CA: Sage.

Taylor, D.W. and Thorpe, R. (2004) Entrepreneurial learning: A process of co-participation. *Journal of Small Business and Enterprise Development*, 11(2), pp. 203–211.

Thandi, H. and Sharma, R. (2004) MBA students' preparedness for entrepreneurial efforts. *Tertiary Education and Management*, 10, pp. 209–226.

Venkatarman, S. (1997) The distinctive domain of entrepreneurship research. In J. Katz and R. Brockhaus (eds), *Advances in Entrepreneurship, Firm Emergence, and Growth*. Greenwich, CT: JAI Press, pp. 119–138.

Wang, C.L. and Altinay, L. (2012) Social embeddedness, entrepreneurial orientation and firm growth in ethnic minority small businesses in the United Kingdom. *The International Small Business Journal*, 30(1), pp. 3–23.

Wang, C.L. and Chugh, H. (2014) Entrepreneurial learning: Past research and future challenges. *The International Journal of Management Reviews*, 16(1), pp. 24–61.

Wenger, E. (1998) *Communities of Practice: Learning, meaning, and identity*. New York: Cambridge University Press.

West, G.P. and Noel, T.W. (2009) The impact of knowledge resources in new venture performance. *Journal of Small Business Management*, 47(1), pp. 1–22.

Westhead, P. and Wright, M. (2011) David Storey's optimism and chance perspective: A case of the Emperor's new clothes? *International Small Business Journal*, 29(6), pp. 714–729.

Westhead, P., Ucbasaran, D. and Wright, M. (2005) Decisions, actions, performance: Do novice, serial, and portfolio entrepreneurs differ? *Journal of Small Business Management*, 43(4), pp. 393–417.

Williams, A.P.O. (2001) A belief-focused process model of organizational learning. *Journal of Management Studies*, 38(1), pp. 67–85.

Winters, D. and Latham, G. (1996) The effect of learning versus outcome goals on a simple versus a complex task. *Group and Organization Management*, 21(2), pp. 236–250.

Wortman, M.S. (1987) Entrepreneurship: An integrating typology and evaluation of empirical research in the field. *Journal of Management*, 13, pp. 259–279.

Wright, M., Liu, X., Buck, T. and Filatotchev, I. (2008) Returnee entrepreneurs, science park location choice and performance: An analysis of high-technology SMEs in China. *Entrepreneurship Theory and Practice*, 32(1), pp. 131–155.

Yam, R.C.M., Guan, J.C., Pun, K.F. and Tang, E.P.Y. (2004) An audit of technological innovation capabilities in Chinese firms: Some empirical findings in Beijing, China. *Research Policy*, 33(8), pp. 1123–1140.

Yin, R.K. (2009) *Case Study Research: Design and methods* (4th edn). Thousand Oaks, CA: Sage.

Zhao, X., Flynn, B.B. and Roth, A.V. (2006) Decision sciences research in China: A critical review and research agenda – foundations and overview. *Decision Sciences*, 37(4), pp. 451–496.

13 Entrepreneurial learning in the Chinese business context

Lorraine Watkins-Mathys

Introduction

During the past two decades the concept of entrepreneurial learning has become an important theme among researchers studying the phenomenon of entrepreneurship within the context of developed economies. The focus of this research on entrepreneurial learning has been largely on the individual's learning from a personal, contextual and situated learning perspective (Hines and Thorpe 1995; Gibb 1997; Deakins and Freel 1998; Cope 2003; van Gelderen *et al.* 2005; Rae 2005) and predominantly in Anglo-Saxon contexts. Despite a concentrated effort by the Chinese government to promote the growth of SMEs (Millman *et al.* 2008) and innovation through hi-tech science and innovation parks (Watkins-Mathys and Foster 2006), the theme of entrepreneurial learning in the China context has not been explored to any great extent.

Against this background therefore, the aim of this chapter is to examine entrepreneurial learning in the Chinese business context. To this end, the chapter's objectives are as follows. First, to discuss the concept of entrepreneurial learning as found in the extant literature; second, to examine the Eastern mindset and Confucian approaches to learning and entrepreneurship, comparing these to Western approaches to entrepreneurial learning; and third, to illustrate entrepreneurial learning in the Chinese business context using the author's earlier empirical work undertaken among hi-tech entrepreneurs in China (Watkins-Mathys and Foster 2006).

The approach adopted in this chapter is to analyse the theoretical concepts found in the literature on entrepreneurial learning and to illustrate these concepts from insights obtained from qualitative individual and focus group interviews conducted with Chinese hi-tech entrepreneurs. In this respect the chapter offers subjective perspectives given by Chinese hi-tech entrepreneurs that emerged coincidentally (Gibbs 1997) during a research project focused on the role of science and technology parks in promoting hi-tech entrepreneurship (Watkins-Mathys and Foster 2006). The chapter concludes with reflections about entrepreneurial learning in China and makes recommendations for further research.

Entrepreneurial learning: Western and Eastern perspectives

This section discusses entrepreneurial learning focusing in particular on perspectives concerned with experiential and transformational or deep learning (Pittaway and Thorpe 2012; Cope and Watts 2000) that is sometimes also referred to as the 'art' of entrepreneurial practice (Rae 2005: 324), which emphasises a process of learning. This is followed by an examination of Eastern thought, centred on Confucianism and how it differs from the rational, logical thinking inherent in the Western mindset; notably how it adopts a pragmatic and experiential learning approach, from a subjective rather than a rational perspective (Yang *et al.* 2006), where 'the self itself is only realized through the act of experiencing' (Elkin *et al.* 2009: 75). This section also introduces the reader to Chinese-specific aspects found in the literature on Chinese entrepreneurship: first, 'guanxi' and how this is applied to overcome 'institutional holes' (Yang 2004); second, characteristics of Chinese entrepreneurs as perceived by Chinese entrepreneurs themselves (Rozell *et al.* 2011), highlighting their attitudes and behaviours as entrepreneurs. At the end of this section, Western and Eastern concepts of entrepreneurial learning are compared and conclusions drawn about the respective approaches.

Western perspectives

Turning to the literature on entrepreneurial learning, researchers recognise that having the ability to learn is fundamental to developing entrepreneurial capabilities (Rae and Carswell 2000, cited in Man 2006). Moreover, entrepreneurial learning is perceived as fundamental to understanding entrepreneurship because it is linked to opportunity recognition and venture creation (Man 2012: 549).

Drawing on Rae's body of work (Rae and Carswell 2000; Rae 2005), Williams Middleton and Donnellon (2014: 4) identify three major themes of entrepreneurial learning:

1   Individuals are involved in developing themselves personally and socially as entrepreneurs.
2   Individual entrepreneurs learn from context.
3   Individual entrepreneurs turn the opportunity spotted into an enterprise (venture), thereby rendering it into a real opportunity.

Thus, the literature emphasises the importance of the personal and social in developing an individual's human and social capital (Macpherson and Holt 2007; Gibb 1997) that contributes to entrepreneurial capability. Moreover, some argue that entrepreneurial learning is a sense-making process (Weick 1995) – a process that creates meaning through shared social interactions (individuals and social contexts) resulting in the 'intertwining of the cognitive and the social' (ibid.: 38). This perspective chimes with the view that 'learning is a process of self-creation and re-creation' (Hjorth and Johannisson 2009: 60) dependent on the individual engaging with his or her social contexts and other individuals. Thus, these processes contribute to creating a person's identity (Rae 2006) and include a process of 'relationally co-constructing self and other self and world' (Hosking *et al.* 1995; Hosking and Hjorth 2004, cited in Hjorth and Johannisson 2009: 60). Learning, therefore, has the ability to alter an individual's values and beliefs, i.e. transformational learning (Brown and Duguid 1991). Moreover, it is a continuous and reiterative process that involves creativity and creating 'new things' (Hjorth and Johannisson 2009: 57).

Other authors on entrepreneurial learning include aspects of the emotional, and risk to family and individual, and failure, as well as the impact of critical incidents that enable an entrepreneur to develop a 'stock of experience' and learning (Cope 2005, 2010). The role of contextual, experimental and situated learning is emphasised as a learning process that develops entrepreneurial capability (Gibb 1997; Cope 2005; Rae 2006). As already indicated above, cognition is linked to contextual, situational and experiential learning. In particular, the role of critical reflection leading to generative (or deep) learning is highlighted by Cope (2003). Indeed, Gibb (2007) posits that entrepreneurial learning only takes place when the learner is engaged in 'learning by doing' that involves 'processes of problem solving, grasping opportunities, experimenting and making things up, making mistakes, copying and overall by doing' (Gibb 2007: 74). Furthermore, Gibb (2007) argues that learning takes place through a process of internalisation, thereby also linking cognition to the individual's learning in context and experience.

Man (2006) adds a behavioural emphasis to entrepreneurial learning that includes 'learning competences' around being active in seeking learning opportunities, continuously learning, learning selectively and purposely, learning about the business or trade in depth, reflecting on experience and wanting to improve upon it, and putting into practice what has been learned previously (Man 2006: 316). Cope (2005, 2010) adds the investment of emotion brought about by exposing self and others (such as family or partners) to risk when engaged in venture creation, and suggests that the latter induce deeper levels of learning or generative entrepreneurial learning. In other words, learning goes beyond context-related, reflective learning and includes learning how to do things not yet confronted (Gibb 1997; Senge 1990; Appelbaum and Goransson 1997; Cope 2010).

To summarise, entrepreneurial learning is about experiencing learning through action and doing (Gibb 1997; Cope 2005); it involves a process of sense making (Weick 1995), whereby the individual creates self and understanding through social interaction with others (Hjorth and Johannisson 2009); it involves cognition and reflection, or in Gibb's words 'internalisation' (Gibb 2007), that leads to an accumulation of 'entrepreneurial stock'

(Cope 2005). Finally, these processes of entrepreneurial learning combine to produce generative or transformational learning because they have the power to change beliefs and values through the process of creating/re-creating self and others. The main components of entrepreneurial learning are summarised in Table 13.1.

These approaches to entrepreneurial learning have lent themselves more towards the adoption of qualitative methodologies, including interviews focusing on entrepreneurs' stories, biographies (Easterby-Smith *et al.* 1991) and reflections of events, social interactions (Gibbs 1997; Rae 2006), as well as examining the language and discourse used by entrepreneurs during interview (Rae 2006), interpretive phenomenological enquiry (Cope 2003), and critical incident techniques (Taylor and Thorpe 2004; Cope 2010). The purpose of these methodologies has been to gain in-depth insights into the experiences of entrepreneurs as perceived and experienced by them.

Traditional Chinese perspectives on approaches to learning

As stated earlier, there is a gap in the literature that deals specifically with entrepreneurial learning in the Chinese context, and so to this end I have chosen to examine theoretical perspectives focused on the Eastern mindset towards knowledge and learning (Chia 2003), Confucian perspective of learning (Yang *et al.* 2006) and Chinese pragmatism and its relationship to learning (Elkin *et al.* 2009).

According to Chia (2003), Western thought is heavily influenced by Aristotle, thus emphasising knowledge and reason (or logic). This perspective provides a philosophical worldview where a knowledgeable person is seen as more important than someone who can perform a task. This leads to 'the art of doing' being 'overshadowed by the art of reasoning' (Chia 2003: 955). Consequently, theory and practice in Western management literature are often perceived to be at odds due to the superior position of knowledge (theory) versus practice (Yang *et al.* 2006; Chia 2003).

By contrast, Eastern thinking highlights 'particularity and uniqueness' rejecting rules, standards and norms that may be applied in general (Atkinson *et al.* 1987: 137, cited in Elkin *et al.* 2009: 75). Moreover, the Chinese sense of reality may be described as an aesthetic model that is in antithesis to Western traditions of generality and universalism.

The difference in traditional Western and Eastern mindsets may also be seen through respective written languages. Western written languages use an alphabet where 'a set of letters or symbols in a fixed order' are 'used to represent the basic set of speech sounds of a language' (*Oxford Dictionaries* 2013). This lends itself to providing a literal meaning of words that may be generalised and applied universally. By contrast, Eastern written languages adopt an ideographic approach, where meaning is conveyed through abstract symbols that need to be interpreted. This non-literal approach enables people who do not share the same dialect, and who

Table 13.1 Western perspectives on entrepreneurial learning

Western perspectives	Authors	Comments
Learning by doing; situated learning; experiential learning; learning how to do new things	Gibb 1997; Cope 2005; Rae 2006; Hjorth and Johannisson 2009	Emphasis on learning in the moment, from the context, experimenting, trial and error, repeating tasks; applying creativity in the learning process that enables individuals to do new things.
Human and social capital; sense making; creating self-identity	Gibb 1997; Weick 1996; Hosking *et al.* 1995; Hosking and Hjorth 2004, cited in Man 2012; Hjorth and Johannisson 2009; Williams *et al.* 2014	The personal and social are important in developing an individual's human and social capital and contribute to developing entrepreneurial capability. Entrepreneurial learning is a sense-making process – a process that creates meaning through shared social interactions (individual and social contexts) which also includes a process of self-creation that is an ongoing process.
Internalisation; reflection of actions and critical incidents, 'entrepreneurial stock' cognitive learning	Cope 2005, 2010; Gibb 1997	The literature links cognition to contextual, situated and experiential learning; i.e. learning takes place through a process of internalisation and reflection of the learning from context and experience.
Transformational and generative learning	Cope 2010; Appelbaum and Goransson 1997	The processes of entrepreneurial learning (situated, context learning, stock of experience, creating self and meaning through personal and social interactions, including critical incidents) combine to produce generative or transformational learning because they change an individual's beliefs and values through the process of creating/re-creating self and others.
Attitude to, and application of, entrepreneurial learning (behavioural approach)	Man 2006	Includes aspects of being active in seeking learning opportunities, continuously learning, learning selectively and purposely, learning about the business or trade in depth, reflecting on experience and wanting to improve upon it, and putting into practice what has been previously learned.

would not understand each other's speech, to share understanding and meaning through the characters (*Oxford Dictionaries* 2013). Thus, it is possible for Japanese and Chinese people, for example, to interpret the meaning of each other's language through the shared characters. The emphasis, therefore, is on symbols and understanding symbols within a context. Both context and interpretation create meaning and understanding. Simply put, much of Western thinking has been to see the world in rational and objective terms, while Eastern thinking places emphasis on understanding meaning through context and interpretation.

Other characteristics prevalent in Western organisations include a desire to 'control the external environment so that the organisational preference (order and stability) inside the company spreads to the external environment as well' (Elkin *et al.* 2009: 73). Yang *et al.* (2006) refer to the Western perspective on learning as the 'technical-rational philosophy of teaching and learning' (Yang *et al.* 2006: 348) that promotes logical order and generality, and lends itself to universal truths (Elkin *et al.* 2009). Although Elkin *et al.*'s view (2009) is in keeping with the Aristotelian philosophical perspective, the entrepreneurial learning approaches discussed in the previous section do not follow the rational and positivist approach. They align themselves much more to the 'art of doing', interpretation of meaning, reflection, experience and identity.

Turning to traditional Confucian thought on learning, the goal of learning is based on five interrelated areas (Yang *et al.* 2006). These are presented in Figure 13.1, and include: benevolence and morality; intelligence and knowledge; courage and constitution; aesthesis and music; talent and faculty (Guo 2002, cited in Yang *et al.* 2006: 348).

Out of the five areas only one is about knowledge. The other four areas emphasise values, morals, virtues, talents, capabilities, arts and sense of experience (aesthesis). Furthermore, Yang *et al.* (2006) highlight the moral and social obligations of learning under Confucianism and cite the following Chinese to illustrate this – '*Xiu Sheng, Qi Jia, Zhi Guo, Ping Tian Xia*' – which translated means 'cultivate one's moral qualities, set up family, serve for the country, and work towards equality and a harmonized world' (Yang *et al.* 2006: 348). What comes through here is a strong sense of moral duty, notably in relation to others such as family and the world; and striving to create harmony and balance in society through one's position within society and order within a given hierarchy (Yang 2006). This finds resonance with Zhao and Roper (2011), who concur that these values have to be exercised or practised. Their work among managers in China underlined that Confucian values of collectivism and striving for harmony remain strong despite the changes brought about through economic reforms. They concluded: 'The successful combination of a strong Confucian tradition with commercial activities epitomises the ideal of modern Confucian entrepreneurship' (Zhao and Roper 2011: 743).

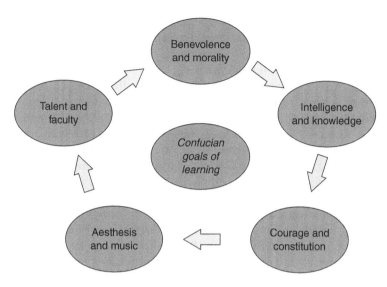

Figure 13.1 Confucian goals of learning (source: adapted from Guo (2002) and cited in Yang *et al.* (2006: 348)).

Turning to Elkin *et al.* (2009), their work on Chinese pragmatism and the learning organisation also reinforced the concept of learning by doing. Moreover, they argue that this is the basis upon which individuals and organisations experience reality. Chia (2003) adds that experience results in 'change and transformation' (Chia 2003: 963).

In summarising these two sub-sections, while notable differences may be observed in the dominant philosophical premises found in Western and Eastern thinking, it may be argued that Western entrepreneurial learning literature discussed in this chapter is much more closely aligned to Confucian thinking because of its interpretive approach. Like Confucian learning it is focused on experiential, reflective and transformative learning that brings in social, personal and emotional dimensions. Confucian learning and values do, however, introduce new dimensions to entrepreneurial learning, not strongly articulated in Western entrepreneurial learning literature. These include a strong sense of moral duty to family and society, a responsibility to create harmony and balance in society, and to practise the art of being through doing, thereby also perfecting knowledge.

China's entrepreneurial context: institutional holes and guanxi

China's modern-day environment has created its own context for entrepreneurship. To this end, this section examines the work around institutional barriers, the role of guanxi and perceptions around the characteristics of

Chinese entrepreneurs, as these have been the focus of a number of studies into Chinese entrepreneurship and provide useful perspectives on entrepreneurial learning. These are then linked to the traditional concepts of learning in Chinese thinking in order to summarise key concepts relating to Chinese entrepreneurial learning in Table 13.2.

Entrepreneurship in China is governed by a nationally developed policy framework that leaves it to provincial governments to interpret and implement the policies at local level, including resource allocation. Different ministries are responsible for respective industries and in turn have different resources available (i.e. each ministry or institutional body has its own resource allocation and activities). However, maximising these resources by combining potentially complementary resources often proves difficult, leaving resources under-exploited (Yang 2004). Overcoming these structural barriers and spotting the opportunities to be seized is something that Chinese entrepreneurs do. Thus, Yan (2004) builds on Burt's (1992) concept of 'structural holes', noting that: 'When these conditions exist, it is up to the entrepreneur to recognize the opportunities and take actions' (Yang 2004: 376).

The gaps in the institutional framework result from having a plethora of institutional rules applying to different industry groups. The difference in unique resources found in these separate industry groups and the lack of connections between these groups of industries prevent individuals from drawing on complementary resources. However, it is precisely these 'holes' or 'disconnections' that spur entrepreneurial behaviour, enabling individuals to overcome continuously changing, ambiguous environments which do not maximise the available resources (Gibb and Li 2003). Like Schumpeter, Yang (2004) argues that imperfections in institutional structures can develop into sources of entrepreneurship because they drive entrepreneurs to spot the opportunities in the 'holes' (ibid.: 373). Furthermore, he suggests that these actions place individual entrepreneurs in a 'network of social connections' (ibid.: 372).

Some authors have tried to understand how Chinese entrepreneurs work through these 'institutional holes' by examining the role of 'guanxi' in Chinese entrepreneurship (Li and Matlay 2006). 'Guanxi' means 'personal favour' (renqing) or exchange of favour, and is based on 'reciprocity', 'responsibility' and 'obligation' (Li and Liu 2010). This takes place within a network where individuals are bound to each other by familial and/or personal ties. It is argued by some that guanxi gives entrepreneurs legitimacy of their enterprise activities and enables them to gain access to resources controlled by local authorities (Tsang 1999, cited in Carlisle and Flynn 2005). Consequently however, as China's reforms strengthen its market economy, the need for guanxi as a means of gaining legitimacy and access to resources diminishes (Anderson and Lee 2008). While there may be mixed views about the importance of guanxi in the Chinese entrepreneurship context, it is, nevertheless, a traditional Chinese concept that is still practised in modern-day China and used to overcome institutional barriers. For this reason, and also that it is linked to aspects of human and social capital, the concept of guanxi is discussed in more detail in subsequent paragraphs.

Li and Liu's (2010) study on guanxi networks and their role in achieving entrepreneurial growth offers interesting insights into the concept. In their work Li and Liu (2010) divide guanxi into two types:

1   embedded guanxi based on personal and social ties (family and *shuren*) discussed earlier in this section;
2   stranger guanxi based on the market or relationships built up through business networks.

They go on to explain:

> [F]amily 'guanxi' and 'shuren guanxi' are highly correlated in the Chinese informal social networks, constituting the embedded 'guanxi' networks, and the stranger 'guanxi' network belongs to, apparently, market 'guanxi'. Considering the aim of this study, we define the embedded 'guanxi' as the 'guanxi' characterized by the responsibility, favor, reciprocity, and mianzi (face-saving), and market 'guanxi' as an interest-based trading or cooperative relationship.
>
> (Li and Liu 2010: 345)

They differentiate, therefore, between guanxi that harps back to the notion of reciprocal responsibility and obligation that manifests itself through showing personal favour and the modern-day business concept focused on a relationship that brings mutual benefit to the business parties.

The results from Li and Liu's (2010) survey data showed that small and new businesses relied mainly on their personal/social guanxi while the medium to large businesses tended to use their market guanxi more (ibid.: 354). This confirmed that market guanxi becomes more important to larger and more mature companies. However, there was no suggestion that social and personal guanxi diminished in the performance of medium and large enterprises. In other words, the positive correlation between embedded (social and personal) guanxi remained positive for small, medium and large enterprises (ibid.: 356). Nevertheless, in order to grow, enterprises need to develop their market networks.

Turning to Rozell *et al.*'s (2011) research on Chinese business owners' perceptions of the characteristics of successful entrepreneurs, various perspectives found in the entrepreneurial literature highlighted in Table 13.1 may be observed. Their focus group research among twenty-five MBA students from Henan University of Finance and Economics, who were also business owners, aimed to examine entrepreneurial attributes and behaviours. They approached this research from a value-belief perspective based on the concept that shared values developed within a cultural context are deemed to influence behaviours (Rozell *et al.* 2011: 63). This approach chimes with the Confucian values perspective discussed in the earlier section, and Rozell *et al.*'s (2011) findings highlight four main entrepreneurial attributes and behaviours.

First, *good communication and networking*, which incorporates embedded networks (guanxi), also refers to being well informed and being able to communicate. These are linked to the human and social capital perspectives of learning.

Second, *exploratory and adventurous* behaviours resonate well with experiential learning and risk taking. This aligns with the perspective of learning by doing, situated learning and learning from critical incidents, which may all be seen as one form or another of experiential learning.

Third, being *knowledgeable, competent and exercising good judgement* chime with the entrepreneurial perspective which picks up on cognitive learning, knowledge, entrepreneurial 'stock' and to some extent reflection.

Fourth, *willingness to learn, determined and resolute, passionate and hard-working* fit well with the behavioural approach based on attitude to, and application of, entrepreneurial learning. It also links to some of the attributes to learning in Confucian learning approaches (courage and constitution).

Table 13.2 summarises the key elements discussed above relating to Chinese approaches to learning and entrepreneurship found in the literature. They draw on the Confucian goals of learning highlighted in Figure 13.1, where moral values (benevolence and morality) are emphasised; attitude to learning (courage and constitution) is likened to learning an art (aesthesis and music) that requires practice and perfecting and in turn develops the learner's capability (talent and faculty; intelligence and knowledge). In addition, Table 13.2 incorporates the modern-day Chinese context for entrepreneurship that draws attention to the role of guanxi and 'institutional holes' but also re-emphasises traditional perspectives: learning by doing (Elkin *et al.* 2009); resolution and hard work to learn; developing knowledge and competency that includes the development of good judgement; and learning that results in transformation (Chia 2003).

The next section draws on the author's own empirical data collection among Chinese hi-tech entrepreneurs in the Beijing and Shanghai area (Watkins-Mathys and Foster 2006). It provides insights into entrepreneurial learning that were obtained coincidentally during the interviews and focus group sessions. The data were gleamed as a consequence of conversations 'drifting' (Gibbs 1997) into areas of Chinese entrepreneurial learning that are noted in Table 13.1, and include the following:

- Learning by doing or the 'art of doing' (Elkin 2009; Chia 2003) and knowledge gained through the 'art of doing' (Yang 2006).
- Guanxi (Li and Liu 2010; Anderson and Lee 2008).

Table 13.2 Eastern perspectives on entrepreneurial learning, including Confucian learning goals

Eastern perspectives	Authors	Comments
Learning by doing; 'the art of doing'	Elkin 2009; Chia 2003; Guo 2002, cited in Yang et al. 2006	Confucian thinking places emphasis on doing in order to perfect and reach the five goals of learning referred to in Figure 13.1.
Guanxi family and business-focused aspects of the concept	Li and Liu 2010; Anderson and Lee 2008	Human and social capital is contained within the concept of guanxi in both familial guanxi and 'shuren' guanxi. Concepts still prevalent in Chinese entrepreneurship literature.
Experience results in 'change and transformation'	Yang 2004; Chia 2003	Learning by doing is the basis upon which individuals and organisations experience reality and this experience gained results in 'change and transformation'.
Behavioural: attitude and behaviour in the face of 'institutional holes'	Yang 2004; Rozell et al. 2011	Noted as using guanxi to overcome institutional barriers but also attitudes and behaviours such as being exploratory and adventurous; being willing and determined to learn (including passionate and hard-working); being knowledgeable, competent and having good judgement. Many of these aspects resonate with practising to achieve the Confucian learning goals.
The importance of moral values, family, serve country and work towards equality and a harmonised world	Guo 2002, cited in Yang et al. 2006; Yang et al. 2006; Zhao and Roper 2011	Striving to create and improve self in line with the Confucian learning goals which emphasise strong morals, virtues and values (noted in Figure 13.1) of benefit also to family and society.

- Experience brings about 'change and transformation' (Yang 2004).
- Attitudes and entrepreneurial behaviour in the face of 'institutional holes' (Yang 2004).
- The importance of moral values, family, serving the country and working towards equality and a harmonised world (Yang *et al.* 2006; Zhao and Roper 2011).

China hi-tech entrepreneurs: perspectives on entrepreneurial learning in the China business context

This section illustrates entrepreneurial learning according to the categories identified in the previous section. Having sifted through the original interview data I provide relevant snippets of conversations obtained from the original individual and focus interviews conducted among a total of fifteen individual interviewees and three focus group interviews consisting of fifteen participants (Watkins-Mathys and Foster 2006). Most of the specific references to entrepreneurial learning that were obtained came from four particular participants who took part in individual and focus group interviews respectively: Dr Xiao, Dr Zhang, Victor and Jack). All worked in hi-tech fields at the time of the research.

Learning by doing or the 'art of doing' (Elkin et al. 2009; Chia 2003) and knowledge gained through the 'art of doing' (Yang et al. 2006)

It was evident from many of those interviewed that they had gained substantial knowledge as a consequence of studying for a Ph.D. overseas and also gaining work experience outside of China. A number had gained knowledge and experience as scientists and/or working in a hi-tech business overseas, like Dr Xiao, a biomedical expert. Dr Xiao recounted that he had left China in 1983 to study for his Ph.D. in Stanford, USA. He remained in the USA until 1994 before returning to Hong Kong, where he stayed for seven years (until 2001) when he and his family moved back to Shanghai with the purpose of running the company he had started in 2000. His subject area, biomedical signal processes, involved him using considerable IT applications (developed and introduced at Hong Kong Polytechnic).

When asked where he thought he had learned his entrepreneurial skills he replied that he had developed them probably as a consequence of being educated and working in the USA and Hong Kong. In particular he attributed his learning from having observed the Silicon Valley phenomenon and working in a market-driven economy in both the USA and Hong Kong. Dr Xiao was keen to point out that he learned by trial and error. Indeed, with regard to setting up his new business in China he had to do everything, from the legal side to setting up and equipping the shell that housed the office premises in Shanghai.

By contrast, there were others, like Jack of Magus Soft, an IT games development company, who had not left China, but had instead worked for a foreign multinational and learned how to conduct market-driven, competitive business within China. Jack spoke about how he applied many of the business practices that he had learned from working for the French company UBI Soft and completing his European MBA in Shanghai. When asked how he thought he managed to run a competitive business that lacked unique intellectual property, he replied, 'the only way to beat the competition is "speed" in thinking about the next step and the next way in which the market is going to develop'. Clearly, Jack had gained his business know-how from doing business the French way and incorporated the market and competitive approach into his own method of running his new business.

Guanxi (Li and Liu 2010; Anderson and Lee 2008)

As a returning overseas Chinese, Dr Xiao provided the capital and initial investment for the IT start-up from his savings and investments outside of China. He was clear to point out, however, that in order to keep the cashflow of the company going he had to focus on outsourcing work for a number of clients, including Shanghai General Motors and other major firms. He won these outsourcing contracts mainly through his Jiao Tong/ Stanford connections. The income generated from this work was used to finance the company's own inventions, which Dr Xiao was intending to sell within the China market. These products were in the security IT sector because it is an area in which he believed foreign firms could not compete well in China because they are government controlled. In his view, foreign firms are easily more advanced in their technology. Talking about his company's start-up, Dr Xia stated that the major challenge to his company was 'not the technology ... it's getting good introductions and connections going with government procurement offices', as they are the gatekeepers to obtaining good government contracts. At the time of the interviews he confessed that he had been struggling to gain insider status and penetrate the right guanxi network for this new product.

Dr Zhang, of Shanghai Magnsoft Consulting Co Ltd, and a start-up company producing software for the pharmaceutical industry, explained that his company worked mainly with private companies because they lacked the necessary guanxi with local government contacts: 'Without guanxi the company won't be able to get contracts with state-owned pharmaceutical companies.' So, in recognition of this, Dr Zhang deliberately focused his business development in the private sector rather than wasting his energy and resources in finding and nurturing hard-to-come-by business contacts in local government procurement circles.

Attitudes and entrepreneurial behaviour in the face of 'institutional holes' (Yang 2004; Rozell et al. 2011)

Both Dr Xia's and Dr Zhang's experiences discussed above highlight the barriers (or 'institutional holes') created by China's industry and local government structures. Dr Xiao's example underlines the importance of guanxi for advancing business within the procurement system. The way Dr Xiao chose to gain time in order to cultivate the right guanxi that could help him break through the local government barriers to contracts was to find alternative sources of income in outsourcing contracts.

By contrast, Dr Zhang of Shanghai Magnsoft Consulting had developed an entrepreneurial business focused on the newly emerging private sector of the pharmaceutical industry because he spotted an opportunity for supplying this new market. Supplying state pharmaceutical companies was not an option without the right guanxi. In this way, he turned a barrier into a business opportunity.

Jack illustrated how he overcame local government bureaucracy by drawing on his contacts gained previously from his former career with Tsinghua State News Agency. These networks enabled him to find a way to navigate his way through the bureaucracy in the Chinese business context. However, Jack stressed that becoming successful was also about creating an attitude among his employees to 'feel as if they are part of a winning team'. This he did by setting clear outcome targets for each employee and enabling them to achieve them.

Experience brings about 'change and transformation' (Yang 2004; Chia 2003)

Jack, from Magus Soft, Beijing, spoke about how he encouraged his employees to become creative through experience and experimentation:

> We don't have expensive computers or a fancy office. We just provide an opportunity and platform for employees to be creative and experiment with their ideas. The company provides plenty of opportunities for employees to add value to their work.

Jack believed that this is achieved by creating a very informal working environment that is target- or output- rather than rule-driven; allowing employees to come and go freely, interacting with each other informally, thereby exchanging knowledge and experience that stimulates new ideas and innovative practices. Jack had learned these aspects from working for foreign firms and had incorporated this experience into the way he ran the company.

Victor, a former state school English teacher, explained that having worked with texts in his previous job as an English teacher for eight years, it gave him the confidence based on his experience of working with texts and indexes to start his own B2B textile search engine, Texindex. The company could provide a text index search for the 200,000 Chinese textile companies operating in China at that time. Furthermore, realising that within the Chinese system he could not reach his ambition of becoming a government official, the only way he could advance himself and his family would be by becoming an entrepreneur. Consequently, Victor used his own experience of working as an English-language teacher as well as his experience of the Chinese system to start his Textindex business.

The importance of moral values, family, serving the country and working towards equality and a harmonised world (Yang et al. 2006; Zhao and Roper 2011)

Among the returning overseas Chinese there was a strong sense of wanting to give something back to China for having sponsored their Ph.D. studies overseas. They felt they could do this by playing a part in promoting China's hi-tech policies and in particular by becoming entrepreneurs, locating in a government-designated science and technology park. Dr Xia's story epitomised this. During his interview he spoke about how when he lived outside China he observed from a distance the changes and developments taking place within China. Watching these changes from afar he decided he wanted to assist with this transformation and so started a company, returning to Shanghai with his family.

Victor of Texindex.com, mentioned in the previous section and whose business was located in Whithub, a hi-tech incubator in Shanghai, explained that his drive for starting his business was linked to an old Chinese value taught to him by his grandfather. He explained:

> The typical Chinese man should improve self, have a good family, educate the family and contribute to the whole of society.

Victor believed that starting his business was a way of improving his former life and being able to improve the standard of living of his family. In this way he would be able to improve self, life for his family and thereby offer his family greater educational opportunities. The latter in turn would enable his family to make a greater contribution to society as a whole. This fundamental Chinese value resonates strongly with Yang *et al.*'s (2006) citation of the Chinese saying, '*Xiu Sheng, Qi Jia, Zhi Guo, Ping Tian Xia*', meaning 'cultivate one's moral qualities, set up family, serve the country, and work towards equality and a harmonized world' (Yang *et al.* 2006: 348). In addition, they saw their hi-tech business making a small contribution to helping China create more jobs through innovation and commercialisation.

Similarly, Dr Zhang of Shanghai Magnsoft Consulting, whose business was to provide software applications for the pharmaceutical industry, explained why he became an entrepreneur. While he had had a good job that had been relatively well paid, he found that he had been hitting a 'glass ceiling' and was unable to progress. Starting up the company gave him and his fellow co-founders the opportunity to make a better life for themselves and their families.

The above examples and extracts from the author's interviews among Chinese hi-tech entrepreneurs in Shanghai and Beijing help to illustrate the Eastern perspectives of entrepreneurial learning discussed previously and summarised in Table 13.2.

Discussion: comparing Western and Eastern perspectives on entrepreneurial learning

This section draws together the preceding sections on entrepreneurial learning comparing Western and Eastern theoretical perspectives and discusses these in the light of empirical insights provided above.

Table 13.3 compares Western with Eastern perspectives on entrepreneurial learning. As may be seen, there are a number of similarities between the two approaches, notably around learning by doing or experiential learning, and transformational learning through experience. In Western thought this is as a consequence of reflection and internalisation (cognition). In Eastern thought it is related more to the 'art of doing' and practising rather than internalisation. There is consequently less emphasis on cognitive learning, although knowledge acquisition through 'the art of doing' (Yang 2006) is highlighted, which does relate to cognition. Nevertheless, the doing rather than the reflection is emphasised.

The concepts of human and social capital are linked to developing entrepreneurial capability in Western thinking. Guanxi could be linked to these concepts, and notably 'shuren guanxi'. Moreover, guanxi based on familial obligations and the notion of reciprocity is used in the absence of a strong institutional framework in the Chinese context (Li and Liu 2010). The latter concept of obligation because of obligation and expectation of reciprocity is not a concept that features much in Western thought.

Explicitly absent in the Western literature reviewed is the emphasis on moral values; working for self-improvement (as noted in the five elements of the Confucian Learning Goals depicted in Figure 13.1), family and striving for harmony within society, which offers a collective orientation to entrepreneurial learning. However, it may be argued that Cope (2010) implies moral duty to family and partners when he points out the emotional risk that creating a new venture poses by exposing nearest and dearest to the risk-taking inherent in the venture creation process. It may also be argued by implication that collective perspectives are also implicit in the sense-making process, as it involves social interactions and team learning perspectives (Weick 1995; Hjorth and Johannisson 2009). Nevertheless, these are not directly emphasised in the Western entrepreneurial learning literature.

Table 13.3 Comparing Western and Eastern perspectives on entrepreneurial learning

Western perspectives	Authors	Eastern perspectives	Authors	Comments on respective approaches
Learning by doing; Situated learning; experiential learning; learning how to do new things	Gibb 1997; Cope 2005; Rae 2006; Hjorth and Johannisson 2009	Learning by doing; 'the art of doing'	Elkin 2009; Chia 2003; Guo 2002, cited in Yang et al. 2006	Similar concepts emphasising the learning by doing; although Chinese perspective highlights practice rather than experimenting.
Human and social capital; sense making; creating self-identity	Gibb 1997;Weick 1996; Hosking et al. 1995; Hosking and Hjorth 2004, cited in Man 2012; Hjorth and Johannisson 2009; Williams Middleton and Donnellon 2014	Guanxi family and business-focused aspects of the concept	Li and Liu 2010; Anderson and Lee 2008	Human and social capital evident in guanxi. However, familial guanxi based on reciprocity and obligation while 'shuren' guanxi more aligned to Western concepts of networks. Creating self through social interaction and learning not prevalent in guanxi. However, noted more in the 'art of doing' concept above, where self-improvement, perfecting the art is emphasised.
Internalisation; reflection of actions and critical incidents, 'entrepreneurial stock' cognitive learning	Cope 2005, 2010; Gibb 1997	Implicit in the 'art of doing'	Yang et al. 2006	Not picked up directly by Eastern perspectives in Table 13.2, but the 'art of doing' involves some reflection and cognitive learning in order to improve the art.
Transformational and generative learning	Cope 2010; Appelbaum and Goransson 1997	Experience results in 'change and transformation'	Yang 2004; Chia 2003	Both note aspects of deeper learning, although Eastern thought linked to 'doing' and less directly to cognition and internalisation producing generative learning
Attitude to, and application of, entrepreneurial learning (behavioural approach)	Man 2006	Behavioural: attitude and behaviour in the face of 'institutional holes'	Yang 2004; Rozell et al. 2011	Some similarities with regard to attitudes and behaviours towards learning noted in both perspectives. In Eastern perspective guanxi and use of guanxi emphasised.
Implicit in emotional exposure of family and partner in risk taking during venture creation process		The importance of moral values, family, serve country and work towards equality and a harmonised world	Guo 2002 cited in Yang et al. 2006; Yang et al. 2006; Zhao and Roper 2011	This perspective largely absent in Western literature on entrepreneurial learning, although implicit in Cope's work that refers to learning produced through emotional experience of placing own family/ partner at risk in entrepreneurship (2010).

To sum up this section, Western and Eastern mindsets have different roots and approaches as epitomised by Aristotelian and Confucian philosophies. However, much of the Western literature on entrepreneurial learning discussed in this chapter finds echoes in Chinese perspectives on learning and entrepreneurship. The main distinguishing feature between Western and Eastern perspectives on entrepreneurial learning is the Chinese emphasis on moral values that places an obligation on the individual to improve self in order to improve the well-being of the family and in turn contribute to the improvement of society. Returning overseas Chinese seemed keen to participate in China's economic transformation (Dr Xia), while home-based Chinese entrepreneurs underlined the moral importance of improving self, family and society (Victor).

The Chinese institutional context (i.e. an economy transitioning from communism to a market economy) promotes and organises resources within specific industry groupings in such a way as to create institutional holes that lead to resources not being maximised across industry and institutional groupings. These give rise to entrepreneurial opportunities in the Chinese context. Linked to this is the belief (albeit mixed) that guanxi legitimises entrepreneurial activities and enables entrepreneurs to gain access to resources. While still in practice, the importance of guanxi is seen to be diminishing as China transitions from a communist to a market-driven economy, although the evidence is that it remains important still for Chinese SMEs (Li and Liu 2010). A number of interviewees mentioned the importance of guanxi as either inhibiting their business progress (Dr Xiao) or in contrast it is seen as an opportunity to pursue business aimed at the private sector (Dr Zhang). In this way, both looked for ways of overcoming 'institutional holes' inherent in the Chinese system but they did this by adopting different approaches (i.e. looking to find the right guanxi for obtaining local government-controlled business contracts or by using guanxi for private business openings).

The 'art of doing' came out as a strong theme through interviewees' highlighting how they gained experience, knowledge and practice in their business or specialist field by working in foreign firms and/or foreign environments. This, together with their drive for self-improvement and guanxi (in many cases), led to transformations in their lives epitomised by starting up their own business (Dr Xia, Dr Zhang, Jack and Victor).

Conclusions

This chapter set out to examine entrepreneurial learning in the Chinese business context. To this end, the chapter has provided an overview of extant entrepreneurial learning literature and compared it to traditional Confucian perspectives on learning as well as more recent contributions to entrepreneurship in the Chinese context; and has illustrated the latter with some empirical insights gleamed from individual and focus group interviews conducted among hi-tech entrepreneurs in Beijing and Shanghai. The approach adopted has been interpretive in keeping with the ontological approaches found in the literature.

Table 13.3 illustrates that many of the theoretical aspects of entrepreneurial leaning found in the Western literature may also be found in Eastern learning perspectives. However, Western perspectives focus on entrepreneurial learning from an individual point of view while China's Confucian value-driven belief system draws attention to the collective obligations of the individual entrepreneur in the learning process. Western literature refers to cognitive learning (reflection and internalisation) explicitly as part of doing and experiencing, while Eastern learning is more focused on perfecting the art of doing in order to achieve the five Confucian learning goals. However, as Table 13.3 indicates, there are implicit linkages to these aspects in the respective concepts.

In the light of the discussions presented, this chapter concludes the following:

- China has its own social, political, economic and cultural context that drives entrepreneurial learning; but, as may be seen from returning overseas entrepreneurs, it also incorporates 'learning' assimilated during study, work and life experiences at home and outside of China, which individuals draw on as part of their 'stock of experience' (Pittaway and Thorpe 2012).
- 'Institutional holes', created as a consequence of the way in which Chinese organise resources for respective industries, provide opportunities for Chinese entrepreneurs to spot ways in which they can obtain resources from the separate entities to increase the resources available (Yang 2004). Guanxi, both familial and market guanxi, play an important role in helping entrepreneurs maximise business opportunities (Li and Liu 2010).
- The Confucian cultural heritage lends itself to meaning-oriented learning and interpretation as well as 'doing' (Chia 2003). Moreover, behaviour and learning is driven by a value-based belief system that places a strong moral obligation on the entrepreneur vis-à-vis society and the collective. Entrepreneurs are expected to have a strong moral character, and a strong sense of loyalty to family and country.

All of the above impact upon identity (Rae 2006), involve risk to self and the individual (Cope 2005, 2010), and influence behaviour and attitudes to learning (Man 2006; Rozell *et al.* 2011).

Finally, entrepreneurial learning in China remains under-explored. This chapter has been able to shed some further light on to the subject from a theoretical perspective and by bringing insights from focus group and individual interviews undertaken with Chinese entrepreneurs. Clearly, the contribution made here is limited and there is considerable scope to explore further and in greater depth entrepreneurial learning within China; to extend the perspectives presented in this chapter that may be of mutual benefit to researchers exploring entrepreneurial learning. In particular, Western researchers may wish to consider the moral and value-driven perspectives found in Eastern thinking, while Eastern researchers may wish to explore in greater depth reflection on, and internalisation of, learning that contributes to generative learning.

References

Anderson, A. and Lee, E.Y-C. (2008) From tradition to modern: Attitudes and applications of guanxi in Chinese entrepreneurship. *Small Business and Enterprise Development* 15(4), 775–787.

Appelbaum, S.H. and Goransson, L. (1997) Transformational and adaptive learning within the learning organization: A framework for research and application. *The Learning Organization* 4(3), 115–128.

Atkinson, R.L., Smith, E.E. and Hilgards, E.R. (1987) *Introduction to Psychology* (9th edn). New York: Harcout, Brace & Jovanavich.

Brown, J.S. and Duguid, P. (1991) Organizational learning and communities of practice: Toward a united view of working. *Learning and Innovation, Organization Science* 9(1), 40–57.

Burt, R.S. (1992) *Structural Holes: The social structure of competition.* Cambridge, MA: Harvard University Press.

Carlisle, E. and Flynn, D. (2005) Small business survival in China. *Journal of Developmental Entrepreneurship* 10(1),79–96.

Chia, R. (2003) From knowledge-creation to the perfecting of action: Tao, Basho and pure experience as the ultimate grund of knowing. *Human Relations* 56(8), 953–981.

Cope, J. (2003) Entrepreneurial learning and critical reflection: Discontinuous events as triggers for 'higher-level' learning. *Management Learning* 34(4), 429–450.

—— (2005) Toward a dynamic learning perspective of entrepreneurship. *Entrepreneurship Theory and Practice* 29(4), 373–397.

—— (2010) Entrepreneurial learning from failure: An interpretative phenomenological analysis. *Journal of Business Venturing* 26(6), 604–623.

Cope, J. and Watts, G. (2000) Learning by doing: An exploration of experience, critical incidents and reflection in entrepreneurial learning. *International Journal of Entrepreneurial Behaviour and Research* 6(3), 104–124.

Deakins, D. and Freel, M. (1998) Entrepreneurial learning and the growth process in SMEs. *The Learning Organisation* 5(3), 144–155.

Easterby-Smith, M., Thorpe, R. and Lowe, A. (1991) *Management Research: An introduction.* London: Sage.

Elkin, G., Cone, M. and Liao, J. (2009) Chinese pragmatism and the learning organisation. *The Learning Organization* 16(1), 69–83.

Gelderen, M. van, Sluis, L. van and Jansen, P. (2005) Learning opportunities and learning behaviours of small business starters: Relations with goal achievement, skill development and satisfaction. *Small Business Economics* 26(4), 97–108.

Gibb, A.A. (1997) Small firms, training and competitiveness: Building on the small business as a learning organisation. *International Small Business Journal* 15(3), 13–29.

—— (2007) Entrepreneurship: Unique solutions for unique environments: Is it possible to achieve this with the existing paradigm. *International Journal of Entrepreneurship Education* 5.

Gibb, A.A. and Li, J. (2003) Organizing for enterprise in China: What can we learn from the Chinese micro, small, and medium enterprise development experience. *Futures* 35, 403–421.

Gibbs, A. (1997) Focus groups. *Social Science Research Update* [online], Winter Issue 19. Available at: http://sru.soc.surrey.ac.uk/SRU19.html (accessed 27 October 2013).

Gibson, C. and Vermeulen, F. (2003) A healthy divide: Subgroups as a stimulus for team learning behavior. *Administrative Science Quarterly* 48(2), 202–239.

Guo, Q. (2002) Essentials of traditional Chinese education thought and contemporary competency education. *Journal of Southern Yangtze University Humanities and Social Science Edition* 1(1), 80–86.

Hao, J., Wei, J. and Yu, C. (2010) An empirical study on paths to develop dynamic capabilities: From the perspectives of entrepreneurial orientation and organisational learning. *Frontier of Business Research China* 4(1), 47–72.

Hines, T. and Thorpe, R. (1995) New approaches to understanding small firm networks – the key to performance, managerial learning and development. *Proceedings of the 18th ISBA National Small Firms Policy and Research Conference*, Sheffield.

Hjorth, D. and Johannisson, B. (2009) Learning as an entrepreneurial process. *Revue de l'Entrepreneuriat* 8(2), 57–78.

Hosking D.M. and Hjorth, D. (2004) Relational constructionism and entrepreneurship: Some key notes. In D. Hjorth and C. Steyart (eds), *Narrative and Discursive Approaches in Entrepreneurship Studies*. Cheltenham: Edward Elgar, pp. 255–268.

Hosking, D.M., Dachler, H.P. and Gergen, K.J. (1995) *Management and Organization: Relational alternatives to individualism*. Aldershot: Avebury.

Macpherson, A. and Holt, R. (2007) Knowledge, learning and small firm growth: A systematic review of the evidence. *Research Policy* 36(2), 172–192.

Man, T.Y. (2006) Exploring the behavioural patterns of entrepreneurial learning. *Education and Training* 48(5), 309–321.

—— (2012) Developing a behaviour-centred model of entrepreneurship learning. *Journal of Small Business and Enterprise Development* 19(3), 549–566.

Millman, C., Matlay, H. and Liu, F. (2008) Entrepreneurship education in China: A case study approach. *Journal of Small Business and Enterprise Development* 15(4), 802–815.

Oxford Dictionaries (2013) [online], available at: http://oxforddictionaries.com/definition/english/alphabet (accessed 30 September 2013).

Pittaway, L. and Thorpe, R. (2012) A framework for entrepreneurial learning: A tribute to Jascon Cope. *Entrepreneurship and Regional Development* 24(9–10), 837–859.

Rae, D. (2005) Entrepreneurial learning: A narrative-based conceptual model. *Joural of Small Business and Enterprise Development* 12(3), 323–335.

—— (2006) Entrepreneurial learning: A conceptual framework for technology-based enterprise. *Technology Analysis and Strategic Management* 18(1), 39–56.

Rae, D. and Carswell, M. (2000) Using a life-story approach in researching entrepreneurial learning: The development of a conceptual model and its implication in the design of learning experiences. *Education and Training* 42(4/5), 220–227.

Rozell, E.J., Meyer, K.E., Scroggins, W.A. and Guo, A. (2011) Perceptions of the characteristics of successful entrepreneurs: An empirical study in China. *International Journal of Management* 28(4), 60–72.

Schumpeter, J. (1975) *Capitalism, Socialism and Democracy.* New York: Harper & Row.

Senge, P. (1990) *The Fifth Discipline: The art and practice of the learning organization.* New York: Doubleday/Currency.

Tang, J., Tang, Z., Zhang, Y. and Li, Q. (2007) The impact of entrepreneurial orientation and ownership type on firm performance in the emerging region of China. *Journal of Developmental Entreprenurship* 12, 383–397.

Taylor, D. and Thorpe, R. (2004) Entrepreneurial learning: A co-participative approach. *Journal of Small Business and Enterprise Development* 11(2), 2013–211.

Tsang, E. (1999) Can guanxi be a source of sustianed competitive advantage for doing business: In China. *Academy of Managment Executives* 12(2), 64–73.

Watkins-Mathys, L. and Foster, J. (2006) Entrepreneurship: The missing ingredient in China's STIPs. *Entrepreneurship and Regional Development* 18(3), 249–274.

Weick, K.E. (1995) *Sensemaking in Organizations.* Thousand Oaks, CA: Sage.

Williams Middleton, K. and Donnellon, A. (2014) Personalizing entrepreneurial learning: A pedagogy for facilitating the know why entrepreneurship. *Research Journal* 4(2), 167–204.

Yang, B., Zheng, W. and Li, M. (2006) Confucian view of learning and implications for developing human resources. *Advances in Developing Human Resources* 8(3), 346–354.

Yang, K. (2004) Institutional holes and entrepreneurship in China. *Sociological Review* 52(3), 371–389.

Zhao, L. and Roper, J. (2011) A Confucian approach to well-being and social-capital development. *Journal of Management Development* 30(7/8), 740–752.

Index

Page numbers in *italics* denote tables, those in **bold** denote figures.

For Product Safety Concerns and Information please contact our EU
representative GPSR@taylorandfrancis.com Taylor & Francis Verlag GmbH,
Kaufingerstraße 24, 80331 München, Germany

Printed and bound by CPI Group (UK) Ltd, Croydon, CR0 4YY
08/05/2025
01864335-0003